# THE END OF THE CENTURY

## The Future in the Past

The Japan Foundation
Center for Global Partnership

KODANSHA INTERNATIONAL
Tokyo • New York • London

Distributed in the United States by Kodansha America, Inc., 114 Fifth
Avenue, New York, New York 10011, and in the United Kingdom and
continental Europe by Kodansha Europe Ltd., 95 Aldwych, London
WC2B 4JF. Published by Kodansha International Ltd., 17-14 Otowa 1-
chome, Bunkyo-ku, Tokyo 112, and Kodansha America, Inc.
Copyright © 1995 by The Japan Foundation, ARK Mori Bldg., 1-12-32
Akasaka, Minato-ku, Tokyo 107. Printed in Japan. All rights reserved.

ISBN 4-7700-2021-X

First edition, 1995

# THE END OF THE CENTURY
## The Future in the Past

# CONTENTS

# PREFACE

The essays contained in this book were first presented at an international symposium, "The End of the Century: The Future in the Past," which was held at Yatsugatake, Japan, in September 1993. The Japan Foundation Center for Global Partnership sponsored the symposium, and the editors wish to express their appreciation to The Japan Foundation not only for its hospitality in providing an ideal setting for a stimulating exchange of ideas but also for its invaluable assistance in expediting the publication of the papers, along with a summary of the discussions. (The original transcript of the discussions was more than three times the length of what is contained in this volume. The steering committee assumes the responsibility for editing the transcript.)

HAGIHARA Nobutoshi
Akira IRIYE
Georges NIVAT
Philip WINDSOR

*March 1994*

# CONTRIBUTORS

Richard W. BULLIET
    Professor, Columbia University Middle East Institute

Ronald DORE
    Research Fellow, Centre for Economic Performance,
    London School of Economics, University of London;
    Professor, Massachusetts Institute of Technology

Curt GASTEYGER
    Professor of International Relations and Director,
    Programme for Strategic and International Security
    Studies, The Graduate Institute of International
    Studies, Geneva

Philip W. GOLD
    Chief, Clinical Neuroendocrinology Branch, Intra-
    mural Research Program, National Institute of Men-
    tal Health, National Institutes of Health, Bethseda,
    Maryland

HAGIHARA Nobutoshi
    Writer and historian

Yehoshafat HARKABI
    Professor, Department of International Relations,
    Hebrew University

William R. HUTCHISON
    Professor of the History of Religion in America,
    Divinity School, Harvard University

Akira IRIYE
    Professor of History, Harvard University

ISHII Yoneo
Professor and Director, Institute of Asian Cultures, Sophia University, Tokyo

Detlef JUNKER
Professor of Modern History, University of Heidelberg

Linda K. KERBER
Professor of Liberal Art and History, University of Iowa

KOSAI Yutaka
President, Japan Center for Economic Research

Julia KRISTEVA
Professor, UFR de Sciences des Textes et Documents, Université Paris VII

KYOGOKU Jun-ichi
Director, The Japan Foundation Japanese Language Institute; Professor Emeritus, University of Tokyo

Dmitri LIKHACHEV
President, International Cultural Fund; Head of Early Russian Literature at the Institute of Russian Literature, Russian Academy of Science

Ernest MAY
Professor of History, JFK School of Government, Harvard University

James MAYALL
Professor of International Relations, London School of Economics, University of London

Edgar MORIN
Director of Research Emeritus of the National Center for Scientific Research, Paris

MURAKAMI Yoichiro
Director, Research Center for Advanced Science and Technology, University of Tokyo

NAKAMURA Keiko
Assistant Director, Biohistory Research Hall, Osaka; Professor, School of Human Sciences, Waseda University

Georges NIVAT
Professor of Russian Language and Literature, University of Geneva

Maciej PERCZYNSKI
> Division Head, Institute of Economic Science, Polish Academy of Science; Chairman of the Scientific Council, Research Center of International Economic Relations, Polish Institute of International Affairs, Warsaw

Fritz STERN
> Professor of History, Columbia University

UENO Chizuko
> Associate Professor, Faculty of Literature, University of Tokyo

UMESAO Tadao
> Advisor (formerly Director) of the National Museum of Ethnology, Osaka

WATANABE Hiroshi
> Professor, Faculty of Law, University of Tokyo

Philip WINDSOR
> Reader, Department of International Relations, London School of Economics, University of London

Michael R. WINSTON
> President, The Alfred Harcourt Foundation; former Vice President for Academic Affairs, Howard University

YAMAGUCHI Masao
> Professor, Institute for the Study of Languages and Cultures of Asia and Africa, Tokyo University of Foreign Studies

YAMAUCHI Masayuki
> Professor, College of Arts and Sciences, University of Tokyo

YOKOYAMA Toshio
> Associate Professor, Institute for Research in Humanities, Kyoto University

(Positions as of September 1993)

# INTRODUCTION

Akira IRIYE

"The End of the Century: The Future in the Past" was the title of the Japan Foundation symposium held at Yatsugatake from August 31 to September 4, 1993. The idea was to gather together some of the leading thinkers from Europe, the United States, and Japan to have them reflect on the world as it approaches the end of the twentieth century.

The Japan Foundation had, in 1983, already held a symposium to assess the meaning of twentieth-century history. The papers presented at that symposium and a summary of the discussions held have been published (*Experiencing the Twentieth Century*, University of Tokyo Press, 1984). As the book clearly shows, however, in 1983 the participants generally shared a rather gloomy view of the contemporary world; they could not but be aware of the suppression of freedom and human rights all over the world, above all in the Soviet Union and the countries it controlled, and of the ever-present danger of nuclear warfare and global annihilation. These phenomena, added to the century's two world wars, the totalitarian excesses of the 1930s, the Holocaust, and other instances of man's inhumanity to man, seemed to overshadow whatever technological, political, economic, and other achievements modern history had produced. Held on the eve of 1984, the symposium participants feared that the kinds of oppression, cynicism, and terror George Orwell had written about so graphically in *1984* were still very much present.

Few then foresaw what was to happen in the world during the subsequent decade. The United States and the Soviet Union concluded nuclear arms control agreements with breathtaking rapidity, the Berlin Wall crumbled, one Eastern European dictatorship after another collapsed, the Soviet Union was dissolved, the United

Nations became an arena for cooperation among all the major powers—all this forced a reassessment of recent history, as did other developments that had only been dimly perceived in the early 1980s: ethnic rivalries in the Balkans, South Asia, the Middle East, and virtually everywhere; the threat of environmental degradation in Eastern Europe, China, and other countries; the "empowerment" of women and minorities in Western societies (as well as a formidable backlash against it); huge waves of migrants and refugees from the Third World to Europe, North America, and even Japan. In recognition of these rapid transformations, in 1992 the Japan Foundation asked the same four scholars (Nobutoshi Hagihara, Akira Iriye, Georges Nivat, and Philip Windsor) who had helped organize the 1983 symposium to plan another one. The result was this Yatsugatake conference, sponsored by the Foundation's Center for Global Partnership. Altogether thirty-one participants attended, coming from nine countries and representing as many as ten disciplinary fields (as well as six area specializations). To maintain some continuity with the 1983 symposium, the participants were drawn from Europe, the United States, and Japan, although "Europe" this time included Poland, Russia, and Israel.

"The Future in the Past"—the idea was to look ahead to the end of the twentieth century and the beginning of the twenty-first from the perspective of the past. But which past? The past of totalitarianism, wars, and atrocities, or the more recent past of liberation, democratization, and international accommodation? Which past phenomena and themes would be more likely to endure into the near future? Could one hope that the horrible disasters of the twentieth century would not recur and that the more hopeful developments during the last ten years would continue? Or would these developments prove to be too fragile, and would the darker forces from before 1983 return to torment humanity?

The participants at the Yatsugatake symposium grappled with these questions. Not surprisingly, a great deal of attention was paid to the collapse of communism in the Soviet Union and Eastern Europe. Could totalitarianism and terror return to these lands? Most participants were cautiously optimistic, believing, as Dmitri Likhachev pointed out, that the collapse of communism meant an end to cynicism and a return to moral and intellectual values, to "natural man," and to "culture." Georges Nivat echoed the same theme, stressing that "historical culture" was what gave hope: the assertion of historical consciousness against fanaticism and manipulative utopianism. Others were more reserved. Fritz Stern reminded the participants that intellectuals had "betrayed their mission" more than once, and Edgar Morin that "techno-bureaucracy" in all countries could militate against democracy. Detlef Junker asserted that social, economic, and ethnic issues in Eastern European countries were such that there was no guarantee that democratization would work. Maciej Perczynski was worried about the persistence of the *homo sovieticus* mentality, seeking to enforce egalitarianism "in distributing poverty." Despite such reservations, there was a general feeling at the symposium that, in the words of Philip Windsor, "we are not optimistic, but have not given up hope."

This hopefulness may have reflected the belief that, if nothing else, the collapse of communist totalitarianism had liberated the individual and restored what Julia Kristeva termed "private psychic space." It is interesting to note that most participants agreed with Kristeva about the regaining of private space as a signal achievement of the last ten years, and at the same time they expressed their concern over the failure of nations, not just formerly communist ones, to solve socio-economic problems which had become, if anything, even more acute in recent years. Had not the gap widened, Ronald Dore asked, for instance, between the rich and the poor segments of society in most industrial countries? Had spiritual freedom been won at the expense of diminished material well-being? If the past could not be changed, and indeed if the recent past was to be a source of satisfaction, where did one go from there so as not to give up personal freedom even as one sought to improve the material conditions of life?

The symposium arrived at no simple answer, but one theme that was often repeated was "sacrifice" (to use Kristeva's word), or "self-criticism," as some preferred to call it. What these terms meant was that individuals and communities must be prepared to be satisfied with less than total comfort and autonomy. Or, to paraphrase Alexander Solzhenitsyn, they would have to drop nineteenth-century ideas of continued progress and adopt "auto-restriction." Both materially and spiritually, people would have to know their limits so as not to create a situation where only a fraction of the globe was free and enjoyed material comfort. Ideally, all should partake of freedom and well-being, although such an outcome should never be arrived at through some manipulative utopian scheme. Thus Kristeva pledged not to "absolutize" any human institution or endeavor but to see them in terms of "a scale of adherences."

Would this mean that we must renounce any idea of a universal solution? Must there be a greater willingness on the part of advanced liberal democracies to share their spiritual and material resources with the Third World?

Third World countries, too, had been making various choices, and that included sacrifices, whether voluntary or enforced. The participants, although they did not come from the Third World and hesitated to speak with authority, were nevertheless quite interested in the growing disparities among those countries. For instance, throughout the 1980s many Asian countries had advanced rapidly in the economic realm but not necessarily in democratization, whereas in Latin America democratization had not brought about increased economic well-being. Yehoshafat Harkabi observed that, in a world where global war or wars in Europe had become less and less likely, "the center of gravity of wars" was shifting to the Third World. At the same time, he pointed to the example of South Africa, Brazil, and Argentina, countries that could have developed nuclear weapons but had chosen not to. These were all examples that fitted well into the symposium participants' concern with the theme of sacrifice.

In this connection, the postwar history of Japan seemed, at least to some participants, to take on fresh significance. Could it be said, as Nobutoshi Hagihara suggested, that by eschewing, under the new constitution, the sovereign right to arm itself, Japan had shown the way for a new definition of nationhood and, therefore, of the international community. Michael Winston thought so, asserting, "There are certainly historical instances where taking the high road turned out to be the smart thing to do and [where] the cynics were wrong." From a different perspective, William Hutchison noted that the United States, by being willing to relinquish its "No. 1" position in certain respects, was in a better position to help develop new identities for its people, and for the rest of the world as well. Kristeva, on her part, insisted that after her generation had "deconstructed" the West through "negation" and "doubt," the time had come "to try to find out and to encourage a sort of revival of our values in order to confront Eastern as well as Western problems."

These were themes that also informed the discussion of other phenomena in the contemporary world. For instance, the development of regional communities and international cooperation implied that sovereign states had to limit their autonomous rights in the interest of the global community. This, it was recognized, was a very difficult proposition in view of the strengthening of nationalistic forces in the wake of the Cold War. The other side of the coin of the Cold War had been what Curt Gasteyger referred to as the disappearance of a "countervailing force"; in the absence of a presumed threat from the Soviet Union, the liberal democracies might lose their incentive to cooperate. The participants tried to understand the implications of the disappearance of antagonistic equilibria and asked if the trend was compatible with national and ethnic diversity. Perhaps, several argued, it would be meaningless to ask whether nationalism or internationalism would prove more enduring, for both were likely to be around for years to come. Morin argued that democracy had to be grounded in institutions and communities and, therefore, that democracy and nationalism were mutually reinforcing. At the same time, however, regional communities would also contribute to democracy's affirmation. James Mayall pointed out that sovereign national entities were not likely to disappear even as cross-national trends might become further accentuated in the near future. Nationalism and globalism were, in his words, linked in "a symbiotic relationship."

Such pairing of opposites, indeed, emerged as one of the ways in which the participants sought to understand the recent past. Besides nationalism and globalism, they pointed to the growing awareness of shared values across nations *and* the deepening of cultural diversity in all parts of the world, to what Kristeva termed "universality" *and* "differentiation." There had obviously emerged an awareness of the commonality of human beings through the turmoil of the twentieth century, but at the same time different segments of humanity had also asserted their individual differences.

The tension inherent in these paired opposites would not go away, but it could be kept under control through, once again, sacrifice: some accommodation between the opposites. Kristeva and others spoke of "eclecticism," even of "the happiness of eclecticism," and these words may well have summed up what the symposium participants were sensing. Many of them welcomed the call for eclecticism, as it implied the negation of totalitarianism, fanaticism, and arbitrariness that had characterized so much of the history of the present century. In his discussion of environmentalism, for instance, Jun-ichi Kyogoku was critical of its fanatical excesses even as he pointed to the movement as one of the most significant developments of recent years. Likewise, regarding the question of the changed status of women in many societies, Kristeva denounced "feminist fundamentalism" and argued for "harmony between men and women." Kerber, tracing women's struggle for recognition through the League of Nations and in the United States, did not wholly agree but indicated that women, too, were willing to make sacrifices, if they were shared by men. Windsor, discussing the evolution of human rights, asserted that while this was a universally valid value, its application varied from one culture to another, each with its own "norms," and that one must respect such variation even as one embraced the universalism of the principle itself. In his response to Akira Iriye's presentation on Third World assertiveness (in which he argued that there had been a viable history of "great power" accommodation with the Third World going back to the 1920s), Richard Bulliet urged the participants to apply the same spirit of accommodation to the discussion of Islam. In his (and Masayuki Yamauchi's) view, Islamic fundamentalism was a misnomer; there were Moslem terrorists, to be sure, but the bulk of those who embraced the religion were not extremists. They would become extremists only if outsiders continued to put them in that category.

The discussions also led to anthropological questions: Would man be the same when there was a growing possibility that humans could be healed of more and more diseases? In an extremely interesting presentation, Philip Gold noted that the advances in molecular biology and genetics in the last several years had been such that scientists today knew a great deal more about the functioning of the human brain and the human mind. The cause of depression, the state of mind that went from one extreme to another in the face of unforeseen circumstances, could be pinpointed and cures found. If so, there would develop a more adaptable personality—another dimension of eclecticism, perhaps. Another scientist, Keiko Nakamura, likewise stressed the need to combine natural with human sciences, toward a more humane science. That, too, was an excellent demonstration of the concern with balance. Yutaka Kosai, an economist, and other social scientists present tended to agree that while the social sciences were not capable of making predictions, they were still useful as explanatory devices. They could no longer claim omnipotence, as they had tended to do in the earlier, golden age of social engineering, but at the same time they could make a contribution to understanding disparate phenomena through a comparative and global approach.

Perhaps one of the most interesting discussions concerned "differences" versus "commonalities." Some, notably Kristeva, stressed differences, and Winston and others commonalities—between the sexes, individuals, cultures, nations. But all agreed that we needed both perspectives, the assumption being that the time was ripe for seeking some balance between "universality" and "differentiation." The symposium was an excellent demonstration of this. As Dore said, "here we are cooperating in having a splendid time...[exemplifying the] sheer sentiments of affection between individuals, the pleasure of working socially rather than in isolation," even as the participants recognized the regaining of "private space" and of "the other" in the process of self-discovery (by individuals, cultures, nations) as a major achievement of the preceding ten years.

So, all in all, compared with the 1983 symposium, the 1993 conference gave evidence of renewed hopefulness, not because humanity was arriving at a golden age but because it had survived the worst disasters in history, not because man had an answer to every question but because he knew his limitations, not because he was totally satisfied spiritually and materially but because he knew how to find happiness in eclecticism. Such an assessment of recent developments sounds modest, but it is strikingly different from the darkness that characterized the 1983 symposium. Perhaps this state of affairs could be summed up by what Windsor said in his discussion of human rights: the question of culture had become somewhat separated from the question of power. The Cold War, the two world wars, totalitarianism—these had been expressions of naked power, violence, and terror. To the extent that they had begun to be replaced by cultural forces, this could be cause for guarded optimism for the future.

The essays and the discussions contained in this volume cannot pretend to offer solutions to the problems of today's world. But the editors hope the book will serve as an example of what some of the contemporary world's leading minds have to say about the recent past from a global, interdisciplinary perspective, which, we strongly believe, will become more and more necessary as we face the future.

# THE COLLAPSE OF COMMUNISM AND ITS CONSEQUENCES

# THE CRUMBLING OF COMMUNISM?

Georges NIVAT

In April 1919 Alexander Blok gave a lecture at the newly founded Volfila, the Free Academy of Philosophy. He called it "The Crumbling of Humanism." The text was published after his death in 1921. In that celebrated text, which sounds like his last will, Blok proclaims the end of the age of Humanism, of Man ethical, political, humanist, and the advent of Man esthetic.... A few days before his assassination by unknown murderers on September 9, 1990, Father Alexander Men said to a friend of his: "Don't you see that I know what kind of mess people have in their heads? If only a few of my listeners, even if one of them, is awakened, is it too few? My impression is that it cannot go on like this, at least for me." The crumbling of communism echoes the crumbling of humanism, which Blok perceived acutely from the very beginning of the century. Father Men was one of those who perceived and hastened the crumbling of communism. Still, he was pessimistic and said once: "The day is coming when we shall be free to speak. What if we find out that we have nothing to say?" Is that forewarning the pang of a man who was struggling alone against the multitude? Or should we take it seriously, and is it authenticated by today's situation? Let us begin with an analysis of the decisive events in Russia over the last two years.

For decades and decades the West has been struggling against communism. It has desired its defeat, although a large part of the West, at various times and in various countries, has also been fascinated by communism, and even by Stalinism. On August 21, 1991, communism fell. The crowd in Moscow refused to submit to the putschists, who represented a return to Soviet communism. On that day freedom of thought made history, and the giant fell. For me personally it was a dramatic event that not only authenticated much of my work on dissidents but changed my life as a Slavist. The fall of that giant reminded me of an event to which I was an eyewitness in Tbilisi in September 1990: I arrived in Tbilisi on the very day that the crowd had gathered in the main square of the capital of Georgia, determined to pull down the statue of Lenin. Of course it couldn't be moved: twenty-three tons is not easy to shift; but at eleven in the evening the municipal authorities decided to give the crowd some help, at two in the morning the idol crumbled and the crowd, including myself, rushed to claim a fragment. Next day nothing was left.

What happened in the case of the statue of Lenin in Tbilisi is of course impossible in that of the social, moral, mental giant of communism: much is left of it even after its fall. But the fall in itself not only is an epoch-making event but it compels us to rethink, and to revise much of our historical thinking. Our understanding of Russia has been forged by two centuries of rather superficial knowledge of that country. A celebrated book, Custine's *Russia in 1839*, has for example played a major role in France: it was inspired by a vigorous hatred, grounded in a superficial account, by a man who knew no Russian, and who had an active sympathy for Poland. George Kennan, in an excellent small book, *The Marquis de Custine and his Russia in 1839*, has written that "even if we admit that *La Russie en 1839* was not a very good book about Russia in 1839, we are confronted with the disturbing fact that it was an excellent book, probably in fact the best of books, about the Russia of Joseph Stalin, and not a bad book about the Russia of Brezhnev and Kosygin." What does this mean? It means that Custine was, and still remains, a key to the understanding of Russia, including communist Russia, or Russian communism at the time Kennan wrote the book in 1971. Has it changed in twenty years? Not entirely.

Although Custine was blind to the birth of a great Russian culture precisely at the time of Nicholas I, his theory of Russia as a country doomed to spying, bureaucratic despotism, and harsh oppression of individuals is still active in our imaginations. Richard Pipes put it another way in his book on Russia under the Old Regime: a country with ever more police and increasing brutality. Custine's theory has been active on two sides: on the Western side but also on the Eastern, Russian side, provoking not only bitter answers, but also a sort of ideological counterattack. Incidentally, in one of the main scenes in his book, Custine meets a mysterious

Russian nobleman who is very probably Chaadaev, the most prominent in the astounding series of self-haters—*heautontimorumenos*, as
the Greeks called them—that Russia has produced.

Let us not discuss Custine, nor the problem of whether Custine
was wrong in 1839 and right a century later. My point is that today
something decisive has happened in Russia, and that the reference
to Custine little by little is becoming obsolete. It is still in use,
because myths are very hard to dismiss, but the curse on Russia may
well have disappeared. Even such a skeptical historian of Russia as
Richard Pipes concedes it now. Custine is becoming obsolete
because that trend toward more and more despotism is now
reversed. It is reversed because a slow evolution of Soviet society
has given birth to new needs and requirements. Soviet society was
moving toward something else, which was alien to it but germi-
nated in its bosom. For that reason Gorbachev's wavering reforms,
which began with a sort of reinforcement of police in the style of
Andropov, then moved to a weakening of apparachiks and concessions to a civil society *in statu nascendi*, went much further than their
author thought: as an apprentice sorcerer, Gorbachev was unable to
master the movement he had released, because society asked for
more, refused a further recourse to coercion against smaller components of the empire (in Georgia, Armenia, and Lithuania), and
demanded not a renewal of the party but a disbanding of it. What
was decisive in August 1991 was mainly the hatred for the party,
and there may have been not only that but a demand for the transformation of Russia. It became clear that Russia was readier for
democracy than was thought, said, and repeated in thousands of
formulae. From 1989 onward, Russian voters have made rather
wise use of liberties, have voted against the supporters of totalitarianism. The April 1993 referendum was confirmation of a political
wisdom which, in my eyes, far surpasses the sagacity of political
leaders in that country.[1] Parliament's leaders were almost sure that
their effort to stop Yeltsin's democratic and economic reforms
would succeed if they were to add a question, which became question No. 2, on the "approval" of economic reforms. A large majority for Yeltsin, a narrower majority for the reforms was the answer.
In spite of a troubled situation, the voters in April put aside the
demagogic arguments of those disguised opponents to reforms
who are active on the political stage of Russia today. How can it be
explained?

It seems to me that the evolution of communism contained

within itself its own rejection. Soviet communism was founded on the ideal of a "new man" (derived from a secularized version of Christianity, celebrated from the twenties both by the regime and *a contrario* by its enemies who, in a way, believed no less in that myth), on the dogma that force could implement total political obedience, a philosophy of scientism (linked with the active destruction of religion) and a philosophy of the "permanent plot," a disbelief in any positive virtues or actions of others, and a permanent militarization of minds. But, because of its "scientist" component, communism developed education, both ideological and technical. An enormous system of technical institutes covered the country. Siberian cities like Krasnoyarsk, which I visited last March, are an impressive conglomeration of institutes and industries.

Pierre Pascal used to explain the rise of revolutionary forces in 1910–14 by the rise of the "new democracy" (that was an expression of Lenin), i.e., a middle class of teachers, veterinaries, engineers, and specialized workers who would no longer put up with the obsolete forms of the Old Regime. It was, according to him, more a question of formal rigidity, and the regime's error was to delay some reforms while it had accepted others: autocracy was attached to old social rituals which a new class of mass-intelligentsia now found unbearable.

Something similar happened under Brezhnev: a weakened "totalitarian regime," which was no longer absolutely totalitarian but maintained all the old formal costumes of totalitarianism. It is important to say that the new "democracy" did not coincide with the so-called Soviet intelligentsia. The intelligentsia, a class of those engaged professionally in ideological and artistic work, had their last say during the period of *perestroika*, which represented their resurrection and their "finest hour," but the "new democracy" is quite different, and not at all characterized by the kind of cleric who has no specialty and yet claims to handle all subjects, as is typical of the Russian *intelligent*. The claim to freedom was implicit in that new class, and could not be satisfied by the party. More surprisingly, and unexpectedly for nearly all observers, the awakening of the working class after seven decades (the "Workers' Opposition" was crushed by Lenin himself in 1921) played a decisive role: the miners from the Donbas, from Vorkuta, from Kemerovo were the real agents of the dramatic turn of events. From the very beginning their strikes (what a new phenomenon in Russia!) demanded the abolition of Article 5 of the Soviet constitution, that is to say, of the monopoly of power for the Party. This was most remarkable. It was inspired by Andrei Sakharov; and it was underestimated at the time by the Western media. What might be termed the "Solidarity connection" assumed a very strange face in Russia, since it happened between one man and distant miners, thousands of miles from the capital. But those miners were the aristocracy of the Soviet proletariat, and they discovered that they could prevent the Soviet economy from functioning. Hitherto they have become the main champions of President Yeltsin in his struggle with a reactionary Parliament.

Nobody really foretold that kind of evolution in Russia because Soviet myths were so deeply rooted, even more in anti-Soviet minds than in the circles of power inside Russia. The extraordinary success of Alexander Zinoviev in the West was not due to the artistic force of his satire but to the fulfillment of a subconscious desire: the "ratorium" pleased a wide public, because it offered a simple, pleasing, anti-Russian interpretation. Zinoviev has now gone over to a very logical admiration of Stalinism and hostility toward the newly born Russian democracy. His *Katastroika*[2] was a mock answer to the reality. Now only cursing was left. Unfortunately Zinoviev is not alone in joining the chorus of those nostalgic for the glorious "Stalinist night," as Siniavski-Tertz calls the sort of pernicious aura which surrounds totalitarianism. Yet this is not the only resistance to the recognition of novelty on the historical stage of Russia: another myth is "revolution from above." Such is the title of an interesting little book by the Soviet historian Natan Eidelman, a specialist in Russian cultural and political history at the beginning of the nineteenth century. Alexander I gave a sort of model of "revolution from above," but an abortive one, when he organized the Secret Committee made up of four young men charged with thinking out the reforms needed by Russia. The most influential of them was Count Paul Stroganov, whose teacher had been the Frenchman Gilbert Romme, an austere mathematician from the Auvergne who became a Montagnard, and committed suicide *à la Caton* before his beheading during the events of *Prairial*. Alexander did not carry out the projects formed by the Secret Committee, nor the plans drafted for him by his Swiss tutor, Laharpe. Revolutions from above last ten years or so and in the end can change things but not minds. Gorbachev's *perestroika* was seen by many as a "revolution from above," and its end as the end of reforms, a momentary return to elemental forces, of which the next stage would be a return to "natural" despotism. Skepticism toward Russian democracy plays its part: it is a serious hindrance.

One might say such arguments are fine, but they concern Russia only, and we need an explanation of a broader phenomenon, the fall of communism itself. So we come to the next stage: was Russian communism Russian or international? The two theses have been in competition, and still are. The thesis that Russian communism was not Russian but imported has been developed by Russian nationalists, the latest being Alexander Solzhenitsyn (although he did it with much moderation and great erudition) and also by adversaries of Russian backwardness, who deplore that the first communist country unfortunately was Russia. Russia, alas! For them it explains the communist defeat in the long run. Had it happened in an advanced industrial country, England for example, would it have been another story? The contrary thesis was brilliantly developed by Nicholas Berdaieff in his *History and Roots of Russian Communism*, a book written in 1933. Berdaieff links Russian communism with the Russian "religious idea," the religious structure of the Russian revolutionary and atheist, and the permanent trend of the Russian intelligentsia toward maximalism. "It is of great importance," says Berdaieff, "for Western people to understand the national roots of Russian communism, its determinism according to Russian history. The knowledge of Marxism will not help." The contempt for the West and its mercantile spirit was an important element in the rapid Russian adoption of that Western doctrine which is known as Marxism. Disputes over the question of whether Lenin was an "alien import" or not have often been of a low level intellectually. There has been much ado over his partly Jewish descent (which was revealed by an orthodox Soviet writer, Marietta Shaginian). In fact he was a typical member of the Russian Bolshevik intelligentsia, combining total unscrupulousness with utopian vision. The Russian writer Soloukhin has written a book against Lenin called *Reading Lenin*, which is now a best-seller, and was first published in the émigré press. He is astonished by Lenin's blunt cynicism, his call to murder and robbery, his manipulation of hatred. In his booklet "The Soviet System in Retrospect: An Obituary Notice" (Columbia University, 1993), Alec Nove reminds us of the main component of Bolshevism: the unleashing of hatred against the intelligentsia and the landlords. In fact, Mao's policy during the Cultural Revolution has helped us to understand what Bolshevism really was, under the mask of the century-old dream of Russian revolutionaries: after the stage of massacre, it protected the remnants of the intelligentsia and the technical aristocracy in return for their allegiance and submission. Michail Gershenzon had already written in the famous collective anti-intelligentsia book *Milestones* (*Vekhi*), inspired by Berdaieff in 1909: "We cannot dare to hope to join with the people—we must fear them more than any State power, and we must bless this power, which with its bayonets and prisons is still able to protect us from the people's wrath." The satirist Bulgakov has shown that hatred, and the coming to power under communist rule of the dregs of the population. His hero Shvonder, from *A Dog's Heart*, is representative of that new lumpen proletariat, acting as the "hegemon." New Russian criticism now makes much of the analysis of "Shvonderism." Stalin's purges were founded on "lumpenization" and received popular support, as Alexander Zinoviev rightly underlined. Fear and enthusiasm were complementary. And an enormous social mobility was a trump that Stalin played with great skill. But it was founded by Lenin, and Soloukhin is quite right to remind us of Lenin's appeal to robbery: "Rob what was robbed." Alec Nove has a subtle answer to the question of continuity between Lenin and Stalin. Stalinism is a continuity, *stalinshchina* is not. That is to say the maniacal and personal psychotic excesses of Stalin are not a continuity. This is dubious, and although Nove quotes the novelist Grossman, he does not listen to Grossman. Grossman discovered, to his own horror, the kinship between communism and Hitlerism. From Lenin to Hitler, from Hitler to Stalin, there is a continuity: the cult of hatred, the contempt for man, the scorn of humanism.

Vassili Grossman saw no other issue out of Leninism than a return to small causes in a Chekhovian manner. Lenin, according to Grossman, preserved the main curse of Russian history: the link between progress and serfdom. Stalin, on this very point, was the continuation of Lenin. Stalinism looks at man as a screw in a mechanism; and on Victory Day, when Stalin gave a toast to the Russian people, he addressed it to the health of all those screws which had played their part. The historian Michail Geller has taken those two words, "screws" and "machine" as the title for his book on the functioning of communist totalitarianism in Russia and the creation of "Soviet man."

One of the best books ever written on that Soviet man is the testimony of a Pole, Herling Grudzinski, in *Inny Swiat* (*Another World*). It is not a manual of totalitarianism but the memories of a Polish *zek.* The book is extraordinarily human and profound, without any hatred, even with love for the Russian people. The author describes a Bolshevik in the camp, a man called Gortsev. "For hundreds of thousands of Gortsevs, Bolshevism is the only religion, and the uniquely possible attitude toward the rest of the world, because it has been instilled in them since their very childhood. For the Gortsevs, the loss of their faith in communism, their unique faith in their life, would have been equivalent to the loss of their five fundamental senses, which allow them to identify, define and appreciate surrounding reality." Gortsev, a former judge and torturer, is slowly annihilated by the inmates of his barracks with the tacit consent of the camp's authorities. One image in Grudzinski's book is extraordinarily vivid: because of their bad diet, many prisoners become temporarily blind: every evening at sunset they walk hesitantly like blind people, waving their hands as butterflies might their wings in the half darkness. No doubt, communism in its fanatical stage was a temporary blindness. Yet at that stage I am not sure that its characteristics are specific of communism: they are common to any blind fanaticism at its height. The point with communism is that it lasted for another thirty years after that moment of culmination. It could weaken but not change. In other words, communism still preserved a core of fanaticism even in its weakened form, even when it seems to be humanized, as once Alexander Dubcek thought was possible. Vaclav Havel is conscious of that paradox, and it is indeed one.

The West has been fighting for decades against the "Evil Empire," as President Reagan used to say, but when that Empire of Evil fell and disappeared, and the West was scarcely happy, many even began to regret the fall of communism, not in its ideological, but in its imperial form. To get rid of the disastrous heritage of that empire is extremely difficult, even from a merely material point of view. Some countries have had to re-create democracies, others have to create democracy. Some small nations have been given the opportunity for the first time in history to grasp independence, and they take all kinds of risks to do so. "It is no fault of theirs," says Havel, "that the opportunity has come up decades or even centuries after it came to other nations." This is a very important point: people on the earth live at quite different stages of history. As we know, a few thousand are still even living in prehistory. A popular illusion in the West is to believe that Marshall McLuhan's global village now lives at the same historical moment because "everybody" watches more or less the same the television program. No mistake can be grosser than that; and in Europe, under the general notion of post-communism, especially in former Yugoslavia, we are now witness to the scale of that error. Hatred is a notion that has disappeared from the Western horizon. The illness of universalism is a Western disease. It may bring new disasters. As Havel points out, people, in their different ways, are trying to correct history, the disasters that resulted from Yalta, and before Yalta from Versailles, and even from previous partitions of this world. The global material civilization does not rule out particular cultures that resist unification and reject mutual understanding. From a certain point of view, although it may look sacrilegious to say so, one may put forward the idea that from Christianity (as understood in the Roman Catholic manner, derived from Constantine) to Islam, from Islam to communism, from communism to United Nations imperialism, we can observe different varieties of the same trend to universalism.

I feel obliged here to quote Adam Michnik, in order to evoke an ally. "The Prague movement that had been the inspiration and witness of an entire generation has turned into an object of derision, a symbol of communist deceit....We should remember that communism was not born in 1945, or in 1939. We should take seriously the motives of those who believed in communism." People were convinced in the East, at some time, that "Western civilization was finished, and that, following the example of the Roman Empire, capitalism would crumble before the dynamic barbarians from the East." Michnik's defensive position today is an illustrative example: the struggle against communism was also ideological, but it was also a difficult liberation from the obstinate and cumbersome "Central Committee in our brains," as André Glucksman once put it. A new generation is now born, which despises the preceding generation's difficult struggle against its own attraction to unity and totalitarianism. But, of course, that temptation may come back in other ways, perhaps in other parts of the world, or in those societies convinced that they are suffering from backwardness. Backwardness, resentment, and utopianism probably will again engender new sorts of Leninism, that is to say of utopian and militarized despotism. Statements such as those of a former Marxist Soviet journalist, Alexander Yanov, who is now an American political scientist, should at any rate be avoided. Yanov, who has made an American career on the denunciation of Russian fascism ranging, according to him, from Soviet generals to such Russian nationalist writers as Solzhenitsyn, is now advocating a sort of American action similar to that undertaken by MacArthur in Japan after World War II. Nothing could be worse than that kind of patronizing approach—worse in its results, or more stupid in its misunderstanding of history.

Another temptation that should be resisted is the temptation to oblivion. A simplistic view is now prevalent: that human history is at all its stages discrete, as philosophers say—that is to say, offers distinct alternatives and breaking points. Any false commitment may lead, according to that view, to a dead end from which the culprit will be compelled to retract. This simplistic view, both mechanical and moralistic, disregards the psychological history of mankind. I was struck on different occasions in Russia by the passionate desire for oblivion. For example, universities have suppressed their chairs of "Soviet Literature," replacing them by chairs of "Twentieth-century Literature" at the very moment when, liberated from ideological dictatorship, they should on the contrary have undertaken a real study of Soviet literature, Soviet law, Soviet science, and Soviet civilization. It should be studied now, before memory is altered, because it is a part of our European civilization, not only of specifically Russian destinies, and a part, more generally speaking, of our world history. One might remark that nothing was more pitiful than the revolt of African students at the Lumumba University in Moscow after the victory over the putsch in August 1991. The new democratic Russia would not pay for them any more, nor would the poor African states which had sent them to the Mecca of communism. They were the remnants of a Third World alliance with the communist utopia.

It was not long ago, in the 1970s, that it was proclaimed that utopia was not a condition outside of man, but was present among living men, even helped to form them. Khrushchev's pretension that communism was on the verge of fulfillment and was about to outstrip America appeared ridiculous only to the West. It had an almost mystical resonance in some parts of the Third World and also penetrated an area of the Soviet psyche. That view of things made the nature of time itself look quite different. The slogan of "true socialism" was in a way part cynical, part thaumaturgic. And true utopianism, that is to say, the real abolition of time, was achieved in a grim variation: the long reign of Leonid Brezhnev. Even that gerontocratic leadership of the Soviet Union was a symbol of an accomplished utopia, as old cardinals in a conclave symbolize eternity in time. Time was abolished, public and private life were gently moving from one anniversary of the Revolution to the next, from one plenum to the next, and so on, in a vicious circle, reminiscent of Hegel's vicious infinity. Interplenum life had no color, no life of its own. Slowly and surely that weakened form of communism was depriving the countries it ruled over of the blood of real life. Everywhere, in whatever sphere of activity, a shadow-life began to prevail: a shadow-economy, a shadow-history, a fake religion. And real life was retreating to the underground, in literature and mores as well as in economy. Clandestine mafias ruled that underground life and have now emerged into the open air. Nothing authentic or true was left. After the crumbling of communism, we were told by the director of Soviet cartography that all the maps published over seventy years were deliberately false at the beginning, ritually false at the end, including the mapping of rivers. We have heard extraordinary confessions about huge lies in sport, in the Stakhanovite movement; we have discovered the monstrous East German clandestine (literally, underground) factories for sportsmen and sportswomen, submitted to chemical and hormonal treatments. Reality was no longer real. That is not in the distant past; that continued during *perestroika*, to the very end of Gorbachev's reign. But archives are now being destroyed, or illegally sold to Western specialists, and research institutions in Russia are torn to pieces by the Western temptation of Soviet scholars. A return to memory will indeed not be easy.

Lenin's mummy has not yet been removed from the Mausoleum.[3] The Russian press has published hundreds of *feuilletons* about that strange mummy, an Egyptian rite in our century. The underground laboratories and sports premises under the Mausoleum, the mysterious lounges for official guests who had to stand on the Mausoleum during the parades have been made the subject of many "revelations." Some of my friends, who had never previously paid a visit, have hastened to see it, afraid that they might miss one of the strangest sights of the century. I myself saw both Lenin and Stalin side by side the year I arrived in Moscow for the first time, as a French student. Stalin was removed a few months later. Lenin's cenotaph and thousands of Soviet ritual statues that have been removed and now lie in huge cemeteries of statues all over the country testify to the enormous legacy of pointless communist symbolism. There is no authority to which they can be escheated!

Dostoevsky's figure of the Great Inquisitor may help us to

understand the legacy of communism. That figure was fascinating until it became reality. His Inquisitor says to Christ: We do not need you any more, go your way, or I shall arrest you and have you burned at the stake. We do not know what Stalin said to his former fellow-Bolsheviks before sending them to torture, public recantation, and murder. But the idea was the same: an ideology, when triumphant, no longer needs its founder, no longer needs sincere and zealous disciples; it needs only fanatical slaves. Dostoevsky's Shingalev adds: "They like to be slaves." The syndrome of Shingalev has played an enormous role in the history of our century, and of the communist movement, but not to the very end, not to the point of victory: neither Tiananmen, nor the "August victory" in Moscow confirmed that prediction of Dostoevsky. "Natural" man, with his love for liberty, has reappeared in places where we thought such a phenomenon had completely disappeared. China is still communist, Russia is no longer. (It makes little difference in our Western policy toward those two countries.) China shows us another stage of communism, a mixture of rigid despotism and broad economic liberty. If Tiananmen is not repeated, will China prove that a successful evolution of communism is possible, a communism in which the whole soul is not withdrawn from man? In Zamiatin's anti-utopian novel *We Show Ourselves*, the comrades in the Ideal City of the Great Benefactor are submitted to a surgical operation, their soul is taken away, and they feel at last free. I suspect that the Zamiatin operation is always doomed to failure, but it may succeed over one generation, even two, or three.

Not long ago, China gave us a terrifying revelation about an extreme form of communist hysteria in its phase of fanatical delirium. It happened during the paroxysmal period of Mao's so-called Cultural Revolution (the object of such enthusiasm in our own liberal society at the time). The Chinese dissenter Zheng Ye concluded after a long investigation, in which he was helped secretly, and at great risk, by many of his fellow-countrymen, in a book called *Red Disaster*, that what is now officially called in China "the three years of natural disaster" were in fact three years of "unnatural disaster." (The same happened in Russia in the twenties, in the Ukraine in the thirties.) The famine was not only deliberate and exploited to the point of utmost cynicism, it also gave birth to ritually organized cannibalism in some parts of the country. The organizers seem to have been local communist leaders. Victims of the Cultural Revolution were eaten in grim ceremonies. Usually their flesh was mixed with pork, so that people should get used to the idea and overcome their revulsion. Cannibalism, as an extreme form of communist fanaticism, makes us think of other religious pagan rites. The Russian writer Andrei Platonov wrote in his novel *Chevengur* that people want to eat communism as a sort of eucharist. Platonov's poetics are based entirely on materializing abstract notions linked with communism, such as food, as flesh, or a place on the earth. Zheng Ye describes three stages of ritual cannibalism under communism, the last one being "hysterical" communism, when inhibition has disappeared and "natural man" has been at last completely erased. Cannibal banquets are then the final stage of the crushing of the class enemy, who must be destroyed as human beings.

That unprecedented inquiry into an episode which might reveal to us some subconscious foundations of communism must also force us to rethink the religious nature of communism. Many people have thought that communism was derived from Christianity. The Russian poet Alexander Blok, in his famous poem "The Twelve," not only uses Christian images (which are numerous in Russian poetry of the beginning of the twenties), but even shows the mysterious figure of Christ walking in front of twelve red guards. My own teacher and *maître*, Pierre Pascal, a French Catholic and French Bolshevik at the same time, who managed to link his two professions of faith for at least five years, thought that communism was a return to primitive Christianity, to the church of the first disciples. In that he was, let us say, a follower of Lamennais, but Lamennais wrote before communism. I wonder whether a more primitive source of communism should not be sought in pre-Christian religion, in a return to the primitive religions of the collective immolation of scapegoats. The French philosopher René Girard has described the mechanisms of that primitive religious mind and the connection between violence and sacredness in *Things Hidden Since the Foundation of the World*. Actually, one Russian poet may have been aware of that link with primitive society. In his novel, Boris Pasternak lends to one of Zhivago's friends a long speech on the theme of the return to tribalism under communism. Socialism, so explains Simushka, was in the nineteenth century mainly a luminous compassion for the poor and the feeble; in the twentieth it became a return to tribal life.

Mark Aldanov, a skeptical novelist, who lived and published as an émigré, has written many novels on the French Revolution and the Russian one. He is the only novelist who has chosen the 9th Thermidor as the center for his meditation. What does Thermidor mean? Trotsky attacked Stalin as a Thermidorian, and that was terribly unreal, a strange and revealing underevaluation both of Stalin and of the sacredness of violence in the revolution. One of Aldanov's heroes says: "The aura that may form around the French Revolution is far more dangerous for humanity than the revolution itself. Revolution will end some day, but the aura will not." In *Two Revolutions*, Aldanov adds, "success proves very little." We might as well turn the formula the other way round: defeat proves very little, at least when we speak of myths, not of reality. And communism, linked with the sacred and with sacred violence, has a mythical nature. "How can one get out of Terror?" asks the Polish historian Bronislaw Baczko in a book on Thermidor. He was struck by the discovery in the documents on Thermidor that the myth of "Robespierre the king" played an important role: anonymous libels accused the Tyrant of planning to marry the daughter of the king and crown himself. Neither is that so strange to us now: Kim Il Sung is the living version of that myth. Communism also tries to perpetuate the violence of its foundation in some sort of communist monarchy.

In conclusion, is communism dead? I am tempted to say: for the time being it is mythologically dead, but it survives in the form of enormous material and human ruins, and those ruins may still fall on the survivors. The disaster of communism has now to be digested by a free Russian, Polish, or Hungarian society, and it is a terrible legacy. But in the next stage, in the next generation, it may be the reverse: communism will be at last completely dead materially, but the myth may reappear. As long as the primitive tribal religion of collective life, as long as the seeds of what Girard calls the "victimarian mechanism" are still hidden in the abyss of the human psyche, the danger is still there, in our subconscious.

**Notes**

[1] The events in October 1993, and the general election in the following December, have not radically changed my view, although it has become clear that discontent in the country may find its expression in some sort of fascism. The fact that the country was able to adopt a new constitution and refused civil war confirms that sagacity. The bad results of the reformers have shown that the old "liberal" intelligentsia is unable to accept political responsibility.

[2] This title of one of Zinoviev's last books is a mixture of *perestroika* and "catastrophe." In a way it predicts the coming to power of Mr. Zhirinovsky, the Russian fascist apprentice demagogue, who received 23 percent of votes at the last general elections.

[3] It has been since, in October 1993. Lenin is now buried in a churchyard in St. Petersburg.

# COMMENT ON
# THE NIVAT PAPER

Fritz STERN

I was privileged to see two drafts of Nivat's rich paper. The major change, I think, from the first to the second was the addition of a question mark after the title, and as a historian I welcome his acknowledgment of uncertainty. In both versions "the consequences" of that collapse are omitted, but we would be remiss if we did not speculate about the consequences of this enormous change.

Nivat concentrates on Russia, raising also the old question of whether Bolshevism was an inherently Russian phenomenon or an alien import. Perhaps it was both—certainly the collapse of communism was at once a Russian and an East European phenomenon. There were many voices, many dramatic events that need to be remembered in this process. Russian thinkers, Russian dissidents, especially in the post-Stalin era, understood the horror and fatality of the regime—and found sustenance in older Russian thought. I remember a visit I made in 1979 to Lev Kopelev, who said to me that he wished to be free *in* Russia even as I was carrying messages facilitating his proposed visit to West Germany that became an enforced exile—and I remember how he walked me to the grave of Anna Akhmatova, with the fresh flowers and scribbled messages on it.

The disintegration of communism should be studied as well in Eastern Europe, where communism had engendered little faith and lacked the constantly invoked legitimacy that the Soviet Union had gained by its heroic survival in World War II. In Eastern Europe there were remnants of civil society that could oppose the regime: the several churches, the strong nationalist traditions. The East European economies were stagnant and life was gray and drab; this material backwardness quickened intellectual dissent and facilitated the alliance of workers and intellectuals. In retrospect one remembers Mirabeau's words of 1789: "The nation's deficit is the nation's treasure."

At horrendous cost the Soviet Union reached the industrial level that Lenin could have envisioned, but it lacked the human and material resources to make the leap to the new technologies of the post-industrial era; a gerontocracy clung to power (as it still does in China). Its radical heir, Gorbachev, thought to reform the party and the economy—and in the process he recognized the need of the other "socialist" states to experiment with their own versions of liberalized communism if they were to survive. He could no more control the reform movement he set in motion than could Luther control his efforts at reforming a corrupt Church. In Eastern Europe, the process of subverting and supplanting the communist regimes gathered momentum. In Poland Solidarity proved the most promising force, and even after its suppression in December 1981, Adam Michnik could write from prison, "this regime is like the vicious dog that loves to bite even though his teeth have fallen out." In the years of communism's decline, which few of us recognized at the time, the signing of the Helsinki Charter, the appearance of a Slav Pope—all these contributed to the growth of opposition and gave moral support to what Vaclav Havel recognized as "the power of the powerless," which power he so stoutly marshaled.

What happened in Eastern Europe in the late 1980s marked a world-historical change for all of Europe—and did so in moral and spiritual terms as well as political and economic ones. A self-consciously peaceful revolution had taken place, a liberation from terror-protected mendacity, and a plunge into the unknown. I agree with Nivat that these events must alter our historical judgments. We must reexamine the very notion of totalitarianism, and the belief that National Socialism and Bolshevism were mirror images of each other—a belief so long resisted and now too easily accepted—is now called into question. That the two regimes ended in such radically different fashions invited reflection: Nivat is right to suggest that Bolshevism carried the seed of its destruction in its beginnings, whereas it is hard to imagine that National Socialism could have collapsed without military defeat; it is equally hard to imagine that it could have compromised with its internal enemies. It is true, of course, that both movements and regimes saw liberalism as their greatest enemy, that they practiced the cult of hatred. But we must remember that they were not the sole enemies of liberalism. As I suggested in a book I wrote many years ago, *The Politics of Cultural Despair*, anti-liberal yearning was a pan-European phenomenon that gathered strength in the 1930s—and it may reappear today in movements both left and right.

I agree that oblivion is a great danger, as is the scattering of archival material. An even greater question haunts people: how should the villains and victims of the old regime be treated? In Russia, and perhaps less in East European countries, communism may be dead but individual communists thrive. To bracket out, as Germans would call it, the period of communism would be a moral failure: the period must be understood, it must be remembered as a warning, and it should recall the great work of the dissidents—however varied, for they were examples of a *civisme* that needs to be reinvigorated in our own countries, as Vaclav Havel in his criticisms of consumer societies has made quite clear.

I note Nivat's mention of Custine and the "curse" of Russia. Let me merely recall that in Germany most especially there were great enthusiasts for the Russian soul, for Russian culture—and resources. At the same time we must recall that in the beginning and for decades thereafter Soviet Bolshevism enjoyed great sympathy in Europe, which had just emerged from the terrors of the Great War, and many Europeans took seriously Bolshevik pretensions at peace and egalitarianism. Stalin's crimes dissipated much of that sympathy, but his leadership of Russian defense against and ultimate defeat of Nazism captured considerable sympathy anew.

The fall of communism will certainly not constitute the end of history and it is certainly not the ultimate triumph of liberal democracy. That collapse deprived the West of a unifying foe, of a kind of moral invulnerability, for in the past Western leaders and Establishment figures could always boast that at the very least "we" were better than the communists, indeed were redeemed by anti-communism. The collapse occurred at the very time when the West (and indeed Japan) was on the verge of its own worst crisis since 1945; a world-wide recession, pervasive corruption in the polity, and general disenchantment with our collective lives. The countries newly liberated from communism are instructed in the virtues of the market and democracy at the very time when the failings of these in the old-established liberal societies become clearer and clearer.

Nivat makes the point that the material legacy of communism

will be gone in a generation, but the myth, now dead, may have new birth. I would add that the two great totalitarian systems corrupted two fundamental longings of our spiritual and psychological lives: the Nazis corrupted the notion of community and the Bolsheviks the notion of greater social justice and a more egalitarian society. I would hope that these longings will find in time new and healthy expressions—though in the meantime people may succumb to nostalgic myths about the regime that had once proclaimed their loyalty to these ideals.

In the beginning of his paper Nivat cites the disturbing words of Father Men: "The day is coming when we shall be free to speak. What if we find out that we have nothing to say?" For the moment we hear many voices, but none with a clear moral or intellectual authority. Before 1989, the great East European dissidents and their followers found inspiration in the values of the Enlightenment, values which had been politically embodied in the American constitution. But even in the short years since 1989, thinkers who can be characterized by Isaiah Berlin's term "Counter-Enlightenment" have made their strident appearance. The parable of the Grand Inquisitor has been invoked, but I would have thought that its central message was different from what Nivat has selected. "I tell Thee," the Grand Inquisitor says to Christ, "that man is tormented by no greater anxiety than to find someone quickly to whom he can hand over the gift of freedom with which the ill-fated creature is born." At the end of this century, the Grand Inquisitor's insistence that men can be governed only by mystery, miracle, and authority has acquired some terrifying plausibility. I would have thought it is the task of liberal societies to struggle against this pessimism, to refute it in public life.

# Discussion:

**Gasteyger:** Following what Nivat and Stern said about the crumbling of communism, Nivat indicated that the seeds of communism may return. I think that is a very important statement because it signals that while we are now celebrating the end of communism, it may not be final. And that leads me to ask two questions.

First, how, in fact, did Russia lose this communism? If communism is basically a Russian phenomenon, in the way we have seen it over the last fifty-five or seventy years linked to the fate of the Soviet Union, or vice versa, that obviously raises a number of questions that have to do with its future and with the question whether or not communism has come to an end. One can also add a larger question by asking how European was communism because, after all, there are still some forms of it around. Nivat mentioned Korea, but I would certainly include China. It is a form of communism that may have different roots and may express a different philosophy and a different economic and political regime, but, still, there it is.

The second question is what does the end of communism, or Russian communism, mean for international order? We have, in a way, lost a countervailing power that was terrible but still stimulated a number of healthy developments, such as European integration or alliance-building, which possibly would not have happened, had there not been this dreadful Soviet power. Now, if antagonism is an organizing principle internationally, and if it provides an element of cohesion internally, one must ask whether the world can live without a countervailing force. Does it have any kind of organizing principles, or is it basically just lost to itself?

This leads me to my final question, whether or not the Cold War was an exception in human history, in international relations. Yet, now it is over, are we not witnessing the resurfacing of experiences we thought were either dead or suppressed by the Cold War?

**Bulliet:** It is notable that with the breakup of the Soviet Union, there are eight Republics that are not European, that did not liberate themselves, Azerbaijan, Georgia, Armenia, Turkmenistan, Uzbekistan, Tajikistan, Kirghiztan, and Kazakhstan. I was recently traveling in Uzbekistan, Kazakhstan, and Kirghiztan. It seems fairly clear that in a number of these republics there is a functioning dictatorship that is little different from what preceded it. It seems clear that the Uzbek state is a communist dictatorship that happens to be free-market-oriented. Since Nivat has given us permission not to include economics in the definition of communism, we can say that.

The phrase "transition from communism," if not to democratic but to liberal society, is one that we think very warmly about in terms of Eastern Europe and Russia. But no one, I think, believes that we have a liberal society emerging in these other republics, and indeed, the inclination of U.S. policy, judging from officials I spoke to in the U.S. embassies there, is that we are actually rather in favor of dictatorships as a bulwark against Islam, and indeed the idea that a communist dictatorship might be preferable to some sort of Muslim state appears to be a continuation of the kind of antagonism that Gasteyger was just speaking of, the need perhaps to have an enemy, even if that enemy is largely imaginary, as I believe in the case of Islam.

In any case, while we can applaud what has happened in Russia and in Eastern Europe, it would be regrettable if we ignored what has happened in the rest of the former Soviet states.

**Kristeva:** I was impressed by Nivat's emphasis on the lack of authority in the fields of political, economic, and spiritual life, even to the extent of the attempt to erase the memory of communism itself. My observation will refer to the last point: religion. Nivat mentioned that religion seems to be the counterweight to communism, and he referred to the Polish example. I agree with his reference to René Girard's thesis concerning "religion as based on the mechanism of the scapegoat," the victimizing mechanism of religion—exclusion, persecution, and worship. I wonder if the development of Christianity, among other religions, has not led also to another conception of religion, a positive one, which is the protection of intimacy, of the private psychic space.

And here comes my question. In spite of its compromise with communism, in spite of the strong connection between nationalism and Russian Orthodoxy, it does not seem that the Russian Orthodox religion now encourages nationalistic war, as has happened in Yugoslavia, for instance. Is this concrete evidence supporting the idea that the Russian Orthodox religion could provide a moral code, on the basis of which some new individual can rise, or some new collective link can be invented?

This could, in addition, be a counterweight to the fanatic Bolshevism that Nivat mentioned. And if we cannot try to find such a support in the Orthodox religion, what seems to be the most effective counterweight to this fanaticism?

**Nivat:** As far as the question of religion is concerned, I think that, of course, the maintenance of religion and of Christianity in Russia has played a huge role, in spite of the fact that the church seemed to be deprived of profound meaning. Tolstoy thought that it would be a great happiness for Russia if the Orthodox form of church disappeared. He disliked religious formalities. But, in a way, only the forms were left during the communist period. Yet those forms played an enormous role, because they were the vector of the return to religion.

There are in Russian Orthodoxy today too many rich phenomena to recall in a few minutes. There are some fanatical obscurantist trends, which to my mind are not at all the majority but do have some prominent figures, even in the hierarchy. There is, I would say, a miraculously changed Patriarch, who plays a very positive role, who for the first time in Russian history since the suppression of the Patriarch by Peter the Great achieved a political role when, on the second day of the putsch, he intervened against the putschists. In secular matters, at the point when nobody knew what the solution would be, he said no.

There is also an ecumenical movement of great richness. But of course what Russia needs, what Orthodox Russia needs, first of all, is the religious challenge of other forms of Christianity, and this is happening now. The development of the Methodist and Baptist churches, which had a huge following in nineteenth-century Russia, are reappearing. This is an extremely positive symptom, because it may facilitate the inclusion of religious man within the citizenry of Russia but not define that citizenship by Orthodoxy.

**Harkabi:** How did such a revolution, correctly described as coming from the people, come without bloodshed? Why did the people behave so magnanimously, without taking vengeance—I would say deservedly—on their rulers? Are these developments symptomatic of something new, or are they accidental? I have difficulty in explaining what lessons we can learn from these facts.

**Nivat:** I think it is difficult for me to answer in the presence of Likhachev. He, indeed, is one of the few men who can answer that question. What must be explained is that it is not pure chance. The absence of revenge, which astonishes you, comes from the Russian soul, and has been described in Likhachev's books. It is a phenomenon in Russian history which is systematically ignored. This is why I began by quoting Custine. Custine had no knowledge of that side of Russian history, just as he had no idea of Russian culture. He was of the same time as Pushkin, but he did not know of Pushkin's existence. So, we may well see a "revolution of the spirit" because of that.

**Perczynski:** I have a question for Nivat because I fully share his view that no doubt we are facing the collapse of communism, but there are some fears as to whether this is a final collapse or whether we will not face some attempts to revive it. In my opinion, we are facing the final collapse, and have probably already reached that point of no return.

But there are some other dangers, and some mixture of ideologies, of concepts, which are anti-communist, but these are not something which we are willing to build in the place of communism. The first slogan of this movement, which I call the populist movement, is "down with communism," but at the same time, down with very many other things—"down with privatization," "down with the market economy," "down with the inflow of foreign capital," "down with foreigners." Although that communist fanaticism is disappearing, extremely powerful new forms are emerging, hampering the process of building a new society.

It is not only a question of nationalism. This is a mixture of ideology and politics, which has really threatened the development of civil society, although it will not bring a return to communism. It is not even encouraged by the previous promoters of the communist society. This is something new emerging now, particularly in Central rather than in Eastern Europe. In Eastern Europe, marks of the old times are more clearly seen; in Central Europe there is a typically anti-communist movement.

What I would like to ask you is: Will the collapse of communism lead to the formation of a new society, which will probably be no better than the old one?

**Dore:** A couple of thoughts are promoted by the question of whether we are really seeing the end of communism or whether there is a possibility of revival. We do tend to think of communism as a unified entity. But we are all, on the other hand, aware of the fact that there was as much diversity among the societies which call themselves communist as there has been among the societies that would call themselves Christian, or, indeed, among the societies that call themselves Islamic.

I think one way of analyzing this diversity is precisely in terms of the dichotomy between liberty and equality to which Morin's paper referred. The sense in which communist society differed from its opponents in the West with respect to liberty and equality can be seen in three dimensions. One is the political dimension of repression of free thought. Another is faith in total central planning of the economy. But the third is the insistence that consumption should be heavily weighted toward what we used to call in Britain the "social wage," namely, free health services, heavily subsidized housing and transport, heavily subsidized basic food, and so on, rather than toward private wages.

I think if one is looking for trends in liberal democratic societies that might lead in the future to a revival of communism, it is not so much in the political dimension, not so much in the revival of some kind of faith in economic planning. Though Kosai's paper (*see* page 81) talks very interestingly about a revised view, about the positive role of government in the economic development of Asia, I think the dimension in which one has to look for tensions, which could lead to a revival of communist thought, is precisely in the provision of the social wage, if you like; what you call in France, "*insertion*," the difficulty of inserting the poor into civil society.

The OECD's recently published employment outlook had, for the first time—and very oddly for a report on employment—a survey of trends in the dispersion of wages in all the OECD countries. It showed very clearly the extent to which the poor have got poorer, in the United States in particular, and the rich have been getting richer.

It does seem that the nature of modern technology is such that if you leave the labour market entirely to market forces, the increasing scarcity of people with high skills, and the increasing superfluity of people who can do only unskilled labour, leads to a big widening in the primary distribution of income. In the OECD's report it is very clear that this is greatest in the United States, and the next greatest widening is in Great Britain, the two most liberal market economies of the West. And the only country where there was no change at all was Germany. Now, it does seem to me that this process can go on for another twenty years, and the tensions which this can produce, unless we too begin to devise ways of increasing the social wage at the expense of private wages, does mean that we shall be back discussing the same kinds of issues as Marx was discussing in the nineteenth century.

**Kerber:** In some ways this comment follows directly, because there is a sense in which it too asks for a category in which we can reclaim some of the elements of communism and in its best form.

Nivat several times used the phrase "return to natural man," that one result of the collapse of communism was a renewed dream of a return to natural man. What are the ingredients of that dream? Because one thing certainly that we have seen in the debris of the collapse of communism has been the justification in terms of what is allegedly natural rather than socially constructed, of an assumption that feminist elements in the old communist dream are to be ignored, and that those elements of feminism which were central to communism in its origins, which by now have seemed poisoned by the old system, have been thrown out. Some of us worry a great deal about how they are to be restored and retrieved in a climate in which they are understood to have been poisoned by their location in the communist system.

The free range of natural man these days in Poland, in Russia, in the former East Germany has meant such things as we don't need day-care, we don't need free access to abortion, we no longer need to ensure the presence of women on national boards, because we saw all that in the time of Lenin and it didn't work. How are we going to rekindle those progressive elements and keep them operative?

**Yamauchi:** I would like to make a comment about the relationship between nationalism in Russia and the fall of communism. The state of Russia is a Eurasian state. The speakers up to now have tended to look at Russia exclusively from the Western point of view, but, being Japanese, I look at Russia from the East, and our perceptions—the way we interpret the fall of communism or the condition of Russian nationalism—appear considerably different.

After the fall of the Soviet Union, the garrisons of the CIS republics were placed on the borders with Iran and Afghanistan. This development can be interpreted or assessed in two ways. It could, on the one hand, be positively interpreted as a stabilizing factor in the uncertain regions of the Middle East and Central Asia, with particular reference to Islamic fundamentalism. On the other hand, on the contrary, despite the fall of communism, it could be negatively interpreted as an indication of the expansionism of the Russian empire.

The Central Asian countries, for example, after the fall of the Soviet Union, except Kirghiztan, are still controlled by "*nomenklatura*," and the power structure still remains. So you could interpret it as a good old communist regime. But they are experimenting with pluralism, sometimes giving rise to two forces. One is the pro-

Western Democratic Party and the other is Islamic revivalism. In Tajikistan, for example, the latter is named the Islam Revival Party, and both it and the Democrats won election.

The Yeltsin administration should have at least watched their experiment in democratization. As things are, the Yeltsin policy, or the Russian Foreign Ministry policy, toward Central Asia, was to support the good old communist regimes instead of giving support to the newly arisen Democratic or Islamic Revival parties. So I feel it necessary to discuss not only the ideology but also the rationality of Russia as a state and its national interests since the empire.

Regarding such experiments in democratization, I think that not only Russia but also Western countries, particularly the EC, lack sufficient patience.

**Gold:** I was wondering, with respect to Nivat's comment, about the fact that the communist regime was characterized by disbelief in any positive virtue or actions in others, and that may have been a mode of looking at the world which lasted for sixty or seventy years and could not have been confined only to a very small group of people but had some consensual validation in a large community. Is there any reason to believe that that general view of the world has changed despite some of the recent positive developments?

From a psychological perspective I can imagine that people who really do not believe in the positive virtues of others may be fearful of doing so because they are afraid of being disappointed; they may not have a positive reservoir of memories in which they felt themselves a recipient of the beneficence of others. It may be a projection of their own aggression, but it seemed like such a pervasive feature of the last sixty or seventy years and such a necessary component of maintaining that regime. Now, I wonder if you feel optimistic that the next generation is not likely to be pervaded by that cynical view.

**Stern:** My first remark is directed to Nivat and it registers a certain unease. In response to Harkabi's question, which I thought was terribly important, on why it is that there has been this absence of vengeance, and whether that says something new, you referred to the Russian soul.

Since this is something that Germans always talk about, I am a little uneasy about the very term "Russian soul," but if we say Russian soul, then that soul has also showed itself in other ways, not just in absence of vengeance, but in atrocities with which we are all familiar. I would myself venture my hope that what Harkabi singled out, which to me is terribly important, is that when in Poland and Czechoslovakia there were these fundamental changes, there was not the outburst of popular revenge at all. I think possibly this relates to what I hope also is a fact, that 1989 may have marked, in a way, the end of a dreadful era that began in 1914 of uninterrupted violence among and within nations, particularly in Europe.

I want, briefly to say a word about Dore's comments. I do not think unemployment alone creates Bolshevism. Bolshevism itself, that is to say, the rise of a Leninist regime in Russia is, I submit, to me as a historian unthinkable without the preceding Great War. That war was both the opportunity and the condition. It is very hard for me to imagine Bolshevism arising out of what I myself referred to as the malaise that now exists, and that is undoubtedly going to grow. There are deep political, psychological, and spiritual crises in our own countries, which in a certain sense we were able to ignore. The Cold War gave the West, and I think particularly the United States, a kind of moral invulnerability. That is to say, whatever was wrong in our countries, one could always say: at least we are not like them; we are better than they are. The absence of a foe is not only politically but, I think, psychologically terribly important.

Finally, once again on the question of the absence of revenge, and the absence of violence. Let me simply say that I also am uneasy not just about the Russian soul but about natural man. I am not sure that I know what natural man is. I do know what human rights are, and those are the elements that need to be protected.

**Nivat:** Well, I thought I would be accused of naiveté over some parts of my paper. Of course, I must say I judge from the Russian point of view, and view Russian Russia as European Christian as far as the Pacific Ocean. Whenever you have that Russian population, you have the Russian mind, Russian habit, Russian way of life. In my paper I did not use the expression "Russian soul." There is a long history of the use of these words since the eighteenth century. Likhachev has used the word "*Russiti*" or "Russianity." Are the atrocities the other side of that Russianity? Probably. What is new is the absence of vengeance in circumstances where we might have expected civil war in Russia. This did not happen, perhaps because of a long political lesson. There are torturers in every street, and there are voices, of course, that advocate that we should hate them and seek revenge. But they have not taken such action so far.

I would like to remind you how often the Western press has

announced that there will be a pogrom in Russia; there has been not a hint of a pogrom. There were pogroms in the outlying areas of Russia, as you know, at the end of the nineteenth and beginning of the twentieth centuries. Some Russians have denied them, others have thought about them. But maybe something has happened and that is the novelty, that lesson of history.

Regarding the question about natural man, I am not a great philosopher. I was thinking of natural man in the Thomist sense, that the junction between Christian faith and antiquity was through the idea of natural man. I think that this idea may not be applied to all countries but may be applied to Russia, and that Russia was submitted to another surgical operation, which was the idea of the new man, a deformation of the new man in Christian faith. Bolshevism is a sort of fake, a false and scornful defiguration of Christian faith. This can be easily illustrated with thousands of examples. Does that mean that natural man is fixed forever? No. It just means that Russian man is part of Christian man, and probably part of that area for which, as Kristeva says in her paper, the idea of intimacy, linked with religious faith, has been the basis of the creation of that culture.

As for feminism, of course, there was a feminist movement in the twenties. There was a Mrs. Alexandra Kollontai. When I was a student in Russia, there were women working hard on the streets, and there were horrible abortions for those who couldn't pay. It was a terrible anti-feminist world. I think that now Russia is creating its own thinking. We must not overrate some—let us say, reactionary—points of view which have a right to exist and do, but which are a minority in Russia, and, I would say, a surprising minority.

Turning to another question, I would like to remind you that there have been democratic elections in Russia, and that there has been a referendum in conditions of pluralism, with very heavy parties representing the old forces. Question No. 2 of the referendum proposed, in spite of the difficulties of reform, an attempt to introduce private property into the economy. And when the reactionary Russian parliament introduced that demagogical Question No. 2, it was sure that it would receive the answer "no." But it received the answer "yes," though with the small majority.

It makes a huge difference that we are now speaking about a country where you can count opinions. It is not what we think about Russia. We can count the voices from St. Petersburg to Vladivostok in that huge country.

As for the diversity of communism: I must confess that this is something in which I am interested, but it would be insolent on my part to speak about Korean or Chinese communism. I am not sure that the diversity in communism is the same as in, say, the Christian or Islamic world. As I said, I believe that there is always that core of fanaticism and cult of political violence, without which it is not communism. It may be socialism, but that is a completely different story.

Utopia may come back. After all, the roots of Russian communism, as Nicholai Berdaieff has said, are in a perverse deformation of the Russian religion. Why did communism occur in Russia? Probably because of that trend toward what Berdaieff has called "chiliasm" or "millenarianism," and the incarnation of which was Leo Tolstoy, that is to say, a sort of new anabaptism that we want the Kingdom of God here and now. The Russian people who voted last April, of course, have learned not to be religiously maximalist, not to demand the Kingdom of God here and now, but the seeds of that may, too, be essentially natural man.

**Windsor:** What has been very clear is that neither of our speakers nor those who raised any points from the floor feel optimistic. What has also been very clear is that nobody has given up hope.

# CAN DEMOCRACY TRIUMPH?

# CAN DEMOCRACY TRIUMPH?

Edgar MORIN

**D**emocracy was born on the fringes of history, alongside the despotic empires, theocracies, tyrannies, aristocracies, and caste systems. It remains marginal, despite the universality of the desire for democracy, yet it is the most civilized of all political systems.

Modern democracy is no full-blown historical formula—it is the product of a volatile history, a succession of fits and starts, over the course of which its principles have been developed and affirmed. The first principle of democracy, that of the sovereignty of the people, straightway implied, in order to ensure that very sovereignty, its self-limitation by the need to observe certain laws and regulations, and by the periodic transfer of power to elected individuals. Reserved from the start for free men, its principle can only be fulfilled when all men are recognized as free and equal in the eyes of the law. Following the democracy of the city-state, the democracy of the nation, bringing together hundreds of thousands or millions of citizens, gave rise to the parliamentary process and introduced the devolution of power—as a safeguard against the inevitable abuse of powers when held in concentration—the guarantee of the rights of the individual, and the protection of privacy. The French Revolution of 1789 established a democratic norm, which was given full expression in 1846 in the form of the trinity—Liberty, Equality, Fraternity. This trinity is complex because its definitions are at once complementary and opposed: liberty alone negates equality and fraternity; enforced equality negates liberty without creating fraternity; fraternity, which must of necessity be fundamental in order that there should be a communal link between all citizens, entails a degree of liberty and reduces inequality, but it cannot be promulgated or given foundation in law. Socialism attempted without success to democratize not just political organization but the socio-economic organization of society. One could be forgiven for believing that the principles outlined above were sufficient to define and to confirm democracy, but it took contemporary experiences of totalitarianism to highlight one fundamental trait of democracy—its intimate relationship with diversity and conflict.

Democracy presupposes and encourages the diversity of interest and of social groupings, as well as the diversity of ideas, which means that it should not simply impose the dictates of the majority but must recognize the right to existence and freedom of expression of heretical or deviant ideologies. Democracy requires a consensus of respect for democratic institutions and regulations, while at the same time it requires the conflicts of ideas and opinions which give it vitality and creativity. But the vitality and creativity of conflict cannot come about without adherence to the democratic law, which controls disputes by substituting ideological battles for physical battles, and which decides the provisional winner of a dispute or competition by means of debate and election.

Thus, democracy, which demands both consensus and conflict simultaneously, is not simply the exercise of the sovereignty of the people, but much more besides. It is a complex system of political organization and civilization which both nourishes and is nourished by the individual's freedom of will, freedom of opinion and expression, and which both sustains and is sustained by the trinity of democratic ideals—Liberty, Equality, and Fraternity.

A complex set of conditions must obtain in order for this system to form and to take root. Democracy is dependent on conditions that depend on its practice (a sense of civil responsibility, acceptance of the rule of democracy). That explains its fragility, and the difficulty of founding democracy after the experience of totalitarianism. The rules of democracy are dependent upon a political and civil culture which decades of totalitarianism have prevented from forming; economic crisis gives rise to an excess of conflict which has the danger of breaching the rules of democracy, while nationalistic aspirations encourage the dominance of a fanatical majority over more peaceable minority groups.

In different parts of the world, a brief flowering of democracy has been followed by the reappearance of systems which are superficially democratic but authoritarian at their core, where a hegemonic body monopolizes power, where sometimes elections are rigged and the mass media is controlled. One is led to wonder whether the current world crisis will not give rise to new hybrid, authoritarian systems, in which democracy is mutilated or severely compromised.

The West is now experiencing grave democratic problems, not simply because the democratization of its democracies is still incomplete, having many gaps and deficiencies, but also because of the emergence of a process of democratic regression. First, the development of a techno-bureaucracy has established the reign of the expert in areas which were formerly the subject of discussion and political decisions. For example, nuclear technology has deprived the citizenry, the parliamentarians, even the ministers of any right to decide on the use of arms—the uses and locations of this new energy source are more often than not decided over the heads of the public at large.

Technicians have invaded territory that was formerly exclusively biological or sociological. In such questions as paternity, maternity, birth, and death, it is already possible to create a child without an identifiable or even a living father, to conceive a child outside the womb, just as it is already possible to diagnose, and to eliminate, a deformed fetus; it will soon be possible to make that fetus conform to its parent's wishes and to social norms. Yet, with the exception of the question of the right to abortion, these problems have yet to enter the political conscience or form the subject of democratic debate.

On a more profound level, the gulf which is opening up between an esoteric, hyper-specialized technician and the average learning of the general public is creating a duality of experts— whose knowledge is moreover highly selective and who are incapable of contextualizing or globalizing what they know—and the uneducated, that is to say, the bulk of the public. This means that we must work toward a democratization of scientific knowledge, toward a cognitive democracy. This task may seem absurd to the scientists and technocrats, and indeed impossible to the public themselves—it cannot be undertaken without encouraging the diffusion of knowledge beyond the normal student age group and outside the confines of the university environment, and, most of all, without proceeding with a reform of thought which would permit a linking together of the different fields of science.

At the same time, the increasing economic competition between nations, particularly in a time of economic depression, favors the precedence of economics over politics, so economics becomes a permanent political problem; with a simultaneous crisis of ideas and ideologies, accepting the preeminence of economics creates a lax consensus which undermines the role of the conflict of ideas which is vital to democracy.

At the same time, too, democracy is regressing socially—after the eradication of basic inequalities that accompanied the era of growth up until the early 1970s, economic competition and the pursuit of productivity have pushed a growing sector of the work force out of the running, while the ghettoization of the immigrant and working classes sets them apart from the upwardly mobile sections of society. The econocrats, who are more than capable of adapting man to fit technological progress, yet quite incapable of adapting technological progress to fit the needs of man, cannot think of new solutions to the problems of reorganization of labor and distribution of wealth. Thus, a dual society begins to form, which, if this democratic deficit persists, will become the norm for society.

By association, the evaporation of grand hopes for the future, the deep crisis of revolutionary thinking, the exhaustion of reformism, the diminution of ideas into workaday pragmatism, the inability to formulate a grand design, the weakening of ideological conflict in favor of conflicts of interest or of racially or ethnically motivated ethnocentric conflicts—all these serve to bring about a sclerosis, a weakening of the democratic process, while supported in their turn by that very sclerosis and weakness. These lead ultimately to the decline of the civic spirit, a retreat into private life, an alternation between apathy and violent revolt, and thus, despite the fact that the democratic institutions remain intact, democratic life ebbs away.

In this retreat of democracy, the major problems facing civilization remain thought of as purely private problems, rather than forming part of the political conscience and becoming the subject of public debate. Thus, those societies which pass for democracies, under many different forms, are faced with the key problem of a deficiency of democracy, that is to say, of the necessity of regenerating democracy, when everywhere else in the world the problem is still one of generating democracy for the first time.

The problem of democracy is a global problem, which takes many different forms. The basic aspiration toward democracy collides with the basic problem of democracy. Democracy depends upon civilization, which in turn is dependent upon democracy.

The years 1989–90 seemed to usher a great flowering of democracy throughout the world, but 1991 and 1992 have been years of regression and of obstacles to democracy. Just as in the past, major crises have threatened the progress of democracy, so the potential deterioration of the global crisis poses a threat to the future of democracy. That future presupposes a progress which is by no means assured. The decisive battle lines have yet to be drawn up in the complex combat between civilization and barbarism.

# COMMENT ON THE MORIN PAPER
## Can Democracy Survive in Latin America, Eastern Europe, and the Territory of the Former Soviet Union?

Detlef JUNKER

U nlike philosophers and systematic social scientists, historians usually prefer specific or rather tangible concepts to abstract formulae. They are reticent to refrain from the factual background of events and activities for the benefit of ascending into the heaven of general theories and structures. Since I am a historian myself, I will try to answer the rather abstract question "Can democracy survive?" by concentrating on two global regions, Latin America on the one hand and Eastern Europe and the former Soviet Union on the other.

The particular nature of the problem provides the second motive for this restriction. After the demise of authoritarian dictatorships in Latin America and the breakdown of the Soviet empire, the people in Latin America, Europe, and beyond are asking themselves whether in the long run democratic systems have a chance of surviving in these two regions of the world.

When we talk about democratization or re-democratization in Latin America in the 1980s, what we mean is the removal of military dictatorships, the creation of civilian governments which derive their legitimacy from general elections, the setting up of representative systems and free competition between rival parties striving for power. Therefore, our understanding of democracy in Latin America is essentially that of an organized system of institutions. The return to democracy in Ecuador in 1979, in Peru in 1980, in Bolivia in 1982, in Argentina in 1983, in Uruguay in 1984, in Brazil in 1988, in Chile 1990, and even in Paraguay in 1989, and in Nicaragua in 1990, i.e., in countries with a tradition of authoritarian governments almost without democratic elements, has to be seen against this background. Even in El Salvador, Guatemala, and

Honduras elections resulted in the creation of civilian governments. However, when I talk about democracy in Latin American countries, I do not mean to imply that after the end of military dictatorships these countries have managed to set up systems governed by the rule of law, create independent judiciaries, provide effective protection of human rights, ensure civilian control of the military, or guarantee an efficient system of government and public administration. Neither does the use of the term democracy suggest that society's opportunities of participation and social human rights have been improved for the great masses, that a more balanced scheme of income distribution has been achieved, that poverty has been overcome or that corruption and clientism have been fought successfully. Such a vast concept of democracy would miss the actual process of democratization, its opportunities and hazards. Yet, it has to be acknowledged that in the current Latin American debate on future prospects of democracy such a wide horizon of expectations is utilized as a means to criticize the actual process of democratic change and dismiss it as detrimental development.

Although the countries south of the Rio Grande are faced with huge problems, a large-scale counterrevolution, i.e., the return to dictatorship, has failed to materialize so far. Castro's Cuba is on its last legs. Politicians in the United States, Europe, and Latin America have called upon Castro to resign and hold free elections. The putschists in Haiti lack national legitimacy and recognition by the international community. In April 1992, Peru's Alberto Fujimori, who had come to power in free elections, staged a coup with the support of the military. By organizing the election of a constituent assembly he is now trying to legitimize his government. Fujimori thus has no real alternative to initiating a process of re-democratization, albeit on his own conditions.

The new democracies' survival so far is less a consequence of the countries' own efforts but is rather due to the total loss of appeal of leftist or rightist dictatorships among their populations. These dictatorships had plenty of time to prove that they were able to create a minimum of prosperity. Probably the nations ruled by them would have put up with the loss of freedom alone, but they were not prepared to accept the fatal mixture of dictatorship and economic misery that occurred in the eighties. In addition, the outright traumatic experience of life under these dictatorships (repression, torture, murder of political opponents), which spared virtually no segment of the population, has led to a change of heart, to progress in the awareness of freedom, including in states which, unlike Uruguay, Chile, or Costa Rica, do not have a longer tradition of democracy.

As a consequence of its breakdown in Eastern Europe, communism, which was once considered the leftist alternative to representative systems, has lost its long-standing appeal for some groups in the Latin American elite. In addition, pressure from the outside has ceased to exist. After the end of the Cold War, communist movements no longer enjoy the support of the Soviet Union, and the United States has stopped promoting rightist military dictatorships. People like the outspoken American Jeane Kirkpatrick have no more reason to write essays with titles like "Dictatorships and Double Standards."

Finally, it must not be neglected that even another variant of Latin American politics, i.e., a form of populism which comprises all social classes and is based on a charismatic leader and parts of the elite, has also lost much of its appeal as a result of its failure in the past. Yet it is also obvious that the democracies in Latin America are confronted with tremendous economic, social, and political challenges which they will hardly be able to meet. Currently, it is not very probable but still conceivable that these unresolved social problems will destroy the present institutional order. For the moment, however, even the anarchist dissolution of national power structures or conflicts, reminding us of civil wars, does not end in dictatorship.

In order to achieve a better general understanding I should now like to make some comments on the economic situation of the region under discussion. In the 1980s virtually all countries on the Latin American subcontinent experienced a period of economic and social decline only equaled by the Great Depression in the 1930s. Thus, people have every reason to talk about the eighties as a "lost decade." The situation in Latin America is extraordinary, because in the economic policy of many states this second Great Depression brought about the change from a development model of import-substituting industrialization based on a policy of protectionism, high tariffs, and state intervention toward a neo-liberalist concept. It was only from the crisis of the eighties that Latin American countries learned the lesson which the United States and the industrialized First World had learned as early as in the Depression of the 1930s.

However, this boost in modernization which Latin America had hoped for by pursuing a neo-liberalist policy goes along with high social costs such as bankruptcies, unemployment, and losses in purchasing power, which further aggravate the economic plight of the middle classes and the population at large. According to some estimates, in 1991 44 percent, i.e., 194 million of the 440 million inhabitants of the Latin American subcontinent, were considered poor, most of them living far below the poverty level. There is hardly any other region in the world where the distribution of income is as unbalanced as in Latin America. Besides costs there has also been some success. It is improbable, however, that neo-liberalist policies will actually help to overcome the debt crisis, reduce the chronic deficit in the balance of payments, and considerably increase Latin America's share in the world economy, the latter having dropped from 6 percent to 3.5 percent in the eighties.

If we add the negative repercussions of neo-liberalist policies on social policies to the other structural problems in Latin American society—rural exodus, drugs, corruption, and clientism, political and criminal violence, rebel and guerrilla movements, the military threat to politics, functional problems of political institutions—we have every reason to doubt whether the hope for economic liberalization and sustained democracy as it was promoted at the end of the 1980s will ever be fulfilled. However, there are vast differences between the countries and subregions in Latin America and the Caribbean. Chile and Uruguay, for example, seem to have the best conditions for a system of sustained democracy. Mexico might increasingly turn into a North American country as a result of its growing economic interdependence on the United States and its migration movements to the north.

Although I am of the opinion that in many Latin American countries democracy—in its stated "minimal definition"—has little chance to succeed, I am even more pessimistic about the general situation in Eastern Europe and in the area of the former Soviet Union, extending from the Weichsel to Vladivostok. I consider it improbable that in this area, with the possible exception of Poland, Hungary, and the Czech Republic, free elections will bring about representative civilian governments with a free press and a minimum of separated powers which will stand the test of time. In the area of the Soviet empire and the Red Army, the transition toward planned economic systems and dictatorship from 1917 to 1925 and from 1945 to 1948 resulted in great suffering, unspeakable violence, civil war, and the degradation of the economy. There is no reason why the reversal of this development should be any easier.

What we have witnessed in Eastern Europe is not the planned transition from one system to another but just the chaotic breakdown of a system.

Of course, in this region, as in Latin America, a possible return to the past has become discredited by the knowledge of the disastrous consequences of despotic regimes. But, as in Latin America, this does not mean that there are no conceivable and realistic alternatives to liberal market economies and pluralist democracies. The dream of the "One World" made up of liberal democracies based on free enterprise and governed by the rule of law, the dream of a great area of liberty and property extending from San Francisco to Vladivostok, was mere pie in the sky. As far as I can see, the choice of the future will be between moderate authoritarian presidential systems without aggressive foreign polices and brutal, ruthless dictatorships marked by expansive foreign policy making.

Possibly the greatest threat to democratic development lies in the potential for destruction of antagonistic nationalism based on ethnic rivalries, which dominate people's energies and passions, is the root cause of wars, and destroys the already limited economic substance of the nations at war. It is this problem of ethnic nationalism that differentiates this region of the world from the Latin American subcontinent.

The nine former Eastern European states consisted of a partial nation-state (the GDR), five nation-states (Poland, Hungary, Romania, Bulgaria, Albania), two multinational states (the Soviet Union, Yugoslavia), and one binational state (Czechoslovakia). Only the five nation-states survived the process of transformation in the east. The GDR became part of the Federal Republic and turned the latter into a nation-state. The bi- and multinational states disintegrated and formed twenty new nation-states, one state with different nationalities but with strong characteristics of a nation-state (Russia) and a disintegrating multinational state (Bosnia and Herzegovina). However, this transformation process did not solve the nationality problem but rather opened a Pandora's box. It is quite possible that even more nation-states will emerge from it. In addition, many of the new nation-states are *nation*-states in name only. Within their borders the so-called titular nation is also seen as the representative of other ethnic minorities. In the case of Kazakhstan the titular nation is itself a minority. Some of these minorities are fighting within their states to create nation-states for themselves; others want to separate their territories and become part of states with their own nationality. Where they stay in their present states and remain in their minority condition, they are fighting for cultural, social, and territorial autonomy and against real or suspected discrimination. The problem of Russian minorities could become the focal point of a new imperialist movement striving to build a Greater Russia. The problem of Serb minorities outside Serbia has already unleashed imperialist forces fighting for a Greater Serbia. A coalition of a Greater Russia and a Greater Serbia would threaten European, if not global, security.

For Eastern Europe and the area of the former Czarist empire, the reemergence of antagonistic nationalist movements symbolizes a return to normalcy. This region's long-standing tradition of foreign rule, the constant threat to its people's ethnic roots as a result of the domination by imperial powers and foreign ruling classes created an understanding of freedom which was not so much seen in connection with sovereignty of the people, with democracy, but with the fight for national liberation. As a consequence of the increasing interdependence of the empire with the Western world of nations in the eighteenth century, reformers and the intelligentsia in the Czarist prison of the peoples started to develop an intellectual tendency toward the concept of freedom and the European ideas of emancipation. This tendency, however, was too weak to break Czarist rule and culminated in the Bolshevik Revolution. Even today, and in spite of the support of Western nations and possibly Japan, reformers and the intelligentsia will probably fail to promote successfully the idea of emancipation and individual freedom against ethnic nationalism and the great social and economic plight in this area.

The second great risk to the democratic idea in this region lies in the breakdown of the former economic and social system which has not been cushioned by a transition process to market economic principles but leads to chaos and abject poverty. I hope that in this respect, too, Poland, Hungary, and the Czech Republic will be exceptions to the rule.

The legacy of totalitarian systems and the lack of personal initiative and individual responsibility seem to block the way toward market economic systems. Russia, in particular, lacks market economy traditions, a proper business culture, and small and medium-sized enterprises. The population expects all changes to be initiated by the state, i.e., from the top down; people expect change to come from poor Boris Yeltsin and allegedly rich Helmut Kohl, whom

German reunification also turned into a beggar. The chronic backwardness of agriculture, the lopsided concentration on the military-industrial complex and heavy industry, the technical backwardness in many sectors, isolation from foreign markets, and huge environmental problems are part of this dismal legacy. The fight for independence in Russia and the other republics of the union and their refusal to make the financial payments required by the central government have further aggravated this situation.

The Russian government's attempt to begin the transition from a command to a market economy with shock therapy, i.e., by liberalizing prices and wages, has so far been a failure. Within two years, the standard of living dropped by 50 percent, inflation is still on the rise, foreign currency is secretly channeled abroad, people's purchasing power is plummeting, and great parts of the population are threatened with misery and starvation. But there are also winners in this state of crisis. Corruption, theft, and other economic crimes have reached unprecedented dimensions. The privatization of homes, factories, land, forest land, and natural resources formerly owned by the state is making little progress. Former communist officials, i.e., the former "nomenclatura," are trying to reap profits from the distribution of state property. They are only prepared to give up political power if they can gain economic power instead.

In economic terms the population is unable to buy former state property on a large-scale basis. In addition, a psychology which is hostile to any concept of private property is further strengthened by such a proposal, because until the breakup of the Eastern Bloc state property was considered the general property of the people, and theoretically every citizen belonged to the group of owners. It has therefore been difficult for the people to understand why they should buy what they already have.

In conclusion, ethnic nationalism and the desperate economic situation make it improbable for the majority of nations of the former Soviet Union to develop into representative democracies.

# STATEMENT
## The Russian Intelligentsia

Dmitri LIKHACHEV

The word "intelligentsia" in other languages is described as "adopted from Russian."

I would define the intelligentsia as an intellectually independent part of society. These are not plainly educated people or thinkers engaged in intellectual pursuits. A critical peculiarity of the intelligentsia is intellectual independence, freedom from party, class, professional, religious, commercial, or simply career-oriented interest.

If, however, his convictions make a member of the intelligentsia join a political party demanding unconditional discipline and actions in conflict with his own opinion, such "voluntary slavery" does not allow him to consider himself as part of the intelligentsia any longer. This is the same as a doctor would stop being one if he were to treat patients contrary to his medical convictions. Equally, a member of the intelligentsia loses his intellectual freedom if he is compelled blindly to follow the dogmas of a certain doctrine or, if out of stubbornness, he refuses to revise his views of the world.

A person not respecting the intellectual freedom of others, persecuting individuals for their convictions, may never be called one of the intelligentsia. Intellectual freedom supposes a respect for this freedom regardless of its manifestations.

The moral factor is very strong here. Intellectual freedom is to a certain extent a phenomenon of morality, while morality is the unique power or force which not only does not impose on a man's freedom but, moreover, guarantees such a freedom. An individual, acting in agreement with his conscience, would not follow any other dictates while he obeys his conscience quite voluntarily. This is a unique attribute of conscience.

Certainly, the intelligentsia, the people who may be called such and not merely thinkers (inevitably present in a certain proportion in any country), do exist everywhere. But, still, the intelligentsia is especially characteristic of Russia. This is not due to a special peculiarity of Russia, or Russians being a special nation, but due to historical circumstances.

Russia always used to have loose (or, as they say now, "transparent") boundaries between classes, and the transition from one social standing to another has been relatively easy. This produced a special base for the emergence of individuals who in essence did not belong to any social group and who therefore were free of any class ideology. In the uneducated strata of society this led to the formation of groups of tramps, Cossacks, various fugitives, withdrawing to the borders of the state, etc. When such individuals, unrestricted by class, were even more free due to a good education, knowledge of foreign languages, and high breeding—they formed the intelligentsia. During all regimes the intelligentsia turned out to be a kind of "internal emigrants."

Inner freedom was to a certain extent characteristic of the Kiev prince Vladimir Monomakh as long ago as the turn of the eleventh and twelfth centuries. He rose above his interests as a prince and lived his life showing concern for the good of the "smerds," as they called the Russian peasants, and for all the population of ancient Russia. This might have been because he was a descendant of the Byzantine empire, which made him less linked with the interests of the Rurikovitches. In addition, he was well-educated, spoke four languages, was familiar with Russian history, and patronized chronicle-writing. Another such member of the intelligentsia, living in the fifteenth to sixteenth centuries was Maxim Greck (Michael Trivolis), a most uncommon monk: a Greek by origin, Orthodox by religion, but an Italian by education.

At the beginning of the eighteenth century a turn toward Eastern Europe did not produce a greater intelligentsia in Russia: Peter the Great liked well-educated specialists and professionals but not free-thinkers.

The first members of the intelligentsia to form themselves into a group were Sumarokov, Novikov, Rhadischev, and Karamzin in the eighteenth century. Their first mass action was the Decembrist revolt. The Decembrists were largely people who voluntarily acted against their own class interests. Characteristically, it was their intellectual freedom that prevented the Decembrists from winning: it did not allow them to unite into one strong party and adopt a common program. Such actions on the part of the intelligentsia were rarely successful, and should not be regretted. While this demonstrates the organizational weakness of the intelligentsia, it nevertheless illustrates their spiritual and moral strength. They were, after all, people of intellectual freedom, destined to create but not to crush others.

The intelligentsia have, however, always been a target for attack by the state. In order to consolidate its power, the state's first action is inevitably to attempt to destroy the intelligentsia and all its sympathizers.

From the moment they came to power, the Bolsheviks arrested, exiled, and deported the intelligentsia, dissolved their study groups and societies, and closed down even the most innocent places where they could meet, such as restaurants, cafés, and scientific societies. They censored attendance at university lectures, shut down newspapers and magazines that published articles discussing general philosophical and ideological problems, and tried to discredit its members in the eyes of the population by falsely associating them with the bourgeoisie and nobility and by organizing false legal trials. They prohibited the study of foreign languages and prevented scientists, writers, and artists from going abroad or exiled them for good. The "secret freedom" of the intelligentsia was what worried the state most of all, especially one that was tyrannical and ideologically unfree.

# Discussion

**Stern:** I want to compliment Junker on his reassuringly specific paper, which was, I thought, very useful. I want to make a comment tying two comments together. I quite agree with Morin that obviously democracy needs to be rooted, so to speak, in national culture, the culture of each nation. And how it evolves historically is terribly important in evaluating the possibilities of a democratic society.

I now want to switch to something else. Likhachev talked about the Bolsheviks not being educated. We ought, perhaps, at some point to realize that the role of the educated, of the cultured, in our century, in the great temptations of totalitarianism, has been quite dismal. Let me hasten to add that in my earlier comment I myself spoke about the heroism of certain intellectuals under certain circumstances. That is the other page, but I think it ought to be understood that we, as members of a privileged class, so to speak, of a cultured class, have certain expectations of how one ought to behave. I think it is part of the record of the twentieth century, of the history of this century, that intellectuals to a very large extent have betrayed their mission.

**Gasteyger:** I was impressed by the question Morin posed. He said democracy will prevail but asked on what level of institutional organization, whether democracy can go beyond the level of the nation-state, namely, on the European level. And that raises the whole issue of the future of European integration moving toward not just an economic and monetary union but to political union. In other words, democracy at the level of the nation-state can survive, but one is doubtful whether it can survive on a higher international European level. And the question, therefore, is about the future of the European Community as a democratically organized community. But how much democracy can the European Community take on without becoming inefficient?

One of the major problems I have, when I look at some features of democracy or democratization, has to do with what I call the democratization of foreign policy making. In other words, that the people become more and more involved in foreign policy making and rightly so—so far it has been in a way exempt from democratic decision making. We see it when we look at the tremendous difficulties the European Community has in formulating anything like a common foreign policy. It is here where one sees the limits of democratic decision making when it comes to highly sensitive, highly diverse, and highly divisive kinds of issues.

So, my question for Morin is, while he said he is a European, does he really think that the European Community and other international organizations will achieve the kind of democracy that legitimates their own existence?

**Likhachev:** Many problems are being discussed in Russia—not only now, but from the beginning of the October Revolution, or rather the putsch. Since that October putsch, we in Russia have been discussing all the problems facing us at this round-table

I think it is impossible to return to communism because you cannot go back to what wasn't there. You cannot go back to nothing. Not only the Russian leaders but all the communist leaders in the world are very immature, or only half-developed in their knowledge. Many of those revolutionary leaders were drop-outs who never managed to graduate from high school. Their level of education was low. Take Lenin and Stalin, Beria, Krushchev, Brezhnev: all of them were very poorly educated. No anthropologist or scholar has ever been a genuine communist. There has not been a single commmunist leader who has read Karl Marx's *Das Kapital* in its entirety, except Lenin. No lies are perfect lies; lies are always partial lies. Conversely, a perfect, complete lie could be transformed into literature or art.

Lies once exposed cannot be used again. For example, in the last eight years I have never seen a paper or a book which susbscribes to Marxism. There are some calls for the return to the Soviet Union in some Bolshevik newspapers, calls for a return to a unified, strong, big state, but in recent years there have been very few public statements in support of communism.

Now, let me mention something most important. The main "protectors of religion" these days are those who were in charge of ideology in the Soviet Union. Many ex-leaders of the party now go to Sunday services. I could mention the names of converts. But these are converts from nothing, because they didn't previously possess any world view from which to convert. For that reason, those people have acted only in their own interests. They are not worthy of the label "intelligentsia." They cannot go back to a world view which they never held; in other words, they cannot return to a communism which they hadn't achieved to begin with.

Now, in the world Soviet republics—Russia, Azerbijan, Turkmenistan, Lithuania, and many others—the most important thing is the question of culture: enhancing their culture, improving their intellectual quality, and inspiring each and every individual to wake up to his or her moral and intellectual worth.

In 1989, at a conference held under the old Soviet system, I was asked about the tasks the nation faces. I answered that the important issue is not economic but cultural, because economic problems cannot be solved in the absence of moral foundations. At that time, in my statement, I said, "It is not existence that defines consciousness. It is the mind that defines existence. It is culture that determines an economy." There were about a thousand representatives present, and not one of them opposed my statement. None of them listened to me, either.

The most pressing problem of culture now has to do with the "reputation of human beings." To wake up to human values and to enhance the dignity of man should be the very foundation of the way we look at things. Without this particular philosophy, we cannot improve Russian society, which is now controlled by the mafia and over which a dictatorship remains. And neither can we ever go back to communism, as it never existed in the first place. That is my opinion why it would be impossible to return to communism in Russia and why the putsch did not succeed.

There is one battle remaining: the war on nationalism. The idea of nationalism fills the ideological vacuum. Characteristically, in the current situation nationalism and ex-communism are predicated on the same foundations: an immature intelligentsia, and imperfect knowledge of history, and an imperfect understanding of culture.

Therefore, what I would like to stress is that truth is visible only to the really wise, or to the genuinely naive. At the birth of Christ, to speak symbolically, there were the Magi and the shepherds, representing two extremes, the wisest and the most naive. The Magi are the wise men, and the shepherds have mastered the mundane details of everyday life.

All other ethnicities of which Russia is composed have discarded communism. What they now need to do is to form or build their own cultures, including religious cultures, and to improve and enhance the levels of their cultures. That is the task that is incumbent upon all the peoples of Russia. Moreover, the entire world should comprehend the tasks facing Russia; that is, conversely, what Russia should not do. It must serve as an object lesson of what the rest of the world should not do. So please watch and try to learn what the Russians should not have done.

**Yamauchi:** While I was listening to Likhachev, I remembered the famous work by Pyotr Chaadaev. Chaadaev once told us the Russian people are the only people to give the world a lesson on what not to do. I think Likhachev repeated Chaadaev's theory quite precisely.

In connection with Likhachev's comments, I should like to mention one problem. Last year two sessions of the Russian Parliament were held, and in the first session the Parliament formally adopted "Russia" as the official name of state. Subsequently, the Parliament rejected this formal title, and adopted Russian Federation Russia. This is very important because Russia is not only a nation-state in its precise meaning, but is also a multiethnic state. This unique characteristic should be remembered when we consider Russian history. Now, I dare say, Russia faces an identity crisis in the formation of its state.

Finally, Junker only mentioned Islamic fundamentalism in his argument about democracy and democratization, but he purposely skipped the problem. We tend to use the term "Islamic fundamentalism" quite broadly and generally, but I think the term is much too vague and ambiguous. Recently, not only in Japan but also in the United States, scholars whose concern is Islam tend to divide Islamic fundamentalism more precisely into extremist, fundamentalist, and revivalist. Nonetheless, even now, not only in the mass media but also in the academic world, people tend to identify the current of Islamic fundamentalism with Islamic terrorism. "Terrorism" has, of course, no connection with Islam itself. I think we should use the term "Islamic terrorism" when we want to indicate such anti-democratic or anti-law or anti-social currents in the Islamic movement.

**Murakami:** Can the members of a community decide to discard democracy in a democratic way? Is such a decision to be regarded as legitimate or valid, viewed from the democratic perspective? This may seem to be self-contradictory, but Morin mentioned or referred to "cognitive democracy" in his paper. I can share the idea, but, still, it seems to me quite possible for public opinion to deny the idea of cognitive democracy.

**Nivat:** I would like to say one word about Likhachev's remarks and his paper on the Russian intelligentsia. Alexander Solzhenitsyn has twice given advice to his Russian compatriots. The first was in

1972 in a letter to the Soviet leaders. He wrote: "At least, let us have spiritual freedom. And you can retain political power. I am not a maximalist." By the way, this was usually misinterpreted as a sort of apology for authoritarianism. In 1990 he gave another piece of advice to his compatriots: "I think now that we shall have democracy, that we have a chance to have democracy, unless the ruins of communism crumble on us." He had changed his mind because of the evolution within Russia. We can see from this that he doesn't think that democracy is an aim in itself. Everyone must have another aim. Democracy is just a way of organizing society.

Coming to the Russian intelligentsia, I would like to say respectfully to Likhachev that, as he well knows, his conception of the Russian intelligentsia was criticized in 1909 by some Russian philosophers, the best known of whom is Berdaieff. He thought the Russian intelligentsia, which was an advocate of progress (and by the way, Dostoevsky or Tolstoy were never considered as such), was bad for Russia because it mixed the sense of justice and the sense of truth, which in Russian are both "*pravda.*"

In other words, they wanted a diversification of intellectual work. I think that today in Russia there is a need for the diversification of intellectual work, that the era of the Russian intelligentsia is over. In Russia we need, on the contrary, to have experts in intellectual thinking, a philosopher and not a sort of charismatic leader, a theologian who is a theologian, and so on. This is also needed for the flowering of democracy in Russia.

**Morin:** It is not random, I think, that all the discussion about democracy turns around the ex-Soviet Union and the new Russia. One little word to my friend Nivat. A philosopher, a theologian—these are not experts. An expert is a specialist technician. A philosopher can utilize the data of the expert. I think the professionals, serious people, are true thinkers, but experts must be at the service of politics and thinkers and citizens.

I want to say that concerning the Soviet Union there is a great misunderstanding about the October putsch. When Lenin decided on the October putsch, it was not for Russia. It was for world revolution. And the tragedy is that the destruction of the first free assembly by the Bolsheviks was the beginning, not of world revolution but of a new totalitarianism in the world. The failure of the culture of communism made for the success of terror and totalitarianism.

Today we can reach both a pessimistic and an optimistic conclusion about the whole process. The pessimist sees the semi-*appa-rachiki* Communists as the nationalist chiefs of the new states, but the optimist sees the self-disintegration of the most powerful power. It is a demonstration of the infinite weakness of infinite power.

I think of Solzhenitsyn, because in his letter to the leaders of the party, he said only one thing: Don't lie. The revolution comes from *glasnost*, in the sense of no more lies, no more distortion of reality, no more deception. The fragility of the totalitarian system is connected with the possibility of the truth.

The question of Europe is very difficult because we have no historical example of democracy outside a nation. I do not think Europe will be a super-nation, but perhaps something new. I think political democratic life can grow. Why? Perhaps when the different national parties become European federations—socialist, democratic Christian, liberal, or conservative—and when the workers' unions are not simply trade unions of various professions, there can be different European unions.

One little thing: You were saying that terrorism is not Islamic fundamentalism. It is true to say that. It is a stereotype, a stupid stereotype. Further, when there is a connection between a strong, intensive nationalist feeling and strong religious fundamentalism, there is the potential for great violence. The Iranian case is not only Shiite religion; it is the connection between that and the great traditional nationalism of Iran. It is fortified by the war against Iraq, because it is the beginning of a long tradition of war.

The forces of association in the world are fighting against the force of dislocation by war. But the decisive bifurcations have not yet ended. It will be another five, ten years. For that reason I said "uncertainty," because new developments may change the direction of history, not only for the ex-Soviet Union, Russia, but I think for the world, too.

# THE CRISIS OF
# THE SOCIAL
# SCIENCES

# THE CRISIS OF THE SOCIAL SCIENCES

KOSAI Yutaka

My assignment is to discuss the crisis of the social sciences in the twentieth century. I feel perplexed—like the undergraduate freshman in an introductory sociology course who is assigned a term paper on a grand theme. To my partial relief, a more specific question has been provided by the organizers of the symposium. The question, which my paper will attempt to answer, is as follows: "The social sciences have largely abandoned their claims to predict (let alone, manage) developments in society and politics and have become increasingly fragmented. Can they rediscover their philosophical roots?"

Before I begin to answer the question, let me briefly discuss the assumptions implied in it. It assumes that the prediction (and control) of social developments should be the role of the social sciences, and that the social sciences should be integrated rather than fragmented. Combining these two assumptions, one can infer that the developments the social sciences should predict are those on a grand scale, rather than those of a piecemeal variety. In addition, the social sciences should, according to the question, be based on philosophical roots which they once had but lost at some point in time.

Several reactions seem possible to these assertions. Two such viewpoints will be mentioned in order to contrast them with the approach to be taken in this paper. These could be termed the representative social scientist's viewpoint (or "positivist," in the broadest sense of the term) and the representative social philosopher's viewpoint (or "existentialist," also in the broadest sense of the term).

Most working social scientists are too busy writing research papers in their respective disciplines to worry too much about the question. If one were to address it, however, he or she would likely

81

reject most of the assertions implied in the question. Many objections could be raised. Failures of forecast, although regrettable, are unavoidable in the process of trial and error; they are a necessary byproduct of active scientific research. Forecasting in the social sciences is the most difficult part of the job, as hypotheses often include many "other things being equal" caveats, experiment is not usually permitted, and adequate statistical data are often lacking. For those who reject the symmetry thesis of Hempel, explanation rather than prediction is the proper role of the social sciences. "Historicism," which is used to predict some grand trend of historical necessity, must remain inadequate (Popper). Only by strict specialization can one accomplish something good in the sciences (Max Weber). Indeed, what are the philosophical roots which the social sciences have lost and must reaffirm? Natural law, Marxism, or the idea of progress? Avoidance of value-laden judgment is the essence of the sciences (Max Weber, again). Or, do philosophical roots refer to the methods used by social scientists? If so, what then is wrong with a working social scientist engaging in a scientific research program which is in a continual process of knowledge growth and forward movement (Lakatos)? The representative social scientist would ask such questions.

From the representative social philosopher's viewpoint, the question posited by this paper is more than justified. According to him, humanity, rationality, and everything else is in crisis; the social sciences are no exception. In spite of the constant success of the respective disciplines, the social sciences have been reduced to mere factual sciences and have lost their meaning in the "life-world" (Husserl). It is high time for the return of a grand theory in the human sciences (Q. Skinner). Crisis can be overcome only by a scientific revolution, and by a shift of paradigms (Kuhn). A new consensus must be attained through reasoned debate in the community of scholars (Habermas). Alternatively, some would maintain (along with Geertz) that social scientists would do well to abandon the ideal of social physics and adopt instead an interpretive approach. The crisis may become permanent, as "the unifying and legitimating power of the grand narratives of speculation and emancipation" has collapsed and as science now has to "play its own game" in post-modern conditions (Lyotard).[1] Such would be the claims of the representative social philosopher.

This paper will take a middle position between the two. Although the progress made in the social sciences in their respective disciplines in recent years has been great, it must be admitted as fact that some predictions by the great social scientists as to developments in the twentieth century have failed miserably. For better or worse, social scientists are divided in their diagnosis of the major issues of the time. The question posed at the outset of this paper is a natural one from the standpoint of an intelligent citizen living in the turmoil and tragedies of this age, and an interesting one from the standpoint of intellectual history.

Additional words on the definition of the crisis of the social sciences are in order. From the representative social scientist's viewpoint, crisis of the social sciences can be defined as the impossibility of maintaining analytical rigor or consistency. From the representative social philosopher's viewpoint, crisis of the social sciences can be defined as a loss of relevance, or of meaning, in the "life-world." When both conditions are met, the term "crisis" can be fully applied. In what follows, crisis of the social sciences will be interpreted as a loss of both rigor and relevance. The paper will be principally concerned with the failure to accurately predict macro-fluctuations. When the failure originates in a lack of rigor at the micro-foundation of the respective theories, a full crisis is said to be under way.

## THE TWENTIETH CENTURY AS AN AGE OF CRISIS AND THE SOCIAL SCIENCES

The twentieth century has been an era of war, revolution, depression, and inflation, and of innovation, growth, and economic development. It has also been an age of flourishing research activities in the social sciences. In this century, the social sciences established themselves as an independent branch among university disciplines, alongside the natural sciences and humanities. Such institutionalization brought about a differentiation of disciplines and specialization among the social sciences, and they came to gain a fair share of professorial chairs and university budgets. In addition, there was a systematization of knowledge, as was shown in the monumental *International Encyclopedia of Social Sciences* (1930–35), edited by Seligman.

An interesting question to consider is how to relate the crisis of the age with the development of the social sciences. To begin, let us rethink the failed predictions made by great social thinkers and scientists on the critical events in this century. The collapse of socialism has betrayed the prophecy of Marx. Wars have repeatedly trampled Spencer's expectation of development from a military to an industrial society. Economic instability in the market economies persisted long after Keynes. The rapid industrialization in some non-Western nations has, to some extent, deprived Weber's thesis of its credibility.

The failure of certain predictions by social scientists does not mean the failure of the social sciences as a whole. There existed other social scientists who opposed the predictions, or who revised and improved the predictions, but there is no denying that the failure of prediction triggered the crisis, at least in some areas of the social sciences.

**Socialism:** Socialism was once regarded by many intellectuals as a more advanced economic organization than capitalism. It was believed that socialism would replace the anarchy of production in the market economy with rational planning and control of economic activities by governments. But now its defects are clear enough. It suppresses individual choice, and thus incentives are lost. The surprising thing is that so many people were unable to recognize such an obvious defect in socialism over such a long period (Buchanan).[2]

The following is one reason why socialism appeared so rational. Suppose that the data surrounding supply and demand functions (elasticities, etc.) are known. One can solve the simultaneous equations and calculate the optimum quantities to be produced and consumed, as well as the corresponding prices. This, of course, is what the market does. According to this view, it is easy to regard central planning—that is, socialism—as a perfect substitute for the market. Taking it a step further, some believe that the "computers" of central planning will perform the function of the market more efficiently, as the computer is freer from noises and frictions.

Criticizing this mechanical view of the market, Hayek proposed the view that sees the market as a "mechanism for communicating information." The "knowledge of circumstances" exists only in incomplete and often contradictory forms and resides in the hands of separate individuals dispersed throughout society. The market is a "process of discovery" in which such scattered knowledge is mobilized.[3] Socialism failed to utilize the scattered information, because individual incentive was lacking.

Sympathizers with socialism could still rest their hopes in politics. By overcoming class antagonism, so they fancied, socialism could realize participatory democracy, and economic defects would be mended more than sufficiently by direct communication among an emancipated proletariat. Unfortunately, "the dictatorship of the official and not that of the worker" (Max Weber)[4] dominated the scene. Weber was right in foreseeing the suppression of individual liberty by the bureaucracy under socialism. The principal-agent problem mattered a great deal. Furthermore, bureaucracy under socialism proved far from rational and efficient when compared with the ideal type depicted by Weber.

**Political Instability:** To see socialism as a rational replacement of the market mechanism, with a huge, efficient computer, oversimplifies the situation. From the start, Stalinism was a phenomenon in "a country that cannot change" (Hoffer), haunted with an historical tradition of despotism and international isolation. Under those circumstances, the transition from socialism to a market economy was bound to be rough. The implication is that the market economy and democracy are not as safe and stable as they appear, when certain conditions are not fulfilled.

The failure of democracy in Germany and Japan in the 1930s and the eventual war in the 1940s—with its concomitant atrocities, Auschwitz, Nanking, and Hiroshima, to name a few—teach us important lessons in this connection. Industrialism has not brought peace, as Spencer expected, but has merely industrialized war itself. It taught the social sciences the fragility of political equilibrium attained within a pluralistic paradigm (Dahl, Parsons) apparently based on the sound micro-foundation of rational political man, as the market economy is based on the rational economic man. The base itself had to be reexamined.

One way to explain this deviation is to emphasize historical continuity and the burden of negative heritage—in the case of Japan, the tradition of Asian despotism and its adaptation in the modern world into a virulent form of ultranationalism (Maruyama). Another is to rely on the psychoanalysis of the anomalous behavior of deprived men at the leadership level (Lasswell), as well as the masses (Fromm). Still another is to highlight the role of the state or dictatorship in critical situations in both the domestic and international arenas (Schmitt).

The defeat of the totalitarian powers in World War II restored the pluralistic-behavioristic views to a position of dominance. An undercurrent of dissonant views survived, however. In the 1950s and 1960s, heterodoxy such as the lonely crowd (Rieseman), the power elite (Mills), and the new industrial state (Galbraith) gradually eroded the classical belief in an independent and public-minded citizen, a movement which culminated in the birth of narcissistic me-ism (Lasch), and brought the end of liberalism (Lowi) and the closing of the American mind (Bloom). The national interest regained its legitimacy in the context of the Cold War, the schism among communist countries, and détente. The state reappeared as an actor in the political sciences (Skocpol), with partially positive results in the form of corporatism (Schmitter, Katzenstein), developmental authoritarianism (Johnson), or as a driving force of history in the form of hegemon and its challengers (Wallerstein).

Socialism failed because of its inadequate micro-foundation—the suppression of individual choice. Democracy proved sometimes fragile in modern conditions due to its eroded micro-foundation—the nonexistence of true citizens. It can easily be taken over by statism or nationalism.

**Economic Instability:** Almost the same story can be repeated in the debate on economic stability. Observing massive unemployment in the 1930s, Keynes attacked the individualistic foundation of neo-classical economics and proposed economic management through monetary and fiscal policies. The 1950s and 1960s witnessed a resurgence of neo-classical economics. Its synthesis with Keynesianism (Samuelson) was the theme of the day. It was at that time that economists believed in their ability to accurately forecast—using large-scale econometric models—as well as their ability to control the economy through the manipulation of the money supply, interest rates, taxes, and government expenditures. However, the simultaneous presence of rapid inflation and massive unemployment in the 1970s forced economists to reexamine the accepted wisdom (Friedman). As in the case of the citizen and the state in politics, the interaction of micro and macro behaviors has come to occupy the pivotal position in the debate on economics.

The current state of affairs in macro-economics can be seen as a continuing fight between two opposing schools—New Classic Economics (Lucas, Barro) versus New Keynesian Economics (Stiglitz, Akerlof, Mankiew-Romer). The New Classicists, now fewer in number, retain their authority through their thoroughgoing pursuit of rationality. Assuming rational expectation and the neutrality of money (at least as far as the change of its quantity is anticipated), New Classicists try to explain why business cycles exist (real business cycle hypothesis). Assuming perfect competition and partial economies of scale, they try to show why economies grow. New Keynesians, admitting the shortcomings of traditional Keynesian theory, which introduced the fixed-price assumption in an *ad hoc* fashion, are trying to reconstruct the system on rational microfoundations. They have found several rational grounds for delaying changes in price-lists (menu costs), for rationing credit (asymmetric information between lenders and borrowers), and for paying state-independent wages (implicit labor contracts). They have further discovered that rational frictions, however small, will produce persistent sub-optimalities and large macro-fluctuations.

The New Classic Economics and the New Keynesian Economics now form the mainstream in economic theory. They share the assertion that rationality in the micro-foundation is essential. The mainstream economists are still, therefore, prisoners of the old religion, stubbornly sticking to the worship of the rationality of individual choice. Their views, having this common base, are converging in many respects. For example, they are working together in building new theories to explain growth and trade. Should we then expect the return of consensus among economists?

To some extent, the answer seems to be yes, but it will be difficult for them to recover the full confidence and credibility in their policy recommendations which they enjoyed in the 1960s. They now know too much about irregularities such as multiple equilibria, time inconsistencies, and rational bubbles. Their policy prescriptions have lost simplicity as a result. Furthermore, other competing schools, such as radical economists, regulationists, post-Keynesians, evolutionists, institutionalists, and decision theorists, are trying to formulate different systems of economics and have affinities more or less with mainstream economics.

**Asian Economic Development:** The Asian economies showed rapid development in the latter half of the twentieth century, in contrast with their stagnation in the first half. The contrast between these two periods may at least partly be attributed to the end of colonial system. So far, however, only Asia (or a part of Asia) has succeeded in rapid growth and industrialization after de-colonization in the post–World War II period. As a result, Japan is no longer the only country among the non-Western nations which has industrialized itself. There has emerged an industrialized corridor in East and Southeast Asia which runs through Japan, South Korea, Taiwan, Hong Kong, Thailand, Malaysia, and Singapore. The corridor shows some signs of widening, so as to include Indonesia and coastal China, as well as lengthening, in order to reach India. Asia will face difficulties if it should continue to grow: population increase and a limited supply of energy, environmental destruction, widening disparity of income among regions, and growing dissatisfaction with authoritarian regimes, to name only a few.

Why has part of Asia succeeded as it has in rapid growth and industrialization? What significance does this phenomenon have for the social sciences?

The mainstream economists tend to interpret the Asian case as proving the validity of the accepted wisdom of classical and neo-classical economics—economic development through free trade (Mynt). Being small countries without strong resource bases, the successful Asian economies accepted the realities of the world market as their given environment—to which they have adapted themselves—instead of trying to revolutionize the world regime so as to build a new international economic order. For the purpose of coexistence with the established world order, they had to be "market-friendly" (*World Development Report*, 1991). Government intervention did occur. They could not, however, totally distort the price structure if they were to continue to live by foreign trade. To expand exports they had to utilize the one factor they possessed in relative abundance—labor supply—instead of jumping straight into enterprises which require capital-intensive technology; as a result, labor-intensive industries grew, and income distribution stayed relatively equal in the process of industrialization. Education spread relatively quickly over the whole population in order to meet the demand for labor. Monetary and fiscal policies were kept basically sound so as not to disrupt the smooth development of international commerce.

The picture painted above has much truth in it, especially when East and Southeast Asian economies are compared to the large countries in Latin America. The success of the former was an historic event, which gave impetus to liberalization and the opening of the economies in China, India, and other developing countries.

Many subtle and important questions, however, remain unanswered. One is related to the role of the state. The domination of the economy by the government has not taken place; for the most part, government policy has been market-conforming instead of market-repressing in the industrializing Asian economies. On the other hand, there is no denying that government plays some active role in the process of industrialization in the region. The task of defining the nature and function of government involvement in the economy of newly industrializing Asia needs further clarification.

Take the case of Japan. An efficient bureaucracy and well-developed relations between government and the business sector are everywhere in evidence (Murakami, Aoki). At the same time, complaints about the non-existence of a central decision making body have frequently been heard (van Wolferen). The criticism echoes Maruyama's characterization of the Japanese fascist state during the war as "a system of irresponsibility." The national economic plan in Japan appears to be an effective tool in forming consensus and ensuring cooperation among the people. Still, the text of the plan is full of empty "visions" couched in very general terms. It is, of course, indicative rather than imperative; it is decorative (Komiya) and ritualistic so as to be reminiscent of the theater state described by Geertz with respect to Bali in the preceding century.

Another area to be scrutinized is the relationship between individuals and society. If Max Weber's thesis is to be believed, modern industrial capitalism was a product of economic rationalism which spread among the masses. But many Oriental religions are "contemplative and orgiastic-ecstatic" in nature and have no bridge to "the practical action of the workaday world," causing the masses "to remain stuck in magical tradition."[5] The statement points to the great difficulty in modernizing, as well as industrializing, non-Western societies. Did this prediction fail? If so, what was wrong with the thesis?

In many societies in Asia where rapid industrialization is taking place, family ties still remain strong, compared to the marked tendency for disintegration prevalent in some advanced countries. Strong family ties apparently shield family members from emotional isolation and help in the children's education; but corruption based on nepotism, exploitation of infants, and the subjugation of women persists. Every society has its own virtues and vices; this shows that development experiences are not single-tracked but vary from nation to nation.

Asia is not one. Its culture and societies are diverse. Many social relations which are not considered "modern" still exist in Asian societies, including Japan. The successful industrialization of some Asian societies which have non-modern, non-Western characteristics shows the need for rethinking the hitherto accepted concept of modernization.

**The Quest of Micro-foundations for Macro-fluctuations:** What this section will try to show is that the big events of the age—macro-fluctuations—such as revolution, war, and depression and inflation, as well as the emergence of the newly industrializing areas, provided the opportunity for the social sciences to be reexamined and, in particular, gave rise to a renewed search for the micro-foundations of their accepted views. In this sense, the crisis of the age and those of the social sciences were mutually interactive. With respect to the social sciences, the lack of not only relevance but also of rigor was thoroughly reexamined.

In this section, the importance of incentives based on individual choice, of "democratic personalities" (Lasswell), of rational expectations, and of rational frictions has been rediscovered through our scrutiny of the failed predictions. In these cases, errors can be mended by reintroducing the more rational micro-foundations. In the fourth example, seemingly irrational micro-foundations appear to coexist with higher performance. We will be forced to search for the meaning of micro-foundations in greater depth.

AN IDEAL TYPE OF SOCIAL SCIENCE AND ITS EROSION

In the preceding section we started from the events of the current century and discussed the reactions of the social sciences to them, focusing on rethinking the relevancy as well as the rigor (micro-foundations) of the theories concerned. In this section the opposite direction will be taken. Starting from the social sciences, we will look into their internal difficulties and then into their relations with the phenomena of the outer world.

An ideal type of social science consisting of two pillars—methodological individualism and social relations centered on contract will be presented. It cannot be overemphasized that the picture here presented is too simplified properly to convey the realities of the social sciences. Methodological individualism, for example, is nothing but a heuristic device, which to some extent helps social scientists to promote the rigor of their analysis. It is not a principle that must be precisely applied at all times. Still, it is hoped that the picture presented below will serve as a point of reference for later discussion.

The social sciences as we know them were shaped around the turn of the century. Methodological individualism broadly interpreted was shared by many of the founders of the social sciences at that time; the marginal utility theory of Marshall, the *Verstehende Soziologie* of Weber, and Wallace's study of political consciousness, for example, all had "the individual and his action as the basic unit" (Weber)[6] in common. The assumption of rationality and emphasis of the Pareto criterion in welfare analysis follow from the adoption of this basic unit. The social relations which most naturally but not necessarily fit in with individualism are those based on contracts. As contracts can be made freely among a multitude of individuals at many levels, the pluralist view of society prevails widely in the profession. The view is completed by the theory of market equilibrium (Walras) and by studies on political process (Bentley).

In the broader perspective of history, methodological individualism would be regarded as well-matched with political individualism (although Schumpeter denied their logical tie), with the rationalization of life (Weber), and with the movement from status to contract (Maine). It apparently is better suited to the *Gesellschaft* than to the *Gemeinschaft* (Tönnies). Sciences and society seem to correspond with each other.

The crisis of the social sciences lies in the disintegration of this unified self-portrait. It also corresponds with the crisis of modern society.

**Erosion of the Ideal Type:** One of the basic questions the social sciences seek to answer using the above information is: How can a society be formed on the basis of contracts between rational individuals? And another question follows from that: What kind of society will it be? The questions have many ramifications. But there is no denying that Arrow's (Im)possibility Theorem and Sen's Paretian Liberal Paradox were a great shock to the naive belief in the democratic process of forming society based on individual liberty. It may well be that we need something more than rational individuals in order to build a sound society; for example, Rawlsian principles of distributive justice. Researchers are finding more difficulties in separating efficiency issues from equity considerations. Formerly it was believed possible to attain maximum efficiency at first and then distribute the fruits as equally as required, without impairing the efficiency, by means of lump-sum taxes. However, it is now widely agreed that any tax will have disincentive and distortion effects; progressive taxes are a disincentive to work and saving, and lump-sum taxes are impossible. The supply-side economics of neo-conservative governments succeeded not so much in promoting productivity—as it promised to do—as it did in scaring people with tales of the efficiency-damaging effects of the redistributive policies of the welfare state. Philosophical schism has thus been even more sharply defined.

Methodological individualism tends to put the individual ahead of the society. That point has been justifiably disputed. Durkheim, well known as an anti-psychologist, wrote that "although society is nothing without individuals, each one of them is more the product of society than he is the author."[7] According to G. H. Mead, "selves and minds" exist and develop "within, or in terms of, the social process of experience."[8] These theories show the sophistication and refinement of naively conceived methodological individualism, as the general equilibrium theory improves over the simple supply and demand analysis. A more direct attack came from structuralism, which aimed at "totality," regarding "social life as a system of which all the aspects are organically connected" (Lévi-Strauss).[9]

The social sciences have inherited some positive images of modern society (as well as observations on its anomalies) from the work of preceding generations: from theology to metaphysics to science (Comte), from mechanical solidarity to organic solidarity (Durkheim), in short, from premodern to modern. The idea of progress is implicit but visible in these expressions.

But should we still continue to speak of the narrative of emancipation in order to legitimize the social sciences? "Progress," "freedom," and "emancipation" are difficult words to define and difficult concepts to measure. Anthropology is accumulating circumstantial evidence which takes us beyond Rousseau's image of the happy barbarian; this evidence downgrades the simple-minded belief in the superiority of modern society and seeks positively to define the "authentic" system of non-modern societies.

As discussed in the previous section, some non-Western countries have made rapid progress toward industrialization, while maintaining some of the non-Western, premodern characteristics of their societies. This finding leads to other findings—that modernity is not complete even in the West, and that those remaining non-modern features play positive roles in the system of advanced societies.

The social sciences are faced with the fundamental need to reconsider the basics which underlie the external and internal pressures. This reconsideration should involve rethinking the implicit assumptions contained in ideas such as modernity, progress, and rationality.

**Contract and Trust:** The point above is further exemplified by the examples of contract and trust.

The establishment of property rights and contract based on mutual consent plays a key role in civil society as well as in the working of a market economy. Their functions should not be exaggerated, however. Durkheim was quick to point out that "a contract is not sufficient by itself, but is only possible because of the regulations of contracts, which is of social origin." Contracts have to be under pressure "that arises from morals."[10] Leibenstein regards contracts as incomplete, because a contract cannot cover all the possible contingencies, a circumstance which impels him to assert an X-efficiency. Contracts in many cases are relational (MacNeil).[11]

This brings us to the problem of trust. Contracts are respected only when other parties are trusted. According to Luhman, trust is a device for the contraction of complexities. The outer world is too complicated for the system to cope with, as the latter's rationality is limited. The system saves itself the effort and cost of searching into the environment by utilizing trust. So the theory goes.

But should trust be regarded solely as a device to contract complexities? Much attention has been paid in sociological discussion to the trust the layman puts in abstract principles and an expert system, reflecting the clear need for such trust in modern society. But there is another type of trust, that is, trust in individuals, which was important in premodern societies, and which is still at work in modern and modernizing societies. In Japan, for example, person-to-person commitments are extensively utilized in labor management, as exemplified in small group activities on the shopfloor. Personal trust does not aim at the contraction of complexities but seeks to deepen the intimacies based on mutuality of experience and of "self-disclosure" (Giddens).[12] Personal trust facilitates communication within the group but may hamper intercourse between groups. Its role as an element of organizing society should be further reexamined.

CONCLUDING REMARKS

How can the crisis of the social sciences be overcome? There seem to be three directions for us to take. First, we might invent a new philosophy which integrates the social sciences, as was the case in the age of Hume, Rousseau, Kant, Smith, and Hegel. Progress in the life sciences and ecology may someday enable us to formulate a new concept of value, in a form which is free from value-judgments.

The second possibility seems to be to accept the crisis as a permanent state, as an unavoidable condition of post-modernity. The social sciences can be legitimized only by a patchwork of scattered and fragmentary narratives. However deplorable, this does not mean that the world will return to barbarity (Lyotard).[13]

The third way lies somewhere in between. Efforts to restore the single-tracked view of social development should be abandoned. On the other hand, the world should not be left to wallow in chaos. By mobilizing all weapons available, and by critically reexamining the implicit premises of existing knowledge, one might build a model of the "multilinear" development of society, as conceived by Professor Yasusuke Murakami, who passed away on July 1, 1993.[14]

We cannot know beforehand what we will know in the future (Popper). After having located the current position of our discipline, we should go back to our desks and set to work meeting the demands of the day in our profession, as directed by our old master.

**Notes**

[1] Jean-François Lyotard, *The Postmodern Conditions*; quoted from A. Easthope and K. McGowan, eds., *A Critical and Cultural Theory Reader*, Toronto Univ. Press, 1992, pp. 189–91.

[2] James Buchanan, "Economics in the Post-socialist Century," *Economic Journal*, 101 (Jan. 1991).

[3] F. A. Hayek, "The Use of Knowledge in Society," *American Economic Review*, 35 (Sept. 1945), reprinted in his *Individualism and Economic Order* (Routledge and Kegan Paul, 1949).

[4] Gerth and Mills, eds., *From Max Weber: Essays in Sociology*, Oxford Univ. Press, 1946, p. 50.

[5] *Ibid.*, pp. 288–89.

[6] *Ibid.*, p. 55.

[7] E. Durkheim, *The Division of Labour in Society*, English translation, MacMillan, 1984, p. 288.

[8] G. H. Mead, *Mind, Self, and Society*, University of Chicago Press, 1934, p. 50.

[9] C. Lévi-Strauss, *Structural Anthropology* I, English translation, Basic Books, 1963, Penguin Books edition, p. 365.

[10] Durkheim, *op. cit.*, p. 162.

[11] I. MacNeil, "The Many Features of Contracts," *Southern California Law Review*, 47, 1974.

[12] A. Giddens, *The Consequences of Modernity*, Stanford Univ. Press, 1990 (Chaps. 3–4). N. Luhman, *Vertrauen*, 1973 (Japanese translation by Ooniwa and Masamura, Keiso-shobo, 1990).

[13] Lyotard, *op. cit.*, p. 192.

[14] Yasusuke Murakami, "The Japanese Model of Political Economy," in K. Yamamura and Y. Yasuba, eds., *The Political Economy of Japan*, Vol. 1, Stanford Univ. Press, 1987.

# COMMENT ON
# THE KOSAI PAPER

Ronald DORE

It is hard for a commentator to know how to begin when pre-sented with a paper like Kosai's. One can only admire the breadth of perspective and sympathy, the enormous scope of the background reading, the leaps of the imagination which enable him to recognize the consonance between the ideas of Maruyama and van Wolferen, or of Komiya and Geertz. If I had read only half of the authors he quotes I would be making these comments with rather less diffidence, but my only defence is to try to make a virtue of our simple-mindedness, and confine myself to one or two points.

To begin with, I can only echo Kosai's puzzled response: What crisis? I do not see around me social science colleagues suffering from an acute attack of angst. In fact I can only think of one exam-ple, an Italian who had spent most of her academic life giving lec-tures on the Soviet economy and explaining to the faithful the superior virtues of central planning. She was in deep trouble because she was being forced to change fields. But most social sci-entists I know are happily carrying on with what Kuhn called nor-mal science. They are not looking for new paradigms and by and large see no need to do so. They may occasionally read some of the authors Kosai quotes, but most for intellectual gymnastics than because they think that they may discover something that changes their way of life or their basic assumptions.

But perhaps there *ought* to be a sense of crisis because there is so much bad social science around. Kosai is a charitable man, and he gives no hint of the fact that the trouble with a lot of social science is that it is of low intellectual quality. One of the consequences of that is that too many social scientists, especially economists, seem to have no interest in life but to distinguish themselves from the herd by demonstrating just how exquisite their own intellectual talents are—

but that is a theme I will return to when I make a few comments on Kosai's discussion of relevance.

## NORMAL SOCIAL SCIENCE

If one were to spell out the basic assumptions on which most social scientists operate, I think they would go something like this. First, objectivity, value-freedom, is as important in social science as in physical science but much, much harder to attain. One of the most important criteria for judging the quality of a social scientist's work is the extent to which he manifestly strives for objectivity by constant self-examination and by listening particularly attentively to critics whom he knows to have value positions different from his. And that is why some of the worst social science is sectarian—what Maruyama called octopus-pot science: little groups like the Society of Socialist Economists in Britain, or the rational choice school of political scientists in the United States, groups made up of people who write for one another and rarely read anything written by anyone else because they know, with absolute certainty, that the rest of the world is wicked.

Second, I would think that most social scientists operate with a model in which pursuing explanation and seeking to make predictions are not, as I think at one point Kosai seemed to suggest they were, alternative pursuits but part of the same search for recurrent regularities, generalizations arrived at by induction, causal connections, laws, or whatever one chooses to call them. Explanations are in terms of general "if so and so, then, other things being equal, such and such" propositions. Explanations which seem satisfactory about past events lend credence to such propositions. The application of such propositions to particular present and future situations yields predictions, and from the falsification of those predictions one learns better propositions. With the generalizations available in the early 1970s, most economists would have said that as inflation rises, savings ratios fall. In fact, in all the industrial countries in the mid-1970s, the opposite happened. So the general propositions were revised. There were actually—amazing as it is to relate—a few bold spirits among economists who actually went out and talked to people who were doing the saving and arrived at some new general propositions about the relation between savings and inflation which actually spelt out the micro-mechanisms—generalizations based on assumptions about what went on in people's minds when they took the decision to save or spend. Alas, alas, these were a small and unorthodox minority. The vast majority continued to believe that social psychology should be left to the social psychologists, and their job was to do wonderful time-series regressions with official statistics for savings and inflation and polish up the coefficients in their equations on the curious assumption that for all intents and purposes the future was sure to be very much like the past.

As for the failure of social scientists to predict big events—the "oil shock," the fall of the Berlin Wall, the collapse of the European Exchange Rate Mechanism—I don't think many social scientists are much shaken by that, nor should they be. Surely, the difficulty of predicting such events is of the same kind, though magnified thousands of times, as the difficulty seismologists have in predicting earthquakes or meteorologists in predicting the weather—the sheer difficulty of collecting and synthesizing the necessary information, as well as the imperfection of the laws which tie that information into predictions. The fact that meteorologists get the weather wrong is not seen as putting in doubt whether or not the physics and the chemistry which underpin meteorology are not exact, law-seeking sciences.

The third characteristic of normal science for the social scientist is—I think Kosai is right in saying—methodological individualism and, a necessary consequence of that, reductionism. When the economist chooses to stick with his official statistics for the prediction of savings rates and says that he will leave the investigation of the psychology of inflation to the psychologists, he is not usually, I think, denying that the micro-mechanisms of individual behaviour elucidated by the psychologist underlie and give causal explanations for the movement of the macro-economic variables which he studies—any more than the meteorologist denies the relevance of basic physics although he himself does not do any basic physics. All he is saying is that there has to be specialization, and he chooses to make his money doing what he does and not something else.

WHO IS A SOCIAL SCIENTIST?

So that is my simple-minded paradigm of empirical, positivistic social science: strivers for objectivity; dealers in falsifiable propositions which they would love to give the status of laws; methodological individualists and reductionists. My first reaction to Kosai's paper was to ask: If one were to say, people who conform to my paradigm are social scientists, those who don't are not, who would be excluded?

Among the writers whom Kosai quotes, I think there are three groups. First there are the Durkheimian sociologists who insist that there are social facts which are irreducible to facts about individuals and fiercely deny my methodological individualist and reductionist assumptions. They, it seems to me, are the *Nihonjinronsha* of the social sciences. *Nihonjinron* seeks to prove that the Japanese are different from everybody else. These holistic sociologists seem to be concerned above all with the integrity of sociology as a discipline, as having something very special which distinguishes it from any other discipline. But in practice when they do sociology, as opposed to doing theory, it seems to me that—like Durkheim, indeed, examining suicide—they are just as much methodologically individualist as anybody else.

The second group are those—Geertz is the one Kosai particularly quotes—who disclaim the law-seeking objective, my second criterion. What they are about, they say, is conveying to their readers some sense of what it is like to be a Bali musician or a Moroccan trader, to give a feel for what goes on in their minds. Fine, that is what novelists do, too, though most novelists do it better. But I do not see any reason for insisting that people who earn their living in social science departments have to be doing social science rather than writing novels.

The third group among those discussed by Kosai who would be excluded are the social philosophers, and this, I imagine, they would willingly accept. What Rawls and Nozick are about is finding some kind of rational foundation for our values, a pursuit which is quite different from doing social science. Good luck to them. It would be nice if they could succeed.

There is a fourth group to whom Kosai does not refer, but who must, it seems to me, be included in any survey of social science: the historians. If Mayall's paper is not social science I don't know what it is. The authors he quotes—the Kennedys, the Hobsbawms, the Gellners, the Kedouries—are, it seems to me, doing about political structures exactly the same sort of analysis of causal interrelations and identification of trends as Kosai does when he talks about long-term trends in the Japanese economy.

## CRISIS OF RESPONSIBILITY?

The *Economist* had a piece recently about the vast growth in numbers and prestige of economists. In spite of their demonstrated incompetence, their authority vis-à-vis politicians and businessmen seems to continue to grow. But there is one consequence of having influence. It becomes more difficult to be conscientiously honest, and absolute honesty is an absolute prerequisite for good social science. When Kosai appears on television and is asked how far the rise in the yen will slow down the recovery of the Japanese economy, he knows that if he says "a great deal" then more people just about to take out a bank loan to expand their business will hesitate, more people just about to buy a new car will decide they had better save the money instead because they might lose their job. What he predicts will, if only at the margin, affect the outcome. If he really thinks the effect will be great, he has the choice between being a good social scientist and a bad citizen or vice versa. So when a Kinsey finds that 65 percent of married Americans have sex outside marriage, he knows that if he publishes that fact he increases the chance of that 65 percent rising to 85 percent; he helps to change the "norm." A demographer who discovers that 70 percent, or whatever it is, of illegitimate children born to mothers under eighteen are black, in a society where white people hold simple and derogatory stereotypes which they apply to all people with black skins, knows that he will be reinforcing those stereotypes if he publishes his results.

The dilemma—having to choose between social scientist honesty and good citizen dishonesty—seems to me a real one for many social scientists, and one which grows in acuteness as social scientists increasingly acquire prestige. I think it is a reflection on our capacity for self-reflection that it is *not* usually counted as a crisis in social science. It ought to be.

RELEVANCE AND RATIONALITY

I was fascinated by Kosai's discussion of trends in economics, of the coming together of the neo-classical and the neo-Keynesian economists in studies of growth and trade. But I ask myself, having recently read a paper by one of the most eminent of those integrating trade economists, Baghwati, chief economic advisor to the GATT, exactly what contribution have these economists made in recent years to our international trading system which is at all comparable to the contributions economists like Keynes made in setting up the Bretton Woods system. We have, he said, to rethink the theoretical foundations of trade theory in order to defend free trade from the current, historically the fifth—or was it sixth—assault it has undergone, this time from the demand for, not free, but "fair" trade. So what have trade theorists been doing all this time? Algebra. Algebra of ever-increasing elegance, sophistication, and incomprehensibility to the layman. And so, by and large, have those micro-economists who deal with the labour market or the theory of the firm. Macro-economists, for the most part, still to have a foot in the real world; they do their fancy econometrics for the learned journals, and they run predictive economic models and talk on television about trends in the economy, and sometimes what they publish in the journals actually affects the way they talk on television. But as for the rest of the economics tribe, there seems to be some kind of law; the more sophisticated the algebra, the more it is a source of wonderment to their colleagues, the more it is deemed to justify a professorship at twenty-seven and a Nobel prize at fifty, the less it has relevance to the real economy that most of us work in and that the macro-economists talk about on television.

Why should this be? What has happened to relevance.

I think one has to seek an answer in the social structure of the social sciences. As Kosai points out, specialization of the social sciences is relatively recent. Adam Smith called himself a political economist and so did Marshall. Specialization began to set in only when salaried university teachers finally took over from gentlemen amateurs at the beginning of the twentieth century. That is when disciplinary departments start competing for university budgets. And one way they compete for budgets is by competing for prestige.

And how do they do that? By and large there are two ways. They can seek respect but from whom? Here there is something of a dilemma akin to that of, say, Bantu tribes under British rule: Should they behave in such a way as to gain approval from their immediate rival tribes, or should they be more concerned with the approval of the more remote paymaster and law-and-order master, the British authorities? Should the discipline, that is to say, define itself primarily in terms of virtues universally acknowledged by all its academic rivals—shared notions of genuine scholarship, say—or by speaking to, and offering authoritative opinions on, topics which are dominant concerns of the lay society, helping to make the world a better place? Should they, in other words, emphasize their claim to intellectual excellence or to relevance?

## ACADEMIC VALUES AND SOCIAL VALUES

The two are often in conflict—as one sees nowhere more clearly than in contemporary economics departments. Thanks to money and markets, much of the subject matter economists deal with can be quantified. Hence it becomes amenable to mathematical manipulation, the more complex forms of which require a level of brainpower with which the majority of the population is not endowed. Hence claims—more often implicit than openly asserted in any vulgar manner—that economics exhibits greater intellectual excellence than other social sciences. These claims are reinforced by high academic performance requirements for students entering university economics departments. Thence a spiralling process: bright students choose economics because being accepted for economics is one way of letting the world know that you are bright, and the choice of economics by bright students reinforces the subject's reputation as the place for the brainy. At the same time, the way in which the tribe defines itself externally is in constant interaction with its own internal values. Thus has been bred the sort of disciplinary culture which dominates most of our economics departments today, a culture in which a scholar's prestige among his fellows is in inverse proportion to the number among them who can understand his algebra.

Which in a way is splendid, because it does make for genuine internationalism. A paper on, say, "Endogenous firm efficiency in a Cournot principal-agent model"[1] or, to quote another recent example, "Optimal investment by the principal in order to increase the probability of favourable states of nature in the principal-agent model with moral hazard,"[2] will be read with equal avidity by the tiny band of the elect, whether their university is in Oxford or Idaho, Yokohama, or Lagos. But that very universality is evidence of the extent to which this intellectual brilliance is bought at the price of real-world relevance, because a lot of the things which determine how economies actually work—institutions, patterns of social relations, norms of right and wrong—are *not* universally the same everywhere. What these elegant pieces of games theory strip out are not only all the things that make real-life situations interesting but all the things it is necessary to take into account if one is to make real-life situations intelligible. The fact that principal and agent in Lagos are often uncle and nephew, that Yokohama principals are often business firms engaged in some R&D joint venture with the firm of their so-called agent, that an Idaho principal is often some junk-bond-issuing asset stripper, etc.—such differences, for the theorist, are neither here nor there. Facts are, as they say, "stylized" out of all connection with recognizable reality. The objective functions of economic actors are pared away to the most basic material welfare maximization. Only with uni-dimensional man can the discipline flourish.

This, you might think, is precisely where the sociologist comes in. One would have thought it was precisely in resisting such attempts at the uni-dimensionalization of man that the sociologist should have a role to play.

And indeed some of them do play such a role, but it is remarkable how the scale of values which elevates the exercise of intellectual ingenuity over the deepening of our understanding of human behaviour spreads from economics to other social sciences. There are now whole departments of sociology in the U.S. where the core of an acceptable Ph.D. has to be some fearsomely complex regression analysis. Now, I should say that some of my best friends do regression analyses. In spite of their tendency to rule out of consideration factors not easily amenable to quantification, they are relatively harmless; and they do sometimes tell one something about the real world—if only what not to believe. A recently published article by a student of industrial relations[3] replicated an earlier study which purported to show that the productivity growth record of firms was quite closely correlated to measures of worker morale. In this second go round he found, for some productivity measures, slightly more significant results; the only somewhat worrying thing was that he had substituted random variables for the earlier researchers' measures of worker morale. The earlier researchers declined an invitation to comment on his results.

When I say that an obsession with regression analysis is relatively harmless, I mean relative to other manifestations of economist-envy such as the use of uni-dimensional concepts of man in formal game-theoretic models. The aggressive rational choice theory school of political scientists was the first to go down this path, and many in sociology departments are prone to follow them. One of the longest entries in any year's social science citation index is the work of Axelrod[4] on how cooperation can result from the pure unadulterated self-interest of players of the prisoner's dilemma game, provided they expect these games to go on for a long time. It now seems to have become *de rigueur* for any social scientist writing about any form of cooperation to include deferential acknowledgement of the work of Axelrod if he wants to be taken seriously. I heard a paper at a recent conference on the social basis of the welfare state which hardly got beyond Axelrod.

Now, most of us, including the author of that paper, are engaged in acts of cooperation many times a day. But in a world which even invented the hotline so that U.S. presidents and Soviet chairmen could talk to each other, it is hard to think of examples of everyday cooperation which fit the basic requirement of the Axelrod model, that the cooperating parties have no way of communicating about the terms of their cooperation—except his actual paradigm situation of partners in crime held incommunicado by the police and having to decide whether and how to confess, a situation in which most of us do not often get involved.

That for a start. A further few moments of reflection on our cooperating behaviour would probably reveal to us that our motives for cooperating are complex; self-interest may indeed play an important part—two heads are often better than one for both headowners; help given now may be requited later. But does not friendship often play an important role? Or the intrinsic pleasures of sociability to be found in group rather than in solitary work? Or shared commitments to an organization? Or to a cause? All of these elements, crucial, for example, for any practical person trying to set up an agricultural cooperative in the Sudan or in Wisconsin, are stripped out of the theoretical models. In fact, the only way the models *can* be made to work is by making the actors uni-dimensionally self-interested men. Furthermore, since the calculus won't work unless pay-offs can be reduced to single parameters, their concept of self-interest also has to be uni-dimensional—measurable either in months of prison sentence avoided or money gained. Show me the man or woman who has actually taken the "findings" of a game-theory exercise of this sort and used them to make either a successful prediction or prescription and I might alter my view that games, however theorized, remain games.

## THE REAL-WORLD CONSEQUENCES OF ACADEMIC SOLIPSISM

Ignorant philistinism and a travesty of the way we proceed, a member of the rationality-obsessed social science mainstream might say. We use explanations in terms of pure self-interest only as a first rough-cut approach. We see just how much we can explain in those terms because in most cases that's the most important thing, and then we can get on with examining the role of less important factors in actual situations. But how often do they actually take the close examination of actual situations as a starting point? Instead, their empiricism is much more likely to be casual and selective. What they are much more likely to do is to abstract from the real world some salient feature—like the fact that it is harder to sack workers now than it used to be, and stylize it into a constraint that adds an extra spice of complexity to the theoretical elaboration of their rationality-driven models.

And, what is more, they frequently go on to make real-world diagnoses and draw real-world prescriptions from such models. A paper at the same welfare state conference as I have already mentioned used principal-agent theory to devise an incentive scheme for the social services which would lead to greater democratic responsiveness. The ultimate principal is the public; the agents are the welfare workers, the doctors and nurses in the hospitals. The trick is to devise electoral and budgeting systems to provide monetary rewards, and monetary sanctions for those who, respectively, please or displease their public. Somehow the author had missed the fact that we live in a culture which does actually expect doctors and nurses to be motivated in their work by something a little more than their expectations of financial reward—by sympathy and concern for their patients as persons, by some sort of commitment to relieving pain and making the sick healthy. It seemed not to have occurred to him that the surest way of killing that commitment was a niggling financial sanction system.

I said, "we live in a culture where doctors and nurses, etc." I should have said, "still, for the moment, we live in a culture where..." because the patterns of incentives we set up don't just use existing motivations. They selectively foster some kinds of motives and cause others to wither. They actively shape individuals' patterns of motivation. It will be interesting to see what historians say about what has happened, particularly in Britain and America, but also in countries like Japan where the social sciences are heavily under American influence, to work motivations, as a result of the deliberate cultivation of individualism under the regimes of Reagan and Thatcher. Britain, in particular, once explicitly cultivated an ethic of public service and relied a good deal on that ethic to maintain honesty as well as efficiency. One by one—the civil service after the Rayner reforms; the universities and the BBC as they are thrust deeper and deeper into the market; now, thanks to the recommendations of a government committee presided over by the Chairman of British American Tobacco, even the police—their salary structures have been altered to reflect a new ideology which would have had almost any member of either the Attlee or the Churchill cabinets turning in his grave: a belief that the ethic of public service is nothing but naive hypocrisy, that men and women can never be satisficers, and are always maximizers about money, and that it is indeed money and only money which can evoke effort.

It will be interesting when historians come to analyse it to see what role they ascribe to the social scientists who provided the theoretical legitimation for these assaults on the quality of British public life by bottom-line-oriented businessmen.

But a more important question is whether this trend will grow or whether can we expect that social scientists will rediscover their humanity, begin actually to examine the complexity of motives which can drive men in universities and government offices and hospitals as well as in supermarkets, and cease to try to remake the world in their own self-image as ruthless self-interested maximizers. Kosai's final remarks about two things—the recent revival of interest in the economic-growth-promoting role of government, particularly Asian governments, and the recent interest in the role of trust, not only in making contracts possible but also in affecting their real-life meaning—are signs of hope. Whether they really are grounds for long-term optimism remains to be seen.

### Notes

[1] S. Martin, *Journal of Economic Theory*, 59, ii, 1993.

[2] M. A. Waller, *Journal of the Operational Research Society*, 44, ii, 1993.

[3] J. W. Straka, "Is poor worker morale costly to firms," *Industrial and Labor Relations Review*, 46, ii, 1993.

[4] Robert M. Axelrod, *The Evolution of Cooperation*, New York, Basic Books, 1984.

# Discussion

**Harkabi:** Even in the natural sciences we have areas which do not deal with prediction at all and still deserve to be sciences. Take geology. In the human sciences, history is a science. It does not have to do with prediction. Archaeology is a science. It has nothing to do with prediction. Now, it seems to me that the hallmark of science is explanation, that is to say, to explain events. However, explanation does not apply to all human knowledge because part of human knowledge is another approach, and that is the hermeneutical approach of understanding, and not explanation, and it cannot be banished from the domain of science.

How can we reconcile these two approaches, the hermeneutical approach and the explanatory approach? It seems to me that we cannot go back to what is called the "Vienna Circle," that is to say the positivist Vienna Circle of approaching whole science in a unitary way. Science does not allow a unitary way. All social and political sciences have to start with an attempt to define what is the world order in which we are because in different world orders you will have a different economy, a different sociology, a different social science, a different political science.

**Winston:** The social sciences, like natural science, take place in a context, social, institutional, ideological and so on. While it is rather obvious to state that, in the case of communist societies, there was a great intrusion of value ideology into the pursuit of social sciences, it is often overlooked that in the United States the Cold War also had an impact. There would be disagreement about how much impact, and certainly many American social scientists like to believe that through all of that period nonetheless there was a free market of ideas. I do not agree, particularly since I know some social scientists who were hounded by the FBI because of the kinds of problems that they chose to study. So, for the sake of trying to make connections between some of our presentations, it may be interesting for us to pursue the line of inquiry into how the social sciences in areas that are presumptively independent of something like the Cold War were, in fact, affected by it, and by implication, then, after the Cold War is over, what might be the impact in terms of a new kind of social science.

**Morin:** First, I think there is a lack of consciousness of the limitations of sensitivity in social science. Sensitivity cannot be extended indefinitely because it is impossible to make experiments as in the science of physics. There is too much complexity to understand all the interactions, and it is impossible to find general laws. The second point is that the patterns of sensitivity dominant in the social sciences have become obsolete. They are the patterns of the physics of the last century.

Third, each social science is much too enclosed in itself with the exception of history. Sociology is closed, and you have compartments of sociology that are closed and too specialized. If you take the most sophisticated economics, the most mathematically sophisticated economists with a Nobel prize, and so on, it will be an unrealistic economics because account is not taken of the interactions between economics and non-economic factors and events. The fourth point in this framework of excessive specialization is the inability to contextualize and to globalize, and now it is absolutely necessary to understand the globalization of the problem.

The fifth and final point is the lack of flexibility, the lack of self-consciousness, the lack of self-criticism, the self inside the story and the society. With the fifth point I return to my first point because I say that social scientists must think and must not only be objectivists.

**Percezynski:** We are expecting too much from social science. I do not see any crisis in the social sciences. On the contrary, I think that we are facing rather a flourishing period in that field of science with many new developments. During these last decades, certain really important dogmas in social science have been abolished and new ones are emerging.

Keynesian dogmas have also been abolished, and I fully support Kosai's argument that what we are facing now is a very good combination of the Keynesian approach to micro-regulation with something which was lacking, the search for rationality at the micro level, and that stream of economics is developing with good results. I do not think that we have a right to ask social scientists what will happen. What will happen is not a scientific question. The scientific question is what will happen if something in the environment changes, not what will happen, other things being equal, because the other things are not particularly willing to be equal.

I can give you an example of something that was ridiculed in the scientific world, which is the first Report of the Club of Rome, where they predicted that the planet will only survive another thirty to a hundred years because the natural resources are going to be exhausted. This was ridiculous. Nothing happened. We have plenty of natural resources, surpluses rather than shortages. While their idea of zero growth was really ridiculous, I think they contributed a lot to the social sciences because in fact they warned what might happen if other things were equal. Probably they were a catalyst to the invention of energy-saving technology, raw materials conservation, pushing into the scientific revolution all the dangers predicted in the Club of Rome elaboration. It seems to me that really what is now necessary is to deepen that way of thinking, to try to include in the analysis all the things which are not willing to be equal, and not to answer the question of what will happen but to find out what are the possible options and which options may materialize.

**Stern:** I come from a field of history where for a hundred years there has been a debate whether we are scientists, whether history is a science or not. I think I find myself rather comfortable in the thought that we are both, which I think is the view of a good many historians. Certainly, the dream of a hundred years ago of somebody like Bury and others who thought history could be a science has been very largely abandoned, and that leaves us freer to borrow from the social sciences, to borrow from literature and philosophy, than to be hemmed in by a somewhat narrow view of our task. Max Weber said over and over again that no great work can be done without passion. Passion, it seems to me, suggests value or, in Dore's excellent exposition, it suggests a degree of non-rationality, which is very important.

And picking up another phrase of Dore's, the malaise of the social sciences, at least as far as I can judge it in my own country, is their distance from actual life. There is an orgy of quantification. There is a daily exemplification of what White had called the "fallacy of misplaced concreteness," and the trivialization of a narrow kind of social science is, indeed, lamentable. But I would say—particularly in light, again, of what Dore said about how social scientists, economists in particular, vie with one another (the less readable, the less accessible, the more preeminent)—that one might have to think about the crisis in our universities that we breed these people, we reward them, and I think that is something to keep in mind. As a motto for that, at the end I would simply echo what Morin said: A social scientist is not exempt from being a thinker.

**Bulliet:** One social science that has not been discussed at all in either of the papers is anthropology, in which the question of responsibility—when you are describing, analyzing, interacting with a culture other than your own—has been a serious crisis in the field, and some anthropologists have reached the point where they do not really feel that it is appropriate for anthropology to be pursued in the way it has been because of the inevitable interference you have when you are doing the observing.

When I was in Kirghiztan recently they had just introduced a new currency, the first of the post-Soviet republics to introduce a new currency in Central Asia, and they had introduced it not because anybody wanted it in the country of Kirghiztan but because the International Monetary Fund had directed them that if they hoped to survive in the world they would have to introduce a new currency. So you had a populace that had new money in their hands, and when they saw it, they thought it looked like sweet wrappers. You had an entire country acting almost pathetically on the basis of what some economists told them they should do. It was almost as if you were observing some kind of anthropologically described cult that if they did what the IMF wished, if they said the words "democracy" and "liberty" enough, the United States and the world would come and rescue Kirghiztan from its apparent inevitable collapse. And the pretense or assumption of authoritarian or authoritative conclusions that you have in some social science milieus get to a point of being a sort of neo-imperialism that must be very carefully scrutinized when you look at these things in a cross-cultural context, considering that the world social science community is primarily drawn from the Western world or the G3 world.

**Junker:** Harkabi mentioned that we should reconcile the traditions of explanation and understanding, and I still believe that we have this rich model of methodology of Max Weber, and this is precisely what he was doing. You can find all the elements in Max Weber and in the more solid German hermeneutic traditions. You can find this very basic distinction between the realm of facts and values, and though it is very complicated I still believe it is the very essence if you think about scholarly social science; and you find the concept of objectivity. Of course, it is not a fact but a regulatory idea, and even that you can find in Max Weber, and I cannot think of a historian or a social scientist without starting with objectivity as a regulatory idea. I do not know what else should be the basis of our profession.

**Yamauchi:** It is often said that the social sciences could not predict, for example, the collapse of the Soviet Union or the end of the Cold War. It is true that Sovietology, which was based on the old framework of social sciences. failed to deal with such issues. Some scholars paid attention to and analyzed the problems of Central Asia and the ethnic regions of the Soviet Union, and they knew already in the 1980s that the Soviet Union was in danger of a crisis. It cannot be denied that, within the old social sciences framework, much of the research and many suggestions were ignored.

So one lesson is that there should be a coalition of regional studies and social sciences, and, in addition, anthropology should play a role, as mentioned by Bulliet. It is true that the tradition of European intellectualism has laid the major foundation, framework, and theories of the social sciences, but as new facts arise and events occur over time, we should be ready to remodel our paradigms to cope with the ever-changing environment.

**Yamaguchi:** There are myriad ways of looking at society—some religious approaches, poetry and other forms of art—but the social sciences have tended to cut off all other approaches. We should be open-minded about other approaches. We should not be bound or blinded by our own individual disciplines, and perhaps we should not be bound by ideas originating in Europe or any particular regionally generated ideas. We should be flexible in creating a new set of frameworks according to the nature of the issues.

**Watanabe:** Likhachev says a sheer lie is all right: it can become a novel or a work of art. In a sense, it is respectable. But a half-lie is the most terrible thing, he said. Now, among many social scientists there are many, many differences and different theories. One believes one's own theory is true and others are not true. This means, I think, that some social scientists or, at worst, all social scientists are half-lying, unconsciously or consciously. An unconscious lie may be worse than a conscious lie. I wonder what this half-lying social scientist can do for the prosperity and democracy of the people in the former socialist countries.

**Nivat:** I think that the social sciences are mainly linked with one stream of European thought, and that is positivism. We have in Europe different approaches, other approaches, which are usually completely ignored and negated by social scientists. I would say that there is another Europe, not only geographically speaking, because in a way Russia is another Europe, but also spiritually speaking. Dostoevsky's impact on Western Europe, his spirituality and his sociological views, which are based on the idea of culpability, which, I suppose, has no sense at all in social science, has only in psychiatry found an equal until today and has played a role in the liberation of Russia through certain circles of dissenting philosophers. This, of course, has found an equal in the thought of Solzhenitsyn, and it was in that sense that he said "Do not lie," which, of course, applies to a religious sphere and not to a scientific one.

**Harkabi:** It seems to me that great, very great advance has been made in the philosophy of science in recent years, and that is a field in which there is great fertility, and what we can learn there is that there are so many streams in social philosophy, giving expression to many, many streams of thought. It does not mean that we have to accept any of them, but we should examine them all. The lesson we can learn is that there is no one dominating view nowadays. There are different streams, though I would divide them into two main arch streams, one that points at science as an explanation, and the other is science as an attempt at comprehension.

There is always a danger in ourselves, as we study a certain period, that we shall freeze what we have studied and pay little attention to subsequent developments. For instance, in some periods economics served the social sciences as a type of scientific approach. Nowadays economists write for economists and that has nothing to do with reality.

Now, furthermore, we always take as an archetype some kind of science as *the* science. For many years it was physics. Nowadays physics has lost because there are two schools of thought within physics. It is not as unitary as it has been, and what I wanted to warn against is the idea of seeing prediction as the hallmark of science. It is not. There are many parts of science which are not based on prediction.

**May:** I think there are three bodies of thought that at least have some bearing before we close this subject. One is referred to in Kosai's paper, and that is the idea that you test the scientific quality of thought not by the predictions it yields or by your ability to test it but, rather, by the kinds of questions that it produces, by the quality of the next set of questions produced.

Second—again something that is referred to briefly in Kosai's paper which seems to me to illustrate that and answers some of what Dore says—is the work of Amartya Sen, which addresses some dimensions that economics has tended to treat simply as externalities and to say that economic analysis, even in the most refined forms of algebra, ought not to dismiss the ethical dimensions either on the side of values, the anthropological side, or the consequentialist side, i.e., what's the effect of it.

The third is the argument, which is not exactly what Yamaguchi was talking about but which I think is influential, that we are handicapped by our effort to reduce to explicit, almost mathematical logic, findings or insights that often really are products of a kind of gestalt, and we have to convey the truth by metaphor or analogy because we cannot convey it by explicit logic, whether mathematical or verbal.

**Dore:** Can I respond to one or two of the things that have come up in the discussion? I would grant prediction is not the objective of social science, to be able to tell when socialism is going to come. That is not what it's about. But I would agree with Perczynski that making predictions and seeing how far events falsify them is one of the ways in which one reaches explanations and understanding, and for that reason predictions have an important part to play in social science. It mustn't be frozen.

Well, I'm frozen at the Vienna School level. I prefer to say that I bought a suit of clothes from the Vienna School. I have always found them comfortable. You know, they fit me well, they allow me to do the things that seem to me worthwhile, and I see no particular reason for changing them, or for changing my definition of what social science is, which I bought with those clothes.

Now, that is not to say that I would ignore or negate a lot of the things that are done by other people who occupy jobs in social science departments—hermeneutics, the ability to give one a kind of holistic sense of what it is like to be a different kind of person in different times and different places, which not only enriches human life but is a source of hypothesis for social science, too, and that also seems to me a highly valued activity.

If I can take up just the final remarks of Stern about the implications for university structures of the crisis in the social sciences, I think it is precisely because of these university structures that we have this crisis of relevance, this dichotomy between doing social science which is appreciated as being intellectually excellent, on the one hand, and doing social science which is manifestly relevant to the things that the society around one wants to know about, on the other.

This dichotomy, it seems to me, was not there when social science was the work of the gentlemen amateurs. It is something that sets in as soon as social science gets located in disciplinary departments in universities. Disciplinary departments in universities are competing with each other for prestige in order to compete for budgets. Everybody wants budgets. Disciplinary departments turn into tribes as soon as they have their own way of socializing the young, like these ten-year periods of graduate study that you have to go through in order to become a political scientist or an economist in the United States. This is the way of reinforcing the tribal loyalties. These tribes are in competition for money. How do they compete? They go along to the vice chancellor or the provost, the rector, or whatever, and they say: Look, we are more relevant than they are. We are more relevant to what goes on in society. "Fine!" says the president, "then you go out into the market and you sell your services and you can earn money for the university and support the work of genuine scholarship, the pursuit of truth, the pursuit of intellectual excellence that is carried on by your colleagues who win the Nobel prizes." So you don't go along and claim that you're relevant. You go along and claim that you are intellectually excellent. As an economist you are more intellectually excellent than the sociologist. And how do you do that? Well, you point to things like the number of Nobel prizes, you point to the SAT scores in the United States, in Japan the *hensachi* of the students who enter your department, and you also point to the undoubted mathematical complexity of the productions which are prized within that discipline.

The one thing about mathematics is that you cannot get away with waffle, and we all know that dispensing with waffle and getting the answers right, getting your equations right, is somehow intellectually more stretching and is an occupation of which only a small number of us are capable of at the highest level. It is, it seems to me, this IQ scale in which the social sciences compete, and it is because of this competition that there is this emphasis on totally irrelevant model building which has a distorted view of man at its base, and a distorted view of man which, because of the prestige of these people, is fed back into society and gives a kind of justification for the Thatchers and the Reagans of this world, who want to turn man into the sort of greedy rational model which is at the basis of the economist model.

If I may just apologize for not referring to responsibility and just ask Kosai if he would say something about how honest one can really be as a social scientist in telling the world what one's findings are if one knows that those findings are going to have an effect on what happens in the world. I keep on seeing Kosai's face on the television screen, in the newspapers and, because his economic models are better than anyone else's and because he has better judgement and insight than most, he is always being asked whether the recession going to get worse or better. I'm sure he is aware that he has a choice between being an honest social scientist and a bad citizen or a good citizen and a dishonest social scientist, and I would just like to hear his reflections.

**Kosai:** I think prediction is quite important because the failure of prediction makes a depression worse or inflation worse, or there might be war because of the failure of prediction. So what I am saying is at least the failure of prediction requires a review of our social scientists' works, whether it is rationally grounded or not.

As to the second point, erosion of objectivity or social science being polluted by value judgment or the dominance of the establishment value, I do not have a good answer how to avoid such a risk. We should be conscious of what our value judgment is. This is a short defense line, I realize, but, still, that is as much as I can say.

I think social science should keep its rational structure in order to raise the probability to predict, but rationality—the concept of rationality—should be widened, as Dore said. Passion, ethics, and not just money but other considerations should be included in the concept of rationality. If we can succeed in that direction, I hope that people would not make fools of economists like me.

# TECHNOLOGICAL REDISTRIBUTION OF THOUGHT AND MEMORY

# DOES COMPLEX TECHNOLOGICAL INFORMATION ALIENATE US FROM OUR HUMANITY?
## Lessons from the Study of Despair

Philip W. GOLD

Beliefs regarding fundamental questions such as "What are the factors that make life worth living?" generally remain stable for centuries. Such stability allows time for a thorough testing and integration of the ideas that are central to a people's concept of what is worthwhile and true.

Some fear that the rapid emergence of complex technology as a major force in our lives will lead to a poorly integrated scientific reductionism that will insulate us from the truths of our past and obscure what is most precious about our humanity. I believe, on the other hand, that our only security lies in the facts of our lives: hence, I feel we are obliged to integrate whatever information we can reliably validate to facilitate our intellectual, moral, psychological, and physical integrity.

To illustrate the potential role that scientific information can play in providing a beneficially comprehensive context for understanding one of life's enduring questions and dilemmas, I shall attempt to integrate humanistic and scientific concepts regarding the problem of depressive despair. I shall suggest, moreover, that recent advances in the biological sciences need not stand in opposition to humanistic, intuitive understanding; rather, the two can work together in a complementary, if not synergistic, fashion to raise new questions for one another that would not have otherwise emerged, and to illuminate what each has learned using their distinctive methodologies.

The problem of depression and its principal manifestation, despair, has become one of the main foci of my life as a scientist and physician. For many years, I have felt that there can be no greater challenge than to help an individual who finds life unbearable reaffirm a will to live. At times, I have asked myself, "What good is our knowledge if we have not yet learned a reliable way of articulating to those in despair a compelling case for remaining alive?"

I initially thought that I could learn to effectively approach the problem of despair by acquiring a clear perception of my own psychological organization and agendas and an extensive fund of knowledge from a variety of humanistic disciplines. Viewed in this way, my life and work became virtually synonymous, because I felt that whatever I learned and whoever I became could be brought to bear on the problem of despair. It was as if I were preparing myself for a career in applied literature and philosophy, where some assimilation of collective wisdom could be therapeutically applied to a broad range of desperate individuals to bring them willingly back to an affirmation of life.

Over the years, I have painfully learned that this is not necessarily the case: neither a large inventory of reasons for living; a coherent, flexible, and realistic vision; the cultivation of empathy; nor a sympathetic and abidingly supportive stance could be consistently counted on to reach individuals in despair. Rather, the apparently impersonal disciplines of physiology, neurobiology, pharmacology, and molecular biology also have become relevant to understanding the problem of despair. Gradually, and perhaps at times reluctantly, my colleagues and I came to observe time and again that the kind of tortured hopelessness and self-excoriation characteristic of the most desperate individuals very often occur in those unfortunate enough to be affected by a convergence of adverse psychological, environmental, biological, and genetic factors. In this regard, we have come to disparage no information that might be relevant to this most fundamental of human problems, regardless of the perspective from which it derives or the kind of temperament that generated it.

## CLINICAL PRESENTATION OF DEPRESSIVE DESPAIR

Depressive despair is a universal experience that transcends culture boundaries. Although it can take many forms, I shall restrict the present discussion to the despair that occurs in the context of a major depression. Although definitive data are not available, it is my impression that this form of despair is more common than generally accepted and that it accounts for a majority of instances in which individuals reach a point in life where life seems unbearable for sustained periods of time. It is also my sense that it is in the context of a major depression that the majority of suicides occur among individuals who have concluded that their lives are of no value and that those around them would be better off without them.

In the United States, it is estimated that 13–20 percent of the population has some depressive symptoms of varying intensity at any given time. The classic and most severe form of depressive despair, melancholia, belies the suppression of thought and feeling suggested by the term depression; rather, melancholia more closely approximates a state of pathological hyperarousal. Psychologically, this hyperarousal presents as a state of organized anxiety, especially attached to one's sense of self: typically, the profoundly depressed individual feels either like a burden to others or the object of their disgust, and is hopeless about the prospects for this worthless self for future gratification in either love or work. Because these feelings rarely yield to the individual's most carefully constructed arguments countering such feelings of inefficacy and despair about self, the sense of helplessness is exacerbated. Consequently, shame deepens and a vicious cycle is initiated that can lead to suicide.

Melancholic depression is also classically associated with inhibition of physiological events that are associated with restorative functions, including sleep, eating, tissue growth, and sexual function. Patients with melancholia often suffer from insomnia, decreased interest in food, with loss of appetite, and decreased interest in sexual activity. These phenomena have often been attributed to the stress of the depressive despair *per se* and secondary physiological changes associated with that stress rather than to primary biological factors that potentially contribute to the establishment or maintenance of the depressed state.

## PSYCHOLOGICAL VIEWS OF THE SUSCEPTIBILITY TO DEPRESSIVE DESPAIR

Many psychological theories have been advanced to account for an increase in susceptibility to depressive despair. Psychoanalytic theory suggests that chronic exposure in childhood to a hypercritical, exploitive, or emotionally unresponsive environment not only complicates the task of developing an intact sense of self but also interferes with its maintenance as one grapples with the inevitable disappointments of life. A child who grows up in such an environment frequently feels that nothing he or she does is good enough, but is reluctant to abandon the hope that they can earn the blessing of those around them. Rather, they imagine that if only they can acquire special qualities or relinquish behaviors and feelings that disappoint others, they can avoid their constant fear of being abandoned. Hence any loss, sadness, or setback must be disowned, and sights refocused on the perfection of the self.

Children caught in this cycle of hurt and repressed feeling rarely allow themselves the experience of grieving, which involves acknowledging and experiencing the sadness and anger that accompanies a loss and sharing it with others. Hence, they rarely seem to process the array of emotional memories associated with a lost relationship or a heartfelt disappointment. In losing the capacity to grieve, they seem to lose the capacity to get over what has hurt them the most. And though the emotional memories associated with these painful events tend to remain hidden, they often emerge reflexively in adult life whenever there is a particularly sharp disappointment or critical loss.

This reflexive reemergence of emotional memories in adult life, most often in the context of disappointment, motivates the further elaboration of defenses to ward off the contingency or awareness of loss. Paradoxically, these defenses often make the individual even more vulnerable to painful emotional states associated with a loss of self-esteem and personal efficacy. For instance, if the defense involves an assiduous avoidance of controversy, it could inhibit freedom of expression and the appropriate exercise of assertiveness in protecting self-interest and self-respect. In addition, a disowning of feeling is tantamount to a betrayal of one's real self, an act that is invariably associated with a sense of demoralization about self. As the impaired capacity to grieve produces an ever-increasing burden of unprocessed losses and disappointments, the defenses that weaken self-esteem contribute to a progressive demoralization with self that can ultimately overwhelm an individual's wish to go on living.

## LITERARY AND PHILOSOPHICAL DIMENSIONS: THE POTENTIAL IMPACT OF A SPECIFIC VISION OF LIFE ON THE SUSCEPTIBILITY TO DEPRESSIVE DESPAIR

Over the years, visions of reality have been depicted in artistic works that convey the artist's perception of the elements of reality he or she has a readiness to perceive. This vision encompasses the artist's conception of the ideal, the disparity between the ideal and reality, and the tension between the two.

The psychoanalyst Roy Shafer has written that the comic, romantic, tragic, and ironic visions of reality have recurred over time in the work of literary critics and philosophers; he argues that these categories are not so much the product of their collective ingenuity as they are a distillation of the typical workings of the human mind and imagination discerned in mythic and artistic productions. These visions differentially shape expectations in life and the sense of the place that glory, disappointment, ambiguity, sadness, risk, and triumph play in human affairs. As such, they interact with other aspects of life experience, learning, temperament, and biological predisposition to bias an individual's response to external reality and inner experience, and hence toward or away from the contingency of depressive despair.

Shafer sees the comic vision as seeking evidence to support fundamental hopefulness. It endorses the notion that virtually no dilemma is insoluble, no obstacle insurmountable, no evil so unrelieved that it is irremediable, no suffering so intense that it cannot be unmitigated, and no loss so final that it cannot be compensated. While laughter and gaiety are not considered essential to the comic, worldly gratification and security are.

The romantic vision sees life as a quest or a series of quests. The quest is often heroic and perilous. Its objective combines some or all of the qualities of mystery, grandeur, sacredness, love, and possession of or fusion with some higher power or principle. The seeker is an innocent adventurous hero, and the quest ends with exaltation after crucial struggles. Idealization is an important aspect of the romantic. The romantic hero is more concerned with overcoming external obstacles and injustices than confronting a potentially disturbing inner world that partially consists of a reservoir of painfully charged memories and potentially distorted memories of an earlier world and less exalted self.

Shafer characterizes the tragic vision as one marked by an acute awareness of the great dilemmas, paradoxes, ambiguities, and uncertainties pervading human action and subjective experience. The tragic vision embraces the absurdities, mysteries, inescapable dangers, and inherent contradictions of existence. It recognizes and celebrates the elements of defeat in victory, and of victory in defeat; the loss of opportunity inherent in every choice and by growth; the inevitable clashes between passion and duty; the pain that is intermingled with pleasure, and the pleasure that can arise in the context of pain. Those imbued with a tragic sense of life know the renunciations inevitably associated with gratification, the necessity of action in the face of uncertainty, and the burden of unanswerable questions and incomprehensible afflictions. They know also the probability of suffering while learning or changing, and the frequency with which it is true that the greatest growth comes during times of the greatest adversity. Allied with the tragic, but partially mitigating its intensity, is the ironic vision of life. This vision reflects a readiness to seek out internal contradictions, ambiguities, and paradoxes. While the tragic vision aims at seeing the momentous and tragic implications of people and events, the ironic vision considers the same material, but aims at some detachment, keeping things in perspective, taking nothing for granted, and readily spotting the antithesis to any thesis so as to reduce the claim of that thesis upon us.

Comic and romantic visions exemplify idealizations that have sustained many through times of adversity and inspired many to acts of heroism. However, from a psychological perspective, the comic and romantic visions can also be viewed as an effort to ward off an awareness of one inevitable and inherent susceptibility to great sadness and uncertainty. Moreover, by their emphasis on the triumph of individual and collective will over external or internal adversity, and their endorsement of the perfectibility of the self and its fate, the comic and romantic visions are antithetical to the grieving process, and hence may tend to entrap individuals in an inner world where the inevitable losses of life cannot be effectively integrated without great shame.

The tragic and ironic visions facilitate the process of grieving in a way that the comic and romantic cannot: neither disparages the inevitability of loss and sadness in life or espouses a perfectionistic ideal where triumph over adversity and attainment of a relatively unambiguous, pain-free existence are seen as the ultimate and perhaps only appropriate aim of living. An aesthetic of the tragic and ironic visions is that individuals can continue to celebrate the beauty of existence and the wonders of an interior life and external connections despite being surrounded by unanswerable questions, ambiguous dilemmas, and the certainty of loss and death. Viewed in this way, each life is infinitely valuable despite, and perhaps even because of, its immense vulnerability, where everything, including the capacity to create and appreciate beauty, can be lost in an instant. To those imbued with a tragic sense of life, we are bound together in these realities, can derive comfort from our shared fate, and can take pride in the willingness to acknowledge the truth of even those things we may be least inclined to acknowledge. Such an intellectual view can serve as a foil to the all-or-none thinking of an individual suffering from the throes of depressive despair and the conviction that he or she is entirely worthless and beyond redemption.

## FINDINGS THAT SUGGEST BIOLOGICAL FACTORS IN THE SUSCEPTIBILITY TO MELANCHOLIA AND ITS PATHOGENESIS

Although few doubt the role of early life experience, psychological factors, and world view on the susceptibility to melancholia, a growing body of clinical, biochemical, genetic, and pharmacologic data indicates that biological factors also influence this susceptibility in a significant way.

Patients with melancholia show consistent physiologic changes in systems subserving sleep, appetite, reproductive function, and in brain modulation of pituitary gland hormonal secretion (neuroendocrine regulation).

Individuals with melancholic depression not only consistently complain of subjective despair, but also of sleeplessness, usually manifested as an involuntary early morning awakening when the depression is most severe. It is at this time that suicide is most common. Physiologic studies of sleep in patients with melancholia reveal decreased time spent in deep sleep, an increase in rapid eye movement sleep (the stage associated with dreaming), and a significantly reduced latency between sleep onset and the first rapid eye movement episode.

Patients with melancholia also lose pleasure in eating and often are frankly anorexic. Weight loss is a frequent concomitant of melancholia, and in the elderly can be life-threatening.

Patients with melancholia show a consistent decrease in sexual interest and activity. In addition, there is frequent interference with the hormonal repertoire required for successful reproduction (e.g., the cessation of normal menses in depressed women).

In addition to the hormones of reproduction, the secretion of a variety of other hormones is abnormal in melancholia. The most notable is a hypersecretion of the adrenal steroid, cortisol, the classic fight or flight hormone that is normally released during physical or emotional stress. This hormone raises blood sugar and enhances cardiac function during threatening situations. Concomitantly, the secretion of growth hormone, which ordinarily enhances the deposition of circulating amino acids into the building of muscle and other tissues, is diminished.

Depressed patients show indices of an increase in the activity of the sympathetic nervous system, manifested by small but significant increase in heart rate and blood pressure. A physiologic concomitant of this activation is an increase in circulating levels of the catecholamine, norepinephrine, the principal neurotransmitter of the sympathetic nervous system.

The increased likelihood for individuals with major depression to have first-degree relatives with melancholia also supports the idea that biological factors play a role in the susceptibility to this disease. Data from studies in twins show that 65 percent of monozygotic (identical) twins will both be affected by a major depression, while only 14 percent of dizygotic (non-identical) twins will be both afflicted with this disorder. Epidemiologic studies also indicate a seven- to eight-fold increase in the incidence of melancholia in first-degree relatives of individuals with manic-depressive illness.

Clinical studies show that 90 percent of individuals with melancholic depression will respond to treatment with the prototypic class of antidepressants known as the tricyclics. These agents are not acute acting mood-altering drugs but rather act slowly and tonically over several weeks to putatively correct the underlying biological defect in melancholia. Tricyclics are not sold as drugs of abuse on the street, because they do not influence mood except in individuals who have an established depression. One of the striking experiences for a clinician treating depression, especially one whose career spans the era before antidepressants were commonly used, is the capacity of these agents significantly to influence aspects of the depressive process that intrude upon self-concept and one's view of the world without the necessity for comprehensive learning or psychological reorientation. It is as if these agents simply neutralized a biologic charge that influenced all thought and feeling, uncovering a self-concept and world view that lay below. And although data clearly indicate that the treatment of melancholia proceeds best by a combination of psychotherapy and pharmacotherapy, it is a testimony to the biological contribution to melancholia that these agents are so consistently effective in this disorder.

## WHAT THE BIOLOGIC ABNORMALITIES IN MELANCHOLIA SUGGEST ABOUT ITS PATHOGENESIS

The hypersecretion of cortisol that is consistently seen in melancholia is the biologic marker that led us to one of our major clues regarding the potential pathogenesis of depression. It has been known for some time that the secretion of cortisol from the adrenal glands is under the control of chemical messengers produced in the hypothalamus, an area of the brain that controls hormonal, reproductive, ingestive, and possibly affective phenomena. The hypothalamus lies at the base of the brain, just above the pituitary gland, which lies outside the brain. Hypothalamic hormones traverse a short specialized bloodstream circuit to stimulate the pituitary gland to release hormones into the bloodstream that control thyroid, gonadal, and adrenal function. The hypothalamic hormone that controls adrenal function, corticotropin-releasing hormone, has only been recently discovered and was only sequenced after decades of painstaking work with extracts taken from tens of millions of bovine hypothalami. Studies from our laboratory and others have shown that it is the hypersecretion of corticotropin-releasing hormone that is responsible for the hypercortisolism of depression.

A variety of experiments have shown that corticotropin-releasing hormone is released not only to stimulate the pituitary-adrenal axis, but also at critical brain sites to coordinate a variety of physiological and behavioral processes that facilitate successful adaptation during stressful situations. These include not only activation of cortisol secretion but also activation of the sympathetic nervous system and facilitation of pathways that promote arousal, cautious avoidance, anxiety, increased vigilance, and focused attention upon the threatening stimulus; in addition, corticotropin-releasing hormone causes inhibition of pathways whose function, though crucial for long-term survival, subserve processes whose facilitation would diminish the likelihood of survival in a life-threatening situation. These neural pathways are involved in so-called vegetative functions such as feeding (by a direct effect on hypothalamic ingestive centers), reproduction (by inhibiting the hypothalamic stimulus to reproductive behavior and the hormonal repertoire necessary for normal reproductive function), and growth (by activating the release of a hormone that inhibits growth hormone secretion).

The hypersecretion of norepinephrine in patients with melancholic depression as an index of increased sympathetic nervous system activity is also thought to reflect hyperfunctioning of the locus ceruleus-norepinephrine system located in the mid-pons regions of the brain stem. The locus ceruleus is a very small area of the brain stem, but it sends nerve terminals that innervate billions of neurons throughout the central nervous system, including critical sites thought to modulate mood, anxiety, and arousal. Stimulation of the locus ceruleus in experimental animals produces fear, avoidance behavior, and inhibition of grooming and feeding. Data from our laboratory indicate that the corticotropin-releasing hormone and locus ceruleus-norepinephrine systems participate in a positive feedback loop in which each stimulates the functional activity of the other.

## RELATION OF MELANCHOLIA TO
## THE GENERALIZED STRESS RESPONSE

The coordinated series of central and peripheral events that occur after the concomitant activation of the corticotropin-releasing hormone and locus ceruleus-norepinephrine systems closely resemble the generalized stress response (or fight or flight response) first described by Selye over fifty years ago. Although Selye used a different vocabulary taken from a different physiologic perspective, he described a stereotypic behavioral and physiological series of events that consisted of enhanced arousal, anxiety, and focused attention and a concomitant inhibition of programs subserving sleep, feeding, growth, and reproduction. This remarkably consistent response to threatening situations was so highly conserved from one species to the next and so necessary for the survival of the organism when acutely threatened that it is not surprising that a dedicated biochemical and anatomical system has evolved for its coordination.

The striking parallels between the generalized stress response and melancholia has led us to suggest that the pathogenesis of melancholia reflects a generalized stress response that has escaped its usual counterregulatory restraints. This observation links the clinical manifestations of melancholia as a state of pathological arousal to the principal neurobiological systems known to subserve arousal. Hence, during a normal generalized stress response, acute anxiety confers an adaptive advantage during the stress of a fight or flight situation; in melancholia, loss of flexibility in the regulation of this arousal leads to a chronic state of organized anxiety that seems most tenaciously attached to the sense of self-representation; hence, the melancholic individual is overwhelmed with concern about his or her grave deficiencies and hopeless character flaws. Similarly, the adaptive temporary suspension of vegetative functions like eating and sexual behavior facilitates survival during an acute fight or flight response; however, it becomes maladaptive in the depressed individual who awakens early each morning, stops eating, loses weight, ceases all sexual activity, and ceases ovulating. Parenthetically we have recently found that every known class of effective anti-depressant drug, regardless of the putative mode of action, significantly decreases the rate at which the corticotropin-releasing hormone gene encodes corticotropin-releasing hormone, apparently by increasing the efficiency of the genes that encode restraining factors. Such pharmacologic data lend support to an hypothesis that a pathologically activated stress response is involved in the pathogenesis and symptom complex of melancholia.

Because melancholic depression does not seem to be an exotic defect but rather a dystregulation in a system of responses that are supposed to occur repeatedly each day for brief periods of time, melancholia does not present as a bizarre spectacle, but rather as an accentuation of the upsetness, anxiety, and discouragement that each of us experiences repeatedly during our lives. What is lost is the modulation of the response, so that it proceeds in a profoundly exaggerated fashion for prolonged periods of time. It is a consistent clinical observation that the process, once established, becomes autonomous and is not ordinarily amenable to volitional intervention. This fact clearly intensifies the sense of helplessness and hopelessness that the melancholic depressed individual experiences and intensifies the shame of an individual already feeling ineffectual, if not worthless.

## CHARACTERISTICS OF THE GENERALIZED STRESS RESPONSE THAT MAY BIAS AN INDIVIDUAL TOWARD DEPRESSION: TOWARD A TRAGIC VIEW OF BIOLOGY

It is clear that the generalized stress response evolved not to promote comfort or the quality of life but rather the fear, cautious avoidance, decreased exploration, and inhibition of restorative functions that must occur if an organism is to survive an acute physical threat to life. In this regard, perhaps because the meaning of evolution seems to be survival rather than the production of organisms with a strongly established sense of well-being, the brain seems especially well organized to generate anxiety and other forms of behavioral inhibition. Far more neurons seem devoted to this function than to any functions that can be construed as conferring a sense of well-being upon the organism.

The anxiety-generating elements in our central nervous systems seem uniquely capable of showing sensitization to the informational substances that ordinarily set them into motion. Put another way, if an organism grows up in a dangerous or anxiety-provoking environment that repeatedly activates the generalized stress response, the intensity and duration of the response to a given stimulus rises progressively over time.

To the best of our knowledge, the human central nervous system does not seem particularly capable of distinguishing between a physical or psychological stressor, so that our heart rates, blood pressure, and cortisol levels are just as likely to go up after someone hurts our feelings as when we are pursued by a dangerous animal or person. In a complex interpersonal system where feelings can get hurt all the time, this means that there will be frequent activation of stress-responsive, arousal-producing neurotransmitters that subserve the generalized stress response and a potentially progressive increase in the intensity and duration of stress responses.

In the light of the phenomenon of sensitivation, one of the potential consequences of a particularly intense and prolonged activation of the generalized stress response is a clinical syndrome resembling melancholic depression. In this regard, data show that the tendency for melancholic depression rises with age, and that in patients with recurrent bouts of depression, the severity, frequency, and duration of episodes increases progressively with time. Our laboratory has shown that corticotropin-releasing hormone itself is one of the most potent sensitizing agents in the central nervous system.

With the exception of individuals who possess a strong family history of depression, a depression-prone individual has not been identified. However, Kagan et al. recently described a sub-set of children who from infancy on show a reduction in the threshold for stress-mediated activation of the corticotropin-releasing hormone and locus ceruleus-norepinephrine systems, as well as behavioral hyper-responsiveness to age-appropriate novel stimuli. Hence, such children in infancy show a markedly exaggerated response when placed halfway across the room from their mothers. At three years of age they hyper-respond to sudden, loud, unfamiliar sounds. At eight years of age they show increased subjective distress in association with exaggerated cortisol and sympathetic nervous system response to tasks requiring arithmetic calculations. Whether such children with an apparent abnormality in either the threshold for activation or in the counterregulation of the stress response have a higher susceptibility to depressive despair will be a question of considerable interest.

## THE FUTURE OF SCIENTIFIC INVESTIGATION INTO THE SUSCEPTIBILITY TO DESPAIR: APPLICATIONS OF THE REVOLUTION IN MOLECULAR BIOLOGY

The past thirty years represent the first time in human history that we have actually been able to operationalize the idea that biochemical factors can influence parameters that we consider to be most influential in defining our humanity and can play a role in our susceptibility to despair. These have largely come about through the disciplines of physiology, biochemistry, and pharmacology. The last fifteen years have seen extraordinary advances in molecular biology, a discipline that stands to truly revolutionize the biological sciences, and perhaps not only our concept of despair but our fundamental concept of our humanity.

Molecular biology concerns itself with the organizations, properties, functions, and vicissitudes of the molecule(s) that transmit an organism's biological heritage from one generation to the next. The principal molecule that contains the genetic codes is deoxyribonucleic acid (DNA). DNA is found in the nucleus of each living cell. In multicellular organisms that reproduce sexually, somatic cells (all cells except sperm and egg) contain two non-identical copies of DNA, one derived from each parent contributing DNA to its offspring. Each time a somatic cell divides, it passes on an exact replica of these two copies of DNA to the next generation of somatic cells. Sperm and egg cells each contain one copy of DNA. When a sperm penetrates an egg, the resulting fertilized egg, or zygote, contains two copies of DNA that are derived from the sperm and egg respectively.

The building blocks of DNA consist of four relatively simple bases. These compounds, called nucleotides, consist of adenine (A), cytosine (C), thymine (T), and guanine (G). The chemical identity of a specific strand of DNA is conferred by the sequence of nucleotides that are arrayed in a linear fashion. Three nucleotides in sequence (a codon) encode a unit called an amino acid (e.g.,

UCU = serine, CUC = leucine, UUC = phenylalanine, GUA = valine, AGA = arginine, etc.). These codons are virtually the same in all forms of life. There are a total of 20 amino acids, and these serve as the building blocks of larger molecules called proteins. In this regard, amino acids are analogous to letters in an alphabet and proteins are analogous to words consisting of a specific and unique sequence of letters. Proteins can consist of approximately one hundred to tens of thousands of amino acids. It is noteworthy that no codon specifies more than one amino acid; hence the genetic code is not ambiguous. Consequently, knowing the dictionary and the rules for its use, we can translate the entire nucleotide sequence of DNA ultimately into an unambiguous amino acid sequence.

A gene is defined as that sequence of DNA that encodes the amino acid sequence for one protein. The gene also contains sequences that influence the time, place, and rate of expression of that protein, and specific sequences that mark parameters such as the start site for construction of the protein and the stop site (like a period at the end of a sentence). Genes are arrayed in linear contiguity with one another and line up on very large segments of DNA called chromosomes. There is a total of approximately 250,000 genes in the human genome located on 46 separate chromosomes.

Every cell in the human body contains the same number of nucleotides potentially encoding the same number of amino acids and proteins. However, only a fraction of the genes in any given cell are actively encoding at any given time and many regulatory factors work to either activate or repress the expression of a gene in a given cell. The differentiation of a cell into a specific cell type (white blood cell, muscle cell, skin cell, neuron) is determined by the repertoire of gene products that are produced by the cell at any given time. Neurons are the most complex of cells, and a given neuron can simultaneously express as many as twenty thousand genes to direct the synthesis of twenty thousand diverse proteins.

The amino acid sequence of a given protein confers upon that molecule its shape and charge, which constitute its destiny. Within a given cell, proteins that are the mirror image of each other are frequently joining hands in a lock and key configuration to form a specific confederation that signals an alteration in the function of the cell. Thus, the protein could function as an enzyme that links with specific chemicals to markedly alter the rate of a chemical reaction, and hence the biologic activity of the cell. The protein could also bind to certain regions of DNA to influence the rate at which a given gene is expressed or whether a given gene is turned on or off in a given cell. The protein could be expressed on the surface of the cell and receive messages from other cells that alter the metabolic function of the recipient cell. Proteins also constitute the fundamental building blocks of all cells and are the substances that respond to foreign organisms (antibodies). Working together, the unique series of proteins specific to each cell type maintains the functional integrity of a given cell; they also serve directly or indirectly as informational substances by which one cell communicates to another in order to orchestrate the various parts of the organism to work together to maintain internal homeostasis; finally, they allow the organism to respond to threats from without either directly or by orchestrating changes in behavior and physiology in order to maintain its fundamental organization. Proteins, in short, provide the physical and behavioral identity of the organism and allow it to function in a sustained and organized fashion.

Even a single nucleotide substitution, deletion, or addition into the tens of thousands of nucleotides that might compose a single gene could result in the encoding of an abnormal protein. For instance, suppose in the middle of a gene a given codon were to mutate from UCU (serine) to UUC (phenylalanine). The substitution of serine to phenylalanine could conceivably change the shape of the whole protein and, as a result, its unique chemical identity. Hence, if the protein served as an enzyme, the specific enzyme activity could fall or be abolished and cellular metabolism altered in a profound way; if it served as an intercellular signal, the signal could be lost and an important mode of regulation between cells severely compromised; if it served as a structural component of muscle, the muscle could be impaired; or if it served as a growth factor for cell division, cell division might become abnormal or unregulated.

The revolution in molecular biology offers us for the first time access to the instruction book that mobilizes the necessary substrates and assembles them in the appropriate sequence and configuration to build a fly, a bird, or a human being, and to allow that organism to reproduce a facsimile of itself. Almost daily, more is learned about the fundamental organization of DNA and techniques are advanced that speed our capacity to decode the instruction book. The human genome project, which has as its aim nothing less than sequencing or decoding the entire human genome, should be completed in less than a decade.

## THE USES OF MOLECULAR BIOLOGY IN MEDICINE: APPLICATIONS TO UNDERSTANDING AND TREATING INBORN ERRORS OF METABOLISM

As expected, molecular biology is having a profound impact on the biological sciences and on medicine. A good recent example is the discovery of the genetic and biochemical defect in muscular dystrophy. This illness was discovered at least a hundred years ago, was known to run in families, and compromised muscular function in an unknown fashion that often led to death within the first few years of life. Thousands of biochemical and physiological studies had been conducted on patients with muscular dystrophy to no avail prior to the advent of molecular biology.

It was assumed that the pathologic defect in patients with muscular dystrophy lies in a single gene that encoded a single protein of the many that are normal constituents of a given muscle, but finding this protein had eluded scientists for many years. However, recent advances in the capacity to locate subtle differences in DNA sequences from one individual to the next paved the way for the discovery of the defect in muscular dystrophy. These techniques were applied to the study of a number of multigenerational families that contained many members affected with muscular dystrophy. Application of the newly developed techniques for isolating subtle differences in the sequences of long stretches of DNA along the genome revealed a segment of a given chromosome among affected individuals that showed a unique pattern in response to a battery of cleavage enzymes that clipped DNA at specific points that was not present in any of the unaffected members. After painstaking analysis of the putative region conferring susceptibility to the illness, a specific alteration in a single nucleotide sequence was discovered in a gene that had not even been previously discovered, identified, or cloned (isolated as a discrete entity from the mass of other DNA constituting the human genome). The isolation of the gene and the sequencing of its nucleotide sequence allowed the construction of the protein encoded by that gene on the basis of advances in molecular biology over a decade ago allowing the translation of gene sequences in cell-free systems. A protein was isolated that had never before been identified. Readily available techniques were applied that allowed the identification and quantification of that protein on the basis of unique chemical properties possessed by that protein alone. The protein, which was named dystrophin, was found to constitute less than 1 percent of normal human muscle tissue, an amount undetectable by current techniques applied to the problem of identifying a protein whose sequence had not been definitively determined.

Scientists all over the world are attempting to perfect the means to insert correct versions of defective genes into the cells of patients with genetic diseases in a way so that the gene will function in a normal fashion to deliver normal copies of a defective protein at the right place and at the right time. Genes can be engineered with regulatory sequences that serve not to encode the sequence of amino acids that will appear in a protein, but, rather, to determine in which tissues they will be expressed and to what regulatory elements they will respond. Vectors, or carriers, are being tested, including a variety of viral agents that infect cells with various sequences of DNA. These viral vectors can be transfected with a normal copy of a defective gene for potential insertion into cells that lack the normal gene product. Most scientists feel that it is only a matter of a few years before gene therapy techniques will be perfected to allow the successful treatment of inherited genetic diseases like muscular dystrophy.

## THE POTENTIAL USES OF MOLECULAR BIOLOGY IN STUDYING COMPLEX DISEASES LIKE CANCER AND AFFECTIVE DISORDER

Muscular dystrophy and a few hundred other inborn errors of metabolism represent a specialized group of diseases that seem mediated by a single defective gene. Susceptibility to many other diseases, such as cancer and major depression, is probably encoded in many genes so that many things have to go wrong in a redundantly regulated system before the illness expresses itself. Moreover, complex illnesses like cancer and depression probably require not only a series of gene defects but also a predisposing environment that stresses the organism in specific ways before the consequence of the series of genetic defects becomes apparent. For instance, certain genes in the genome that encode proteins that serve as growth factors promoting cellular division (oncogenes) are normally active only early in life during differentiation and development but are shut off in adult life. Some individuals seem susceptible to having these turned on in adult life, possibly because of a combination of a lack of a normal tumor-suppressor gene that encodes a protein suppressing the expression of the oncogene, infection with a virus that activates the expression of the oncogene, and/or exposure to a carcinogen or radiation that damages the regulatory region of the oncogene or the tumor-suppressor gene. It is thought by some that the development of the malignancy may also require failure of immunologic tumor surveillance, requiring yet another defective gene or genes for the development of full-blown disease.

A qualitative similar "multi-hit" chain of vulnerabilities may be required for the development of a full-blown melancholic depression. Candidate genes include those that encode the genes that are involved in the counterregulation of the stress response, those that are responsible for activating the genes that produce the informational substances that activate the stress response, genes that encode membrane receptors that bind these information substances to transduce their message, genes that encode second messengers that convey the message carried by the intercellular message to another part of the cell, and so on down the line. Because an adaptational response like the stress response is so important for survival, it is likely to be regulated by a redundant series of modulators so that many have to fail before homeostasis is disrupted. Other processes that may be involved include the proteins that mediate the sensitization of cellular substrates to effectors of the stress response and the genes encoding informational substances encoding the sensory material that the individual must process in order to form judgments about the outside world. Clinical experience also suggests that a genetic predisposition may not necessarily result in a clinical depression unless an individual is exposed to a chronically predisposing environment that is excessively stressful or overwhelming in one of many ways. Thus, the genetic defect(s) may be in genes that play sufficiently subtle roles in maintaining the homeostatic economy of the organism that a pathologic process becomes manifest only when the individual is exposed to environmental extremes.

## THE STUDY OF THE BIOLOGY OF COMPLEX BEHAVIORAL TRAITS AND ITS POTENTIAL FOR ALTERING OUR CONCEPT OF OUR HUMANITY

Clinical experience tells us that the susceptibility to depression is clearly enhanced by psychological and environmental factors such as childhoods associated with relentlessly demanding expectations and perfectionistic standards that diminish the capacity of individuals to attend to their feelings and grieve for what is lost. Before biological factors were elucidated in depressive illness, these were thought to constitute the sole risk factors, and a depression-prone personality with a prototype life experience was posited. We know that depressive illness can afflict any individual if the biological susceptibility is sufficiently great, regardless of the quality of early experience, the organization of personality, the sophistication of world view, and the apparent psychological stamina. And we may be on the verge of identifying biological markers and linkage to specific genes that signify susceptibility to the development of major depressive illness.

What, then, do we make of an illness that infiltrates those parameters that we consider definitive of important aspects of our humanity, as well as those aspects that are systematically influenced by the illness. Parenthetically, with respect to depression, these include not only self-esteem and one's estimate of future prospects but also subtler aspects of thought and feeling that can be altered by a process that systematically biases toward hyperarousal. For example, depressed individuals often seem much less likely to take risks on behalf of themselves or others because of a sense of heightened vulnerability. They often seem unable to celebrate the happiness or success of others because these indict their own perceived failures to adequately influence the course of their lives. And they often seem inhibited from either giving or receiving because of excessive concerns about depletion or being controlled by their indebtedness to others. These parameters, in a fashion analogous to more obvious ones such as self-esteem and hope for the future, also seem to change in some individuals with the adequate pharmacological treatment of the depression without extensive psychological exploration. Are human characteristics such as generosity, the willingness to take risks, and the capacity to em-pathize with the happiness of others also significantly influenced by biological parameters, and is our biological heritage, manifested in the linear sequence of our nucleotides, more influential than our cultural, intellectual, and religious heritage?

A corollary to this question regarding the role of genetic factors in the symptom complex of illnesses such as major depression is the role of our genes in mediating phenomenon such as the aging process and conferring a bias toward complex traits such as temperament (e.g., arousability, obsessionality). Recently, scientists at the National Institutes of Health in Bethesda, Maryland, identified a variation in the nucleotide sequence of a region in the X chromosome that occurred only in male homosexuals but not in their heterosexual siblings. This variation may not correspond to the actual altered gene but may be many thousands of nucleotides away so that considerable work could be required before a gene conferring susceptibility is identified. It is possible that this gene product will encode a single protein that transduces the effects of a male hormonal signal in many areas of the brain and periphery.

The revolution in molecular biology raises many ethical, philosophical, and practical considerations that no previous generations have had the opportunity or responsibility to confront. One of the major questions is how to deal with information that might reveal susceptibility to developing complex traits such as specific sexual preferences. Should a family that strongly opposes homosexuality be able to apply such information to determine the fate of a pregnancy? What should ultimately become the fate of genes that confer susceptibility to complex illness such as cancer and affective illness? Should they be systematically weeded from the gene pool by not allowing fetuses that carry these genes to reach full term? Will complex traits such as the capacity for disciplined application of effort, delay of gratification, and various forms of aggression and anti-social behavior be traced to the presence or absence of a pattern of specific genes, challenging currently held ideas regarding personal responsibility and the historical, societal, and interpersonal factors that shape character? And will our fundamental concepts of heritage change in the light of our capacity to delineate our biological heritage encoded in the sequence of billions of nucleotides?

It is difficult to know what the next generation will be facing in the light of access to the code of the instruction book for biological organisms. On the one hand, I suspect this generation will be asking the same questions we have always asked about the meaning of life, suffering, change, and the death that we must all face. Perhaps it will also be a generation that more acutely realizes its common humanity, aided by the explicit fact that the nucleotide sequences from one individual to the next differ only infinitesimally. It may wonder why so much has been made of exceedingly subtle alterations in skin color and other morphological differences when the fundamental templates are nearly identical. The next generation may also develop new approaches to the dilemma that our brains are organized as much for the generation of anxiety and the aversion of novelty as for anything else. Such an organization, promoting survival in the wild, may contribute to the penchant human beings have for identifying the subtlest distinctions among themselves and using these distinctions as a way of segregating various groups in the name of reducing anxiety about external threat and annihilation. As we learn to manipulate the genes that encode this anxiety, perhaps we may be able to produce subtle decrements in the propensity we have to view human differences with suspicion and fear. At the same time, I believe the fundamentally tragic and ironic aspects of existence will obviate the emergence of any simple answers that will spare us much trial and error, soul-searching, ambiguity, and the endless successive approximations that we must make in the search for elusive truths.

## DOES ADDING A BIOLOGICAL PERSPECTIVE TO UNDERSTANDING HUMAN EXPERIENCE NECESSARILY LEAD TO AN IMPOVERISHING REDUCTIONISM?

Many argue that introducing biological concepts in an effort to understand despair introduces a reductionistic perspective that disparages the wonder of the human spirit. Others argue that minimizing biological concepts in an effort to understand mind represents an endorsement of the view that consciousness, feelings, and ideas have supernatural origins that survive the death of the brain. Compromises between these extremes have been advanced that incorporate both scientific and less empirical, more intuitive perspectives such as the mentalism of Nobel prize winner Roger Sperry. This concept depends upon the idea that all biologic systems contain emergent properties that surface at each new level of complexity. To Sperry, conscious phenomena are emergent, functional properties of brain processing that obey higher-order laws not yet existent at the level of their constituent material, neuronal, and electrophysiological processes. An additional feature is that these higher order brain processes have active, central roles as determinants in shaping the flow pattern of cerebral excitation. Sperry compares the emergent laws governing consciousness to a protein that follows the lower-order chemical laws pertaining to proteins, but, when it is part of a single cell, is obliged, with all of its part and partners, to follow along a trail of events in time and space determined largely by the higher-order dynamics of the cell. In this way, the protein assumes a more complex existence, in which it obeys not only the laws that bind atoms, molecules, and amino acids together but the logic that maintains the integrity of the cell, its capacity to reproduce, and its role in the overall economy of a yet more complex system. If either the cell or the organism is broken into its constituent parts, its unique organization is lost; therefore it has not been and cannot be reduced to its parts.

According to this model, thoughts and feelings cannot simply be reduced to brain physiology or written off as supernatural wonders but, rather, serve as emergent properties of complex systems that determine the form of an inner self that in turn is responsive to and can modulate lower-order processes. In this regard, I see the despair of depression, in part, as a disorder in which perturbations of low-order arousal processes impair the integrity of the intact self, which reflects higher-level emergent properties of complex interactions between biological organisms and the social, psychological, and physical environment.

Human sadness is a complex emotional and cognitive state rich in texture and nuance. As such, it is a higher-order emergent process that cannot be reduced to its constituent parts. Conversely, major depression is a relatively monochromatic, constricted state in which there is a perseverative focus on the worthlessness of self, the inevitability of rejection, and the futility of life. To view depression as an intrusion of pathologic arousal on sadness is not an attempt at reductionistic materialism, but rather to be fully appreciative of the higher-order functions that go into making a thinking and feeling human being. Seen in this light, an understanding of despair requires the integration of information from many sources, dimensions, and levels of complexity. It requires an understanding of the personal history of the individual, the burden of sad, painful memories, the degree of abuse, frustration, or loss, and the quality of love. It requires an understanding of medical, biochemical, and genetic factors that ultimately will include an assessment of the functional integrity of a variety of genes that encode complex parameters such as central nervous system arousal and the flexible modulation of stress-responsive neurotransmitters. We cannot afford to be threatened by or lose a single fact, no matter how formidable the onslaught of information may seem. Sifting through the facts and making the imperfect judgments regarding which we can afford to relegate to secondary positions requires a capacity to bear imperfection and loss without undue shame, and the humility to know that though we may not get it right in our lifetime, we might at least be placing a single brick into the infrastructure of an edifice that will continue to dazzle with its ever-increasing wondrous emergent properties.

## SUMMARY

An integration of time-honored humanistic and intuitive knowledge can be made with contemporary scientific knowledge to enhance our capacity to approach an age-old problem like despair with greater compassion, tolerance, objectivity, and efficacy. What we learn as clinicians from sharing the suffering and pain of those in despair and as students from the artistic and mythic creations of the past can be effectively united with what science can teach us about the organization of our minds and bodies and the nature of our humanity.

We now know that despair can occur in individuals regardless of their world view, psychological organization, and their capacity to relate to others. We also know that the cardinal manifestations of despair that intrude upon the characteristics we see as definitive of our humanity reflect, in part, a pathological alteration of central arousal systems rather than simply a character structure biased toward disgust, fear, and withdrawal. Moreover, factors such as the capacity for sharing, the willingness to take risks for others, and the capacity to empathize with their happiness can also be temporarily, yet significantly, influenced by biological parameters.

The generalized stress response that seems altered in melancholic depression is an apparent reflection of a central nervous stem that is biased toward generating anxiety, avoiding novelty, and seeking shelter. As we learn to understand better the organization of this system and the factors that contribute to its activation, we may be able to modify our capacity to view subtle differences between ourselves and others with suspicion and fear. Moreover, knowing that only infinitesimally small differences exist between our genome and that of others, while showing 99 percent overlap with the genome of the chimpanzee, should further bring us together and help us acknowledge our connection to all living things.

Far from alienating us from our humanity, science may help educate us more about what factors influence our development, character formation, and temperaments. In the case of depressive despair, science can work hand in hand with humanistic techniques in ameliorating its terror. And because despair represents the loss of one's real self to the coloration of a pathological hyperarousal, science can help to provide us with the greatest human gift of all: reuniting an individual with his or her true self. What could be farther from insulating us from the truths of our past or obscuring what is most precious about our humanity?

# COMMENT ON THE GOLD PAPER
## A Proposal for Biohistory

NAKAMURA Keiko

Scientific research can never be completely divorced from cultural values simply because the research is being carried out by human beings, who naturally are affected by their own social values. At the same time, the knowledge acquired in scientific research can contribute to a shift in cultural values as well as innovation in technologies. Many people, however, have observed that despite the material gains technology has brought in modern times, there is very little appreciation of the deeper understandings that science can provide about life and nature.

Through his research and clinical work on depressive despair Gold has provided us with an excellent illustration of how science can teach us about the nature of humanity and can change our cultural values. Based on this proposition of the relationship between science and culture, I propose a new field which I call "Biohistory."

Molecular biology has shown us that the genomes of all living things contain DNA, and suggests strongly that all have evolved over the past three billion years from common ancestors. While since the beginning of life many things have been born and many things have died, all of the 300 million types of living organisms that exist today are part of one interdependent ecological system, a fact that genetic research substantiates. Thus, human beings cannot be considered separately from other animals, plants, and microbes but rather as one in the flow of life. All forms of life bear a relationship to one another. And yet while molecular biology views life at a micro-level, the purpose of modern biology is not strictly the research of molecules. Rather, it takes us further to enable the understanding of the shape, life cycle, and history of all living things. Therefore, a reading of the history and experiences which have shaped life is a relevant and important part of modern biology.

Molecular biology looks at the microscopic world, yet in most humans curiosity about nature also extends to the macroscopic world, the world that can be easily observed. Utilizing both these viewpoints, we can achieve a better understanding of the fundamentals of natural phenomena and better read the history of life. The combination of natural history and molecular-based biological science may be denoted by the term "biohistory." We propose this terminology as a tool for presenting a unified vision of nature, life, and humanity in a format that is relevant to the experiences of human beings. Biohistory refers to the traditional biological areas of study into life and living phenomena, with the added dimension of illustrating how the information gathered in these fields affects society.

Furthermore, biohistory emphasizes the importance of contact with nature itself, without which biological research has little meaning. This approach is similar in many ways to natural history. Natural history also examines living things in detail, and is concerned with the study of their history and life. However, natural history observes living things from the outside, and considers plants and animals separately. Therefore, a major difference is that while modern biological science considers all life together as one current in history, in natural history the human being becomes the objective observer, distinct from the current. It is biohistory which brings the human being back into the fold. The objective of biohistory, therefore, is to derive a contemporary understanding of life and the relationships between living things through the combination of modern biology and natural history.

Application of the recombinant DNA technique and nucleotide sequence analysis can reveal the history written in the genomes of all living things. Comparison of the results of genome analysis illuminates the interrelationship of humans with the rest of the living world. Genome is a fascinating substance, because it has various characteristics. It can be fully analyzed by scientific methods, in addition to representing both the species and the individual in all living things. The genome possesses complex characteristics representing universality, diversity, and individuality at the same time.

However, reading the history of life is not solely the domain of the scientist. In order to answer profound questions about life, human beings, and the interrelationships characterizing nature, knowledge of a broad range of areas including philosophy, literature, art, and music is necessary. Science today is compartmentalized to such an extent that the overall vision is lost. It is the purpose of biohistory to recapture this vantage point.

This field also naturally invites participation by the general public, as the "miracle of life" has been a subject that has sustained people's fascination throughout the ages. As a further advantage, the study of living things is relatively easy for the non-scientist lay community to assimilate. Finally, this field is at a stage where the scientists themselves are beginning to recognize the advantages of receiving social feedback and cooperation from other disciplines. For all these reasons, it is proposed that biohistory be a new field of study.

Based on research in biohistory, I believe "Life" itself will take its place as the key concept of the next age, as outlined in the following chart.

| Age | Key Concept | Relationships Between Nature, Human Beings, and Technologies |
|---|---|---|
| Ancient Times | Life | (Nature, Human Beings) Humanistic and institutive knowledge |
| Greek Ages Medieval Ages Modern Times | Reason | (Nature) (Human Beings) (Artificial World) Products of science and technology alienate us from nature and humanity |
| 21st Century | Life | (Nature, Human Beings, Artificial World) Integration of humanistic and institutive knowledge and scientific knowledge |

# Discussion

**Kristeva:** I would like to make a very concrete observation on the basis of the fascinating papers by Gold and Nakamura. It is an observation related to my own practice, a very concrete experience with depression, a disease on which I have been working for years now in a famous French hospital, Salepetrière Hospital. I have worked with a group of researchers, biologists, psychiatrists, and psychologists. Our conclusions, published in a book translated into English as *Black Sand*, are not contradictory to Gold's observations, but I would like to ask him his feelings about them very briefly.

To our mind, depression is, of course, determined by biology, namely by serotonin transmissions, and we treat patients with anti-depressants. But it is affected by two major factors that are not biological, the first one being the object relation, the relationship between the patient and the other—therapist or parent or whatever person from the patient's social surroundings.

The second observation and the second factor of depression seems to us to be a special economy of linguistic capability and precisely a dislocation between linguistic sense, on the one hand, and the instinctual drives, on the other hand, which give the depressive person the impression that his language does not express his feelings, that there is a void between language, meaning, and emotional experience. In this context, aggression, for instance, is turned back to the self instead of going to the object, and I would like to link this with an earlier discussion. We talked about the absence of revenge in some social contexts, mainly in the Russian context. In the light of this experience with depression, we can perhaps say that if we observe an absence of revenge it is maybe because depression is what takes the place of revenge. Here is a linkage between our psychological concerns and our social concerns.

In Salepetrière Hospital, we have organized an interdisciplinary seminar—which follows the sense of Nakamura's recommendations—between neurobiologists, psychiatrists, and psychoanalysts. To my mind it is a unique experiment in broad interdisciplinary connections. Going back to Dore's earlier observation, we are not at all content with the notion of frozen rationality, but we are trying to elaborate a more subtle approach to it, which is, of course, necessary when biology and psychology try to share the same field.

**Iriye:** I think we have been presented with a very noble vision of what could happen in the near future. That is, Gold and Nakamura presented a vision where science and the humanities can cooperate together to create a nobler vision of humanity, one which I would welcome as a vision which I assume is transcultural or cross-cultural.

We spent some time in the first session talking about the cultural diversity and the relevance and irrelevance of different visions, but it seems to me that here what is discussed transcends cultural boundaries and is, as Harkabi was saying, a globalizing vision. I would certainly share the sense that if this were to come about, that sense of coming together or cooperating between scientists and humanists, it will be a great way to promote global civilization, bridging the gap which C. P. Snow talked about in the 1950s.

Can we expect that to happen? That question is specifically what the humanists and others that Nakamura talked about ought to conceptualize. Now, when Nakamura says that the people who appreciate music and literature, etc., must be brought into it, what can we do? That is, people with general humanistic backgrounds or historians and social scientists and so on. Are they to cooperate with the natural scientists, biochemists, and molecular biologists, etc., to create some kind of an agenda which may have policy implications? I think we should probably discuss the implication that we might be saying that we will need experts in this, just as we will need scientific experts and technicians. Are we going to be training those in the humanities and social scientists to do this job for us? If so, would this create the kind of problem Morin was talking about yesterday, creating yet another cadre of experts, with the implications for that specialization for the future of democracy?

If we are not going to be training social engineers but we are addressing ourselves to the general public, as Nakamura said, can we expect the general public—everybody throughout the world, billions of people—to equally appreciate scientific discoveries as well as music and literature? I think that is a very noble vision, which I fully share. But I just wanted to see how that will specifically work out in the twenty-first century.

**Kosai:** I was much fascinated by Gold's remarks. At the same time, I am somewhat confused, so I would like to ask two questions. First, suppose someone is in a depression and does not value himself at all. He believes he is a very sinful person, and then Gold came and helped him to make him believe in his value. But suppose he feels himself a sinful man, this might be the first step to being a good Christian. In that case, why do you help him? Or someone fearing God very seriously, will you help him to mitigate his fear? This is my first question, a very simple one, but maybe misdirected. But the question is the value system: Has the fear or depression already some value in the choice of a life course and so on? In that case, how do you judge whether this fear is valueless or whether it is very valuable. This is my first question.

The second question is as a social scientist heavily burdened with our earlier value judgment discussion. If Gold could show that value is biologically founded, then social scientists can be freed from the value judgment discussion completely. We can believe in a common human value which is incorporated, and the situation will have changed drastically.

**Gold:** It is a very provocative and important question, and I think it underlines the relative imprecision of our language and concepts regarding these most important and difficult issues. I can only answer it from the perspective of my own scientific culture and clinical experience, and I think one of the reasons that I focused on depression is that I think it is the best studied clinical entity. It is relatively homogeneous. That is, if you are a clinician in practice and you see hundreds of people with depression, you will see many of them, despite enormous disparities in their backgrounds and life experience and philosophies, giving the same kind of clinical presentation. It can only come after a lot of experience because there are no tissue markers—we cannot take a blood test and say this person is depressed; we cannot definitively document biologically. There is not a gene that will clearly tell us that this is a depressive individual.

But I imagine that everyone in the room here, economists, political scientists, gets a feel for the cards when they work with certain concepts and paradigms year in and year out over and over again, of dealing with something that has some organized core to it, that is not simply a random presentation. So, as a clinician, when I see someone who feels very badly about him- or herself, there are certain tip-offs or features that distinguish that feeling tone from humility—a sense of awe, the way a religious Christian might feel in the presence of a complex universe and divinity; a feeling of shame that does not seem to make sense in terms of the person's experience when a certain coloration seems to overtake self-representation. It is different from the way it had been before, which is systematically biased toward shame and self-derogation and hopelessness, and it is still only an estimate that it is a clinical entity.

I am sorry I cannot be more precise, but I can just tell you that I have a sense, at any rate, of when I'm dealing with that kind of clinical entity and when I am dealing with something that seems more intrinsically an intellectual, philosophical, or emotional conviction.

The relative reproducibility or similarity of depression from one person to the other and his or her responsiveness to given classes of drugs suggest a coherent underlying biological alteration. In one part of my paper I suggested that it is not necessarily reductionistic to try to identify that biological alteration because that biological alteration interferes with the person's humanity. It is a coloration that I think insulates the person from their capacity realistically to assess to what extent they feel a genuine humility in the face of the world or the universe, what the relationship is between themselves and others. To me that is part of the tragedy, but it also makes it exciting to bring on a biological perspective.

We now have very rudimentary, imprecise, imperfect means of trying to get a sense of factors that go beyond what we traditionally considered can shape the way a human being presents himself and thinks about himself. It is another parameter to consider and to humble us, I think, with how little we know about it.

**Kerber:** As we think about the seriousness of depression and its drift toward suicide, my assumption is that in time of war suicide rates are said to go down, and if that is so then I wonder if you have any reflections on that relationship.

**Gold:** I do not know the data but I will give you just an intuitive response. During times of crisis a stressor can be really noxious if it results in a situation where an individual is disparaged, humiliated, disconnected from a social context, and which fills that individual with a sense of hopelessness about future prospects.

Other kinds of stressors may not necessarily have that kind of noxious impact. During wartime, for instance—and people have vividly described this many times—there is a wonderful sense of solidarity, a union against an external enemy, an interdependence that is a life-and-death one in which bonds are formed never to be broken. Affirmations of love and friendship and solidarity are made that do not ordinarily occur in other kinds of context.

In that regard—and this is a question only for philosophical speculation: What is it that is most important to human beings?—some of the things that really bind us to the world and make life most worthwhile and least unbearable can occur in these kinds of extreme situations that bring us together, connect us to others, give us a sense that we have a purpose. Ironically, in the tragic vision, I suppose these can occur under the most horrifying kinds of circumstances. I could have other speculations about how that kind of arousal from a chronic external source, which is different from the internal sense of arousal that has no flexibility that occurs in depression, could paradoxically actually insulate a person from a certain kind of despair.

**Likachev:** To Gold's very interesting and important report I would like to add one thing. All criminals are, almost without exception, pessimists. This does not mean all pessimists are criminals, but criminals are all pessimists. So far as my association with criminals can tell, all criminals have been pessimists. Each one of them, if you look at them individually, is a professional. They justify their actions in the following terms: There is no justice in the world. There is no goodness in the world.

In individual psychology what is important is the social condition surrounding it. That is to say, the pessimistic psychological condition is very contagious. It contaminates individuals, but even social groups and society's elite get contaminated by pessimism, and this is one source of great danger.

**Windsor:** In discussions, the word "skills" that Gold used disturbed me. Obviously, we have to have skills in coping with circumstances, but skills in becoming a person or skills in acquiring self-regard, it would seem to me, is a different kind of question. In approaching that question and having read with interest the three kinds of visions, it seems to me that it is essential in this regard to acknowledge tragedy and that the horrors of this century are, in very large part, due to a wish not to acknowledge tragedy—to, as it were, engineer tragedy out of existence.

Gold is absolutely right, it seems to me. I could not agree with him more that part of what is the communist legacy goes back to the romantic movement and the post-Enlightenment avoidance of tragedy, which became characteristic of modern thinking. The acknowledgment of tragedy is essential not only to curing, or hoping to cure, people who are depressed in the way described but also to a world in which it is possible to create this humanistic culture, combining the scientific knowledge that we have and the acknowledgment of what we can never know. That is to say that our life is tragic because at the end of the day the only place at which truth and knowledge meet is in the certainty that we will die. But otherwise there is no relationship between truth and knowledge. We do not even know whether we are free or not.

I think behaviorist reductionists basing their view on inadequate knowledge can easily say we are not free. But we do not know whether freedom of the will is only an act of faith. We do not know whether death is the end or not. We have to decide how we approach these questions, but the approach to these questions is itself part of the acknowledgment of tragedy; and the acknowledgment of tragedy is exactly the opposite from the pessimism which is being discussed just now. Life is tragic, and provides for optimism or hope. What it does not provide for, and I think this is the danger in what Gold and Nakamura have been discussing, is that we could try to engineer ourselves, to manipulate ourselves into humanity, whereas the precondition is already there. It lies in our not knowing the truth but using our knowledge to cope with that situation.

**Bulliet:** I am struck that, if one goes back to the initial question whether complex technological information alienates us from our humanity, we do have to ask whether what we have heard is representative or whether it is a singular instance in which you can see complex technological information coming together with humanity.

It seems to me that while we can look with a certain optimism toward some of the things that have been said, nevertheless, at the same time, our culture, world culture, seems to be increasingly absorbed with images of technological dystopia, of the loss of human agency as technology becomes increasingly complex with a division in the labor force between an increasingly small minority who understand things and a larger group that has no hope of understanding them.

Certainly, the great scientific breakthrough of the twentieth century has been in the biological sciences and, to some degree, in that area it might be possible to redeem the sciences from the great tragedy of physics in having unleashed nuclear weapons upon the world, which has created so much of the depression about technology and humanity. But I wonder with Iriye how this is to be brought about: How does technological knowledge come to be disseminated among populations that are not seemingly inclined toward receiving it? I am also struck by the history of the phenomenon of the double truth—the notion that you get to one set of truths through science, rationality, difficult processes and another set of truths through religions, myths, metaphors, etc. While, ideally, these coincide—and one might hope for a science like biohistory to become universally recognized—the greater likelihood is that a science of this sort will be popularized, metamorphosed into non-scientific forms, something in the way that Darwin's observations turned into Social Darwinism. The question is whether this can be done in a benevolent way or whether these discoveries and advances in biotechnology will go the way of so many other scientific advances and simply add to, on the one hand, a measure of despair, which is what has been talked about, and, on the other hand, a measure of perversion of the scientific core and simply contribute to the sense of technological dystopia that seems to me is a dominant theme in popular culture.

**Winston:** The question that occurred to me was that of the social implications of Gold's findings in terms of at least one aspect of what this conference is about—the future in the past. What I want to ask is whether Gold would speculate that in contemporary societies of very different types and forms it might be possible that more of them, in terms of their very structure in what they are going through now, have generated the interaction of multiplying stressors so that the societies themselves become psychopathogenic.

At one end of the scale we have societies that are becoming more and more industrialized and urbanized into megacities. The impact of technology makes people feel less and less significant, even though they can control much of the environment in that kind of situation. At the other end, in large parts of the world societies are undergoing various forms of disintegration because they are unsuccessful in dealing with the challenges of modernization, where we see increasing numbers of people migrating to new environments, their cultures under breakdown, and then particular populations being subject either to systematic discrimination or reactions to them because of other stresses in the society.

There has not been much discussion of that from a socio-psychological perspective that I know about. So I am raising that question—not about one particular type of society since it is obvious that in the contemporary situation, from the most developed to the least developed, there are multiplying stressors that are interacting in different ways because of these changes.

**Yokoyama:** I have been rather fascinated by the combination of Gold and Nakamura. Gold has drawn back a curtain and allowed us to peep behind the scenes, revealing all varieties of phenomena and human societies which have been understood and discussed by people in the humanities, but what Nakamura has revealed is some sort of reason and cause-and-effect relationship. But I must remind the audience that there is some tricky business behind this glittering discovery of science.

As a friend of mine once pointed out, in the rather staggering development of bioscience, what is very conspicuous is that science tends to choose topics which it would take at least two months but not more than one year to solve, and which in due course give rise to suitable academic papers. There are some other more serious questions which one would think would take ten years or twenty years to try to solve and may never be successfully resolved. Such questions have been very carefully avoided by the scientists. That is the problem.

But to take things more optimistically, I think Nakamura helped me quite a lot. Having now observed a sort of basic limitation in scientific discoveries of cause-and-effect in the workings of human nature, we have still attained a stage in which we can enjoy varieties of knowledge, and enjoy this sort of scientific discovery in a more sober sense, keeping a certain detachment from whatever scientists do. So the message which I received from this combination of talks is very simple: there are two messages that we can receive from modern biochemistry or molecular biology.

One strong message, which is very simple, as Gold said, is the declaration of the basic homogeneity of mankind. People in the humanities tend to emphasize very tiny differences between each individual and different cultures and nationalities, but if we reach down to the level of DNA, the homogeneity is staggering.

The second message is again pretty grand, concerning closeness to nature and the basic homogeneity of varieties of life. This also can be enjoyed, according to Nakamura's fashion, and I can give you one example. A recent discovery, really an accumulation of more than thirty to forty years of study, tells us of an area where chimpanzee groups and some tribes live. The family structure—if I may use the word "family"—on both sides is quite similar. In another region there are some examples, although different from the former one, of a similar type of family being observed between apes and mankind.

**Dore:** I find the work which Gold records exceedingly impressive, but I do wonder about the use of words like "the revolution in molecular biology," etc. I do ask myself what is really new because, after all, the fact that biological factors have been involved in depressive illnesses, although there have been a few sort of dyed-in-the-wool Freudians who have gone on denying it, for a long time has been pretty universally understood. I mean I remember that wonderful psychologist Manslow, who did so much to elucidate our common humanity, saying in one of his books: "Anybody who has had more than one child and seen the differences in personalities and capacities between his own offspring, and is still capable of denying the probability of there being biological factors in the formation of personality, must have his eyes closed."

As for molecular biology and the fact that whereas we have hitherto had all kinds of means of pharmacological intervention in curing depression or, as Windsor put it a bit tendentiously, manipulating ourselves back into humanity, the fact that there are now drugs that can manipulate one back into humanity seems to me a great advance. But the fact that we have now, in addition to the pharmacological methods, the possibility of genetic manipulation, we have also the possibility of fetal diagnosis and abortion, which might add new weapons to the armoury, but does it really change the fundamental problems that Kosai raised of when one is entitled to intervene and when one is not?

Depression seems to be clear because, as Gold said, there is a general consensus in our society as to what is pathological, and this ought to be a good thing. But levels of aggression are different. I am often struck by the fact that it is impossible to translate the American word "aggression" into Japanese in any easy way. If you translate "American aggressive marketing" using the same word as when Hosokawa said "Japan committed an act of aggression," you are not conveying it. The Japanese word is "positive" rather than "aggressive."

Now, the actual level of expected aggression in Japanese and American society, of "aggressiveness," is different, and are we ever going to get to the state where it really is a social problem of deciding what is a permissible level of aggression, what is a pathological level of aggression, and are we going to face really new problems in that respect? But my basic question is: What is really new in adding the genetic to the pharmacological instruments for altering states of mind?

**Murakami:** What I am going to say is related to the technological dystopia which was raised by Bulliet. In 1980, a symposium like this was held in Stockholm and I was one of the participants. I proposed the idea of the "right of ignorance" or the right not to be well informed as one of the fundamental human rights, and I was accused almost unanimously of being an enemy of democracy. But still I rather stick to that idea because if there is a one-way flow of technological information from experts to the public, if the public or the people are well informed by an expert or a group of experts, they are forced, so to speak, to share the idea or the value system or the methodology of the experts. That is not, I think, the true end or true purpose of cognitive democracy, which Morin proposed, but, in many cases, just the dissemination of the experts' idea to the public. That is what I am against.

**Nakamura:** In the last session we talked about the crisis of social sciences. We should not discuss simply the crisis of the social or natural sciences but that of science in general, whether social or natural. As I suggested in my paper, scientists tend to be regarded as dangerous people. That, to me, is one reason why science and technology have failed to take root in a wider social context. What most impressed me in Gold's paper was that he said his patients appeared strange, but once he identified the causes of this strangeness he came to look at his patients more humanely as human beings. And, similarly, I want you to look at scientists as genuine people, if only to avoid the danger of plunging into dystopia. So do not look simply at science and technology themselves but look also at scientists.

Second, in connection with the comments of Yokoyama and Kosai, I do not think life itself has value *per se*, but if you study DNA, you are struck by the presence of universality, diversity, and individuality. The factors exist in the same genome, and nowhere else can you see the coexistence of individuality, universality, and diversity.

These points are important not simply for the understanding of life but for society at large. So if we can identify the wisdom of the coexistence of these three factors in the body, then we could utilize that knowledge in social problems. But, again, I do not see that the genome itself has value.

Now, on the theme of looking at the future in the past, my idea is that you have to have a very long-term view of what the past represents. We have to go back not simply to the origin of human beings but to the origin of life. We have to have a much longer view of the past than we are accustomed to.

**Gold:** I must say that I found the comments very provocative, and I am not really fundamentally in disagreement with any of them. I think what they have stimulated in me is the sober recognition that the more things change the more they stay the same, that I do not really necessarily believe that we are entering an entirely new world where we will be grappling with age-old problems in fundamentally different ways, that the tragic nature of things still holds. There is technological dystopia, there are opportunities for developing new metaphors or at least elucidating what has puzzled us over the millennia.

Perhaps my enthusiasm for what we are learning about depression reflects my own personal intellectual and scientific history. I think certainly Freud mentioned that there may be biological factors in behavior, and none of us would disagree. To me it is rather thrilling that we are beginning to identify specific informational substances, stereotype physiological responses that are going awry, and are groping to understand mechanisms of psychotropic drug action that influence life and death matters with respect to behavior and parameters of feeling, such as shame and anxiety about the self. That would have been unheard of ten or fifteen years ago, even though people have been speculating about it for a long time, and I think it is only the tip of the iceberg.

Without being a great enthusiast for molecular biologists, I must say that there really is, at least in the short term, a certain kind of revolution in cracking the genetic code and having access to the instruction book that dictates and regulates the molecules that constitute our physical being, that gives us an opportunity to study biological systems, and especially the brain, in ways that had not been heard of before.

I think in that regard certainly it is wonderful that we have pharmacological interventions for the treatment of depression and anxiety, but these are such gross sledgehammer approaches to try to alter biological systems. You give a chemical by mouth that is supposed to affect a single molecule in the brain; it bathes every cell in the body, it influences the functional activity of every cell. You give it in a thousandfold concentration in order to get it to that cell, and you hope against hope that over several weeks it will begin subtly, awkwardly, but fortunately at times, influentially, to alter the system and promote homeostasis.

With molecular biology you have access to the code book for every single distinct protein that constitutes a living organism and the potential to modulate the expression of that protein in a specific cell anywhere in the brain or anywhere in the body. You have an opportunity to screen the human genome. This sounds very anti-humanistic, and it actually does frighten me, but it is possible, for instance, to take a hundred criminals or aggressive individuals, screen the genome, find a consistent alteration in a nucleotide sequence that changes the identity of a protein, the sequence of that protein, and find out that it influences the secretion of a hormone that influences aggression.

That kind of approach raises all kinds of ethical problems, whether you delete that gene from the gene pool by aborting the fetuses or utilize gene therapy. In a sense, in terms of what Iriye was saying, there is a likely idea that there is a universality of science, that molecular biologists across the globe are talking to each other with the same vocabulary, but the data may generate many more questions than they solve, and they are going to generate imprecise answers that really will throw us back on imponderables about what genes we are going to select and promote and how we might actually change the phenotype of the organism in ways that we could never hope to do surgically, pharmacologically, with a discreteness that was beyond imagining fifteen years ago.

Now, from my perspective as an enthusiast and looking at the world in a very focal way, spending time working with people who have pathological hyperarousal and anxiety and watching the wonder of what it is like to see an individual who experiences life through that prism return to his humanity and discover elements of self and the capacity to relate to others and to give and to take in a wondrous way, this question occurs to me: Suppose we begin really to understand the repertoire of genes that influence arousal levels and the capacity for anxiety. This is a lunatic statement about future evolution, but I ask myself the question why is it that, although we are empathic human beings capable of love, we can view another human being whose suffering we can at least partially understand and who is doomed without doing everything we possibly can to ameliorate his condition? I think one reason—there are many, I am sure—is anxiety.

People are afraid of letting go of what they have. They are afraid of being depleted. They are afraid of being left with nothing, feeling small. These are the most aversive kinds of human experience. Anxiety is coded in the bone and the brain is organized to generate it, and I think when we get to the point where we can begin to manipulate the genes that are encoded in ways that release individuals from the bondage of a certain kind of anxiety, then we may see—and this is highly utopian, and I am embarrassed to say it, and I do not really believe it—but we may see the initiation of a new phase in human evolution.

# CAN WAR STILL BE AN INSTRUMENT OF POLICY?

# CAN WAR STILL BE
# AN INSTRUMENT OF POLICY?

Yehoshafat HARKABI

As long as armed forces and weapons exist they are liable to be used. However, not every use of violence and incident of bloodshed deserves to be designated as war. The constituents of traditional definitions of war are its being a means adopted by states (at least statelike entities), using armies, involving hostilities of a considerable magnitude and duration. Many other cases of collective violence are excluded, otherwise the meaning of war becomes diffused as every act of violence is called a war. I maintain that we may be entering a turbulent world, not a peaceful one, which will not necessarily be riven by interstate wars. The incidence of international wars, especially among the developed countries, has already declined, entailing some devolution of the institution of war and a reduction in the resources devoted to it. These changes have been ushered in not pursuant to an ideological blueprint or following normative improvements but rather by the impact of political realities. Evidence of these trends has already emerged. However, we should be careful not to drift toward the common blunder of "presentism"—being excessively impressed by present trends and extrapolating them into the future, whereas, eventually, they may prove to be short-lived. Indeed, only a theoretical analysis of the origins of such trends and their raison d'être, can give us some confidence that they are not a passing phenomenon.

The role that war plays is shaped by the prevailing world order. Thus, the question about the future of war equals the question of what kind of world we live in. The term "world order" is neutral, as it does not mean that world order is orderly. Anarchy, too, is a kind of order, and the recent disorders in Eastern Europe and elsewhere are part of the present world order. World order is our conceptualization of the main traits of each age in terms of the structure of the political international system and of the modes of behavior between the political entities of which the world consists. The late Professor Hedley Bull differentiated between "international order," which applies between states, and "world order," which is wider in its connotation and includes—besides the political relationship between states—the main social and cultural attributes of the age. In every age since the formation of an international system of states, there has been a world order of sorts.

The expression "new world order" does not mean the arrival of the millennium but only that changes have emerged important enough to make the present world order different from the previous one. World order is a dynamic phenomenon as a mixture of old and new ingredients, and each world order deserves both the adjectives "new" and "emergent."

There are two main approaches in tackling the new world order: The first assumes that the new world order was inaugurated by the collapse of the Soviet system. Thus, it examines the influence of the end of the Cold War on the international system. Its approach is political and diplomatic, and it deals with contemporary world politics. The second tries to explore the basic components in the international infrastructure that preceded the upheavals in Eastern Europe and enabled them. Its approach aspires to be more metapolitical. The first deals with international "currents"; the second with international "undercurrents," whose influence is more profound. I shall try to lean toward the second approach.

The effort to diagnose the characteristics of world order should be a central task of the political sciences. Such an effort should not only be descriptive but analytical, identifying the constituents that have molded this kind of order. True, the characteristics of the prevailing world order can be ascertained only with hindsight. However, we should make such an effort now, even if the results will be mostly conjectural, recognizing that history's logic does not necessarily follow our reasoning, and reluctant to ensconce ourselves in the comforts of an historically agnostic position.

In the social and political sciences we can establish predispositions which cannot be given the form of laws that apply to all cases but only to the majority of cases, and thus be of an approximate probabilistic nature. Hence, one exception that is sufficient to falsify a law in the natural sciences does not refute an assertion of a tendency in the social and political sciences. Individual cases of war do not disprove a proposition stating that there is a decline in international wars.

## MAIN TRENDS IN THE EMERGING WORLD ORDER

**Market Economy and Democratization:** Competition between nations will revolve more on economics and technology than on territory, domination, and power. Conflicts that may ensue from such competition will probably not escalate into interstate wars. Commercial competition has other means at its disposal than the resort to violence. There are fierce divergences on commerce between the United States and Japan; it is improbable that they will become violent.

In this trade competition the developed economic giants or blocs will be the main players; the share of the less developed countries in these commercial transactions may prove to be small. In the past, every country was important at least in terms of its own region. In modern trade all countries are neighbors, and states will lose the importance their location conferred on them. The end of the Cold War may weaken the motivation and preparedness of the developed countries to aid the no longer needed underdeveloped countries, which may thus be left to their own devices.

**A Very Heterogeneous World:** The world has always been heterogeneous in terms of economic and technological developments. Thus, within the general world order there will be varied patches of local orders. It will be an extremely complex, fragmented, and hybrid world. Security entanglements will be regionalized. This complexity is not the result of our subjective limitations in understanding current developments but follows from the multiplicity of states, each wrestling with some particular plight. In the past, watching Moscow spared us the need to peruse the developments in its satellite states. Now each of them calls for special attention. We are bombarded by incessant news about a motley sequence of events, including acts of violence, both communal and political. We can hardly digest all this news. Modern mass media may have made the world a global village, but it is an extremely baffling one. Leaders' agendas are overwhelmingly burdened with insoluble problems and dilemmas. It is humanly impossible for them, even with the best assistance, to cope with all that happens. By necessity leaders will neglect whatever seems to them of lesser urgency.

**Wars Less Likely:** Historically, changing boundaries or quarrels over contiguous territories have been the main reason for launching wars. Yet the geographical division of most of the globe is congealing and becoming stabilized as many societies become resigned to living within their present boundaries. Of course, there are exceptions. This crystallization of boundaries is normatively reflected in the proscription of conquest. Previously, conquest conferred legal title to property, as was promulgated by Vattel, the protagonist of the legal principles of the Westphalia settlement. Proscribing conquest is now embodied in international enactments, such as the famous Security Council Resolution 242, enjoining "the inadmissibility of acquiring territory by war," an idea that was reiterated by President Bush—"the acquisition of territory by force is unacceptable"—in his speech on August 8, 1990, announcing American readiness to resist the Iraqi conquest of Kuwait and to deploy troops in Saudi Arabia.

The Iraqi attempt to occupy Kuwait may prove an exceptional case. Paradoxically, despite the unsatisfactory end of this war, the frustration of Iraqi aggression and the punishment visited on Iraq may in the future have a "demonstration effect" of discouraging leaders, especially in the less developed countries, from initiating war. There are not many countries that could withstand the punishment inflicted on Iraq.

Aversion to war is not so much a reflection of an increase in morality, but rather that conventional weaponry—and not only nuclear weaponry—has become very destructive, and this has been reinforced by the fear of escalation and nuclearization of war. The cost of war has become exorbitant. Memories of recent wars have produced a public revulsion against the idea of war. Television bringing war into people's home has reinforced this repugnance. A decline in the trust afforded leaders may produce resistance to follow them to war, unless such a war is considered by the public to be justified. Many recent wars have proved a disaster for their initiators. (In previous centuries there was a high correlation between initiating war and winning. It has been reversed in this century.) This decline in war can be considered a manifestation of progress in the course of humanity.

New factors causing international tensions and quarrels may emerge, such as demographic pressures and the urge to migrate, ecological disputes, and cultural antipathies. What form they will take is not clear. Nevertheless, the world is not going to shed its main characteristic as state-centric. States' sovereignty has been curtailed, but states have not been superseded by another political structure. Thus far, states and their alliances—not cultures and civilizations—have been the actors engaged in wars. We have to differentiate between the issues on which wars are waged and the nature of the belligerent parties. The parties have been politically organized bodies, which in recent centuries have been states. Ethnicity and culture can be an issue, but only political organizations, functioning as even rudimentary states, can engage in wars as distinct from riots and pogroms.

**Wars Between the Major Powers Improbable:** The end of the Cold War has made a war pitting the major powers against each other unlikely. Europe, which historically constituted the main battlefield for wars and was recently considered the potential main battlefield between East and West, has been pacified.

The main fear that haunted the West was a conventional invasion of Western Europe by the Red Army. The recent upheavals in the Soviet Union and the republics into which it disintegrated deprive them of the capacity and the desire to expand. Actually, it can now be evaluated that the Soviet Union lost, many years ago, the capacity to launch a conventional war because of its internal demoralization. Its leaders lost their legitimacy in the eyes of the public, and would have failed to enlist the support of their people in going to war. Without a modicum of national consensus, war nowadays is impossible. War and expansion can no longer solve the former Soviet states' domestic quandaries. Only nuclear war, which involves relatively few operators, is still a theoretical possibility, but its probability has always been small, and more so now.

**From International to Internal Wars:** It should be noted that there is no international war at present. All cases of fighting are at present internal. There are some cases of simmering irredentism in Central and Eastern Europe, but it is doubtful if they will erupt into fully fledged interstate wars (more probably they will take the form of civil strife and persecutions). These states hope to join the European Community as the only solution to their economic difficulties. This inhibits them from aggressive behavior between themselves lest they jeopardize their admittance to the community. Thus, vagaries of nationalism are partially restrained.

In cases in which the integrity of a state has not congealed, a rebellion or internal strife may erupt and develop into a civil "war." This becomes a war once the parties are recognized as politically separate entities. So long as these states' internal disarray does not threaten other countries, the world may prefer to observe these unhappy countries' predicaments with some equanimity, bearing in mind that the developed countries, which could intervene, are also overburdened with grave domestic problems that compete for attention and resources. As long ago remarked by Raymond Aron, humanity has learned not how to eradicate conflicts, but rather how to localize them, and thus marginalize their significance to the rest of humanity.

**Wars in the Third World:** The center of gravity of interstate and internal wars may have moved to the Third World. Because of the big powers' penchant for extracting themselves from regional conflicts, small powers may perhaps feel more free to embark on war. However, they will not be in a position to maneuver between the superpowers, call on them for help, or pass them the bill. Only in exceptional cases can wars between lesser powers affect world order. Otherwise, they are likely to be isolated and almost ignored, as happened, for instance, in the long and disastrous Iran–Iraq war. Thus, their damage will be more internal than worldwide. There is no longer danger of world wars, only localized parochial wars.

The recent war against Iraq has demonstrated the merit of sophisticated weaponry and will incite states to acquire it. However, small states' acquisition of modern technology will not necessarily have an equalizing effect in their confronting the big powers; apart from quality, small states cannot escape the tyranny of quantities they cannot afford. States' vulnerabilities grow, and a major power's sting can be very painful.

**Intervention:** Memories of unsuccessful intervention may discourage future intervention. The world community finds it easier to intervene in interstate cross-border invasions than in intrastate conflicts. Interventions in intrastate conflicts may be costly in terms of the considerable size of the forces needed and the casualties they incur. Furthermore, the question of how to adjudicate between the claims of adversaries in internal controversies, and what settlement is just and can be imposed, is very confusing. Readiness to intervene in internal wars is dependent on the leading states' evaluation of the importance of the case and of the dangers of not intervening.

Interventions may be effective the earlier they take place. Yugoslavia has been allowed to languish, and on the whole has been treated as an unimportant suburb of Europe.

By default, the decision in such cases may be to leave the traditional way in which conflicts have been determined and boundaries traced by letting the parties "fight it out." Thus, the "realistic order" is allowed to prevail over the hitherto "formal order," which has become artificial and anachronistic. Arrangements to resist the "realistic order" may also be short-lived, as the local balance of power may eventually shape the outcome. The developments in Somalia may discourage further interventions on humanitarian grounds. Instead of intervention, the world community may threaten and use the capacity of inflicting punishment as means of deterring aggression, by the destruction of power stations, of which no country enjoys redundancy.

## THE DANGER OF NUCLEAR WEAPONS

**Nuclear Strategy:** Nuclear strategy was developed as a theory on the paradigm of the confrontation between the United States and the Soviet Union. As a theory it was a success. However, it was enmeshed in grave contradiction, as the threat to activate nuclear weapons and launch a nuclear war meant causing a devastation that in a showdown between the superpowers would be graver, at least in the short term, than the harm caused by the aggression that provoked the initiation of a nuclear war. If a nuclear war becomes suicidal, meeting what provocation is worth committing national suicide? Thus, no coherent doctrines on the first use of nuclear weapons could be derived from its theory. The relevancy of writings on nuclear strategy based on confrontation between the superpowers lapsed with the collapse of the Soviet Union. Most of this literature will be abandoned on shelves in libraries, to the great dismay of its authors.

With the decline in the danger of nuclear war between the big powers, the danger of its use by small nations and even by terrorists still lingers. Terrorists may perhaps acquire a bomb, and may use it as means of vengeance or blackmail. It is remarkable that so far proliferation has been much smaller than envisaged in the sixties and seventies. Some threshold states like Argentina, Brazil, and South Africa have relinquished their efforts to become nuclear, and submitted to mutual and international inspection. Probably the NPT Extension Conference in 1995 will exert fierce pressures on the states recalcitrant to adhere to the NPT. The Iraqi example has manifested the weakness of IAEA inspection, however, and paradoxically it will reinforce IAEA authority and the efficiency of its inspection.

The theoretical nuclear strategy of small nations has not been developed. This is not accidental, as such confrontations cannot be generalized as those between the superpowers, since the local concrete circumstances are its main inputs. Thus, there can hardly be a general theoretical nuclear strategy for small powers because each case is special.

The confrontation between the superpowers constituted a "closed system" in terms of the non-existence of a super-superpower that could intervene and change the situation. By contrast, a confrontation between small nuclear powers, or a mixed situation of only one party possessing nuclear weapons, constitutes an "open system" by virtue of the possibility of intervention, even nuclear, by the superpowers. Thus, small powers' nuclear strategy must include in its reckoning such an intervention, and this complicates the whole issue. The possibility of such a forceful intervention may have a deterrent effect on the behavior of a small state planning to acquire nuclear weaponry and, more so, eventually use it.

**Security Council Resolution 255:** Perhaps the best means of discouraging small powers from developing nuclear capability is by the Security Council's permanent member nuclear states underscoring their undertaking pursuant to Security Council Resolution 255. As this resolution is not well known, I shall allow myself a small digression to explain it.

In the deliberation on the 1968 NPT agreement the non-nuclear states posed the question: Why should they forswear developing a nuclear capability if they were not assured protection against a nuclear threat, nuclear blackmail, and even the use of nuclear weapons against them, by a small nuclear power? They demanded that the nuclear superpowers solemnly undertake to act forcefully, even nuclearly, against such an aggressor. The superpowers refused to guarantee an automatic response against such an aggressor state. Instead, on June 17, 1968, each of the representatives of the United States, the Soviet Union, and the United Kingdom (then the depository states) made identical declarations:

"Aggression with nuclear weapons, or the threat of such aggression, against a non-nuclear state would create a qualitative new situation in which the nuclear weapon states which are permanent members of the United Nations Security Council would have to act immediately through the Security Council to take measures necessary to counter such aggression or to remove the threat of aggression in accordance to the United Nations Charter which calls for taking:

"effective collective measures for the prevention and removal of threats to peace, and for the suppression of acts of aggression or other breaches of the peace....

"any State which commits aggression accompanied by the use of nuclear weapons or which threatens such aggression must be aware that its actions are to be countered effectively by measures to be taken in accordance with the United Nations Charter to suppress the aggression or remove the threat of aggression."

This undertaking was formalized on June 19, 1968, in Security Council Resolution 255: "...aggression against a non-nuclear-weapon state would create a situation in which the Security Council, and above all its nuclear-weapon state permanent members, would have to act immediately in accordance of their obligations under the United Nations Charter."

This resolution accentuates the "open system" nature of confrontation between small powers by virtue of the possibility of intervention by the nuclear superpowers. The question posed is whether the superpowers will honor their undertaking and act immediately and forcefully. We cannot be sure. However, it would be a mistake to discard such a possibility, not because of their philanthropy but because it is in their own interests to abide by it. One case in which a small state gets away with the use of nuclear weapons will signal to all states that it is worthwhile possessing and even using such weapons, culminating in a world of nuclear anarchy. The strength of Resolution 255 stems from the possibility that the superpowers would have acted in accordance with it, even without such a pledge. Furthermore, France and China may in the future join the undertaking of this resolution.

It is of great importance to make Security Council Resolution 255 absolutely known to the public, emphasizing the superpowers' resoluteness in their undertaking. The nuclear superpowers should even publicize their readiness to include "rogue states" in their targeting program. It seems that President Clinton followed this line in a speech in his July 1993 visit to South Korea, threatening to destroy North Korea as a state if it used its nuclear weapons. It may seem farfetched now, but once such dangers materialize, leaders of the superstates may be impelled to react more forcefully than they now credit themselves.

The NPT definition of a nuclear state was one that had exploded a nuclear weapon before January 1, 1967. Thus, one atomic device, even non-operational, sufficed. This should not be valid any longer. States should be reminded that articulating nuclear threats while possessing a bomb or a small arsenal may summon a preemptive nuclear attack by the superpowers. Thus, it is ill-advised—and, I believe untrue—to argue that one Iraqi atomic bomb could have sanctuarized its aggression. Had it been true, it would have goaded other potential aggressors to acquire a bomb and shelter behind it.

**Reduction of War Tensions:** The end of the Cold War has already allowed states to reduce their military outlays and plan further cuts. The fact that military industries are encountering difficulties in marketing their products indicates the slowing down of the arms race in general, though there are some exceptions. This generally calmer climate could have been improved had nations and public opinion differentiated between "dangers" ("risks" or "hazards") and "threats." A country can draw a list of acts by its neighbors detrimental to its security and well-being. These constitute "dangers"—but not necessarily "threats"—that this state has ascertained its neighbors are harboring. A "danger" is a theoretical injurious course of action, irrespective of whether it has been adopted by a prospective enemy as a concrete policy. By contrast, a "threat" exists only if it is the policy of a "threatening" agent.

For instance, the establishment of the State of Israel was considered by many Arabs as a terrible act of aggression that could be remedied only by undoing what had been accomplished—by the destruction of the Israeli state. They were well aware that such a goal contradicted the main tenet of international law on which the League of Nations and the United Nations had been founded—respecting the integrity of existing states. At that stage the objective of the destruction of Israel was a "threat," abetted by a host of preparatory steps. However, history is a learning process, and the general Arab position started to change, even if not completely. This change enabled the peace with Egypt and the present negotiations. Thus the idea of the destruction of Israel is now mostly a "danger" for Israel, and will remain so because of the existence of the Palestinians and the Arab states.

The possibility of a conventional Soviet invasion of Europe was initially a "threat." Because of the internal weaknesses of the Soviet state that have recently been revealed—the internal demoralization of the regime and the impossibility of enlisting the support of the Soviet peoples for such a military adventure—this erstwhile "threat" was demoted to a "danger" to Europe and the United States, because of the sheer existence of the Soviet Union.

Paradoxically, because the real threats have so dwindled, nations may resort to listing the "dangers" they may face as if they were "threats," thereby justifying their military efforts. Thus, differentiating between "threat" and "danger" by the bureaucracy and intelligence services—and no less by the public—is of the utmost importance for the purpose of reducing anxieties. Historically, it seems, mistaking a "danger" for a "threat" has been more common than the opposite. Of course, the relationship between "threat" and "danger" is not uni-directional, with "threat" becoming "danger" but not vice versa. Yet for a "danger" to become a "threat" there is generally a need for a strong irritating factor or event.

**The Need to Think "Internationally":** A big problem that faces us is the gap between the exigencies of international life as they come into being and the modes of thinking to which we have been inured. We tend to think nationally and parochially but not internationally. In the past foreign affairs interested only a minority. Goals were in many cases defined in possessive terms of acquisition of assets, mainly territory. The style was heroic. Leaders decided what they wanted to procure for their state and then elaborated a strategy to attain it. Strategic calculations were confined to the examination of how adversaries could thwart these efforts, and how to overcome them. This thinking was self-referential, i.e., our private well-being served as the measuring rod to gauge situations and outcomes.

This is no longer adequate. Our age is post-heroic. We live now in a dense and intertwined world in which, when molding external policy, we shall first have to consider how the world order constrains or enables us to achieve our goals. The attitude of the rest of the world toward our policy will impinge decisively on its feasibility. *Thus, before thinking "nationally" we shall have to think "internation-*

*ally.*" Using Arnold Wolfers' terminology, "milieu goals," which define the kind of world order we prefer, will supersede "possessive goals" of what assets we covet. National interests of the big states will be shaped by the terms of the kind of world order they would like to prevail. Thinking "internationally" is the intellectual and emotional awareness that a mature national policy should include wider considerations than the narrow considerations of allegedly direct national interests.

In many cases in the past, mistakes stemmed from parochialism and from the failure to consider the international ramifications of our problems. For instance, Saddam Hussein's mistake resided in confining the calculations of the invasion he had designed to resistance by Kuwait while ignoring the possible international reaction to his venture.

The need to think internationally is patently clear in the case of lesser powers. However, what is characteristic of the present period is its validity for the United States. As evidenced in the last Iraqi crisis the United States did not want to stand alone, which militarily it could, but used its best endeavors to enlist the support of the United Nations and the world community. It is not the calculus of power that constrains the hegemon but the climate of opinion inside the United States and in the world at large.

The need to think internationally, or to have an international outlook, stems from a series of changes and innovations: neither the security nor the prosperity of states is dependent on their exclusive efforts, and geography can no longer insulate a country. Most countries that have tried to live in isolation are currently in the throes of opening themselves to join the world community. Communications have made us aware of events in all parts of the world and have made our societies and states permeable to the rest of humanity. We are the only species that knows about the other members of their species. (The alligators in Florida know nothing about the crocodiles in Kenya.)

**The Problem:** My basic assumption is that every kind of world order is linked to a corresponding mode of thinking, a mentality, a mindset, or a political culture. People in every age have constituted an "epistemic community." This idea is not new. It was presented in a grand fashion by Auguste Comte. Man is a thinking being and the ways in which mankind thinks and behaves are correlated, mutually reinforcing each other.

Our cultural legacy has not prepared our minds to think internationally. By reading literature or listening to folktales, by empathetically identifying ourselves with the challenges of its heroes, we have vicariously enlarged the scope of our experience and enriched our grasp of the intricacies of the human condition. Literature, concentrating on the feelings of individuals and their ordeals, or at most the adversities of some collectivities, could not make the same contribution in the international domain. Even international events like wars and battles were described in novels from the vantage point of an individual. (Tolstoy's description of Pierre's experiences at the battle of Borodino and Stendhal's description of Fabrizio's bewilderment at Waterloo are cases in point.) Literature, myths, and legends have sensitized us to *interpersonal* problems but not to *international* quandaries.

The question this poses is: How will we rise to "thinking internationally"? We are no longer living in an aristocratic regime in which decision making could sometimes, if not always, be of high quality and independent of the public level of understanding. In democratic regimes an island of wisdom can no longer last if surrounded by an ocean of stupidity. Thus, if we want to ensure high-quality policy, we have to elevate the level of political and international thinking of the public.

We cannot introduce ourselves and the public to thinking internationally by preaching the need to transcend national, parochial, and narcissistic thinking. People cannot identify themselves with humanity. They tend to identify themselves with their particular reference groups, their communities, their religions, nations, and states. However, they can identify themselves with humanity's dilemmas in its grappling with how to organize itself and shape the relations among the entities into which it has been divided. People are capable of manifesting empathy toward the adversities humanity has had to face, since these do not set them at loggerheads with their narrow loyalties and their patriotism. The destiny of humanity may then appear not so much as foisted on mankind, but as its own enterprise, in the making of which mankind has collaborated. It will make us more alive to the difficulties of molding the world order according to our liking, more alive to the untoward outcomes that may ensue from our designs, thus limiting our idealistic expectations without disheartening us.

There is a general feeling that the world is at an historic turning point. The problems this poses are: First, to identify the main changes that are taking place in the world community and the configuration of the emerging world order that these changes engender. Second, to ask ourselves how to encourage the development of those factors and modes of thinking that may support and even improve the positive changes in the world order, including averting war. Third, how to introduce these modes of thinking into our educational system and propagate them among the public.

# COMMENT ON
# THE HARKABI PAPER

Ernest MAY

H arkabi's argument is learned, lucid, and persuasive. It is not, however, unchallengeable.

He asserts that the apparent and probable trend is toward significantly lessened use of war as an instrument of policy. Noting that the past century and three-quarters have seen only two giant wars, he comments, "individual cases of war do not disprove a proposition stating that there is a decline in international wars." I am reminded of the legendary Foreign Office mandarin who retired in the 1950s, observing with satisfaction, "Every weekday morning for fifty years, I predicted that on the next day there would be no great European war. In all that time, I was only wrong twice!"

From the data we have, one can draw the inference that Harkabi draws. With equal logic, we could compare the scale of World War II with that of World War I, note the shortness of the interval between the two, especially as compared with the interval between World War I and the Napoleonic Wars, and say that the observable trend is toward international wars of increasingly devastating violence.

Projecting the alternative trend lines, one might forecast, at one extreme, *no* international wars. At the other extreme, the forecast might be eventual violence obliterating or nearly obliterating civilization: perhaps not the pinging Coke bottle of *On the Beach,* symbolizing the extinction of humankind; perhaps, however, a world like that envisioned in *A Canticle for Liebowitz,* where monks treasure fragments of blueprints that to them are mysterious remnants of a lost age.

If the happier trend line develops, future historians will probably offer explanations foreshadowed in Harkabi's paper and in John Mueller's arresting book, *Beyond Doomsday.* Taking account of the increasing destructiveness of war, historians may say states use all-out military force as the final resort for adjusting balances of power. They found alternatives, and/or internal evolution in states capable of large-scale warfare militated against such resort. As Kant wished, polities evolved eventually to give overriding voice to citizens who believed (a) that *their* interests would be adversely affected by war and (b) that, except in extraordinary circumstances, the killing of others contravened moral logic. Possibly—though Harkabi voices skepticism—historians may say that polities in particular states evolved toward surrender of sovereignty and the creation of successful peace-keeping, peace-enforcing institutions at supranational levels.

If the more dire scenario develops, historians re-creating events after some new (and more aptly named) Renaissance might explain the cataclysmic wars of the twenty-first century as evidence of a state system unable to accommodate revolutions in military technology. States played "chicken" and did not brake in time. An alternative explanation could be the biologist's: for all their art and finery, humans turned out to be another species that succumbed to becoming too adept at intraspecies aggression.

(If your inner voice says, "But these are fantasies from Cold War days," recall a few facts. At the time of Ronald Reagan's "Evil Empire" speech and the KGB's hysterical "Operation Ryan," presuming preemptive nuclear war, the United States and the Soviet Union each had about 10,000 nuclear weapons targeted on the other. Now that the United States and Russia are collaborators, almost allies, they target only 3,000 warheads on one another. France today possesses more nuclear firepower than was possessed by the Soviet Union at the time of the Cuban missile crisis. So does China. An Indian general asserts that the moral commonly drawn in the developing world from the recent Persian Gulf War is "do not challenge the United States until you have operational nuclear weapons.")

Suppose that the actual future brings neither peace as Kantians have dreamed of it nor war as Europeans and Americans have known it in this century. Suppose events follow one of the alternative courses sketched by Harkabi. Or some other: a new era of limited wars such as we sometimes imagine of eighteenth-century Europe or a long era comparable to the late Victorian period or the late decades of the Cold War, when major states displaced their antagonisms, spilling mostly the blood of mercenaries or aliens in territories of marginal interest to most of their people. Or an era with no modern precedent except in areas where empires disintegrated with no nations immediately replacing them, as, for example, China when under warlords, or parts of Africa now. In such an era, war could have all other attributes except that of being waged by territorial states. One can imagine—if only with difficulty—a world where major armed combatants (even nuclear-armed combatants) include Hezbollah and the Medellin Drug Cartel.

How would we historians explain trends leading neither to war's obsolescence nor to more and deadlier world wars? Our first recourse would probably be to ascribe to states, territorial and non-territorial—or to the human species—a prudent concern for survival. But when we began to explain *why* history had taken such a turn, we could find ourselves at a loss. For the theories that provide our presumptions about what is *normal* in international relations do not make much allowance for adaptive behavior, and they make almost no allowance for *variably* adaptive behavior—that is, for the possibility that, at a given moment, two interacting states may be functioning in two different systems, competing (if at all) for different stakes, and following differing norms.

We are handicapped now in imagining the theories on which future historians may draw because we do not in fact have a body of political theory adequate to explain the history we have already experienced. The great age of modern political theory ran from the Renaissance to the Romantic period. From Machiavelli to Mill, many of the greatest minds of the Western world coped with questions of how power and authority could or should be pursued, maintained, expanded, or shared, whether within states or among states. Despite the coincident expansion of the European world, these thinkers nearly all supposed a comparatively static universe. For Machiavelli and almost every later writer on interstate relations, power was a constant. There was just so much. If one prince gained, another lost. From Bodin to Mill, most writers concerned with the internal functioning of states supposed that one set of institutions or norms would be ideal for all circumstances. The absence of imagination about possible changes is suggested by writings about war before the industrial age. A late eighteenth-century novel, eerily accurate in envisioning a great Anglo-German war right around 1914, pictured a war fought entirely with eighteenth-century weaponry and tactics.

The Industrial Revolution swamped political theory—and theories concerning war. The best minds turned to the natural sciences. The few that focused on relationships among human beings tended to concentrate on transactions in goods and services. Marx and Engels, Weber, and a few others constructed theories that took some account of economic and social evolution. Weber analyzed the corresponding evolution in some political institutions, particularly officialdom and bureaucracy.

Nevertheless, it is probably not an exaggeration to describe our understanding of politics as at or about the level of our understanding of chemistry before Lavoisier. As historians, we can describe some evolutionary trends that seem certain or nearly certain to continue. We have no framework for connecting them. We and our colleagues in the social sciences have no web of generalizations on the basis of which to offer even speculative predictions. And if we pause to think, we recognize that what we do know is at odds with the theories usually invoked.

We know that values and normative criteria guiding political behavior have not been constant either over time or within particular periods. Classical theories of international relations, tracing back to Machiavelli, suppose states maximizing their relative power. But political power has never been clearly measurable. It does not come in BTUs or megawatts. Statesmen have often acted on differing conceptions of power. Hitler and Churchill in 1940, for example, had different notions about the ingredients of power, leading the one to rate the United States as a decisive force in a new world war, the other to discount it as too ethnically and politically fragmented to make its potential weight felt. In many states, from the Spain of Philip II down at least to the Britain of Anthony Eden and Harold Macmillan, crucial internal divisions concerned the relative contributions to national power of land-controlling forces on the one hand, and sea-controlling forces on the other. And these are merely ambiguities relating to power to make war. How much more ample are ambiguities relating to what Joseph Nye labels "soft power," where ideology and culture are in play. Every relevant concept—power, interest, peace, war, order, anarchy—has changed, is changing, and has differing meanings from state to state and within states. How can we generalize about the movements of these conceptual quanta?

Even if we had generalizations about the evolution of ideas, how could we relate them to generalizations about institutional evolution? Most of our political theory comes from periods and societies where power and status derived primarily from location within political hierarchies. In Europe by the seventeenth century this was as true for clergy as for laity. But the eighteenth century saw the sprouting of alternative hierarchies. In the twentieth century, in many parts of the world, these alternative hierarchies have grown to levels where they offer individuals opportunities for power and status equaling or surpassing opportunities offered by the state. In the United States only a small minority of the elite seeks reward and satisfaction in political or governmental careers.

Changes in concepts and values have interacted with institutional changes in ways that are hard to reconcile with any generalizations seemingly useful for forecasting the future. In one example, regarding nuclear proliferation, existing theory suggests precisely what Harkabi prescribes. One should suppose that states will be concerned about the armaments of their competitors and their own security. Hence, the right formula for non-proliferation is to stop any proliferation and to provide all non-nuclear states with iron-clad security guarantees. But what is our experience? We know of two cases in which states capable of becoming nuclear powers chose not to do so. We know of one other which became nuclear, then de-nuclearized. The first two are Italy and Argentina. The third is South Africa. Was external security the determinant in any of the three cases? Answer—No. Italy had precisely the same rationale as France for having its own *force de frappe*. And the Italians had the French example before them. Argentina elected not to proceed with nuclear weapons when its rivalries with neighbors were more intense than earlier and when it was at odds with a power already nuclear-armed—the United Kingdom. South Africa shut down a nuclear weapons program in which it had an immense investment at a time when it was arguably at its most insecure.

What were the common determinants, if any? One probably was at the conceptual level. Even by the early 1960s, when the Italian decision was made, awareness of the destructiveness of nuclear and thermonuclear weapons had blurred traditional conceptions of war and peace and traditional understanding of the relationship between military force and state power. In France it was widely understood that investment in the *force de frappe* might render the French state *less* capable of actively defending its interests. General André Beaufre observed, "Metternich said that one can do everything with bayonets except sit on them. With nuclear weapons, one can do nothing but sit on them."

A second determinant was chance political interplay within evolving domestic institutions. In all three countries, *internal* priorities argued against heavy investment in nuclear weapons. Elections and other political processes—in which external security issues played minor parts—brought into critical posts leaders with little or no interest in developing or retaining such weapons.

How to take these examples and generalize even for the immediate future? Will Ukraine become the world's third-ranking nuclear power? Will North Korea defy President Clinton's threat of condign punishment? Who can say?

World War II came when and as it did because many wise heads—even in Germany—supposed that no state would risk another Great War, given the horrible costs of the war yet in living memory. The Cold War derived some of its character from a supposition that coldly calculating statesmen would be deterred from acting as Hitler had only if faced with the certain annihilation of their nations—and perhaps not even then. These examples are reminders of two truths. First, it can be horribly costly if we derive a wrong assumption from our answer to the question, "Can war still be an instrument of policy?" Second, we *have* to have some working assumption of what is the right answer to that question. Otherwise, we cannot make decisions about, among other things, the future of our own national military forces and missions to be assigned to the U.N.

Benedetto Croce once argued that historical research should always address urgent theoretical questions. I can think of few or none more urgent than that exposed in Harkabi's paper.

# Discussion

**Gasteyger:** I do not want to go into the question of how we define world order, lest we create more disorder in our discussion. One can certainly interpret world order in ways other than Harkabi. Let me start rather with two very small comments—or questions, if you like—and then make two more substantial ones. First of all, the question that obviously worries all the Europeans: whether or not Yugoslavia is going to be the rule or remain the exception. If you [Harkabi] call it a "suburb," obviously this will not please very many people in Europe, in the suburbs of Europe. But if you think of Central Asia, wars are going on, and I deliberately call them wars. They go on probably because Central Asia is on the outskirts of the Soviet world and because very few people can do anything about what is happening in Central Asia, although I think this is very wrong.

Harkabi argues that today we are faced only with internal war. Now, again one can argue at great length whether the war between Azerbaijan and Armenia is an internal war; it would have been one in the Soviet Union, but today, at least by international law, it is unfortunately an international war, and there are many other examples.

I have one more major argument and that is the distinction between "war" and "violence." I am not absolutely sure how important it is. What is important is the objective that you want to achieve, the scope of the violence or the war, the kind of weapons that you use, the solution or the settlement that you want to achieve, the consequences of either war or violence. In the end, what is most important is whether or not the difference between war and violence makes any impact or difference for the people affected by it. So I think we should probably look much more closely at this distinction and check whether it is useful. I have only one criterion by which I suppose one could make it sensible, and that is who are the actors involved: state actors versus non-state actors. That may be one answer to the question as to whether there is much of a difference between the two.

The second major point I would like to raise has to do with the Cold War as a harbinger of nuclear deterrence. Obviously, I suppose that nobody would doubt that nuclear war and nuclear deterrence have been mutually reinforcing. The nuclear deterrence has occurred to degrees that nobody could consider to make any political, let alone military, sense. The nuclear deterrence has in my view falsified our idea of war, and its avoidability. First of all, it created certainty in the East–West context. It was what Larry Friedman rightly called, "a political stability." But the very moment the Cold War ended, and with this obviously also the sense of legitimacy, if there ever was one, of nuclear deterrence, we realized that the stability was an artificial one, and that all those elements that we thought had been buried under the stability, in Europe at least, are now coming back. And here is, in fact, the past coming back to some extent—not to the full extent, because a number of other things have happened such as European unification that surely have made war less likely, or even impossible, in the European context.

Second, nuclear deterrence has created not a Third World, but two worlds, namely, the world within nuclear deterrence and the world outside. As you said rightly, wars have moved to the Third World. Well, they had moved already before the end of the Cold War, and precisely because the Third World was left outside this nuclear deterrence.

Third, I suppose that the American–Soviet rivalry gave a wrong or historically short-sighted assessment of the nature of the conflicts we have been dealing with, particularly in the so-called Third World. We discover today that the origins of many of these conflicts in the developing world, and possibly also in Europe, antedate the Cold War, or have very little to do with it. When we review many of the internal or external conflicts all over the world, we see that many of them had very little to do with the Cold War. Otherwise, they would more or less have been solved.

War certainly does not pay any more as an instrument of politics. This is something we should have realized a long time ago, but is it accepted by everybody? My question is rather: What is going to be the role of military power in international relations, as distinct from the role of war? When we look at the world, we see that there is much more military power around than any of us probably realizes.

**Iriye:** I appreciated greatly the contributions by Harkabi and May. It seems to me that they are in agreement on one very important point, which is the need of education. Harkabi said that we should be teaching our students the history of world order. With that observation I am in full agreement, and with May's point that we should also be teaching our students how to theorize or how to propose theoretical perspectives on past events. I think we are all doing so in a sense, mutually educating and so on. And I think the importance of education, particularly as we face the twenty-first century, keeping in mind what we discussed earlier, seems to be more important than ever.

I was very struck by the last paragraph of Harkabi's paper, in which he points to the fact that we are at an historic turning point, and he mentions three characteristics of that. We ought to identify the changes that are taking place in the world and encourage those developments that would support the positive changes in world order, and we ought to impart a new mode of thinking. As Harkabi so eloquently put it, in thinking nationally we must think internationally. That sense of internationalism ought to be communicated through educational efforts. And this is a very eloquent statement. Yet, what strikes me about this is that these are the kinds of statements one finds in the first postwar period, that is, the post-1919 period, when the League of Nations was created and immense amounts of effort went into creating an internationalist mind. Such statements here could be found almost verbatim, duplicated by many spokesmen at the League of Nations, and elsewhere. They all stress the role of education, they all stress the role of a new international order.

I cite this not to say that, well, this kind of optimism proved to be premature, that the 1920s were followed by the disasters and atrocities and aggressions in the 1930s. It would be too simple to say that this kind of idealism or internationalism cannot bear fruit. I would rather argue from this that there is a continuity. This continuity really impresses me. It seems to me to point to the continuity in the nobility of the human spirit, that there has been, despite ups and downs, despite the vicissitudes and aggressions, a history of this international-mindedness.

I think, therefore, the agenda today is not to create anew from nothing an internationalist awareness but to harp back to the legacy of the 1920s. There was once a very good beginning, and, obviously in the 1920s, there was a kind of international order, particularly a very solid, well-defined world order in Asia and the Pacific in the 1920s.

Now, it breaks down. Why? In this connection I would like to raise a question about Harkabi's distinction between risks and threats. He cited the Israeli–Arab and the NATO–Soviet examples.

If I may introduce the Chinese–Japanese example here, it does seem to me that a fairly well-defined world order in Asia in the 1920s, which old Chinese and Japanese and other Asians supported as a manifestation of the new internationalism, broke down because Japan broke it. Why did Japan destroy that very hopeful beginning of world order in Asia? In Harkabi's terms, we can say that the Chinese were not really posing any threat to Japan, but the Japanese military thought there was a potential threat from China, and they therefore engaged in a preemptive attack. That is the explanation, I think, for the Japanese aggression in China, starting in 1931. Therefore, we need to consider these questions, risks, and threats as a state of mind, as well as in terms of the physical realities of strategic plans. Sometimes what one perceives in the neighboring states—not in terms of real threat, but in terms of an imagined threat—seems to be very dangerous. And if only to prevent that kind of thing from happening again, it becomes all the more important to cultivate an internationalist mind.

**Bulliet:** Harkabi has entitled his paper "Can War Still Be an Instrument of Policy?" and, while it appears to say "no," it seems to me clear that the answer he gives in his paper is "yes." It is simply that it cannot be an instrument of policy on the part of those entities that will make up the world order—Europe, Japan, North America, possibly Russia. But, as he states, in the Third World it will still be an instrument of policy. He points out, "Only in exceptional cases can wars between lesser powers affect world order. Otherwise, they are likely to be isolated and almost ignored, as happened, for instance, in the long and disastrous Iran–Iraq war."

What you get is an atomization of the world order that essentially says, "with respect to large categories of nations, war can be, very probably will be, an instrument of policy which the constituent actors in the world order will look at at arm's length; they will supply the weapons, but they will not intervene or participate." The Iran–Iraq war is an excellent example of that, a war which virtually everyone in the world wanted both sides to lose, hoping both sides would manage to destroy one another.

I see no reason why wars of this sort will diminish. Indeed, I think they are likely to increase. Certainly the level of armaments going into Third World countries from major arms suppliers is not decreasing, at least in the part of the world that I know best, the Middle East.

Perhaps it is of no consequence to Europeans, Japanese, and

Americans whether two African nations or two Middle Eastern nations or two Southeast Asian nations go to war with one another. But with respect to the other topics we are discussing in this seminar, topics dealing with migrations and refugees, topics dealing with the environment, topics dealing with human rights, any number of the major topics that we have as world problems at the end of the century will be profoundly affected by Third World wars.

And simply because we have a world order that allows the most powerful, economically and militarily, entities not to wage war upon each other and not to use war as an instrument of policy, that does not mean, in my view, that one should simply dismiss wars in the Third World as trivialities or simply petty tragedies, because they will eventually all affect us in these larger, more powerful entities through the other impacts they have upon categories of experience outside the actual battlefield.

**Nivat:** I will add two words. The first is about the impact of the civil war in former Yugoslavia. From the point of view of, say, European or French opinion, we had forgotten what war is about, although it is not so far away, and some of us had experienced war in Algeria. Yet we had forgotten what that kind of violence is. So, war is incomprehensible. I am always shocked by an expression frequently used by political thinkers, and even philosophers, and the mass media at large that it is a scandal there should be a war two hours' flight time from Paris, which supposes that if it is three hours, the scandal is less, and if seventeen hours, there is no scandal at all.

Of Yugoslavia, we knew nearly nothing. We knew Yugoslavia as a place where you could go for holidays. We had forgotten Ivo Andric's books, and especially his *Letter from Sarajevo,* which depicts in the middle of the 1920s an atmosphere of terrible fear. The Jewish hero of the book says to Sarajevo: "I leave you, because I cannot live in the atmosphere of hatred of your town." I wonder, in listening to Harkabi's paper, whether the "Yugoslav tribes" have returned to the love of war, because war is not launched only for national or regional interests. I am sure that among the regions of Yugoslavia there is some love of war. With the danger of nuclear war that love of war had disappeared. With non-nuclear war, it will reappear. And you have warriors, after all, who love war.

My third point is about teaching. I didn't understand very well what is implied. Does it mean teaching pacifism? The history of world orders is a history of wars. I think of myself as a European, and a European is a child of Jerusalem, Athens, and Rome. Of course, the first foundation of education should be the law given on Sinai. But that law probably is of no use for non Judeo-Christian cultures. If we look at the history of cultures, we see that wars have played a great role in the creation of all cultures, defeats as well as victories.

**Harkabi:** Let me remind you, I did not speak normatively. I spoke analytically. I did not say that non-intervention is desirable. But we are facing a tragic world in which there will be a lot of turbulence, and people will be hesitant to intervene. Therefore, what I described as a course is not normative, not pacifism. I won't mention it even, but will simply describe how the human race strived with the problem of how to arrange its relations. I would describe the tragedy of a pluralistic world, the fact that God produced many nations. That was a big problem for the Bible. Then they invented the story of the Tower of Babel to explain all problems that come from the multiplicity of nations.

**Mayall:** I wanted to make an observation about the likelihood of intervention in this new turbulent world that you have described. There are certain reasons which would support your argument there. One you have just mentioned is certainly the reluctance of Western industrial democracies to take casualties in causes which are not their own. But the other is purely financial. Just to give one example: The British are not involved, in the military sense, in the peace-keeping operation in Somalia, but that operation is now the most expensive U.N. peace enforcement exercise. The British contribution is 8 percent, which is considerably more than its average payments for the normal U.N. budget in an ordinary year. They are extremely reluctant to see that kind of expenditure go on for very long.

Despite that, I am not so confident that there will not be interventions in the future for two reasons. One is, and I will put it in parentheses, the kind of moral reason, or, rather, randomly moral reason, and that is sometimes called the CNN factor. The allies in the Gulf War have, in my view, been doing the right thing in the end in providing safe areas for the Kurds. They did not do it as a result of government decisions but rather because of the pressure of public opinion. The same is true of Somalia for different kinds of reasons. That kind of thing is likely to continue to happen.

The second reason is more problematic and also relates to Somalia. In previous international orders, there were always areas of statelessness. There were states, and then there was a *terra nolius,* which on the whole lay beyond the state system. It does seem that in our present international order there is an extreme reluctance for states, both great and small, to tolerate statelessness. Of all of the resolutions passed by the Security Council in the last four years, only the Somalia one was unanimous. Even the Chinese, who were extremely reluctant to accept any kind of universalist role for the international community, voted for operation "Restore Hope," perhaps on the grounds that it was so small—but, in fact, it is very expensive—and the grounds given were that it was unique.

The present system may not be able to tolerate statelessness for very pragmatic reasons, because in areas of chaos that become semi-criminalized will be located the modern equivalent of piracy. That raises, in my view, a moral question. If there is going to be intervention, then we must have military intervention by the great powers. We have to think about the criteria which should govern that intervention. It may well be that if you have to go into an area of statelessness, you have to face up to the possibility—which no one will face up to at the moment—of effectively creating some kind of international administration to secure the use of force, which Harkabi claims to be legitimate.

**Junker:** I would like to address the problem May raised about the poverty of theory to adequately describe perhaps the world order and war, and I would like to start with a quotation, nearly verbatim, of Bismarck. He once remarked that the normal state of international affairs or international order is fluidity. Now and then, it seems that if the international order is frozen for a while, then it goes back to its natural state, that is, fluidity.

During the Cold War, it seemed to all of us that there was a frozen *status quo*. Now we are back to fluidity, and obviously what we need is a theory which is able to explain changes in our times. As far as I can see, the only method is the typological approach. In the nineteenth and twentieth centuries there have basically been four typological approaches to create order. The first is the balance of power. The second is hegemony, the exercise of hegemonical power. The third is authorized suppression, Nazi rule over Europe and other things. The fourth is collective security. Obviously our helplessness in the present situation of disorder is because we have elements of all four types at the same time, on different levels.

**Kristeva:** I have some very brief remarks; one is empirical, and the other more epistemological, about Harkarbi's notion of world order.

I was very impressed when you spoke about the necessity to think internationally. You asked how to do this practically and suggested some educational programs including history, on what happened in the past. You said that literature cannot make the same contribution in the international domain, because, I suppose, literature emphasizes what is personal, eventually national, or very egotistic. If we try to develop a world order which is not universalizing and vandalizing, but which takes into account the differences, I propose the inclusion of literature in your educational program. I will give an example of the important role literature can play. Last year we organized a six-month literary program on French and Dutch television about the European novel as a way to European understanding. We had the work of five writers from the past (Dostoevsky, Cervantes, Kafka, Voltaire, and Joyce) discussed by modern writers. The conclusion was that although literature is national or even egotistic, comprehension of those particularities helped mutual understanding in the sense of not neutralizing but differentiating this world order.

My second remark is in connection with the assumption in your paper that people "tend to identify themselves with their particular reference groups, their communities, their religions, nations, and states," which means that they do not care about an abstract mankind. But this first remark brought to my mind the great woman philosopher Hannah Arendt, her criticism of the universality proposed by the French Enlightenment, and her emphasis on the national identity and national state. It seems to me, and I would like to have your feeling about this, that you take a step beyond the conception of Hannah Arendt to which I just referred when you try to reconcile this exigency for national recognition with the necessity of a universal link. I understood your argument in the sense of the French Enlightenment, in the sense of what Montesquieu called "*esprit general*," which means the sense of criticism and understanding of the differences of others but not an acceptance of the unity of the participants.

This acknowledgment of a sort of new understanding of universality differentiates between what you called "risk" and what used to be "threat." People who do not accept this notion of universality, I suppose, in Israel do not think that Arabs are "a risk" and not "a threat"; and they will not accept, for instance, actual negotiation, which is presumably your position. So, in my mind, you go further than Hannah Arendt's recognition of nationality, and you try to reconcile the necessity of this national recognition and universality in order to build a differentiated world order. And maybe this is what we require in order to avoid war.

**Perczynski:** I would like to add an additional element to the discussion, which I think is still missing. In the contemporary theory of international relations, the concept of international security is usually regarded as a category composed of three elements, that is, the military element, the political, and the economic one. Usually there is an almost common agreement that two elements, the military and political ones, are diminishing in their importance, while the economic one is increasing.

What does that mean? Once President Bush said that there are no more enemies in Europe, but there is a common enemy and a common threat. It is the threat of de-stabilization. In the peaceful area of Europe, there have been tremendous successes, tremendous progress in the military and political dimensions of international security. But there is a big asymmetry between this component and the economic one. There is a growing discrepancy between the Western and Eastern parts of Europe, although politically, militarily, they are becoming closer. This is dangerous. It cannot last for too long because it produces frustrations, which may start the de-stabilization process and push people to violence. And when violence becomes conflict and conflict becomes war, is very difficult to judge.

Until the economic component is introduced into the picture and we gain more symmetry in that old concept of international security, I do not think we will live in a safer world.

**Stern:** Just two points. One, simply to underline, with great emphasis what Iriye said, using the Japanese–Chinese situation of the 1930s as an example. I must confess that I was not persuaded, as others have already pointed out, by your [Harkabi's] distinction between threat and danger. If I translate this into, as it were, educational terms, I would have thought that one of the things that one would have wanted to teach is that history records the misperceptions of people—misperceptions of their own interests and misperceptions of the intentions of others—so that I can only echo exactly what was said before, that what may appear to some as a danger, others can either intentionally or non-intentionally escalate into a threat.

The other is a minor point, but it has not been made before: You emphasized as a great deal U.N. Resolution 255, which I thought was important and interesting. Do you really believe that resolution would necessarily be carried out, that is to say, that the nuclear powers would in fact intervene in the situation which is provided? In short, would this U.N. resolution, which is on paper, would this be a deterrent or not?

**May:** First of all, I think that Gasteyger and I should have a side discussion about the future role of nuclear weapons because I am by no means persuaded that they have disappeared along with the end of the Cold War. This connects with Harkabi's point. In some way some of the most interesting propositions about nuclear weapons were those of General Galois, who argues that they were essentially the weapons of the weak against the strong. And that is likely, I think, to be explored in some detail in the future.

To approach the problem by typology, as Junker observed, may work, but actually I doubt it. The theory that we apply tends to be at best an international systemic theory, that is, to assume that forces in the international system and forces that have to do with the foreign policy or security interests of states are determinants. As I look at the historical record, I see very few instances anywhere where that has in fact been the case. I do not think we have a set of generalizations that comprehend the reality of what is happening; key terms like "power" and "interest" tend to get defined in domestic terms, and vary from time to time, and are different across international borders and within institutional and political structures that are fluid. It is that fluidity—conceptual, institutional, and political fluidity—about which we are incapable of generalizing. And I am not happy with general systemic typologies, such as balance of power and hegemony, as ways of explaining what happened or getting some sense of what might happen.

Just an observation on Kristeva's point. This institutional fluidity is not just internal to states but develops also across states; our theories do not take account of the development of transnational communities. There are communities of military people who feel more in common with one another across national frontiers, even if they are using translators, than they do with people in their own societies. And this applies not simply and literally in cultural circles but also even in the kinds of circles where decisions are made.

**Harkabi:** I was asked if Yugoslavia is an exception to the rule. I do not believe there is such a simple answer, because it depends on conditions. But I would say that Yugoslavia perhaps is not the only case in which a conflict was allowed to fester, and the big powers would say: "Let them stew in their own juice; we cannot intervene, let us leave it to the traditional forces of history." By imposing a certain order, you impose something which is artificial, and there is no assurance that it will last for long.

So all through history there was a formal order, and then, from time to time, it was disturbed by a realistic order, which meant that one side became stronger and therefore expanded. No border in this world was traced by justice or by some kind of sophisticated reason, but simply is a result of the process of history.

Now, war. I am afraid of a metaphorical use of the word "war"; war between generations and war between father and sons, and cultural wars. It is metaphorical and it distorts the meaning, because war is bloodshed. And, therefore, I stress the need to prevent a semantic evasion about what is war, and to see it, to follow the usual explanations, the usual definitions all of which stress that war is not simply identical with violence. It is a kind of violence in which states participate. Revolt is not war. Revolt becomes war when the other side gets political recognition. I will not go into the legal definition of war, which is even more restricted. Therefore, I don't see any escape but to stick to the technical definitions of war. When I was asked to analyze it in my paper, I referred to that technical definition of war, and not to the metaphorical use of that expression of war.

Now, about deterrence. Nobody can prove that there was no war in Europe because of nuclear deterrence. We always know if deterrence fails, but we do not know when it succeeds, because there is a possibility that there was no intention to attack. It is my feeling that a lot of intellectual and very important, interesting, elating energy was invested in the theory of deterrence. There is a lot of Talmudic discussion among the people who know the details of deterrence. It is important, but we cannot decide whether deterrence is the reason that there was no war in Europe. We have perhaps to differentiate between different periods, because it seems to me that in the later period it was not deterrence but simply the weakness of the Soviet Union, which started before 1989.

Let me discuss now what professionals call stability. Stability is still very unclear, but let me quote somebody who is very much on the right, Colin Gray. He said stability is a mythical expression. How do we know, how can we measure, the question of strategic stability?

Now, it was said that what I discuss is reminiscent of World War I. Perhaps; I did not live at that time. But the fact that certain ideas were then mentioned is not so bad. For instance, we use biblical expressions such as changing swords to ploughshares, and that is already an antiquated expression. From time to time we resurrect an old expression, although I do believe there is a big difference between what I described and post–World War I.

I know that what I suggest is very limited. But I will challenge others: Do they have better suggestions? Let me say this: I never mention the word "Israel" in my course. After one course, a student of mine said, "After attending your course, I can never vote for the Likud." This is simply because I brought my students to see the wider problems, to combat what I called "provincialism." There is provincialism in Israel, when Israelis think that their problem is only the Palestinians; it is not the Palestinians; it is much wider than the Palestinians. And it seems to me that in our world, it is important even in a small way to widen our horizons, not only to teach others but to teach ourselves.

I was asked whether I am sure that the big nations will intervene, according to U.N. Resolution 255. No, I am not sure. But I do believe that they would have intervened even if there were no Resolution 255. If there is one instance of a small nation achieving its aim by using a nuclear bomb, then all the world will go nuclear, and the Galois vision will be proved. This would be a huge disaster for the world because then we shall have a nuclear anarchy.

I describe things in realist terms, or so I try to persuade myself. I try not to pontificate or preach to others. We can call non-intervention a "scandal," but we see terrible things and we do not intervene. That is a scandal. But, let me say, I do believe that there will be many such scandals, because nations will be hesitant to intervene. And the United States will be hesitant to intervene in all small wars in different places. I am afraid the experience of Somalia will discourage other interventions on humanitarian grounds because of the United States' experience. The Somalis attacked the Americans instead of considering them benevolent saviors.

Now, about literature. Surely literature has broadened our wisdom and human experience for, vicariously, we have been involved in different situations in which we did not participate by reading about human experiences, human predicaments, and human dilemmas. However, literature cannot describe international situations in such a way. When we read, we identify with the heroes or with the situation. History books do that because they describe nations, but not novels.

It seems to me that our minds are more developed in interpersonal affairs, and less in international affairs. It flows in greater part beyond the horizon of humanity, because it is not part of the daily life. I see here some kind of an imbalance between interpersonal wisdom and international wisdom. How can we impart international wisdom to people who are geared only to interpersonal wisdom?

Returning to refusal of intervention, I know, for instance, by reading Arab intellectuals that they are very afraid of marginalization of the Middle East, that in case there is an armed conflict in the Middle East, the world will get sick and tired of the Jews and of the Arabs, and say: To Hell with both your houses! Personally I doubt it, because of other considerations: the arsenals in the Middle East, and the possibility of a big conflagration if war starts between the Jews and the Arabs. This means that the world will have to be judicious in deciding where to intervene and where not to intervene. There are many conflicts now going on and there are places in which there is no intervention.

Now, I doubt if one can call the Armenian-Azeri affair an international one because it is in a region which is still within Azerbaijan. But it is becoming an international war; in other words, it is an interesting case, which all of us have to think about. The last big international war, apart from the American and the allies' intervention in Iraq, was the Iran–Iraq war. There have been many other small conflicts, but no international wars, and I do think this means a decline in international war.

# THE
# DISPLACEMENT
# OF
# POPULATIONS

# MIGRATION: THE "CRISIS OF OUR AGE"?

Curt GASTEYGER

The world seems to be taken again by surprise: ever since the end of the Cold War migration has constantly moved up on the international agenda. A report, published by the U.N. Population Fund, warned that this unprecedented migration "could become the human crisis of our age."[1] Migration rates now amongst the major concerns of the industrialized nations. At least it is there where it is most talked about. They feel their political stability and economic well-being is threatened by growing floods of people moving in from the overpopulated South and emigrating from the undernourished East. If today's migration seems still just manageable—though basically unwelcome—tomorrow's migration promises to become unmanageable. It will then turn into another and major source of international tension, if not global disorder, even more so as nobody has a ready-made answer how to cope with it.

Literature on migration in its various aspects abounds. Most authors rightly emphasize that migration is not a new phenomenon. It has determined and permeated human history at all times. In fact, without migration there would hardly be civilization. The diffusion of the agricultural revolution, for instance, would not have taken place without migration and, as its consequence, the meeting and intermingling of different kinds of civilization.[2] Europeans tend to forget that in more recent history they were at the top of the emigration scale. The nineteenth century saw the first major demographic explosion with worldwide ramifications. Its center was Europe where the first industrial revolution began. From here people by the millions began to emigrate westward. They did so under "the push of internal demographic pressure and with the advantage of technological superiority—which in one form appears in superior military power."[3] Average annual overseas emigration from Europe amounted to about 377,000 during the period from 1846 to 1890, and about 911,000 between 1891 and 1920. All in all, some 40 million Europeans emigrated, mainly to North America and Australia, with some additional millions settling as colonizers, if not occupiers, in Africa and Asia. It is useful to remember that this nineteenth century was not merely one of peaceful emigration but also one of imperial expansion.

The tide is now moving the other way. To be sure, Europeans have had their share of migration also after World War II. And so had the Japanese. In contrast to previous times, much of the migration was not voluntary: millions of people, mainly Germans and Japanese but also many others, were forced to leave their homesteads. "Economic migration," though at a slower pace, continued in a westward direction.[4] But the real change began in the 1950s and 1960s. It was then that migration became a worldwide phenomenon. It was caused by three major developments: the process of de-colonization; the globalization of the East–West conflict with, at its core, Soviet–American rivalry in what became to be known as the "Third World"; and the second industrial revolution in North America and Western Europe.

Needless to say, this is a somewhat simplified categorization of a highly complex phenomenon. But the main point here is to ask if and to what extent the Cold War in all its global ramifications has been a catalyst of international migration and what its ending may mean for the future of migration and hence for international order. Before giving at best a tentative answer to the questions, it may be useful to see what distinguishes present-day migration from its predecessors.

## NEW DIMENSIONS

If migration as a social or civilizational issue is nothing new, some of its dimensions certainly are. In many ways these new dimensions are a result, or a reflection, of a rapidly changing international environment. Both interact as they do in such related fields as demographic growth, environmental degradation and economic development. In the case of migration we can distinguish, with some degree of simplification, at least six developments that have gained in importance and scope over the last decades: globalization, differentation, acceleration, commercialization, internalization, and discrimination. These are evidently short-hand descriptions for highly complex processes. Still, they help us to distinguish major trends and thus also to grasp the phenomenon of migration in its proper proportions and consequences.

Nobody would dispute that migration is an issue of global dimension. In a sense, it has always been as it occurred practically in all parts of the world, though obviously at different phases and to different degrees. Today, global communication and international mobility have made it universal: the former providing the incentive, the latter the means to migrate. Any overview of global migrationary movements leaves no doubt that few regions, if any, are still left outside the ever-growing streams of migrating people. Thus developing countries are being increasingly drawn into global networks of migration. As many as 70 million persons, mostly from developing countries, are today either working (legally or illegally) in other countries. Over 1 million persons emigrate permanently to other countries each year.

This number is bound to increase as a result of a still-galloping demographic growth in regions as populous as Africa and South Asia. At least 1 million people seek asylum every year, and over 12 million refugees live *outside* their homelands, compared with about 2 million in the 1950s.[5]

The important points here are not only the huge figures (behind which human hopes and human tragedies are all too often hidden) but the fact that the "network" of migratory flows between sending and receiving countries is getting ever closer, and answers how to disentangle it ever more difficult.

The second new development may be called "differentiation." It has to do with the fact that "new, unexpected groups keep coming up which need to be dealt with, such as the displaced, exiles, poverty affected, unique humanitarian cases, environmental refugees and asylees."[6] Whether or not these "new groups" become important or permanent is less relevant than that they reflect what we called a growing trend toward differentation. The term "migration" has become, at best, the common denominator for a highly diverse number of movements and people "changing places." Thus, a widely accepted typology of international migration identifies today at least six different kinds:[7]

—permanent (settlers), including persons admitted under family reunion schemes;

—temporary contract workers, normally semiskilled or unskilled, who remain in the receiving country for finite periods;

—temporary professional transients, professional or skilled workers who move from one country to another, usually as employees of international and/or joint venture companies;

—clandestine or illegal workers whose entry may or may not be sanctioned by the receiving country's government;

—asylum-seekers who cross borders and appeal for status on grounds of political discrimination; and

—refugees as defined by the 1951 U.N. Convention Relating to the Status of Refugees.

The distinction between some of these categories is not always easy. Also, in recent years, it has become an issue of hot debate whether or not it is possible, or even desirable, to distinguish between political and economic asylum-seekers, i.e., those who seek asylum because they do not wish or cannot return to their home country because of the political situation there, and those who merely want to be granted "asylum" because of the poor economic conditions in their home country. As the latter group more often than not has little chance of being granted asylum, more and more immigrants claim asylum for political reasons. Here again the distinction between mere asylum-seekers and refugees becomes diffuse. This is particularly the case in Europe after the breakdown of communism in its eastern part and the decline of political repression there. To this development, as it is clearly related to the central topic of this paper, we will have to return.

The third development of more recent date is that of acceleration. Arnold Toynbee's statement about the "acceleration of history" has become such a commonplace notion that one hesitates to invoke it here again. In retrospect, however, one wonders whether the Cold War has indeed "accelerated" history. There are some good arguments which can prove that it rather has, in some important ways, slowed it down. What we have been witnessing in the few years since its end would seem to bear witness to this: it is now that we see history either truly gathering momentum or in fact catching up with itself.

In any case, migration with its many roots and causes clearly shows acceleration of almost staggering proportions. This has, of course, to do with demographic growth. East and Southeast Asia, but also some parts of Black Africa, are growing so fast that migration flows, even in the short term, can be expected to grow accordingly, though nobody can accurately predict their flow, direction, and scope.[8]

But there are other causes which may push migrationary movements still further. Environmental degradation and water scarcity are two of them; economic marginalization and unemployment two others. Wars, today mostly internal ones, wreak havoc on populations and force them to flee. Ex-Yugoslavia and Abkhazia are but the most recent proofs thereof.

Paradoxically, the first stages of "economic take-off" tend to increase rather than to slow down migration. This is, for instance, the experience of some Maghreb countries where students and skilled labor acquire the knowledge and the means to emigrate to more promising lands, mainly Western Europe. Such and similar experiences should make us cautious in seeing in economic development—however desirable—a, or perhaps even *the*, main answer to slow down or even prevent massive migration.

The fourth development relates to what we call, for lack of a better expression, "internalization" of migration. Migration within a given country or region is again nothing new. During World War II, Stalin moved millions of people whom he considered to be a political liability into the vast spaces of Central Asia; and the Chinese Communists sent the Han people to Tibet and Sinkiang lest the local minorities there become too independent-minded. But as a consequence of de-colonization and a growing number of conflicts, changes in regime, and wars, the focus of internal migration has shifted southward. The list of countries of which substantial numbers of people have been—or are presently being—displaced is as impressive as it is depressing (Table II). Half a dozen countries—Sudan, South Africa, Mozambique, Afghanistan, Sri Lanka, and Ethiopia—count more than 1 million displaced persons each. The total figure worldwide is difficult to ascertain but certainly in the order of 20 million.[9]

It needs little imagination to realize the tremendous human suffering and misery linked with such figures. And yet it would seem that this form of migration, in almost any sense burdensome and disturbing, is largely ignored or at least underestimated in Western countries. These internal migrants are rarely a matter of "international concern"; most of them do not qualify as "international refugees" entitled to some assistance. Still, they presently form the bulk of migration—both as a living testimony of the sins of a recent past and a future responsibility of mankind.

Fifth, we are witnessing a new and ever-expanding trend toward discrimination. This may be too harsh a term for the various kinds of acts, policies, and laws that are being introduced to regulate irregular immigration and to stem the ever-growing flow of migration. As a recent report states: "Since the beginning of the 1990s, faced with a growing influx of usually spontaneous claims for asylum and with continuing illegal immigration, several OECD countries have taken steps to discourage abuse of the asylum-seeking procedure and to align national policies in this respect."[10] Discrimination here has at least a double meaning. Many of these measures seek merely to establish criteria by which the various kinds of "asylum-seekers" can and must be distinguished. Illegal immigrants must be deterred in order to offer better treatment to the legal ones. In order to achieve this, various methods are being tested and applied. They are seen and explained as matters of self-defense as well as lying in the interest of the immigrants themselves. In the first half of 1993 alone, several European countries—amongst them France, Germany, and Austria—have stiffened their immigration laws, and others are likely to follow.

Almost inevitably, some of these measures verge on discrimination in its pejorative sense. They do so when immigrants are not being granted the kind of treatment to which they are entitled by virtue of their status, origin, work, or income. Protective measures, legitimate and adequate at the beginning, may escalate into xenophobia that bars the possibility of gradual integration of foreigners into the indigenous society. However repugnant and unjust, such discrimination will probably gain in importance and acceptance. The trend is clearly visible in many European countries; Asian countries with expanding economies but strong national cohesion—like Japan and South Korea—may follow suit, and so may the United States and Canada. All this seems to be the fruit of a growing frustration of both national administrations and indigenous populations with a phenomenon of global dimensions for which they find no answer except that of self-protection, however discriminatory and elusive.

Finally, commercialization. This is probably the most depressing and revolting part of migration. Inducing people to emigrate and making them pay for it has become a "business" of staggering proportions. It is as scandalous as it is global. Who does not remember the unfortunate "boat people" from Vietnam trying to escape a revengeful communist regime with the help of "guides" who extorted from them their last possessions only to leave them to their fate in the open sea? Examples of similar exploitation, treachery, and ensuing misery abound today. Wherever there are people who, for reasons of political persecution or economic poverty, want to leave their homeland, there are others who try to make money out of it. Migration as commerce with human beings is one more sorry testimony to the insatiable materialism of our age. Few are the means to limit, let alone to suppress, it.

## MIGRATION AND THE END OF THE COLD WAR

Nobody would dispute that the Cold War has something to do with migration; and so has its end. The confrontation between an assembly of totalitarian communist regimes, from the Elbe to Vladivostok, with democratic societies in the West, and its extension, spurred by the rivalry of the two superpowers over major parts of the globe, were not just the source of a seemingly unending arms race and conflict of all kinds. They also became a major source of migration of all kinds. Without unduly simplifying a highly complex issue, we can distinguish at least three kinds of migration directly linked to this Cold War and its side-effects:[11]

First, a constant stream of refugees fleeing from communist rule. The exodus from East Germany, brutally interrupted but not stopped by the erection of the Berlin Wall, was probably the most massive and politically the most explosive Cold War migration in Europe. Hundred of thousands of Hungarians and Czechoslovakians left their country in 1956 and 1968, respectively, after it had been reoccupied by the Soviet Union. There was a continuous flow of people from Poland and the Balkans, mostly Germans. And there were, from the late 1960s onward, thousands of Jews, Germans, Armenians, and Greeks emigrating from the Soviet Union.

On the whole, these refugees from communist rule were welcome in the West. They were seen and treated as victims of a despicable and inhuman system. At the same time their flight—often enough under dramatic circumstances—was depicted, if not celebrated, as testimony to the superiority of the Western democratic way of life. The United States, in particular, favored refugees from such communist or Soviet-oriented countries over those who came from countries which the U.S. administration considered to be allies or friends.[12] This bias became particularly evident vis-à-vis Central America after the Sandinistas had taken over in Nicaragua: as statistics show refugees from this communist-inspired country, under Moscow's influence, were given preferential treatment over those leaving El Salvador or Honduras, both close to the Reagan administration.

In sum, then, migration associated with the East–West conflict was a highly politicized affair: humanitarian considerations, while no doubt present if not prevalent, were helped along by political calculations. Migration became an ideological tool as much as a simple humanitarian concern.

Second, where the Third World became the theater of "proxy wars" between East and West, and the Soviet Union and the United States in particular, migration occurred in a massive way. Surprisingly enough, the Korean War seems almost an exception to what was to happen in connection with the wars in Vietnam and Afghanistan, both in terms of internal and external migration. A look at Table I makes this point as clearly as anything else. Most of the countries listed as major theaters of internal migration have been either the stage or the object of the East–West conflict, however defined. In addition to the two countries already mentioned, we find on the list Mozambique, Ethiopia, Angola, Somalia, El Salvador, Nicaragua, Cambodia, Guatemala, and Honduras. If we add the tragedy of the Vietnamese "boat people" and that of the Eritrean refugees in Sudan, we recognize the full dimension of the human cost linked, directly or at least indirectly, to the Cold War.

The list would be incomplete if we did not mention the people who fled or emigrated from two other communist countries, Cuba and China. In the former, Castro's rule has led to a constant and often massive outflow of people; the latter had its Tibetan tragedy and the massacre on Tiananmen Square as the most spectacular but by far not the only causes of migration—a migration, incidentally, whose scope we do not fully fathom but which is certainly more important than most people assume.

Third, the end of the Cold War as a strategic and ideological confrontation between two socially opposite systems has added a new "Eastern dimension" to migration as we have known it so far.[13] For once, migration contributed to the breakdown of at least one particularly rigid communist regime, that of the former German Democratic Republic. It was no minor affair that another communist-controlled country, Hungary, opened the Iron Curtain and thus the floodgates to the West for the thousands of East Germans trying to reach the "other Germany." A human wave was thus set in motion, its crest piercing the Berlin Wall in November 1989.

Next, and closely linked to this, was the peaceful revolution within the communist countries themselves. Revolutions, whether peaceful or violent, are notorious producers of migratory waves—

from the French Revolution in 1789 via the Iranian revolution in 1979 to that in Eastern Europe in 1989. In the case, first, of Eastern Europe and then of the Soviet Union, the end of totalitarian rule meant two things at the same time: the liquidation of oppressive regimes and, with it, the tearing down of the barriers to freedom of movement. Together they altered both the motive for and the nature of emigration. People leaving Eastern Europe do so not to flee a hated regime or escape persecution. Today, they do so primarily for socio-economic reasons. The collapse of communist societies left an economic legacy of often-disastrous dimensions. Prospect for rapid economic reforms and recovery are slim. The attractions of a seemingly prosperous West are almost irresistible precisely because with a Europe no longer politically divided, its economic division is being felt even more painfully. The most visible example of this is Germany, whose political unification did not stop but rather encouraged migration from East to West.

Still, the massive exodus from the former communist world—that many people feared—has not as yet happened. The overall picture of East–West migration is a very mixed one.[14] It shows various kinds of movements, both legal and illegal; refugees here and internal migration there. There are gypsies from the Balkans and refugees from former Yugoslavia. Emigration from the former Soviet Union has not attained major proportions. It would, however, be imprudent to assume that it is not going to happen sometime. The revolutionary process in many now independent republics of the former Soviet Union (henceforth FSU) has not run its course. Nor have the many actual and potential civil, ethnic, and religious conflicts. For the time being it would seem that the major concern here relates to internal migration.[15] One has simply to remember that some 80 percent of the FSU's internal borders are artificially imposed or created. Some 25 million Russians live outside the Russian Federation; other minorities abound in almost all the other states of the FSU.

Attempts to correct these borders and eject unwelcome minorities will inevitably lead to migration. And so will conflicts associated with it—to witness those in the Crimea, Ossetia, Abkhazia, Nagorno Karabakh, Tajikistan, and Moldova.

Whether or not such internal migration will, at some point in time, spill over international borders remains to be seen. It would be surprising if it did not. In other words, we may be only at the beginning of what we called the "Eastern dimension" of international migration. And to this "Eastern dimension" we may well have to add a "Chinese wing." We will briefly return to this later.

The upshot of it all is, first, that the Cold War and its end have profoundly altered the patterns, directions, and consequences of international migration, and, second, that Western attitudes toward people coming from the East (i.e., former communist-ruled or "-inspired" countries) has changed. Many, if not all, of these people are no longer considered to be "friends" fleeing the camp of an erstwhile adversary. They now are at best tolerated, at worst unwelcome and sent back. Moving from the status of a welcome "friend" to that of an unwelcome "foe," from a "victim" to a "nuisance," shows how perceptions of and attitudes to migration have changed in what used to be such a seemingly simple East–West context.[16] It needs little foresight to predict that East–West migration is almost bound to become an additional liability in relations between the former West and the former East. It needs even less vision to anticipate this if indeed the floodgates were to open on the increasingly porous borders of the FSU.

## FROM THE END OF THE COLD WAR
## TO THE END OF THE CENTURY

The post–Cold War era is still in its infancy. Within only four years the world has moved from euphoria to pessimism—both understandable and excessive. Hopes of a "new international order" were grounded too much in a rapid renaissance of international institutions, on the reform of basically bankrupt regimes in the East and corrugated political systems in the West, and in the inexhaustible learning capacity of political leaders. Of course, none of these hopes came true. What took most people by surprise was the discovery that obsession with the Cold War had pushed to the background some of the fundamental changes in international society and the global environment that now, after its end, had come suddenly into the open. It seems that only now, no longer preoccupied with an unending arms race, mutual nuclear deterrence, and a global strategic rivalry, mankind finds time to turn its attention to the developments that have been partly recognized and partly ignored for a long time. In this sense, if in no other, the Cold War was an historical and thus an exceptional period of history.

This is true also for migration and some of its major causes. One of them is demographic growth. It is, of course, no new topic on the international agenda, but one cannot somehow escape the impression that its full scope and importance is only now dawning on us. And yet it is one of the very few, if not the only, domain in which long-term predictions have been surprisingly accurate.[17] They tell us that within the present decade (i.e., from 1990 to 2000) the world population will increase by about 1 billion (from 5.292 to 6.261 billion according to a U.N. medium-average estimate), that 80 percent of it will live in the "developing world" (i.e., outside the OECD area), and that 80 percent will be under the age of twenty. Such figures compel us to draw some conclusions also for the future of migrationary trends. They become particularly relevant if we include in the calculation the enormous economic and social disparities between the various regions of the world and the numerous political and ecological causes that are likely to cause such migration.

It was said before that the Cold War itself and its end have contributed to migration, both internal and international. It is to be hoped that some of their aftereffects will gradually subside. This may be true for Vietnam, Afghanistan, Ethiopia, and Central America. At the same time we discover that many conflicts attributed all too readily to the East–West competition have much deeper roots, and are at best only partly related to it. This is true for most of the ongoing conflicts from Eastern Europe to Central Asia, from Vietnam to southern Africa, from the Middle East to the Sahara. Almost all of them are, or are likely to be, sources of migration. What is new here is that these events are taking place in a new international environment that, for lack of a better word, we may call "more relaxed." The disciplining effect of the Cold War, with its rewards and sanctions, provided a setting in which everybody can do more or less what he pleases without sanctions but with the expectation of reaping more immediate, because localized, rewards. Old scores can be settled with impunity and new gains attained in the name of self-determination.

The practical result of both is either conflict or fragmentation, or the two combined. In almost all instances it also means migration. The specter of India's breakup, or of a tribalization of Africa with, at its end, some two hundred "states," may look as improbable as the breakup of the Soviet Union a few years ago. The least we can say is that the world in its present phase of gestation, unpredictability, and ungovernability is replete with centrifugal forces but short of disciplining and unifying institutions.

The second development that has gained in importance after

the end of the Cold War is economic marginalization. The prime example of this is no doubt Black Africa. A different but no less disquieting one is the FSU. Regions like the former Third World retained some relevance as long as they were considered to be the object or the stage of Soviet–American strategic competition. As such they could hope or bargain for some political support and economic aid. They were bound to lose one or both with the end of the competition. They find themselves today at the margin of public attention. They are left to their own devices, with regimes which derived much, if not all, of their legitimacy from playing the East–West game and using the Soviet model to justify their one-party rule at home.

The FSU is another, though different, case of economic marginalization. It has never been a full partner in the global economic system. It remained the main outsider, if not opponent, of the Western-dominated world economy. Today, Russia and the other CIS countries are at best prospective members of what they had rejected until recently. They are *demandeurs* for financial and other assistance, and play no, or only a marginal, role in international economic organizations. If and to what extent the countries of South Asia—from Myanmar to Pakistan—can be seen as full and supportive members of the international economic community, seems questionable to many. In some respects they, too, are marginal. And yet all these regions and countries are of particular importance when it comes to demographic growth and possible political fragmentation. Both are major reasons for migration and, in the case of countries like India, of migration on a grand scale.

Moving still further east we will have to address a third development before the end of this century. Under the heading of migration, it has so far not raised much concern: the movement of millions of Chinese within the country itself and possibly, if not probably, beyond its borders. It is here that we may see exemplified, on a mass scale, what other developing countries have experienced and are experiencing, namely the dramatic consequences of uneven economic growth on the one hand, and a "softening-up" of political control on the other. To date, migration in China, where it is taking place, has been mainly internal and, relatively speaking, limited. It would be surprising indeed if the many new centers of wealth in cities and economic regions were not to attract a massive stream of unemployed or underemployed peasants still making up for some three-quarters of the population (i.e., some 880 million).

It would be equally surprising if millions of Chinese were not to follow the time-honored tradition of emigration the moment the political authorities either relax or lose control. Already today there is clandestine, if not simply illegal, emigration of thousands of Chinese seeking their way to distant and more prosperous countries. An apparent trickle now, it may grow into a stream of yet unheard dimensions tomorrow.

Combined with the other developments mentioned here we can thus detect at least three new and major sources of migration, both internal and international: political fragmentation in major regions, economic marginalization of many Third World countries, and, more specifically, a combination of both political change and economic disparities in China. They will sooner or later compound the issue of population movement, be it called migration or mobility, transfer of people or "ethnic cleansing."

## SOME TENTATIVE CONCLUSIONS

The world is on the move. It will surely be more so as the century draws to a close, and again more in the next one. As a social phenomenon this is nothing new. What is, however, new are, first, its dimensions; second, its diversity and origins; and third, the fact that the international community has failed so far to devise policies for coping with this ever-growing mass movement in ways that are both politically manageable and economically sustainable. It can, of course, be argued that migration of whatever kind should not or cannot be controlled. This may be so—or may have been the case so far. The question is at what point the international community will either wish or be compelled to regulate an ever-growing stream of people in search of a better life, decent jobs, or greater security. That point will be reached if and when migration is commonly considered to be a threat to international order or national societies.

Several countries, particularly European ones, already perceive migration to be a potential threat to their own internal order. This concern could widen into an international one. Western Europe after World War II further expanded the network of political, social, and economic entitlements. Their origins date back to the nineteenth century. Rapid though unequal economic development was first helped and then sustained by cheap labor migrating from the poorer countries of southern and southeastern Europe, partly also from northern Africa in the case of France, from the Commonwealth in the case of Britain. This network of social security and political participation, of free access to education and cheap health care, came under stress as economic progress slowed down or came to a halt, while at the same time migration of all kinds grew. "Multifarious social changes, many apparent before massive immigration but often unnoticed until later, have undermined assumptions about the current and future quality of life. Higher rates of crime against property and the person, renewed social conflicts, long-term unemployment, housing shortages and greater unpredictability in solid relations have occurred in most industrialized societies in the West."[18]

This is an apt description of the profound changes in Europe. They influence people's perceptions of, and attitudes to, new waves of immigration. Foreigners—migrants—are, rightly or wrongly, seen as being at least partly responsible for such changes or accelerating them unless stopped. If migration on the scale we must expect to occur in the years to come appears so intractable and socially so explosive, it is precisely because its potentially negative effects are being perceived ever more as a threat to Western societies, their welfare and security, if not survival in the sea of ever-growing populations in the South. If such perception should prevail and migratory floods from the South cannot be properly channeled or controlled, a backlash is to be feared in the form of xenophobia, if not racism already brooding in some Western countries.

Measures to stem or control the stream of undesired immigrants have so far been taken almost everywhere on a purely national basis. International efforts have not been particularly successful or are inadequate. As so many other issues of recent concern—like drug trafficking, organized crime, environmental degradation—migration, or perhaps rather its nature and scope, is as much a matter of perception as an objective fact of life. This makes consensus-building amongst sending and receiving, rich and poor, populous and small, culturally homogeneous and culturally diverse countries very difficult. And yet, if migration is going to be one of the great challenges of the future—as we think it is—then any piecemeal and purely national solutions are likely to aggravate rather than alleviate the problem.

Pessimism about the world's incapacity to deal with the migration issue may be premature. As always, states and politicians will act when the challenge is imminent, and action cannot be avoided any more. In the case of migration action should begin today. More likely it will be taken tomorrow or in a few years. To rely on a resumption of economic growth with a corresponding upswing in job creation and on the emergence of a more stable and conflict-free international environment is asking for a lot of optimism. There are all too few signs which would justify it and too many which don't. Temporary expedients are no solutions. If refugee and migration issues are to be addressed effectively, a broad and coordinated range of measures that relate to the underlying causes of population movements and their effect is necessary.[19]

The international community has yet to grasp the double fact that migration is a global issue and therefore needs a global response. The measures which the latter involves, both on a national and, more importantly still, on a global level are recognized and feasible. They range from an improvement of governmental migration structures to programs supporting the return of migrants, from concerted immigration policies amongst the receiving countries to the promotion of economic-social betterment in the sending ones.[20] But above all the response can emerge only on the basis of a clear recognition that migration is no longer—if it ever was—a tool in ideological confrontation or a pretext for attaining political or other ends but the offspring of human misery and human expectations. The end of the Cold War should facilitate such recognition and the end of a terrible century prompt us to act on it. Otherwise, the prediction, quoted at the beginning of this paper, may well come true: migration will be the source of a major crisis of our age.

## Notes

[1] United Nations Population Fund. *The State of World Population 1993*. New York, 1993.

[2] Cf. Cipolla, Carlo M. *The Economic History of World Population*. Penguin Books, Harmondsworth, 1976, pp. 18ff.

[3] Cipolla, *op. cit.*, p. 115.

[4] Cf. for a useful overview Loescher, Gil. "Refugee Movements and International Security." *Adelphi Papers*, No. 268 (Summer 1992).

[5] Cf. Appleyard, Reginald T. *International Migration: Challenge for the Nineties*. International Organization for Migration, Geneva, November 1991.

[6] Appleyard, *op. cit.*, p. 21.

[7] Widgren, Jonas. "International Migration and Regional Stability." *International Affairs*, Vol. 66, No. 4/1990, pp. 749–66.

[8] Appleyard, *op. cit.*, p. 8. Cf also SOPEMI. *Trends in International Migration*. Continuous Reporting Systems on Migration, OECD, Paris, 1992.

[9] It remains to be seen to what extent "internal migration" within the FSU, particularly that of expatriate Russians, will become an important factor.

[10] Cf. report cited in note 8 (*Trends...*), p. 29.

[11] Cf. for a good overview of the various causes and objectives of forced "migration": Weiner, Myron. "Security, Stability and International Migration." *International Security*, Vol. 17, No. 3 (Winter 1992/93), pp. 91–126.

[12] Thus, "(A) national Security Council Paper entitled 'Psychological Value of Escapees from the Soviet Orbit' stated explicitly that it was American policy to 'encourage defection of all USSR nationals as well as of "key" personnel from the satellite countries' as this would inflict 'a psychological blow on Communism' and 'though less important...material loss to the Soviet Union' in so far as the emigration constituted a brain drain of professionals and a loss of manpower skills." Quoted after Loescher, *op. cit.* (note 4), p. 36.

[13] Cf. Wihtol de Wenden, Catherine. "Le choc de l'Est, un tournant historique pour les migrations?" *Esprit*, juillet 1992, pp. 101–11.

[14] Cf. Table III.

[15] Cf. Segbers, Klaus. "Migration and Refugee Movements from the USSR: Causes and Prospects." *Report on the USSR*, November 15, 1991, pp. 6–14, and Titma, Mikk/Tuma, Nancy B. "Migration in the Former Soviet Union." *Berichte des Bundesinstituts für Ostwissenschaftliche und Internationale Studien*, No. 22/1992.

[16] Cf. Hassner, Pierre. "*L'émigration, problème révolutionnaire.*" *Esprit*, juillet 1992, pp. 96–100.

[17] Poursin, Jean-Marie. "*La population mondiale en 2150.*" *Le débat*, No. 75 (mai-août 1993), pp. 36–61; cf. also Table I.

[18] Heisler, Martin O./Layton-Henry, Zig. "Migration and the Links Between Social and Societal Security" in: Woever, O./Buzan, B./Kelstrup, M./Lemaitre, P. *Identity, Migration and the New Security Agenda in Europe*. London, 1993, p. 156.

[19] Pinto-Dobernig, Ilse R. "South–North Migration: The Challenge of the 1990s." *PSIS Occasional Papers*, 2/1991, p. 52.

[20] Cf. e.g., Purcell, James N. "The World Needs a Policy for Orderly Migration." *International Herald Tribune*, July 8th, 1993.

**Table I. Development of the World's Population (%)**

|                    | 1950 | 1990 | 2020 |
| ------------------ | ---- | ---- | ---- |
| Africa             | 9.6  | 13.0 | 20.0 |
| Asia               | 58.8 | 61.7 | 57.9 |
| European Community | 10.1 | 6.2  | 4.3  |
| Japan              | 3.3  | 2.3  | 1.6  |
| Latin America      | 6.6  | 8.6  | 9.5  |
| U.S.A.             | 6.1  | 4.7  | 3.9  |

**Table II. Selected List of Significant Populations of Internally Displaced Civilians**

(as of 31 December, 1990)

| | | | |
| ----------- | --------------------- | ----------- | ------- |
| Sudan        | 4,500,000  | El Salvador | 400,000 |
| South Africa | 4,100,000  | Nicaragua   | 354,000 |
| Mozambique   | 2,000,000  | Uganda      | 300,000 |
| Afghanistan  | 2,000,000  | Cyprus      | 268,000 |
| Sri Lanka    | 1,000,000  | Burma       | 200,000 |
| Ethiopia     | 1,000,000  | Peru        | 200,000 |
| Lebanon      | 800,000    | Cambodia    | 140,000 |
| USSR         | 750,000    | Guatemala   | 100,000 |
| Angola       | 704,000    | India       | 85,000  |
| Liberia      | 500,000    | Colombia    | 50,000  |
| Iraq         | 500,000[1] | Turkey      | 30,000  |
| Philippines  | 900,000    | Honduras    | 22,000  |
| Somalia      | 400,000    |             |         |

1. The number of displaced Iraqis increased considerably in 1991, to as many as 2 million people.

**Source:** Gil Loescher. "Refugee Movements and International Security." *Adelphi Papers,* No. 268 (Summer 1992), p. 71.

**Table III. Stocks of Foreign Population in Selected OECD Countries, 1980–90[1]**

|  | 1980 | 1981 | 1982 | 1983 | 1984 |
|---|---|---|---|---|---|
| Austria | 282.7 | 299.2 | 302.9 | 275.0 | 268.8 |
| % total population | 3.7 | 3.9 | 4.0 | 3.6 | 3.6 |
| Belgium[2] | – | 885.7 | 891.2 | 890.9 | 897.6 |
| % total population | – | 9.0 | 9.0 | 9.0 | 9.1 |
| Denmark | 101.6 | 101.9 | 103.1 | 104.1 | 107.7 |
| % total population | 2.0 | 2.0 | 2.0 | 2.0 | 2.1 |
| Finland | 12.8 | 13.7 | 14.3 | 15.7 | 16.8 |
| % total population | 0.3 | 0.3 | 0.3 | 0.3 | 0.3 |
| France[3] | – | – | 3,714.2 | – | – |
| % total population | – | – | 6.8 | – | – |
| Germany[4] | 4,453.3 | 4,629.8 | 4,666.9 | 4,534.9 | 4,363.7 |
| % total population | 7.2 | 7.5 | 7.6 | 7.4 | 7.1 |
| Italy[5] | 298.7 | 331.7 | 358.9 | 381.3 | 403.9 |
| % total population | 0.5 | 0.6 | 0.6 | 0.7 | 0.7 |
| Luxembourg | 94.3 | 95.4 | 95.6 | 96.2 | 96.9 |
| % total population | 25.8 | 26.1 | 26.2 | 26.3 | 26.5 |
| Netherlands | 520.9 | 537.6 | 546.5 | 552.4 | 558.7 |
| % total population | 3.7 | 3.8 | 3.8 | 3.8 | 3.9 |
| Norway[6] | 82.6 | 86.5 | 90.6 | 94.7 | 97.8 |
| % total population | 2.0 | 2.1 | 2.2 | 2.3 | 2.4 |
| Sweden[7] | 421.7 | 414.0 | 405.5 | 397.1 | 390.6 |
| % total population | 5.1 | 5.0 | 4.9 | 4.8 | 4.7 |
| Switzerland[8] | 892.8 | 909.9 | 925.8 | 925.6 | 932.4 |
| % total population | 14.1 | 14.3 | 14.4 | 14.4 | 14.4 |
| United Kingdom[9] | – | – | – | – | 1601 |
| % total population | – | – | – | – | 2.8 |

1. Data as of December 31 of year indicated extracted, except for France and United Kingdom, from population registers.

2. In 1985, as a consequence of a modification of the nationality code, some persons who formerly would have been counted as foreigners were included as nationals. This led to a marked decrease in the foreign population.

3. Population censuses on 04/03/82 and 06/03/90. The figure for the census of 20/02/75 is 3442.4.

4. Data as of September 30 up to 1984 and in 1990 and as of December 31 from 1985 to 1989. Refers to Western Germany.

5. Data are adjusted to take account of the regularizations which occurred in 1987–88 and 1990. The fall in numbers for 1989 results from a review of the foreigners' registers (removing duplicate registrations, accounting for returns).

6. From 1987, asylum-seekers whose requests are being processed are included.

(Thousands)

| 1985 | 1986 | 1987 | 1988 | 1989 | 1990 |
|------|------|------|------|------|------|
| 271.7 | 275.7 | 283.0 | 298.7 | 322.6 | 413.4 |
| 3.6 | 3.6 | 3.7 | 3.9 | 4.2 | 5.3 |
| 846.5 | 853.2 | 862.5 | 868.8 | 880.8 | 904.5 |
| 8.6 | 8.6 | 8.7 | 8.8 | 8.9 | 9.1 |
| 117.0 | 128.3 | 136.2 | 142.0 | 150.6 | 160.6 |
| 2.3 | 2.5 | 2.7 | 2.8 | 2.9 | 3.1 |
| 17.0 | 17.3 | 17.7 | 18.7 | 21.2 | 26.3 |
| 0.3 | 0.4 | 0.4 | 0.4 | 0.4 | 0.5 |
| – | – | – | – | – | 3,607.6 |
| – | – | – | – | – | 6.4 |
| 4,378.9 | 4,512.7 | 4,630.2 | 4,489.1 | 4,845.9 | 5,241.8 |
| 7.2 | 7.4 | 7.6 | 7.3 | 7.7 | 8.2 |
| 423.0 | 450.2 | 572.1 | 645.4 | 490.4 | 781.1 |
| 0.7 | 0.8 | 1.0 | 1.1 | 0.9 | 1.4 |
| 98.0 | 96.8 | 98.6 | 100.9 | 104.0 | – |
| 26.7 | 26.2 | 26.5 | 26.9 | 27.5 | – |
| 552.5 | 568.0 | 591.8 | 623.7 | 641.9 | 692.4 |
| 3.8 | 3.9 | 4.0 | 4.2 | 4.3 | 4.6 |
| 101.5 | 109.3 | 123.7 | 135.9 | 140.3 | 143.3 |
| 2.4 | 2.6 | 2.9 | 3.2 | 3.3 | 3.4 |
| 388.6 | 390.8 | 401.0 | 421.0 | 456.0 | 483.7 |
| 4.6 | 4.7 | 4.8 | 5.0 | 5.3 | 5.6 |
| 939.7 | 956.0 | 978.7 | 1,006.5 | 1,040.3 | 1,100.3 |
| 14.5 | 14.7 | 14.9 | 15.2 | 15.6 | 16.3 |
| 1,731 | 1,820 | 1,839 | 1,821 | 1,949 | 1,875 |
| 3.1 | 3.2 | 3.2 | 3.2 | 3.4 | 3.3 |

Numbers for earlier years were fairly small.

7. Some foreigners permits of short duration are not counted (mainly citizens of other Nordic countries).

8. Numbers of foreigners with annual residence permits (including, up to December 31, 1982, holders of permits of durations below 12 months) and holders of settlement permits (permanent permits). Seasonal and frontier workers are excluded.

9. Numbers estimated from the annual labor force survey.

**Source:** *Trends In International Migration.* OECD, SOPEMI, Paris, 1992, p. 131.

**Table IV-A. Inflows of Foreign Population into Selected OECD Countries, 1980–90[1]**

|                          | 1980  | 1981  | 1982  | 1983  | 1984  |
|--------------------------|-------|-------|-------|-------|-------|
| Belgium                  | 46.8  | 41.3  | 36.2  | 34.3  | 37.2  |
| France[2]                | 59.4  | 75.0  | 144.4 | 64.2  | 51.4  |
| Germany                  | 523.6 | 451.7 | 275.5 | 253.5 | 295.8 |
| Luxembourg               | 7.4   | 6.9   | 6.4   | 6.2   | 6.0   |
| Netherlands              | 78.5  | 49.6  | 39.7  | 34.4  | 34.7  |
| Norway[3]                | 11.8  | 13.1  | 14.0  | 13.1  | 12.8  |
| Sweden[4]                | –     | –     | –     | 18.3  | 14.1  |
| Switzerland[5]           | 70.5  | 80.3  | 74.7  | 58.3  | 58.6  |
| United Kingdom[6]        | 69.8  | 59.1  | 53.9  | 53.5  | 51.0  |

1. Data, except for France and United Kingdom, taken from population registers. Asylum-seekers are excluded.

2. Entries of new foreign workers, including holders of provisional work permits (APT) and foreigners admitted on family reunification grounds. Does not include residents of EEC countries (workers and family members) who have not been brought in by the International Migration Office (OMI).

3. Entries of foreigners intending to stay longer than six months in Norway.

4. Some short-duration entries are not counted (mainly citizens of other Nordic countries).

(Thousands)

| 1985 | 1986 | 1987 | 1988 | 1989 | 1990 |
|------|------|------|------|------|------|
| 37.5 | 39.3 | 40.1 | 38.2 | 43.5 | 52.3 |
| 43.4 | 38.3 | 39.0 | 44.0 | 53.2 | 63.1 |
| 324.4 | 378.6 | 414.9 | 545.4 | 649.5 | – |
| 6.6 | 7.4 | 8.3 | 9.0 | 9.1 | – |
| 40.6 | 46.9 | 47.4 | 50.8 | 51.5 | 60.1 |
| 14.9 | 16.5 | 15.2 | 16.4 | 14.0 | 11.7 |
| 13.4 | 19.4 | 19.0 | 24.9 | 28.9 | 23.9 |
| 59.4 | 66.8 | 71.5 | 76.1 | 80.4 | 101.4 |
| 55.4 | 47.8 | 46.0 | 49.3 | 49.7 | 52.4 |

5. Entries of foreigners with annual residence permits, and those with settlement permits (permanent permits) who return to Switzerland after a temporary stay abroad. Includes, up to December 31, 1982, holders of permits of durations below twelve months. Seasonal and frontier workers (including seasonal workers who obtain permanent permits) are excluded.

6. Entries correspond to permanent settlers within the meaning of the 1971 Immigration Act and subsequent amendments.

**Table IV-B. Inflows of Asylum-seekers into Selected OECD Countries, 1980–90**

|  | 1980 | 1981 | 1982 | 1983 | 1984 |
|---|---|---|---|---|---|
| Austria | 9.3 | 34.6 | 6.3 | 5.9 | 7.2 |
| Belgium | 2.7 | 2.4 | 3.1 | 2.9 | 3.7 |
| Denmark | 0.2 | 0.3 | 0.3 | 0.3 | 4.3 |
| Finland | – | – | – | – | – |
| France | 18.8 | 19.8 | 22.5 | 22.3 | 21.6 |
| Germany | 107.8 | 49.4 | 37.2 | 19.7 | 35.3 |
| Greece | – | – | – | 0.5 | 0.8 |
| Italy | – | – | – | 3.1 | 4.6 |
| Netherlands | 1.3 | 0.8 | 1.2 | 2.0 | 2.6 |
| Norway | 0.1 | 0.1 | 0.1 | 0.2 | 0.3 |
| Portugal | 1.6 | 0.6 | 0.4 | 0.6 | 0.2 |
| Spain | – | – | – | 1.4 | 1.1 |
| Sweden | – | – | – | 4.0 | 12.0 |
| Switzerland | 6.1 | 5.2 | 7.1 | 7.9 | 7.4 |
| United Kingdom | 9.9 | 2.9 | 4.2 | 4.3 | 3.9 |

1. Provisional data.

**Source:** *Trends In International Migration.* OECD, SOPEMI, Paris, 1992, p. 132.

(Thousands)

| 1985 | 1986 | 1987 | 1988 | 1989 | 1990 | 1991[1] |
|------|------|------|------|------|------|---------|
| 6.7 | 8.6 | 11.4 | 15.8 | 21.9 | 22.8 | 27.3 |
| 5.3 | 7.6 | 6.0 | 4.5 | 8.1 | 13.0 | 15.2 |
| 8.7 | 9.3 | 2.7 | 4.7 | 4.6 | 5.3 | 4.6 |
| – | 0.1 | 0.1 | 0.1 | 0.2 | 2.5 | 2.1 |
| 28.8 | 26.2 | 27.6 | 34.3 | 61.4 | 54.7 | 50.0 |
| 73.8 | 99.7 | 57.4 | 103.1 | 121.3 | 193.1 | 256.1 |
| 1.4 | 4.3 | 6.3 | 9.3 | 6.5 | 4.1 | – |
| 5.4 | 6.5 | 11.0 | 1.4 | 2.2 | 4.7 | 27.0 |
| 5.6 | 5.9 | 13.5 | 7.5 | 13.9 | 21.2 | 21.6 |
| 0.8 | 2.7 | 8.6 | 6.6 | 4.4 | 4.0 | 3.0 |
| 0.1 | 0.1 | 0.2 | 0.3 | 0.1 | 0.1 | – |
| 2.3 | 2.8 | 3.7 | 4.5 | 4.0 | 8.6 | 8.0 |
| 14.5 | 14.6 | 18.1 | 19.6 | 30.0 | 29.4 | 26.5 |
| 9.7 | 8.5 | 10.9 | 16.7 | 24.4 | 35.8 | 41.6 |
| 5.4 | 4.8 | 5.2 | 5.7 | 16.5 | 30.0 | 57.7 |

**Table V. Estimates on Asylum Applications in Europe, North America, and Australia, 1983–91 (Rounded Figures)**

|  | 1983 | 1984 | 1985 | 1986 |
|---|---|---|---|---|
| Europe | 75,000 | 110,000 | 178,500 | 214,700 |
| IGC Countries | 65,400 | 98,300 | 164,400 | 194,200 |
| Central, Eastern, and Southern Europe | 9,600 | 11,700 | 14,100 | 20,500 |
| North America | 25,000 | 31,400 | 28,400 | 41,900 |
| Canada | 5,000 | 7,100 | 8,400 | 23,000 |
| U.S.A. | 20,000 | 24,300 | 20,000 | 18,900 |
| Australia | – | – | – | – |
| Total | 100,000 | 141,400 | 206,900 | 256,600 |

**Source:** *The State of World Population, 1993.* United Nations Population Fund, 1993, p. 34.

**Table VI. Inflows from Some Central and Eastern European Countries into Selected OECD Countries**

| Country | Australia | | | | Germany[1] | | | | |
|---|---|---|---|---|---|---|---|---|---|
|  | 1987 | 1988 | 1989 | 1990 | 1987 | 1988 | 1989 | 1990 | |
| Hungary | 717 | 1,201 | 1,003 | 806 | 8,938 | 12,966 | 15,372 | 18,400 | |
| Poland | 7,036 | 9,231 | 15,985 | 16,551 | 158,220 | 313,792 | 455,075 | 370,172 | |
| CSFR | 922 | 866 | 1,089 | 1,354 | 9,101 | 11,978 | 17,130 | 21,000 | |

1. Foreigners and Germans (mainly ethnic Germans, "*Aussiedler*")

**Sources:** *Australia:* Australian Bureau of Statistics. *Germany:* Statistisches Bundesamt. *Netherlands:* Centraal Bureau Voor de Statistiek. *Sweden:* Statistics Sweden.
**Source:** *Trends In International Migration.* OECD, SOPEMI, Paris, 1992, p. 94.

| 1987 | 1988 | 1989 | 1990 | 1991 | 1983–91 |
|---|---|---|---|---|---|
| 203,150 | 243,950 | 321,900 | 461,100 | 599,400 | 2,407,700 |
| 172,250 | 220,450 | 306,900 | 426,100 | 544,400 | 2,192,400 |
| 30,900 | 23,500 | 15,000 | 35,000 | 55,000 | 215,300 |
| | | | | | |
| 61,100 | 102,000 | 122,000 | 109,600 | 100,500 | 621,900 |
| 35,000 | 45,000 | 22,000 | 36,000 | 30,500 | 212,000 |
| 26,100 | 57,000 | 100,000 | 73,600 | 70,000 | 409,900 |
| – | – | 500 | 3,600 | 16,000 | 20,100 |
| 264,250 | 345,950 | 444,400 | 574,300 | 715,900 | 3,049,700 |

| | Netherlands | | | Sweden | | | |
|---|---|---|---|---|---|---|---|
| | 1988 | 1989 | 1990 | 1987 | 1988 | 1989 | 1990 |
| | 192 | 303 | 309 | – | – | – | – |
| | 725 | 1,096 | 1,307 | 1,500 | 1,500 | 1,700 | 2,000 |
| | – | – | – | – | – | – | – |

# COMMENT ON
# THE GASTEYGER PAPER

YAMAUCHI Masayuki

The world today is overflowing with migrants and refugees. Migration was a phenomenon in Europe at the very start of the modern era, prompted by the exigencies of disaster and war. But it was the startling development of rapid and safe methods of long-distance transportation that stimulated it to the proportions we know today.

Migration in the twentieth century increased largely as a result of the introduction of long-distance train and bus services. These trends were further accelerated by the advent of jet passenger planes in the 1970s. In Japan, for example, the introduction of the jumbo jet in 1971 occasioned a sudden rise in the number of persons entering and leaving the country (*see* Table I). In 1977, the total distance covered by regular air routes worldwide (excluding the Soviet Union) stood at 332 billion kilometers; by 1986 this had risen to 603 billion kilometers—nearly doubling within a decade.[1]

No country is free of migration. In the world today, the number of people working outside their native country, both legally and illegally, has risen to 70 million. Some of these people were unquestionably forced out of their mother countries by political oppression. The majority, however, have migrated for other reasons. To borrow a phrase from former U.S. President George Bush, they have been "drawn in" by the power of the market—by the peace and order it provides. Since the 1980s, "false refugees" requesting application of the Convention Relating to the Status of Refugees (1967) have appeared in large numbers. Unlike the Kurdish or Somalian refugees, whose political persecution has been recognized, these are "economic refugees." The 7,400 Indochinese currently in Japan are mostly political refugees; but it is fair to say that the 55,000 Indochinese refugees in Hong Kong are economic refugees. It has already become difficult to make a simple distinction between "migrants" and "refugees" since, fundamentally, people who ought to be considered migrants or foreign workers claim to be refugees.

The new migration symbolized by the economic refugee raises several important issues. In 1991, the number of people actually termed refugees reached 20 million. This figure can be supplemented statistically with another 30 million. In other words, approximately 1 percent of the global population was in an unstable and fluid condition. Two years later, that figure had increased to 70 million. The background to this included such structural considerations as North–South income differentials, and demographic imbalances. For example, the population in the South has increased annually by 100 million. By complete contrast, the annual rate of population growth in Japan as of 1990 did not exceed 0.42 percent: if this continues, by the year 2010 the population should start to decrease. Generally speaking, a country's relative attractiveness to refugees depends on such factors as: (1) affluence compared with the refugees' native country; (2) ease of transportation access; (3) liberalism of the host country's legal procedures, and the magnanimity and generosity of its people. Without changes in the "structurization" of North–South relations, migration will not stop and the curtain will fall on a twentieth century that might well be called "The Century of the Refugee."

## MINGGONG MENGLIU AND HEIHAIZI

In June 1990, China's top leader, Deng Xiaoping, averted Western sanctions with the following words: "If China were to collapse, 10 million people might flow out to Thailand, 100 million to Indonesia, and 5 million to Hong Kong." This was not merely bluster on Deng's part. The changes in the Soviet Union and Eastern Europe entailed massive migrations. If China, with its 1.13 billion people (21 percent of the world's population of 5.3 billion), were similarly to undergo a great crisis, then this would unite the "globalization" and "internalization" of migrations referred to by Professor Gasteyger, unquestionably triggering a crisis of global proportions.

Already, due to the uneven development of the domestic economy, Chinese cities have been inundated with the "blind movement of unemployed workers (*minggong mengliu*)," or surplus laborers from the countryside. This phenomenon occurred in the spring of

1992; but its most famous occurrence was in the spring of 1990 when, in a single day, 2 million people from Hunan Province and from the Guangxi thronged into Guangdong Province. Buried by this avalanche of blind movement, the provincial capital of Guangzhou was thrown into chaos. The local authorities forced the laborers back; but this was a crisis born of "reform" and "liberalization," and the draw of the urban economy. The phenomenon derives ultimately from the remarkable imbalances in wage levels, an important source of latent instability in Chinese society.[2]

In spite of the official "one child (*duhaizi*)" policy, the Chinese population continues to increase by 16 million each year—this is as much as the population of metropolitan Tokyo or, for that matter, of Australia. Within a decade, a generation of Chinese will be born on the mainland whose numbers are equal to the entire population of Japan. Moreover, it is known that this population explosion includes some 15 to 17 million "invisible babies" (*heihaizi*) not recorded in the population registers. The birth of these extra "unwelcome" children contravenes the government's "one child" policy, rendering the families liable to fines. The parents therefore conceal these births from the authorities, with the result that the children carry no nationality. In the eight years from 1982 to 1990, their numbers increased at an average annual rate of 1.8 million. In ten years, a community of "invisible babies" had quietly come into existence in China, greater in number than the entire population of Australia.[3]

At the close of the twentieth century, these "invisible babies" will enter the work force and seek employment, forming the kernel of a huge surplus labor force roaming the mainland. Eventually, by one means or another, they may be forced out and abroad. This will mean the linkage, in East Asia, of the "globalization" and "internalization" of migration. Once before, when "false refugees" caused great social problems in Japan, the Chinese government promised to take back any who could be determined to be Chinese; and they kept their promise. It remains to be seen, however, what policies can be adopted in the future to deal with "invisible babies" unregistered as Chinese citizens, who try to enter Japan as "false refugees."

## HORIZONTAL AND VERTICAL MIGRATION

Refugees currently come principally from the ranks of former communist countries and from developing nations, but across Europe and East Asia, three common patterns may be discerned.

The first pattern, characterized by the migration of refugees to the advanced countries from the former communist countries and from developing nations, is that of vertical migration. The Indochinese "boat-people" who tried to enter America and Canada; the Chinese "false refugees" and the Iranians who aimed for Japan; the people from Romania, or the former Yugoslavia, or Turkey who applied for refugee status in Germany: these are all examples of vertical migration. The refugees migrating from "South" to "North" are thus being taken in by the advanced countries: a new North–South problem.

The second pattern is that of horizontal migration between developing countries or among former communist countries. Refugees cross national borders on the same continent, entering neighboring countries with similar economic conditions. Because this is a horizontal migration to a country at a similar level of development, it means that before the receiving country has dealt with its own low level of economic development, it is saddled with the burden of the refugee problem. In Asia and Africa, countries generating massive numbers of refugees are at loggerheads with the countries taking them in. The Kurdish refugees flowing out of Iraq crossed borders into Iran, Turkey, and Syria. The 150,000 Somalian refugees who left their country as a result of the turmoil there are also a case of horizontal migration. The potential for tragedy in horizontal migration can be seen in the plight of the 200,000 Ethiopian refugees who fled from Ethiopia, found refuge in Somalia, but then had to return as "double refugees."

The third pattern is compound migration. Following the end of the Cold War and the disintegration of the Soviet Union, some people returned en masse as refugees (or forced immigrants) to the countries they thought of as ethnically "ancestral." The Volga Germans who moved from Central Asia to Germany or the Russians from Central Asia who sought refuge in the Russian Federation are examples of this sort of compound migration, in which the newcomers are of the same ethnic identity as the country taking them in. However, one could say that along with the differences in economic level, a generation raised in Central Asia or Siberia is imbued with the customs and lifestyles of that place, and differs entirely in ethnicity from its host community in Germany or Russia. This sort of migration, which has a strong vertical component to it, is compound.

The distinctive historical traditions and social values of the people receiving immigrants or refugees are readily apparent. With the exception of ancient times, Japanese history is barren of any such experience. The United States was from the beginning a country built by immigrants, a country built by accepting refugees. Germany and other European countries have a utilitarian dimension to their history of taking in immigrants and refugees: it has facilitated freedom of belief and the transfer of technology. For example, it is no exaggeration to say that after World War II, Germany was reborn with the help of the refugees known as "*Vertriebene*" (expelled people), who were driven out of such former Eastern territories as East Prussia and Schlesien, and returned to Germany proper. They also supplemented a German population decimated by the war. Now, however, due to the influx of foreign immigrants and refugees, unemployment in Europe has risen and citizens' lifestyles are threatened. It is this that will generate the problem of "discrimination" to which Gasteyger refers.

In particular, the refugees referred to as "*Asylbewerber*," or "petitioners for asylum," seek political asylum in Germany on the grounds that they are persecuted for their religious or political beliefs in their native country, but in reality they are almost all economic refugees. In 1990, the cases of 148,842 such *Asylbewerber* were investigated, and the number of those recognized as "meriting asylum" came to only 6518. This was no more than 4.4 percent of the total.[4]

The reason Huguenot refugees from seventeenth-century France were taken in by England, Switzerland, and Germany was that they were "welcome guests," valued for their contribution to the transfer of technology in such fields as printing, clock-making, and textiles. At the end of the seventeenth and at the beginning of the nineteenth centuries, some 20 percent of the population of Berlin was French. But the refugees migrating vertically from Asia and Africa to the advanced countries in the late twentieth century are "unwelcome guests," who worsen the problems of employment and housing.

The refugees engaged in compound migration inside the former Soviet Union are relatively compatible with respect to language, educational level, beliefs, and behavior; or they demonstrate a potential for assimilation. For example, with the disintegration of the Soviet Union, the 25 million Russians outside the Russian Federation found themselves in a newly "foreign" country. Among these, as of 1989, some 3.3 million Russians lived in Central Asia, excluding Kazakhstan. Most of them had hoped to move to Russia before the disintegration of the Soviet Union (*see* Table II). The vast majority live in cities. For example, of the 1,633,000 Russians in Uzbekistan, 701,000 live in Tashkent, and of the 388,000 in Tadzhikistan, 195,000 reside in Dushanbe.[5] These former technicians and skilled workers can hardly be satisfied with the employment they are given as truck drivers or milkers in their new locales in central Russia. It is as much of a mismatch as the case of the refugees from Baku, who wound up living in Russian villages.[6]

Most of the refugees relocating to Europe or seeking refuge there are "brain workers," but few countries have welcomed them. For example, 70,000 researchers left the Soviet Union in 1989, and in 1990 one out of six persons leaving was a scholar, technician, or doctor. But as those in Israel had already learned, the experience and education they had received in the Soviet Union did not translate easily to their new location. Both Russians and Jews, often as not, found themselves forced to begin again, as simple laborers. Thus, in compound migration as well, one cannot expect that migrations across national borders will necessarily entail the transfer of technology or the promotion of scholarship.

## IMMIGRANTS VERSUS THE EXTREME RIGHT

The chief destination for "economic refugees" is Western Europe. From the point of view of Western Europeans looking at these refugees, the key distinctions are, first, whether these are long-term, permanent residents or part of a new influx of transient workers; second, whether they are Europeans or non-Europeans. Recently, the proportion of non-Europeans from developing countries in Asia and Africa has been growing. Cross-linking these two pairs produces the matrix shown in Chart I. If we examine the relationships among the four resultant categories, we can see the structure of the national question a united Europe will be facing in the near future.[7]

First, a clear line can be drawn between citizens of the EC nations (I) and permanent residents from Asia and Africa (II). While the former can enjoy "free space," the latter are still divided by established national boundaries. The European Community, of course, involves only citizens of the various EC nations, and not permanent foreign residents, although their rights of residence and employment are recognized legally by each host country. When European integration is spoken of so idealistically as creating "free space," it does not refer to these Asian and African permanent residents in Paris or Berlin.

Second, consider the permanent residents from Asia and Africa (II) and the newcomers from the former Soviet Union and Eastern Europe (III). The relationship between these two groups is defined by their "competition" for jobs and housing. The classic example here is Germany, with ethnic German residents from outside (*Siedler*), such as citizens of the former East Germany or the Volga Germans, included after reunification. Those from the former East Germany are called "across-the-border immigrants" (*Übersiedler*); those returning from Russia and Eastern Europe are called "outside-the-country immigrants" (*Aussiedler*).

However, in spite of reunification, the economy of the former East German area continues to decline, and fierce competition for employment has ensued between citizens from the former East Germany (*Übersiedler*) who have flowed into the former West Germany, and Turks and others. When five Turkish women and children were killed in Solingen at the end of May 1993, the government authorized constitutional revisions within a matter of days, designed to reduce the flow of asylum-seekers. The integration of Europe and the reunification of Germany have imbued some people with a consciousness of themselves as "Europeans" and others with German nationalism; but the countries of Western Europe will probably experience difficulties similar to the "Islamic problem" faced so far mainly by France.

Third, one must not ignore relations between the permanent residents from Asia and Africa (II) and new entrants or illegal residents (IV). Most of the new influx is made up of people laboring for low wages in poor conditions. It is not just that the permanent residents are improving their social position or affirming their consciousness of their rights, but rather that changes in the lifestyle of the second generation of immigrants raised in Western Europe have left certain categories of work undersupplied, requiring new foreign workers for manual labor. The most likely candidates are those in the weakest position, namely the refugees. In the EC countries, the ones who come to mind are the refugees from the former Yugoslavia.

These Yugoslavian refugees truly deserve protection within the recently growing categories of "economic refugees" and "false political refugees." The majority of the nearly 3 million Yugoslavian refugees are receiving shelter in Croatia, Serbia, Montenegro, and so on; the number in various European countries is approaching 700,000. In particular, over 300,000 are reportedly in Germany. Bosnian Muslims, who cannot find safe haven in the former Yugoslavia, are handicapped by not having a fellow Muslim country they can reach overland, as could the Kurds and Afghanis in the Middle East. Their greatest hope and desire is that Germany or Australia will take them in out of humanitarian considerations. It is timely and appropriate that the EC countries, acting out of just such humanitarian considerations, are extending immediate temporary relief to these Yugoslavian refugees without launching investigations of each individual. It will be quite some time, however, until the Yugoslavian civil war is brought under control and refugees or evacuees are able to return.

Why, then, are migrants and refugees the object of discrimination? The reason is that they live, by the thousands and tens of thousands, in permanent communities that foster an independent identity. They are no longer easily assimilated into their host community, nor do they give themselves up to the cause of national unification. Migrants once showed a tendency to preserve their ethnicity in an alien environment, even to discover their identity in a foreign land. For example, Algerians became strongly conscious of their identity when they resided in France. From 1920 to 1924, some 100,000 Algerian migrants lived in a strange land, being taught daily such phrases as "*nos ancêtres blonds les Gaulois*" (our blond ancestors, the Gauls) and "*la grande Revolution française*" (the glorious French Revolution). When they compared such teachings with their own circumstances, they must have been uncomfortable. The experience of Messali Hadj, the founder of the nationalistic Algerian People's Party (*Parti du Peuple Algérien*), illustrates the problem well. Born in Tlemcen in 1898, Messali Hadj served as a soldier in World War I, and was impressed with French affluence and culture as he was exposed to it in Bordeaux. Algerian nationalism was born when Messali Hadj and immigrant Algerian workers founded *L'Etoile Nord-Africaine* (The North-African Star) in Paris in 1923.[8]

The same level of discrimination that was inflicted on Messali Hadj and his compatriots is now being inflicted on Algerian immigrants by the neo-fascist movement led by Le Pen. This movement, ironically, is attracting the support of two groups formerly opposed to each other. In the first group are workers who used to be loyal supporters of the French Communist Party, but who now find, living near their neighborhood, a number of poor Maghreb immigrants, maintaining their own religious creed and ethnicity. The second group is called the "*pieds noirs*" (Black Feet). These are the descendants of the "white" colonialists in Algeria, who were forced to return to France like refugees themselves after independence. They fled without a penny after Algerian independence was achieved in 1962. Maltese, Italian, Spanish, and Corsican blood flows in their veins, but they seem to feel more French than any French person in Paris. Le Pen regularly obtains 30–40 percent of the vote of suburban areas where Maghreb immigrants or refugees live.

Racism of the kind that goes hand-in-hand with anti-Semitism has appeared in other countries. The neo-Nazis and skinheads supporting the recent violent activities in the reunified Germany; the National Front in England; the extremist "white power" groups in America: all proclaim themselves "ethnically" or "patriotically" as the "true" Germans, Englishmen, or Americans. Extreme right-wing parties have mushroomed in these countries, as if to match the growth in the number of refugees. Examples are the Freedom Party in Australia, the Vaams Blok in Belgium, the Falangists in Spain, and the Northern League in Italy.[9]

In Japan, there are no such ostentatious, attention-grabbing groups. That is not to say, however, that Japan has escaped from this problem. Only recently, Japanese "angry young men" clashed with Iranians. This came immediately after Yoyogi Park was reopened for public use: it had been closed for a while by the authorities irritated by the Iranians' "unlawful occupation" of the park. One might say that the appearance of such "angry young men" in developed countries is in part a reaction to the horizontal or vertical migration of workers brought about on a large scale as a result of contemporary world capitalism.

ONE'S HOMELAND OR A STRANGE LAND?

A particular cause for concern is the massive flow of refugees from Bosnia-Herzegovina. This goes beyond the "Islamic issue," which revolves around differences in daily customs or religious observances. Rather, it is to be feared that a "Muslim national question" will develop in the center of Europe. The reason EC leadership, unlike that of the U.S., has adopted a consistently passive attitude toward military intervention in Bosnia-Herzegovina is that the fear of a Muslim migration ("Muslim" in the national sense). Some relief, however, is provided by the fact that at present there is no massive flow of Muslim "economic refugees" into Western Europe from Central Asia or Kazakhstan. They do not seem to be inclined to leave their national region (something I have touched upon else-where[10]), so it need not be feared that Uzbekis or Azerbaijanis will soon be appearing alongside Algerians and Turks in Paris or Berlin.

Germany has revised Article 16 of its constitution. It was decided to recognize the right of political asylum, but to repatriate economic refugees. Foreigners constitute 7.2 percent of the total German population. The largest subgroups are the Turks (30 per-cent of foreigners) and the "Yugoslavs" (12.3 percent). In the 1980s, less than 20,000 people came to Europe each year in the hope of obtaining political asylum. This gradually increased, and by 1992 the figure had reached 550,000. In Germany alone, which had been accepting two-thirds of EC political asylum-seekers, the number of applicants in 1992 reached the astounding figure of 440,000 (see Table III). These were the *Asylbewerber* we encountered above. Given these circumstances, the German decision is under-standable.

Voices have been raised both inside and outside Germany to the effect that this refugee policy, on the part of traditionally generous Germany, is a backward one. Sadako Ogata, the United Nations High Commissioner for Refugees, has had this to say on the sub-ject: "I favor constitutional revision, as a means of strengthening the system of protections and preventing their abuse. It is to be hoped that the provisions of the Convention on Refugees will be sufficiently incorporated into the new constitution."[11]

The German standard for accepting refugees is the extent to which those seeking asylum or residence exhibit a compatibility with the classical conception of a nation-state as a community that must preserve its "purity." Under current German law, dual citizen-ship is forbidden. Those wishing to become German nationals must give up their current citizenship and must pass an examination, cer-tifying conversancy with German customs, language, culture, and institutions. However, a high standard is set in order to regulate the numbers eligible for German nationality. Turkish farmers who have just shot through a course in elementary German, or Bosnian Muslims who know only a smattering of German, find it difficult to "become German."[12] Still, to the extent merely that Germany shows that it has standards for "becoming German," it is more straightforward than Japan, which has no such standards for "becoming Japanese."

However, there are certain people who have no command of standard German, who are better, in fact, at conversational Rus-sian, but who can obtain residence unconditionally. These are the

Volga Germans sent off by Stalin to Central Asia or Siberia: two million of them altogether, some 950,000 in Kazakhstan alone. Approximately 104,000 returned to Germany in 1990, another 150,000 in 1991. All in all, it is calculated that 600,000 Volga Germans have been repatriated. The argument could be made that, compared to the overly sophisticated Muslims from large cities such as Istanbul or Tehran, these Volga Germans cannot adapt to urban life; but that argument does not work here. The constitution holds that even if they are living in a foreign country, people of German descent are German.

But today, when multiculturalism is so highly valued, can we really acknowledge special rights based on biological distinctions of "race" and "extraction"? Can one really call people who can't speak German, Germans? Figures compiled in 1990 show that only 48.7 percent of Volga Germans claimed German as their mother tongue; 45.0 percent responded that it was Russian, and 1.6 percent indicated that their native language was one of the other national languages of the former Soviet Union.[13]

If they cannot prove political persecution, should not even the Volga Germans be treated equally with other "economic refugees" and sent back to Central Asia? Would that be fair or just? The Volga Germans would still be Germans all the same. Even if we say that one's nationality is not just a matter of blood, but of language and the stuff of daily life—clothes, food, dwelling—still, they are qualified to be called German. Perhaps this question of nationality involves something innate, unquantifiable. Ignore that and one distorts history and reality. It is the same with the "abandoned orphans" in China's Dongbei district, who speak only Chinese but are not Chinese: they are authentically Japanese.

However, this issue is separate from the evidently undesirable fate of the Volga Germans who migrated into Germany. That matter is related, rather, to the "discrimination" referred to by Gasteyger. Recently, it is sad to say, some of their fellow countrymen in the mother country displayed what seemed to be a prejudiced attitude toward the refugees. A woman who had rented a house to these "resident nationals" from Russia, told them, claiming to represent neighborhood opinion, that they were "Germans who had come from Siberia where they had maintained a pure, German environment: the ones from Kazakhstan are much worse." Those were not Germans as she knew them ("her people"), and she regarded them with suspicion.[14]

The same sort of discrimination also obtains among Russians engaged in horizontal migration inside the former Soviet Union. Twenty-five million Russians live outside the Russian Federation: they account for 17.4 percent of the population of the entire commonwealth. "Internalization" in the former Soviet Union is rather complicated. Russians from the Asian districts, such as Central Asia, continue to be rejected as immigrants or refugees by others who fear for their personal safety, or who worry about the Muslim population explosion or job insecurity. But the spirit of independence and self-sufficiency amongst Russians in the Russian Federation is strong, and they have made no preparations, whether physically or emotionally, for greeting the returning Russians, most of whom were born and raised in Central Asia or the Caucasus. An example of this is the inability to prepare housing for the families of the military returning from Eastern Europe. The animus toward non-Russian internal refugees and migrants will no doubt grow and intensify.[15]

## THE LESSONS OF HISTORY

Migrants and refugees cannot move freely without any trace of the social environment from which they originate. Nor can they begin new lives innocent of any constraints from their surroundings. Their departure has no doubt spurred social transformations in their place of origin; their arrival may instigate qualitative changes in their new community. The immigrants' ethnicity and identity may also undergo transformation, due to changes in their social environment. A feeling of disillusion and discouragement, a sense that "national consciousness" or "we-feeling" is an illusion, accompanies this experience, to a greater or lesser extent. The immigrants get a sense of their own independence within the community, and differences between them and the culture of their host community transpire: in short, a kind of ethnicity. I have already indicated that the Volga Germans who returned to Germany may have experienced this kind of disillusionment and identity-change.

History provides comparative examples. One took place after World War I, when Greeks from Asia Minor—more strictly, Greek Orthodox believers—were repatriated to Greece in exchange for Turkish residents. In contrast to the Volga Germans, whose repatriation was voluntary, and who chose freely between compensation and retaining their possessions, the Asia Minor Greeks were sent back forcibly, with inadequate compensation. Because their freedom as individuals to choose their destination was not recognized, they were refugees whose activities centered on a group: they were close to what is called in German, *Auswanderer*. One might call them "an association of wandering refugees."

On January 30, 1923, a bilateral agreement was signed between Greece and Turkey. Greece and its population of about 5 million were to accept some 1.5 million refugees from Asia Minor. How to provide housing and farmland for the refugees and arrange for employment became a serious problem capable of affecting the whole nation. Whether residing in the cities or the villages, the Asia Minor Greeks had occupied the highest social and economic positions. The city-dwellers in particular included bankers and artisans, and people who were expected to play a major role in the industrialization of Asia Minor.[16] This can be compared with the Volga Germans in the former Soviet Union, who included many intellectuals, scientists, and administrators. When the Asia Minor Greeks returned to Greece, they experienced a rapid drop in social status. On top of that, to the native Greeks who welcomed them, refugees were a major source of budgetary red ink. Some of the refugees who had put down roots in the villages were provided for by land reform or relocation programs, which proved to be a source of friction with the previous residents. Asia Minor Greeks in the cities filled the lowest ranks of the work force, resulting in a lowering of the wages of the older residents who constituted the mainstay of the work force, worsening working conditions, and causing an increase in unemployment.[17] In other words, it caused an economic schism between Greeks and Asia Minor Greeks, the most serious result of which, however, was the racial discrimination experienced by the Asia Minor Greeks.

In spite of commonalities in creed, language, and identity, the Greek host communities welcoming the refugees were, to the newcomers, utterly foreign. These two groups that had achieved and long maintained independent existences, with differing histories and social environments, now began to make contact. It must be only natural for cultures and lifestyles developed by various groups to differ—to say nothing of the fact that many of the Asia Minor Greeks could speak only Turkish, while many others were bilingual. And as far as the Greek language went, they spoke something completely different from the Attic dialect of the mother country. With a distinctive lifestyle and Turkish-sounding names, these Asia Minor refugees made their individuality felt in Greek society. They fostered an ethnic consciousness different from the majority and referred to themselves as "*prosphyges*" (refugees) and "*Mikrasiates*" (people from Asia Minor), different from the Greeks of the mother country. Furthermore, in many cases the refugees settled not as families but in larger group units, isolated from Greek society. One might call it the ghettoization of the refugees.

The rout of the Greek military's campaign in Asia Minor, which led to a conflict of interest between two kinds of Greeks, and to a new ethnic consciousness, became a source of racial discrimination. The mainland Greeks called the Asia Minor refugees "Turkish," and "Turkey-born," and "yogurt-baptized." To these mainland Greeks, the Asia Minor refugees constituted a grave threat to the "purity" of Greek society, and to the unity of the Greek state and people. Discrimination and prejudice gradually took on a political character. Localities passed resolutions rejecting refugees; extremist groups of established residents made murderous attacks on refugees; arson attacks were made on the dwellings of refugees, incited by the newspaper of the fanatical anti-Venizelist group. Such incidents of racial discrimination occurred often throughout both world wars. In 1933, there was even a proposal put forward to absolve mainland residents from associating with such refugees.[18]

It must be borne in mind that the refugees who crossed over from Asia Minor to Greece underwent extensive transformation of their identity. This involved more than a change from believers in the Greek Orthodox faith to "Greeks": it meant the discovery of their separate identity as "people from Asia Minor." Needless to say, this transformation was a qualitative one constrained by the socio-economic network embracing the refugees. In Asia Minor, they achieved broad social and economic, if not legal, success. When they migrated to Greece, they must have developed a new national consciousness. However, it is not possible that this national consciousness was engendered as a result of discrimination on the part of residents of the home country. It was the result of cultivating their independent identity as "people from Asia Minor." For quite some time this was a major cause of deep divisions in Greek society.

## THE REFUGEE PROBLEM AS A DEVELOPMENT PROBLEM

The twentieth century has been "a century of wars and revolutions"; it has also been "a century of refugees." Born of war and political oppression, the nature of the refugee problem is indicated by the deep-rootedness of such concepts as identity and ethnicity. The huge numbers of refugees currently appearing in response to the lures of the market, are, like the migrants, trying to pour old wine into new bottles. According to this way of thinking, it is obvious that anyone who lives and works in a country will come to think of it as their ancestral or mother country and naturally absorb some national sentiment.[19] But it is even more evident that refugees who act as an ethnic group will resist identification with, or assimilation into, the host nation-state. Endeavoring to preserve a separate identity will, in fact, cause great problems for that "nation" or "nation-state."

On top of that, refugee problems stemming from a clash of races must be said to constitute a "new national question," the resolution of which will be extremely difficult. One senses a need for what might be called a "symbiotic philosophy"—principles that can solve these national questions by going beyond the framework of current international law and conceptions of sovereignty. What is especially difficult is the question of how to consider the "lures of the market" by which refugees are attracted. First, one must recognize that most employment opportunities are particularly desirable when they are available in the place where the applicant is born. Unless that obtains, most of the people in the "South" will never escape the status of "drifters." In the worst case they will have to move like just like *Auswanderer*—drifting and working abroad, like a nomadic tribe.

From the standpoint of Marxist economics, labor is a commodity; and from the standpoint of a developing country, it is an export commodity. There are even countries like the Philippines and Bangladesh whose greatest source of foreign currency is earned through their nationals encouraged to work abroad. As we have seen, the Philippines can send out 3 million people without any sign of improvement in its social development. So even if they resort to dispatching their nationals overseas as emigrants or refugees, their economy would still not improve.

As for the problem of overpopulation, either the birth rate must be reduced or great care will have to be exercised in adopting a policy of dispatching migrants and refugees to advanced countries as a means of reducing population. Encased as it is in the shell of cultural relativism, the population explosion is also bound up with religion and custom. Thus, it would appear that neglecting birth control policies is not the fault of the politicians alone. As for what

Japan can do in Asia, one contribution would be to strengthen job-training programs, creating employment opportunities on the spot. This would give a fresh boost to the "Stay-at-Home" policy. In the sense that the refugee and migrant issues are bound up with issues of development, they also constitute "a new national question."

## Notes

[1] Hirano Ken'ichiro, "*Minzoku-kokkaron no shin tenkai: 'hito no kokusaiteki ido' no kanten kara*" (New Developments in the Discussion of Nation and State: the Perspective of "The International Movements of 'People'"). In *Kokusai ho gaiko zasshi* (Journal of International Law and Diplomacy) 88:3 (1989).

[2] Nakajima Mineo, *Mittsu no Chugoku* (The Three Chinas) (Nihon Keizai Shimbun, 1993), p. 121.

[3] Takeda Isami, *Imin-Nanmin-Enjo no seijigaku* (Migrants and Refugees' Aid from a Political Science Perspective) (Keiso shobo, 1991), pp. 238–41.

[4] Ito Mitsuhiko, "*Toitsu Doitsu o mezasu Yoroppa nanmin*" (Refugees Heading for the Unified Germany), *Gaiko Forum* (Forum on Foreign Affairs) (1991:8).

[5] N. N. Guboglo, *Izmanenie etnodemograficheskoi situatsii v stolitsakh soiuznykh respublic v 1959–1989 gg.*, Moskva: Institut Entonologii i Antropologii, 1992. str. 35.

[6] V. Perevedentsev, "What Prevents a Civilized Migration of Russians," *Moscow News*, No. 41, 1992.

[7] Kajita Takamichi, "*Atarashii minzoku mondai–EC togo to esunishiti*" (New Racial Problems—EC Unification and Ethnicity) (Chuo Koron, 1993).

[8] Benjamin Stora, *Messali Hadj (1898–1974): Pionnier du Nationalisme Algerien*, Paris: L'Harmattan, 1982.

[9] "Western Europe Starts Shutting Out the Immigrants," *International Herald Tribune*, 11-VIII-1993.

[10] Yamauchi Masayuki, "*Hinshi no Ribaiasan–peresutoroika to minzoku mondai*" (The Lingering Death of Leviathan: Perestroika and Nation) (TBS-Britannica, 1990).

[11] Ogata Sadako, "*Nanmin gekizo ni yureru*" (Shaken by the Jump in Refugees), *Yomiuri Shimbun* (1993.6.7); morning edition.

[12] *The Independent*, A-VI-1993.

[13] S. I. Bruk, *Nemtsy v SSSR: Sovremennaia Situatsiia*, Moskva: Institut Etonologii i Antropologii, 1990, str. 8. For the history of the Volga Germans, see Jean-François Bourret, *Les Allemands de la Volga: Histoire culturelle d'une minorité, 1763–1941*, Lyon: PU de Lyon.

[14] Yuri Teplyakov/Yuri Shpakov, "Russian Germans," *Moscow News*, No. 19, 1992.

[15] "The Fourth Wave of Emigration," *Moscow News*, No. 7, 1992.

16 Harry J. Psomiades, *The Eastern Question: The Last Phase, A Study in Greek–Turkish Diplomacy*, Thessaloniki: Institute for Balkan Studies, 1968, pp. 60ff.

[17] League of Nations, *Greek Refugees Settlement*, Geneva, 1926, pp. 31–49.

[18] George Th. Mavrogordatos, *Stillborn Republic: Social Coalitions and Party Strategies in Greece, 1922–1936*, Berkeley: University of California Press, 1983, pp. 194–95.

[19] Benedict Anderson, "The New World Disorder," *New Left Review*, 193 (May/June 1992).

**Table I. Departures by Japanese and Entries by Foreigners**

|      | (Departures by Japanese) | (Entries by Foreigners) |
| ---- | ------------------------ | ----------------------- |
| 1960 | 146,881                  | 894,729                 |
| 1970 | 663,467                  | 1,798,333               |
| 1980 | 3,909,333                | 2,326,116               |

**Source**: Ministry of Justice, Bureau of Immigration (ed.), *Immigration Records* (1986), p. 40.

**Table II. Migration from and to Russia (in thousands of people)**

|              | 1961–70 | 1979–88 |
| ------------ | ------- | ------- |
| Turkmenistan | +4      | -84     |
| Uzbekistan   | +257    | -507    |
| Kirghiztan   | +126    | -157    |
| Tajikistan   | +70     | -102    |
| Total        | +457    | -850    |

Central Asia acted as a magnet for people from around all parts of the U.S.S.R. before the mid-1970s. After the mid-1970s the number of people leaving Central Asia was greater than the influx.

**Chart I. Four Categories of Interaction**

Permanent Residents

Europeans                              Non-Europeans

I    EC Citizens                       II   Asian and African
                                            Permanent Residents

III  Former East Bloc                  IV  Asian and African
     & S.U. (East Germans)                 Refugees and
     Illegal Entrants

New Influx

**Table III. Knocking on Western Europe's Door**

People applying for political asylum in each country in 1991 and 1992, in thousands.

|          | 1991  | 1992  |
|----------|-------|-------|
| Greece   | 2.7   | 2.0   |
| Spain    | 8.1   | 12.7  |
| Austria  | 27.3  | 16.2  |
| Italy    | 31.7  | 2.5   |
| Sweden   | 26.5  | 83.2  |
| Britain  | 57.7  | 24.6  |
| France   | 47.4  | 28.9  |
| Germany  | 256.1 | 438.0 |

**Source:** OECD (*The New York Times*).

# Discussion

**Kerber:** There are three issues that are not developed at any length in these papers. The first, and I think the most significant, is that both papers stress the increasing difficulty of distinguishing between migrants and refugees. Both authors subsume refugee into migrant and leave the problem as a single one, so that by the end of Gasteyger's paper, we are dealing with a flow of people who are seeking "better life," "better decent jobs," or "greater security," and they are all part of the same problem, these people knocking on the doors of borders. One comes to identify, I think, in a subconscious way, with the pride of the people who are guarding those borders, keeping out these people who are going to disrupt the internal life of their country. I think we need to pay more attention to the discernment of what is a refugee, and how we can develop an international order in which refugees will find help.

Second, I see a resistance to the notion that it is possible to enter another nationality authentically and permanently, even when the person is a member of a former colony of a metropolitan state. I must ask whether only the United States, Canada, and Australia are to be left in the twenty-first century with capacious concepts of citizenship, in which there is a rich tradition of migration. If you have an order in which the only people who can make a claim to citizenship are those who are born there, is that an authentically liberal and progressive democracy?

And, finally, what I miss in these papers is any consideration of the role of the differences that gender brings to the meaning and situation of refugees. If we look at Gasteyger's list of the categories of migrants and refugees, some are more likely to be male, some are more likely to be female, and the implications of those balances need to be explained at some length. What does it mean when we know that the large majority of adults in refugee camps are by and large adult women, that very few adult men are found in U.N.-administered refugee camps? What does it mean when the boatloads of illegal immigrants recently captured offshore New York are virtually all male? I would like to know what that means in terms of who paid their freight, who was sold into prostitution so that they could have tickets for their boats.

**Windsor:** About categories for Gasteyger's list, we should bear in mind—perhaps a little more explicitly than has been said so far—

the enforced refugee or the enforced migrant. Now, refugees might be fleeing from something, from the threat of torture or starvation, but there are others who do not want to flee and are made to go. Sometimes their numbers can amount to millions. In some countries it becomes partly internal repression and the system of the camps of the enforced displacement of population inside the country, but then that also creates the problem of how then to get out of that particular category inside the country.

It also means, secondly, in terms of the treatment of such people and the problem of their reception in another country that because they have been forced to become refugees, they have been displaced by government authorities. Their identity is very strong, and it is very hard for them to assimilate or to be assimilated. In that sense this is a separate human category, although not a very distinct intellectual category.

**Gasteyger:** First of all, the growing difficulty of distinguishing between migrants and refugees. Refugee status is basically fixed or defined by the Geneva Convention. Therefore, it is an international issue. Now, you may argue that the Geneva Convention on refugees is outdated and needs to be revised, but at least there is an instrument. There is no instrument, no international instrument, when it comes to "migrants." These are still national affairs. Hence the various, almost totally anarchic, kinds of treatment that go from acceptance to the question of citizenship, erecting barriers against some kinds of migrants but letting in others.

Now, to come back to the refugees and, therefore, also, to this very diffused category of asylum-seekers, some asylum-seekers are refugees, and others are not. The problem that we have with these asylum-seekers or with refugees is to be able to distinguish whether they are refugees, and if so, for what reasons. There are fewer and fewer political refugees, for instance, from the former communist countries, but they call themselves economic refugees.

Do you now refuse economic refugees, who come sometimes from extremely dire, downtrodden areas, with no chance of employment, with no chance of economic progress? Do you refuse them? Probably you do. That is what the actual practice is. Political refugees, particularly—and that is why I think the end of the Cold War is so important—have become a very difficult category, too, because it is very difficult to distinguish whether somebody fleeing from Armenia, or from Azerbaijan or Yugoslavia is a political refugee or is a refugee just in the normal definition of the word.

Second, regarding the question of citizenship, you are right in mentioning the United States, Canada, and Australia as the main countries which are immigration-tolerant. However, I do detect some interest in a stricter application of immigration law. I have the feeling that the trend is certainly going against relatively liberal immigration policies everywhere, certainly in the industrialized countries.

The third question, namely, difference of gender and whether it makes a difference when you look at the various categories that I mention in my paper. What you basically need is a labor force, and when you need labor force, you go first for men. And there is clearly a preference for males for a number of other social or economic reasons. There is one problem, however, that we have not yet touched upon, and that is the linkage between one male having immigrated and his family. The experience of the last thirty years is that once somebody has been able to settle, whether from Africa, the Maghreb, or other countries, the chances of his bringing along members of the families, and not just male members but the families in general, are obviously much greater, I would submit, than if you have a woman coming alone. But that is a guess more than an assertion.

Finally, Windsor's point about enforced migrants. I do think this is a category that one should consider seriously, but I have problems in defining who is an enforced migrant. You mentioned yourself that it is primarily an internal problem. And when you look at internal migration, much of it is enforced. Ethiopia is one of the major examples. The second question one has to ask is enforced by whom or by what? You can have natural disasters. I am thinking of Bangladesh, where you have some kind of enforced migration because of the floods. So, again, while I accept this category, I have great difficulties in defining it or in putting it in terms that are politically operational.

**Windsor:** I have in mind a very straightforward and brutal example—the expulsion from Uganda by Idi Amin of the entire East Asian population in Uganda, a case in which Britain behaved relatively honorably for once and accepted them. But that kind of thing has been very frequent. And when you say "enforced by what or by whom?" I had in mind by government.

**Kerber:** One of the things we know is that when people are expelled from their country, or when they are in a situation in which it is too painful to live, the way in which the world is now organized makes it more possible for men to travel freely. So they are privileged in their efforts, however painful they are and however tragic they often are, to cross borders. And yes, then, if they feel like it, maybe they will bring the women back home, but do not count on it.

Some suggest that in the mid-1930s it was more likely that Jewish men got out of Germany than Jewish women, because they could travel more freely and because their families figured they would get jobs when they went somewhere. It is not simply a question of men getting established and bringing women along. It is for us a larger question of what elements in our society favor one gender and bear more heavily on the other. We should avoid using what I think of as the "fake generic"—these terms which say "contract workers" without making clear whether we are talking about men or women, permanent settlers without making clear whether we are talking about men or women, clandestine or illegal workers. I just would like us to refine our terms a little more precisely.

**Yamauchi:** The Geneva Convention defined the status of refugees. But the kind of refugees envisaged at that time was limited to political refugees, people who have had to get out of their country for their political or religious creeds. Today, the concept or definition of refugees has become more varied and differentiated. The Kurdish people expelled by Saddam Hussein at the time of the Gulf War were war refugees. Then in Herzegovina and Bosnia you have a new type of refugees. They may be war refugees or internal strife refugees. And then there are famine refugees, people who have to seek shelter because of starvation in Somalia and Ethiopia. So there are multiplying categories of refugees seeking freedom, seeking escape, for various reasons and motivations, and we need more sophisticated classification.

Migration: Migrants, and how to treat or accept them, is a big problem. Canada, the United States, and Australia are relatively of recent origin, and in a sense their founding fathers were immigrants. Of course, there were indigenous aborigines, and now these states are composed of an intricate combination of immigrants and aborigines. Even Japan, historically older than the United States, in the seventh and eighth centuries accepted many immigrants and refugees. There are strains in our ancestors from Koreans and Chinese who came to Japan and were later naturalized.

One point we should never overlook is the political responsibility of the country that produces refugees, and we must ask who is to be held accountable for refugees. It is a very irresponsible way of settling domestic problems by dispatching the products of their political difficulties. So what I meant by the "stay-at-home policy" is that the original country should endeavor to resolve its problems with the cooperation and assistance of other countries.

Now, gender distinction is quite marked in the Islamic world. If Islamic women should start seeking shelter, of course, that would mean a major social transformation and will have an impact on the distribution of gender among immigrants and refugees. As for this story about men coming first to be followed by women, I for one do not agree with this argument. I think the *Mayflower* included not only men but women, too. The Western frontiers were opened up by pioneers, and the men certainly took their women with them on the wagons.

**Yamaguchi:** Yamauchi has raised an interesting issue about the responsibility of politicians in those countries from where they transport migrants. His point was to get them to practice a stay-at-home policy. From my limited experience, it seems that there are several problems involved in this kind of stay-at-home policy. For instance, the domestic immigration policy of Indonesia has resulted in a large number of migrants from Java to Irian Jaya for cultivation. This has caused a disaster, because those inexperienced peasants have destroyed the soil by practicing a kind of slash-and-burn agriculture. As the forest area is destroyed, this will cause a serious environmental problem.

Another difficulty is related to the experiences in Central and South American countries. Politicians always try to reduce the number of immigrants who are living in marginal areas like mountains surrounding an urban area. But every time they are settled in the cities, the immigrants take over the slums, driving out their inhabitants. So, there is no solution, it seems. There are nowadays really borderless societies, and unless a policy is carried out with international collaboration, it may be rather difficult to succeed in controlling migration.

**Junker:** Historians of the nineteenth century, who have studied migration, especially from Europe to the United States, like to distinguish between push and pull factors—push factors being all the conditions in the land, and the pull factors being the hopes, the visions, the migrants have of what would happen to them if they should come to the foreign country, and both ends of the process have been studied quite carefully.

Now, my question relates to the situation in the receiving countries. Are there any reliable works on the economic effects of this post–Cold War migration which is now going on? Half a year ago I had a long discussion with the deputy mayor of the city of Heidelberg, and he showed me the enormous drain on the Heidelberg city budget caused by this huge influx of several kinds of asylum-seekers, migrants, and so on. The change of the law in Germany was partly effected by the enormous pressure the Social Democratic mayors of the cities placed on the political parties. The most usual reaction I get from ordinary citizens in Germany, who are neither Nazis nor sympathizers, is: "Why are we responsible for the misery in the countries they come from?"

**Watanabe:** My comment is somewhat related to what Junker just said. Whenever I hear from people in the developed countries that this problem, especially that of migrants with economic motives, is serious, I feel somewhat uneasy in terms of ethics, and remember a story of Buddha and a wicked robber. A man was in hell. He had been a wicked robber, and as a result, in his afterlife, he was in agony in hell. One day Buddha, who is of course living in heaven, looked down at hell, saw that man, and remembered that he had done some small good things when he was alive. So he let down a thin thread from heaven to hell to help him. The robber noticed the thread and started to climb up it to heaven. But when he had almost reached heaven, he looked down and saw that many people from hell were following him. He was horrified and shouted that they should not follow him as the thread might break at any moment. As soon as he had shouted, the thread broke and he fell back into hell with all the people who had followed him.

Now, I wonder, how can those people who follow be persuaded to stay at home? What kind of ethical logic do we have to persuade them?

**Mayall:** Listening to Watanabe, I was reminded of a less elevated story which appears somewhere in David Hume, that in a desert with one glass of water and two thirsty people, there is no point in talking about justice. I have no idea really how to weigh these enormously escalating figures of population movement.

I take it that the classifications that we have are for two purposes. One is just to try to help us understand what is going on. But the other is to try to devise discriminatory policies so we can tell the difference between a legitimate asylum-seeker and someone who is just pursuing his own quest, where it would be perfectly justifiable for domestic reasons to turn him aside. But, of course, those kinds of reasonable distinctions will break down at some point under the influx of numbers. What I think one is looking at is, in a sense, that the administrative system is breaking down under the pressure of increased numbers. Now, what I do not know is whether the numbers are of a rate and a volume which will, in fact, destroy the classifications because the system just cannot cope. My suspicion is we are not there yet.

**Yamauchi:** Perhaps what you are pointing at is, I imagine, that figures can play magic, but the figures or statistics do have some importance which we should accept openly. They do not necessarily lead us to discriminatory measures or actions. In order to discuss these matters, we must go back to the basics—figures, statistics. At the same time, it does not follow that we should indiscriminately accept everybody coming from one country into another. Theoretically and policy-wise, is it possible? I do have serious misgivings about it.

Here, beyond merely writing it off as a policy issue, you have to consider the public sentiment in the host country because you have to persuade the citizens to accept these people. One should hope that these opinions are positive, but as a means of persuasion, you need figures and statistics. Statistics, unfortunately, are produced by the government, not by non-government organizations. When a government produces these figures, they are subject to some skepticism. Everyone looks at these figures differently.

**Gasteyger:** I have not yet seen any reliable work appraising the economic costs of migrational immigration. There are clearly economic costs, not just housing these people but also the sheer administration of distinguishing between who is a refugee, who is an asylum-seeker, and who is not legitimate. I am told that the administrative costs of dealing with these issues of immigration have risen to several billion dollars in just a few West European countries and Canada.

Certainly I do not have an answer to the question how can we persuade people to stay home. There is one facetious answer—to tell them that they are not coming to heaven but they may be coming to hell. This is surely not their view, and it is certainly not the view of those who make big business out of migration. We should not underrate the commercial aspect of migration, of those avaricious brokers between the sending and receiving countries. One answer is to try to persuade them that probably their only long-term advantage is in staying at home. That is the answer usually given by a number of countries when they mention aid to developing countries, industrialization, education, etc. But, fortunately or unfortunately, the first phase of industrialization or economic development usually leads to more immigration rather than less. So it is a long-term prospect, and that is not necessarily particularly helpful at the present moment.

There are also political costs. We have to realize that in countries like Germany, France, Switzerland, and elsewhere, the problem of migration, whether a real one or an artificially made one, is becoming a highly delicate political issue. A lot of damage can be done playing it the wrong way.

# CHALLENGES TO
# TRADITIONAL
# IDENTITIES

# THE LONG GOODBYE: REVISION OF TRADITIONAL IDENTITIES IN THE "CHRISTIAN WEST"

William R. HUTCHISON

S amuel P. Huntington, the Harvard political scientist, re-marked in a recent *Foreign Affairs* article that processes of eco-nomic modernization and social change are now weakening the nation-state "as a source of identity," and that "in much of the world religion has moved in to fill this gap."[1]

I imagine that most of Huntington's readers, as people attuned to day-to-day events and analyses in the 1990s, found this passing comment insightful but, withal, not especially surprising. The emergence or reemergence of religion—whether as common piety in Russian churches, or as American televangelism, or as a lan-guage and vehicle for extremist politics—has become a very famil-iar notion for readers of the daily papers.

Yet for anyone immersed, as I have been recently, in earlier his-torical and social-scientific treatments of "religion and national-ism," the proposal that religions, or cultural complexes defined by religions, are now, at the close of the twentieth century, displacing other forms of group loyalty is startling, if not mind-boggling. This is not because of any fault in Huntington's observation about cur-rent happenings. It is rather because his almost casual assertion tes-tifies to a sharp and nearly complete reversal—a reversal either in the actual relationship between religion and other forms of group identity, or else in our perceptions about such relationships.

I think what we are dealing with here is principally—or at least very importantly—the latter. Over the last two decades or so, while the actual, real-world importance of religious loyalties may indeed have been increasing at least incrementally, our perceptions about the role of religious loyalties in modern (or modernizing) societies have been changing radically.

The possessive "our" that I have just used refers principally to historians and social scientists in the Western world. Although my knowledge of the details of non-Western scholarship is imperfect at best, the little I do know makes me doubt whether analysts of Hindu or Buddhist or most other cultures have ever habitually referred to nationalism as "displacing" religion. In the West, however, for a considerable time, that was a common, or indeed the reigning, assertion. Through much of the twentieth century, Westerners in their elite scholarship and to some extent in common discourse, held that in and after the French Revolution, modernization and social change had weakened religion as a source of identity, and that nationalism had—to reverse Huntington's metaphor—"moved in to fill the gap."

There were of course exceptions. For example, monographs on the social history of particular national formations did recognize and study the role of religious ideas and even of religious bodies. Nationalism *as* a religion, moreover, was discussed even in general analyses of the nationalist phenomenon. But it is fair to say that the dominant view around mid-century was that of Hans Kohn, who found "religion as a source of identity" not merely weakened in the nineteenth century but for all intents and purposes obliterated—rendered ineffectual. Kohn wrote of nationalism in the post-Revolutionary era as, quite explicitly, "taking the place of religion."[2]

In Kohn's work and that of most of his colleagues and immediate successors, religion figured as an important predecessor to nationalism and as its frequent challenger (particularly in the form of Roman Catholicism), but beyond that as little more than reminiscence or false consciousness. Bibliographies and encyclopedias of nationalism, from the 1930s up to the 1990s, gave eloquent further testimony to the fact that several generations of scholars had virtually ignored religion as a category that might be useful in the general analysis of nationalism.[3]

It is neither possible nor necessary to expand here upon the reasons why students and theorists tended until recently to ignore the continuing salience of religion—and especially of popular religious belief—in the drama and vicissitudes of Western nationalism. That would be a highly interesting discussion, involving such things as the changing shape and status of social history over the past twenty years, and touching on what Rodney Stark and others argue was an almost willful misreading of the effects of "secularization."[4] For present purposes, however, I need only ask readers to consider the possibility that nineteenth-century Western religion, if it had a voice, would protest with Mark Twain that "the reports of my death have been exaggerated."

We may at least be able to agree, even at the outset, that religious beliefs, religious modes of identification, and in some instances religious institutions remained important after the Revolutionary era, within the developing story of Western nationalism and in the clash of nationalisms. If so, then any exploration of what is new or not new about the current high visibility of religion must consider the extent to which the policy makers of yesteryear—for example, the political managers of wars and imperialism—exploited popular religious convictions and in other ways were induced to take those convictions into account.

As I have acknowledged (but it bears repeating), it is also probably true that in our day an actual situation has been changing. I would not contend that we have merely awakened to religious modes of group loyalty that have been there all along. What has happened, I think—if we can weld "change in perceptions" and "real change" into a single formula—is that the recently heightened prominence of religious forms of identification has alerted us to religious components in earlier nationalism (for example, the American nationalism of McKinley, Bryan, and Wilson), of which we were supposedly aware but which our definitions of nationalism were inclined in principle to underestimate.

## NARROWING THE FOCUS

I have been asked in this paper (more aptly, I guess, "challenged") to ruminate about the uses of history in understanding the role of religion today; and, within that broad topic, to consider "challenges to traditional identities." Perhaps the direction in which my ruminations have moved is already somewhat clear. In any case, I shall argue in the remainder of this paper that current uncertainties about identity in the Western world have been shaped as much by the past history of such anxieties as by the recent events that, quite naturally, impress and transfix us.

I shall concentrate on three forms of identity—national, religious, and "Western"—and contend, as the foregoing discussion would suggest, that these forms of identity not only are, but always have been, intimately related. Their relationship, however, if one eschews any simple reduction of, say, religious identities to political ones, presents itself as extremely complex; so I shall, for the moment at least, narrow the field to a single form of advocacy and rhetoric in which the interactions of the three elements can be observed more vividly, I think, than anywhere else: I shall focus on the "missionary mind" in one Western society, that of the Americans.

Other scholars, within an extremely large body of writings produced between the mid-1930s and the present, have chronicled and assessed this American missionary mind through the speeches of politicians and the work of journalists, poets, and novelists.[5] For that and other reasons (such as the emphases in my own past research and writing), I shall draw principally, though not exclusively, on the expressions of overseas missionaries and their sponsors, together with the ideas of theorists and theologians of foreign missions.

The Americans might be considered, at first blush, to have been so extreme in their missionary pretensions—both religious and nationalistic—as to provide a poor illustration. In this area as in many others, however, Americans have differed from their European cousins in degree or intensity rather than in fundamentals: a recent comparative study of "chosen people" ideologies in a dozen Western societies makes that point abundantly clear.[6] As a people whose national identity depended upon belief in the ultimate triumph, jointly, of the West and of Christianity (or, sometimes, "Judeo-Christianity"), the Americans were archetypal rather than qualitatively different.

## THE NINETEENTH CENTURY: CONFIDENCE NOT QUITE UNLIMITED

During the time of the so-called War of 1812, a prominent Congregationalist clergyman in Massachusetts, Edward Dorr Griffin, offered a confident prediction about the coming Kingdom of God on Earth. Griffin's rendition, though unusually specific about the geography of this event, was otherwise entirely typical for its time and country:

> If the Church, now chiefly confined to two countries [the United States and its current enemy, Great Britain], is to rise from this day forth, where is it more likely to rise than in the United States, the most favoured spot on this continent which was discovered, as I may say, by the light of the Reformation? And if in the United States, where rather than in New England? And if in New England, where rather than in Massachu-

setts, which has been blessed by the prayers of so long a succession of godly ancestors?[7]

By the later decades of the century, the implicit evolutionism in this
kind of assertion, along with its suggestions of linkage between religious and cultural triumph, were regularly made explicit.

One especially famous and widely read illustration of this was a
book called *Our Country*, written by another Congregationalist
leader, Josiah Strong, and first published in 1886. Strong and his
book have often been considered racist because of certain passages
in which the author pictured the Anglo-Saxon "race" as either
absorbing or obliterating all the others; but that objection rests on a
misunderstanding of some ways in which the term race was then
frequently used. Although he cited physical data to show that
Northern Europeans were more robust than others, and that the
Americans were the biggest and healthiest of all, Strong held no
notion of fixed biological characteristics; when others in post-slav-
ery America did revive such notions, he protested. (In the early
twentieth century he joined the anthropologist Franz Boas in trying
to discredit them.) What Strong was talking about was, instead, a
cultural heritage, a mix of Protestantism and constitutionalism that
for him defined the Anglo-Saxon "race" and virtually guaranteed
its future dominance in world civilization.[8]

Strong, who pursued a wide variety of interests—preacher,
writer, editor, social reformer, promoter of "church union"—had
also served as a missionary on the Western frontier; and certainly
the "missionary mind" is evident in *Our Country* and his other writings. The same can be said about the third, rather different, nineteenth-century example that I offer as illustration of the powerful
religious–cultural identity of the Americans: the Columbian Exposition. This event, staged in Chicago exactly one hundred years ago
(May–November 1893), was a multifaceted cultural presentation in
which, despite its cosmopolitanism and its apparent openness to
cultures and religions of the non-Western world, the missionary
motif was pervasive.

This was most directly evident when the Reverend John Barrows, who had organized a "world's parliament of religions" as part
of the Chicago exposition, answered conservative critics of this
enterprise by insisting that non-Christians had joined in reciting
the Lord's Prayer, and that the Parliament of Religions had "ended
at Calvary."[9] But the entire Columbian Exposition conveyed, both

intentionally and unintentionally, a similar message of Western superiority and assumed cultural hegemony. A "White City" of monumental Euro-American design housed the trophies of the West's technological and other triumphs, whereas the exhibits relating to other societies were for the most part relegated to an area dedicated mainly to recreational activities and called "The Midway Plaisance." (The term "midway" has since, by no accident, denoted that part of a fair or circus that is dedicated to amusements, curiosities, and "sideshows.") In perhaps two-thirds of the mottoes carved into its buildings and monuments, the great fair at Chicago made palpable that "vision of empire"—a supreme confidence about the world-conquering destiny of Western culture and religion—that Robert W. Rydell finds in the whole series of world's fairs staged in this era by the supposedly non-imperialist Americans.[10]

Throughout the nineteenth century, in short, conceptions of American identity had strayed regularly and increasingly beyond the limits of a mere "chosen people" ideology. That is, instead of resting with the idea that their society had been divinely but perhaps conditionally chosen to a special vocation, Americans were prone to adopt the more exalted rhetoric of what Conor Cruise O'Brien calls "the holy nation." Holy nations, according to O'Brien, are "chosen people with tenure."[11] Americans seemed frequently, in the nineteenth century, to consider themselves a permanently and unconditionally favored segment of humanity.

Even in these heady, exuberant decades, however, challenges to such identity were already in evidence, and might be deeply and agonizingly felt. Each of the three assertions of American identity that I have cited from different parts of the nineteenth century can in fact be perceived as a stubborn declaration of faith in the face of threats and perils that nearly all reflective persons took seriously and that a few saw as guaranteeing disaster in the event certain remedies (their own) were not adopted.

Edward Dorr Griffin, in 1813, proclaimed his apocalyptic message to a young revolutionary people still fearful of conspiracies against their religious order and still radically unsure about the survival of their republican form of government. John Barrows's "Parliament of Religions," eighty years later, constituted a response, albeit an unusually friendly one, to the challenge represented by non-Western religions and cultures.[12] And Josiah Strong's best-selling volume of the 1880s, even if now remembered as a chauvinistic paean to the strength and future glory of Euro-Christian civilization, was also a modern jeremiad, a warning that dreadful things would happen if Americans did not confront the challenges set before them. Among the fifteen chapters of *Our Country*, nine were focused on an entire litany of "perils"—from "immigration," "Romanism," and "Mormonism" to the dangers stemming from plutocracy, the rise of cities, and "the exhaustion of the public lands."

## CHALLENGE AND RESPONSE IN THE FIRST HALF OF THE TWENTIETH CENTURY

These examples of "threats to identity" may only demonstrate that every society, however proud and triumphant, operates with an undercurrent of fears and a steady succession of naysayers. Significant as elements of continuity may be, however, the differences between the apprehensions of one era and those of another are on the whole more revealing. In the American case, such differences did become evident in the twentieth century.

Until about 1920, perceived challenges to cultural and religious identity, though they mounted in number and volume, resembled those of the American nineteenth century. The naysayers, even though heard "loud and clear" by later historians, in their own time were prophets without honor—or at least were not honored for their naysaying—even among the intellectually elite. But they were, certainly, speaking out in new ways. William Graham Sumner of Yale University, the one-time Episcopal priest who became a pioneer both of American social science and of modern political conservatism, held out little hope for the survival of those individualist values that he thought were essential to Western civilization and its world hegemony. By 1903 he had decided that one must expect "a frightful effusion of blood in revolution and war during the century now opening."[13]

Some leading theologians and theorists of foreign missions also, in this period before World War I, could be found questioning certain premises of Western world-conquering optimism, and doing so quite patently in response to the challenges posed by non-Western religions and cultures. William Newton Clarke, a Baptist theologian and mission advocate, at the turn of the century wrote a critical analysis of the foreign mission enterprise that remained for many years a standard text in Protestant seminaries. Clarke had by no means given up on missions; yet he concluded that the approach to non-Christian cultures had been overconfident, ill-informed, and to a large degree counterproductive. The missionary movement, generally with the support of secular Western governments, had "really expected that vast masses of organized humanity would slide easily and without resistance into the kingdom of God, so that a nation would be born in a day, and born into satisfactory Christian life."[14]

Other influential religious leaders in the early years of the century challenged common conceptions of Western identity by heaping scorn upon secular imperialism and, with Sumner, predicting disaster if Westerners did not pay more heed to their own professed ideals—their *real* identity. The president of the renowned Oberlin College in Ohio, Henry Churchill King, deplored Western "exploitation of the less advanced peoples," along with their too-ready resort, in the course of offering the benefits of their civilization, to a "method of force...at obvious variance with the underlying principles of the civilization so introduced." The West, King asserted, would have to "pay, sooner or later, the full penalty for its deeds of oppression," but even after such restitution the question of Western leadership would remain in doubt. King, who was more optimistic than Sumner, thought the triumph of humane ideals and human equality was inevitable. The point, however, was that if America and the West could not manage to ride this wave of the future they would be overwhelmed by it. The question was not just one of leadership or preeminence. What was at stake for the Christian West was survival as a great civilization.[15]

Before 1920, as I have suggested, such questioning of the premises of religious and cultural expansionism claimed a very limited constituency, probably not much larger than the number of Americans who paid attention to Oswald Spengler's *Decline of the West*. After the experience of the Great War, however, this constituency expanded considerably. Actual opposition to foreign mission activity remained a minority position in "mainline Protestant" churches (which before mid-century sent out nearly all the missionaries). But the minority stance became both more vocal and more trenchant in the wake of a war experience that, especially among intellectuals and the young, had cast serious doubts upon traditional (i.e., nineteenth-century) Western identity and pretensions.

This expansion of dissent and questioning concerning foreign missions was made especially evident in three sets of events during the twenty years following the war. The best-known and perhaps most important of these centered on the so-called Laymen's Inquiry of the early 1930s, a project financed by Rockefeller money that produced a multivolume report on foreign missions and, subsequently, a great deal of controversy. The succinct form of this report, written largely by the Harvard philosopher William E. Hocking, urged many practical adjustments that by and large were not controversial; but it also advocated one ideological shift that was intensely so, precisely because it affected the central and most cherished element in Euro-Christian religious and cultural identity. What the Laymen's Report questioned, however tactfully, was the deep-seated notion that Christianity and Western civilization must either be Number One or else resign themselves to being nothing. More directly, Hocking urged a truly collaborative approach to non-Christian religions and non-Western cultures.[16]

In many other cultural or national settings, such a proposal—especially with respect to equal coexistence of religions—would not have threatened traditional identities. In the context of Christian and Western assumptions that, however recently established, had come to be thought of as eternal verities, the idea of a Christianity that considers itself true, yet does not seek to convert everyone, was simply, as we would now say, an oxymoron.

The other postwar "happenings" of signal importance were (1) beginning in the later 1920s, a steady decline in financial support for missions, and (2) a fairly vociferous reaction against traditional missionary assumptions among young people who were offering their services to the enterprise.

The first of these requires little elaboration, except that one should note that the decline in support began during flush times, before the onset of the Great Depression. The indications are that, whether or not ordinary churchpeople liked the Hocking Commission's recommendations for reform, an increasing number were not comfortable with the aims and assumptions of foreign missions as these were commonly presented.

The second point, youthful protest, will repay a bit more scrutiny. During the 1920s, in the various journals and conventions in which younger missionaries and recruits could express their views, older leaders were subjected to steady criticism—usually but not always polite—in which the central point was that the missionary program must place more emphasis on social amelioration, less on evangelism. Whatever their activities, the young people also argued, missionaries and the directors of the movement must rid themselves of the traditional, inbred paternalism. They should be more in the business of meeting needs actually articulated by those they serve, less in the business of telling those people what to do and believe.[17] Underlying these advocacies, but also brought directly into the discussion, was a conviction that the recent war, together with the botched settlements and terrible recriminations that followed it, had raised serious doubts about the superiority of the so-called Christian civilization.

Among the many impassioned expressions of such convictions, two that reached a broad American readership were articles in the *Atlantic Monthly* by a young missionary educator in Iran, R. C. Hutchison. Hutchison's 1926 article on "Islam and Christianity" began by asserting that in the entire history of Christian efforts to convert or influence others, "no repulse has been more certain, more continuously effective, or more thoroughly disheartening than that which has been suffered at the hands of Islam." The author, seeking an explanation for this rejection, found it in the long history of a "Christian West" that, whatever the merit of its ideals, had in practice behaved no better than Islamic or other non-Christian civilizations. The recent war had demonstrated that this dismal situation had not been rectified in the modern era.

How might it be rectified? Hutchison the following year, in an essay on "Christianity and Proselytism," argued that Christians were truest to their own ideals when willing to offer medical, educational, and other services with no evangelistic strings attached. The young professor, while declaring himself strongly sympathetic to evangelism, also declared that most missionaries would want to continue their humanitarian work even if "never another Moslem turn to Christ, nor devil worshiper leave his fetishes, nor Hindu stir from his ancient philosophies."[18]

There is no evidence that Hutchison's articles had a singular impact. Their significance lay in their very explicit testimony that the war had constituted, for the younger generation, a new and serious challenge to traditional identities—most particularly the "We're Number One" identity that issued in calls for cultural and religious conquest of the world. It was also important that, through the mediation of leading publications such as the *Atlantic Monthly*, a radically different Western and Christian self-image was gaining respectful attention, and probably a good deal of assent, among an educated general public.

Equally daring, but far more thoroughly articulated, was the revisionist thinking of a professor at Union Theological Seminary in New York, Daniel Johnson Fleming. R. C. Hutchison was qualified to express the thoughts of many in the younger generation. Fleming, however, as a senior academic who had spent twelve years in the mission field, was in a position to elaborate similar ideas with far greater authority. He could also, through his teaching of prospective ministers and through a large number of articles and books for the "churchgoing public," exert a deeper and more lasting influence. One cannot determine just how much credit Fleming deserves for the changed outlook that marked the Laymen's Report in the 1930s, an outlook that by the 1960s pervaded the official policy of American "mainline" churches (Catholic as well as Protestant). What is clear, however, is that his ideas were predictive of these later positions at almost every point.

Fleming in his writings of the 1920s demanded (as had preceding reformers, to little avail) that Westerners in religious work accept job descriptions that would make them in all cases "temporary, secondary, and advisory." Going beyond that, he also held that these same job descriptions should in effect be written by the people of the "receiving" culture, not by the mission boards or churches of the West. More broadly, this meant that the "recipients" should define their own needs, should write the agenda. In a trenchant article called "If the Buddhists Came to Our Town," Fleming urged American Christians to pay more attention to their own Golden Rule; that is, to think carefully about the degree of cultural and religious aggressiveness they would sanction if foreigners ran the best schools in Kansas City.[19]

## CONCLUSION: THREATENED IDENTITIES AND THE "RETURN OF RELIGION"

With these and a number of related proposals, Fleming signaled a fundamental change in self-perception and in conventional beliefs about Western and Christian relationships to the rest of the world. At about this point, however, a reader is likely to become querulous: "These rather creative responses to the challenges posed to Western and Christian identity are all very well, but were they not minority responses? And how does this whole, rather Whiggish, chronicle of improved self-understanding and increased cultural sensitivity relate to the issue supposedly before us? How, exactly, does it bear upon the matter of religious resurgence in the last years of the twentieth century?"

The answer to the first of those questions will take us quite far toward an answer for the others.

As I have mentioned, Fleming's outlook did become the governing one by the 1960s in most of the so-called mainline American denominations and in such international bodies as the World Council of Churches. By some important measures, however, it was indeed still a minority response. For one thing, the members of mainline churches were neither as internationally minded nor as liberal theologically as were the denominational leaders and bureaucrats. More significantly (especially with an eye to the second question above), every one of these moves toward a more open theology, every step away from chauvinism, every shift from aggressive evangelism to collaborative service provoked counter-reactions. These reactions frequently took institutional form in the ultraconservative or "fundamentalist" organizations that many people today have in mind when they speak of a "return of religion."

Despite a common impression to the contrary, however, ultra-conservatives also fell short of becoming a "majority" either domestically or in overseas religious operations. The largest grouping of international religious workers has consisted of more evangelicals who reject fundamentalism as well as religious modernism. Operatives on the "far right" are nonetheless numerous and, of course, highly visible and much noticed.

In other words, just as Ronald Reagan's kind of retrenchment (including, by the way, his revival of chosen people rhetoric) must be understood as a form of backlash against decades of liberal advance, the upsurge or new visibility of very conservative American religion represents a protest against decades of step-by-step adjustment to a religiously diverse world and to a revised understanding of American and Western leadership. What is usually called fundamentalism is very centrally a yearning for older identities, whether real or just fondly imagined.

In this respect as well as others, surely, there are analogies to be drawn between the revival of ultraconservative religion in the United States and the rise of similar ideologies or popular movements in other parts of the world. Details and configurations differ, but behind all such advocacies are, for example, rankling objections to allegedly secularizing political and religious leaders, as well as to the modernist social forces they are taken to represent.

It is important, however, that we not fall into the common error of overemphasizing ultraconservative religious movements in the late twentieth-century world; or, worse, ignoring the patent differences between ordinary religion and extreme religion. (Having just spent two months in Indonesia, the largest Islamic country in the world, I have in mind especially the tendency—long-standing, but especially distorting and dangerous at the moment—to make "Islam" synonymous with religious and political fanaticism.) One way, surely, in which we can guard against such errors, and help others guard against them, is to lavish less publicity on reactionary movements—in the United States or elsewhere—and give at least equal attention to the creative adjustments that, to a great degree, fueled these reactions in the first place.

In any broad historical perspective, the long succession of creative adjustments to new world conditions, along with the great religious mainstreams or majorities that nurtured them, deserve as much notice as the peculiarities of extremists, however dangerous the latter may be. The achievements of religious progressives, moreover, and the ways in which these were effected, might well be worth consulting as we look for paths to better mutual understanding in the next few decades and the coming century.

### Notes

[1] Huntington, "The Clash of Civilizations?" *Foreign Affairs*, 72 (Summer 1993), p. 26.

[2] Kohn, *The Idea of Nationalism: A Study in Its Origins and Background* (New York: Macmillan, 1948), p. 574.

[3] The exceptions in this case are to be found in the work of Carlton J. H. Hayes and Salo W. Baron. See especially Baron's *Modern Nationalism and Religion*, New York: Harper, 1947. The leading bibliographies of nationalism were those of Koppel Pinson in 1935 and of Karl Deutsch in 1956. Encyclopedia articles, with bibliographies, are those of Hans Kohn in *The International Encyclopedia of the Social Sciences*, New York: Macmillan, 1968; and Louis Snyder, *Encyclopedia of Nationalism*, Chicago: St. James, 1990.

[4] Stark argues that sociologists and others, believing as a matter of faith that secularization means the death of religion, ignored the evidence that secularization also provokes new sectarian formation. "Church and Sect," in Phillip Hammond, ed., *The Sacred in a Secular Age* (Berkeley: University of California Press, 1985), pp. 139–49.

[5] Of the literally dozens of works on this subject, the most useful as an introduction is Ernest Tuveson's *Redeemer Nation: The Idea of America's Millennial Role*, Chicago: University of Chicago Press, 1968.

[6] William R. Hutchison and Hartmut Lehmann, eds., *Many Are Chosen: Divine Election and Western Nationalism* (to be published by Augsburg Fortress Press in Spring 1994).

[7] Griffin, *Sermon Preached in Sandwich* (Boston: Willis, 1813), p. 33.

[8] Strong, *Our Country: Its Possible Future and Its Present Crisis* [New York, 1886], Cambridge, Mass.: Harvard University Press, 1963.

[9] Barrows, ed., *The World's Parliament of Religions* (2 vols., Chicago: Parliament Publ. Co., 1893), p. 1578.

[10] Rydell, *All the World's a Fair: Visions of Empire at American International Expositions, 1876–1916,* Chicago: University of Chicago Press, 1984.

[11] O'Brien, *God Land: Reflections on Religion and Nationalism* (Cambridge, Mass.: Harvard University Press, 1988), pp. 41–42.

[12] On fears and conspiracy theories in the early Republic, see Roger H. Brown, *The Republic in Peril: 1812,* New York: Columbia University Press, 1964; and David B. Davis, ed., *The Fear of Conspiracy: Images of Un-American Subversion from the Revolution to the Present,* Ithaca, New York: Cornell University Press, 1971. For the World's Parliament: Richard H. Seager, *The Encounter Between East and West at the World's Parliament of Religions,* Bloomington: Indiana University Press, forthcoming Spring 1994.

[13] "War," in *Selected Essays of William Graham Sumner* (New Haven: Yale Unniversity Press, 1924), p. 333. For extended treatments of dissent from the reigning optimism, see T. J. Jackson Lears, *No Place of Grace: Antimodernism and the Transformation of American Culture, 1880–1920,* New York: Pantheon, 1981; and Henry F. May, *The End of American Innocence: A Study of the First Years of Our Own Times, 1912–1917,* New York: Knopf, 1959.

[14] William Newton Clarke, *A Study of Christian Missions* (New York: Charles Scribner's Sons, 1900), p. 172.

[15] Henry Churchill King, *The Moral and Religious Challenge of Our Times* (New York: Macmillan, 1915), pp. 348, 371, 384.

[16] William Ernest Hocking (editor and principal author), *Re-Thinking Missions: A Laymen's Inquiry After One Hundred Years,* New York: Harper, 1932.

[17] Nathan D. Showalter, "The End of a Crusade: The Student Volunteer Movement for Foreign Missions and the Great War," unpublished Th.D. dissertation, Harvard University, 1990.

[18] R. C. Hutchison, "Islam and Christianity," *Atlantic Monthly,* 138 (November 1926), pp. 707–8; "Christianity and Proselytism," *ibid.,* 140 (November 1927), p. 621.

[19] See William R. Hutchison, *Errand to the World: American Protestant Thought and Foreign Missions* (Chicago: University of Chicago Press, 1987), pp. 150–55.

# COMMENT ON THE HUTCHISON PAPER
## The Protestant Influence on Religion and Politics during the Meiji and Taisho Periods

YAMAGUCHI Masao

Hutchison's report, drawing on abundant historical records of nineteenth-century America, makes the following three points: First, American missionary activities overseas are regarded as primarily confined to proselytization with little political motivation. Second, a closer look at the historical facts shows that such missionary endeavors were not entirely free from politics and, third, the facts suggest that politics and religion have closer links than can be judged from superficial appearances.

I am a specialist in neither the history of religion nor in American history. Nor do I specialize in the early Meiji period when Christianity was reintroduced to Japan after more than two hundred years during which it had been banned under shogunal law. I am therefore not necessarily qualified to comment on Hutchison's paper. However, intercultural contact is one of the most important aspects of cultural anthropology, and from this standpoint I should like to present some observations on how the American missionary movement unfolded in Japan and what kind of response it evoked.

By the 1850s the Protestant missionary movement had infiltrated most of Asia, with the exception of Japan. However, the signing of commercial treaties between the Tokugawa shogunate and the United States and other Western powers opened the door to missionaries, despite the fact that Christianity at that time remained under religious sanctions. The first to arrive in Japan, in May 1859, was Liggins of the American Episcopal Church, followed the next month by Williams from the same denomination, who arrived in Nagasaki. In October, Hepburn, an American Presbyterian, arrived in Kanagawa. In November, Brown and Simmons of the American Reform Church appeared in Kanagawa, while Verbeck of the same denomination arrived in Nagasaki. In 1860 the Baptist Goble came to Kanagawa with his wife. Other well-known missionaries who visited Japan at that time include Ballagh and Thompson, who resided in Yokohama.

Thanks to a wealth of documentary materials surviving in Japan and the United States, rapid progress has recently been made in research on these and other missionaries in the early phase of Japan's modernization. Central government posts were virtually monopolized by men from the former western domains of Choshu and Satsuma (now Yamaguchi and Kagoshima prefectures, respectively), which had been instrumental in toppling the shogunate. So the sons of former shogunal retainers, for whom the path to success was closed under the new Meiji regime, often gathered around these foreign missionaries. Thus, local groups of Christians—called "bands"—were formed in Kumamoto, Shizuoka, Yokohama, Tsukiji (Tokyo), and Sapporo. Each band produced many key figures in the modernization (i.e., Westernization) of Japan's intelligentsia. In particular, the school opened by Ballagh in Yokohama, which was then Japan's main gateway for the import of Western civilization, produced outstanding church leaders in the initial stages of the Christian missionary movement, such as Oshikawa Masayoshi, Honda Yoichi, Ibuka Kajinosuke, and Uemura Masahisa. These men joined the Nihon Kirisuto Kokai, the first Protestant church built in Japan, though they were active at slightly different times. They resisted the notion of belonging to a foreign religious denomination and aimed at independence from such organizations. Researchers today believe that all the American missionaries who came to Japan at that time were free from political and colonialist motives, and no political controversy accompanied the Christian movement in Japan in its early phase.

What was a problem, however, was the religious atmosphere in the United States at that time, to which Oshikawa Masayoshi, who traveled there in 1887 to solicit financial assistance toward the running of the Tohoku Gakuin theological seminary (present-day Tohoku Gakuin University) in Sendai, registered quite an extreme reaction. During his stay in the United States he became profoundly depressed by the arrogance of church members he met and was concerned about the zealous advocacy of white supremacy and colonialist expansion he encountered. Oshikawa, it seems, became acutely aware of the close link between overseas missionary work and imperialistic expansion to which Hutchison refers.

In order to spread the faith overseas, Oshikawa, together with Honda Yoichi and fellow zealots, established the Dai Nihon Kaigai Kyoikukai in 1894. In April 1896 he founded another missionary society in Seoul. In 1907 he collaborated with Matsumura Kaiseki in opening the Nihon Kyokai (later renamed Dokai) where a mixture of Christianity and Confucianism was taught. With the militant nationalist ideologue Okawa Shumei and others, Oshikawa was a member of the editorial board of *Michi* (The Way), a magazine published by Matsumura. He thus came to be inclined toward nationalism and pan-Asianism, and his own missionary activities increasingly assumed the flavor of colonialism and expansionism.

When the Manchuria and Mongolia independence movement began in March 1916, Oshikawa, together with Shiba Shiro, Kawashiwa Naniwa, and others, helped to support the campaign. The following year he ran for the thirteenth Lower House election and was elected in his Ehime constituency. In his speech he declared, "the Japanese people, embracing cultural pan-Asianism, should become the leaders of Asia and spread the rule of right throughout the world."

In 1918 he and Okawa Shumei founded a nationalist society called Zen-Ajia Kyokai and the following year he joined the ultranationalist Kita Ikki, Okawa, and Mitsukawa Kametaro in establishing a political organization called Yuzonsha. It is ironic that Oshikawa, who at first was offended by the expansionist ideology he observed in Christian churches in the United States, ended up as a Japanese-type expansionist. Oshikawa's near-ultranationalist stance was not, of course, shared by all Japanese Protestants. They tended rather, like Uchimura Kanzo, to be known as champions of the anti-war movement. But it is still true that there were many, like Honda Yoichi, founder of Aoyama Gakuin University, whose position was close to that of Oshikawa, and they were widely trusted.

Focusing on conditions in one nation, in other words, obviously does not provide an overall picture of world history. In discussing the political expansionism of American missionary work, it is essential to consider conditions in the individual countries that became targets of expansionism. It is, of course, impossible to cover the entire topic in a brief symposium report, much less discuss the situation pertaining in each country of the world. In as much as this symposium was convened in Japan, however, it might have been preferable if Hutchison had discussed whether the American missions in Japan were politically motivated and what the reaction of the Japanese Christians was. Perhaps the above account will help to supplement Hutchison's observations.

# COMMENT ON
# THE HUTCHISON PAPER
## Which Individual for the Twenty-First Century?

Julia KRISTEVA

I was very intrigued by Hutchison's remarks, in which he seeks to define *identity* from the perspective of *religion* or the *nation*. I found his analysis of the "American missionary mind," of Protestant and nationalistic militancy, as well as of different attempts at open-mindedness and adaptation, to be judicious and stimulating. Finally, I am convinced—as Hutchison seems to be at the end of his essay—that the extreme vigilance with which we must approach the various sorts of fundamentalism (notably the Islamic variety) does not excuse us from becoming more familiar with other aspects of these religions, aspects that have most recently defined traditional identities.

As I am not a specialist of the history of religion, but a semiotician and psychoanalyst, I will limit my response to two comments.

My first comment is less an objection than a modified perspective. I do not believe that the "Western mind" can be identified with the theological debates that affected the United States in the nineteenth century. As I said throughout the fictional mode of my novel *The Old Man and the Wolves,* the crisis of civilization that we are now experiencing seems similar to the fall of the Roman Empire, except for the fact that instead of foreseeing the arrival of a "new religion," we are witnessing the return of already known forms of spirituality, as well as the firming-up of different forms of fundamentalism. Hence, if we wish to assess the metamorphoses of the "Western mind," we must consider not only its failings, but also its finesse: its heritage is too complex to be subjected to mere criticism.

In this vein, the Greek, Jewish, and Christian tradition, including its highly distinctive Orthodox, Catholic, and Protestant movements, has developed a notion of "individuality," a notion of what I would call "private life." I do not see this as subsumed by such global notions as "religion" or "the nation." Such a transreligious and transnational approach to identity does not stem from a rudimentary atheism or an oversimplified internationalism. Western private life, which transverses the links of religion and the nation, owes its complexity to Saint Augustine's *Confessions*, Saint Bonaventure's *The Soul's Path towards God*, and Duns Scotus's *ecceitas*, among others, all of which consciously or unconsciously impregnated the concept of the Western individual before it could find an outlet in the idea of human rights.

Although such a concept can descend into selfishness or psychosis, for a psychoanalyst, writer, and woman like myself its singularity is an indispensable legacy. I believe that we must not bury this notion under such labels as "religion" or "the nation." Although religion and the nation contribute to the notion of the individual, they do not encompass it. By way of my second remark, I shall try to ponder the fate of this phenomenon ("the personality," "*ecceitas*").

Three aspects of contemporary life have already influenced the psychical map of the individual, and they will probably have a substantial impact on his development during the coming century:

1. Modern life can be characterized by the loosening or dissolution of family and social bonds, the weakening of authority, and constraints and cohesion in family, nations, states, and groups. Defensive reactions, however, can serve as a temporary antidote to these phenomena. Such reactions consist of community bonding whose only identity comes from efforts to sustain *hatred for the other*.

2. Physiological and genetic experiments (such as organ transplants, artificial insemination, and modifications of genetic inheritance) are changing the notion of human *identity*, an identity that is corporeal and, by way of consequence, psychological.

3. The growth of information, particularly visual information, and the prominence of televised images and video games that go as far as simulating sensation and even actual objects, might give us the impression that the modern individual is developing his imagination. Paradoxically, the sort of imperialism of the image actually hinders the imaginary, which is becoming mechanical and impoverished. Universal setups seem unnecessary, and a "soft core" totalitarianism frees the individual from having to think about his *own* imaginary potential. Thus, an irreducible particularity is swallowed up by a visible generality. What is more, images that *fascinate* supplant words, words that used to ask questions, reflect, and look for *meaning*.

In their practice, analysts are beginning to see what I have called the "new maladies of the soul." (*New Maladies of the Soul*, Columbia Univ. Press, forthcoming in 1994). As a result of the Greek logos, the interpretation of the Bible, and Christian passion, Western tradition has been offered an exceptional hypothesis—that of inner space, of *psychical space*. I have found one of the first outlines of space in the writings of Plotinus, who, in the beginning of the Christian era, transformed Narcissus's confrontation with his image into hands joined in prayer, into an introspection of the self gripped by the Beyond, by the Third Party. The psychical life has evolved throughout Western history, and Freud's discovery put it into new perspective that accompanies the upheavals to which modern life has subjected it.

To sum up, Freud demonstrated the existence of *another physical scene*, the unconscious, which is subjacent to the conscious and subscribes to divergent types of logic that relate to *soma*. *Repression* keeps the unconscious away from the conscious, but unconscious traumas influence the subject nonetheless, and only if we use transference speech to work them through can we soothe suffering and discover the truth of each subject. Although faced with these new maladies of the soul, which are generated by the social conditions I first mentioned, the Freudian question does not disappear; it becomes more complicated.

Modern man suffers less from repression than from *a lack of psychical inscription*. Traumas have become so violent that nothing, or almost nothing *has been represented* in the unconscious. Now, insofar as such a psychical inscription is also a protective device against internal and external attacks, its absence exposes biological and psychological identity to increased attacks. This results in either somatic dangers (psychosomatic illness) or in the fragmentation of psychical unity (psychosis, false-self, borderline, etc.). In extreme cases, a disassociation of drives and language, and of sensations and behavior appears. Such disassociation can end up a sort of endemic autism, an unreachable "black hole" in the heart of psychical life that is a source of anxiety and vital incapacity. *Depression*, as an abandonment of meaning and a relinquishment of bonds, is another variation of such unleashed destructiveness. In a more eroticized manner that extracts an unconscious pleasure from the death drive, drug addiction and its dark shadow of delinquency complete the panorama of these new maladies of the soul.

If I have emphasized both the conditions that result in the dissolution of psychical identity and modern man's incapacity to confront his conflicts, it is because my experience has led me to believe that these dangers are only going to get worse. I am not unaware, however, of the *benefits* that today's individual can gain from the loosening up of authority, unanimity, and social, personal, and organic cohesion. Thus, on the positive side of this evolution, we can anticipate the emergence of *a new sense of happiness.* I foresee an eclectic sort of happiness, which would consist of a greater capacity to adapt to other people and the environment. It would also consist of an amalgamation of different spiritual movements borrowed from various dogmas that are derived from their coherence. The autistic personality or a falsely structured subjectivity would no longer be "individual" but polymorphous; it would resemble a socialized, humdrum perversion. The truth of such a subject would be found neither in the "fringes of society" nor in "transgression," but in a supple plurality of various sorts of pleasure, space, time, and value. The question is, can this occur through other ways than aesthetic sublimation?

Faced with such upheavals, the return to conservative values will probably offer the enticing advantage of saving us from the unknown. The popularity of traditional models (such that they have been propagated by the Jewish, Catholic, Protestant, Greek Orthodox, Muslim, and Buddhist religions) appears as a resistance in the battlefield of this new psychology's emergence, a resistance that sometimes saves us and sometimes kills us off. Might not Confucianism, Taoism, Shintoism, and their substitutes that come from the East, particularly Japan, be better equipped to confront those upheavals than Western models of psychical life?

The strictness of personal, familial, and social discipline may offer a stronger defense against the fragmentation of psychical life, even against autism, the false-self, psychosis, and depression. Moreover, civilizations that have valued the written word more than speech, movement and the body more than the soul, and participation in the cosmic flux more than individual atomism are perhaps better able to confront these forms of personality disintegration than the West appears to be.

For new ways of destroying the soul (brought about by the breakdown of the family, biological experiments, or the reign of the image) will encounter traditional logical structures of disintegration. In these traditions, the absence of "authenticity," masquerades, and cruelty are more frequent and included in social games.

When these old codes of conduct are combined with new sorts of disruptions, they will perhaps make autism and the modern absence of subjective truth less distressing. But who can say if hiding new maladies of the soul in traditional codes will alleviate the tragic element of life? On the contrary, will this lead to an all-too-easy infliction of barbarism?

There is one thing of which I am certain. Although the West has consistently failed to relate to the other (xenophobia and the Holocaust are unbearable manifestations of this), it has been more ambitious than any other culture in its efforts to elaborate a *theory of the other* and a respect of his rights. (*Strangers to Ourselves*, Columbia University Press, 1989) The exquisite theory of the other that Western thought has offered us will become more essential than ever if we wish to confront the identity explosion of the coming century. If we fail to cherish the other, the twenty-first century may, through the help of civilized channels of science and media images, finally become the realization of fascism.

Resorting to religions that have curbed their fundamentalist fringes may allow us to sublimate such mortifying inclinations and form a civilization composed of large groups of people that are threatened by psychosis, as well as by dogmatic or technological suppression. These basic concerns, however, must not let us forget that *understanding of the other*—a goal of such diverse modern thinkers as Heidegger and Freud—requires that we pay attention to each person's individuality. We can do this by creating facilities that care for, educate, and accept other people, regardless of the wishes of any pressure group. Such a desire to *understand* the singularity of each person relies, of course, on religious communion, but the truth is that it goes beyond this and challenges the twenty-first century with a quasi-utopian goal: to protect the individual and to watch over the risks that he incurs, without succumbing to the blackmail, corruption, and submission that entice those who have gained the slightest bit of responsibility.

If democracy still exists tomorrow, will it be an indistinguishable mass of unconscious flux that can be endemically manipulated? Or will it be a harmony (in Heraclitus' sense of the term, which implies "secrecy" and "tenderness") of autonomous individuals? Is it possible to safeguard individuals who are capable of *understanding others* and *understanding themselves* without encouraging the emergence of an elite that is also concerned with understanding itself and understanding others while remaining entirely free from any dogma?

This sort of elite would maintain the stoic legacy of the *oikeiosis*.

In my view, these are the enormous and minuscule questions for which we have no answers, but that we will soon need to ask.

(translated by Ross Guberman)

# Discussion

**Windsor:** I was very interested by this morning's discussion, and it occurred to me this is part of the question of context which is involved here. It was very interesting that we have a Western historian and a Japanese anthropologist to open the discussion, and that a Western historian is talking in terms of religion and the identity as opposed to "the other." A Japanese anthropologist is talking about the development of Christianity in Japan in a particular context, namely the defeat of the shogunate, which, after all, began the Tokugawa period by excluding Christianity from Japan, by slaughtering Japanese Christians, and then ended, in terms of its defeat, by becoming "the other" in terms of those who converted to Christianity after many years of excluding "the other" from the Japanese experience.

Now, to be a bit autobiographical here, I have only recently discovered Plotinus and begun to read him in any proper manner, but I find him overwhelming. One of the things that is very important in this is that "the other" is essential before one can identify one's own identity, and it is the joining of the auterity and the identity in prayer which creates inner space. That is my view of what Plotinus was talking about in these terms.

Now, we have here an image and a way of thinking which can rescue us from what has been an awful pattern of thought, which you might call the "traditional or modern pattern of thought," namely that religion and history are opposed. Religion and history are not necessarily opposed. They became opposed in a certain historical form, but the identification of the "self," the identity, does not depend on religion; it does not depend on history. Religion is not necessarily resistance. It is resistance in a context. That context, I think, is something which one can reconsider in terms precisely of the inner space and the relationship between auterity and identity in that inner space.

What Hegel did, and perhaps quite wrongly, was to put Plotinus into history, and the relationship between "self" and "the other," the thesis and the antithesis, became historical. I think in terms of where we are now—in a sense speaking post-historically—we can talk in terms of those hands joining in prayer which might take religious expression, but the identity cannot exist without the recognition of "the other," and that, in terms of one Western experience and one Japanese experience, seems to me to have been at the focus of the earlier discussion about those two experiences so very different, in which the work that you have mentioned can begin to reconcile what in the past was irreconcilable.

**Junker:** One of the basic problems with religious and national fundamentalism is that they may serve to identify a specific nation or group of peoples, but combined with a sense of mission, or uniqueness, or exceptionalism, they may pose a threat to the uniqueness of others, and what I guess from Hutchison is that he seems to be of the opinion that this relationship is not structural but accidental. I still believe that this is a structural problem of religion and nationalism.

I happen to believe that, as a German historian, my very education was based on the theory of "the other" because this theory of "the other" is the philosophical background to German historicism in the nineteenth century, based on Herder and the romantic notion, and what it means is to extract yourself as much as possible from the prejudices of your own time, your own society and personal situation. So I was fascinated by that, and by what you call "the eclectic sort of happiness" that goes together with the theory of history.

**Hutchison:** Is the relationship between religion and nationalism accidental in the form in which I was presenting it as an American and, explicitly and implicitly also, as a Westerner? I see what you mean in that I seemed to be emphasizing the accidental, that this is something which religion in these particular aggressive formulations has grown up with, for example, the rise of the West. But is the relationship accidental or structural? I give the same answer. Yes, both.

What is accidental in that situation is the historically contingent formulation; for example, the connection between this reli-gious–national amalgamation, on the one hand, and the very recent rise of the West in dominance, on the other. That is what I mean by "historical contingency," and that, it seems to me, has also been ignored, but more often in common discourse, so that Americans, for example, suffer from an illusion of the permanence of the conjunction between their kind of polity, polities of the rise of the West, and particularly the American and Anglo-Saxon, on the one hand, and a particular religious formulation, on the other.

**Kristeva:** Is it possible to develop this internal psychic space outside religion? Of course, religion will continue. The problem is what can be the basis for lay ethics outside religion but without ignoring it. Here I would say that this basis will be the receiving of "the other," but we have to extract this from the religions. Why? Because in my mind the religions have some weak aspects that cannot confront precisely those modern aspects of the individuality I spoke about, these new maladies of the soul, the discrepancy of identity, abortion, free sex, genetic manipulation, and so on.

Religions confront this phenomenon by forbidden codexes that go against such experiments. It is just a refusal, but we cannot sustain this position of a simple refusal. If we try to understand more deeply we have to introduce more complex moral ethical codes, and in this sense a comprehension of "the otherness" extracted from its religious background, which is the origin, is necessary, and this complexification of "the otherness" passes through Freudian psychoanalysis, understanding of what language is, what different levels of meaning are. Meaning is not only one logical system; there are different logical systems in meaning. There are drives, there are sensations, there are feelings that are not cognitive models, etc. This sort of polyphony of the human mind is maybe what this foundation of modern ethics is required to establish. It is a very, very important question, but I am afraid we cannot go further.

Junker said the theory of "the other" was one of the basics of German philosophy and consists in requiring the self to be extracted from its own closure—nineteenth-century romanticism— and even Freud had inherited this. There was a great influence of this philosophy of "the otherness" in German philosophy on Freud, and there were different works showing how much Freud was indebted to Hegel, on one hand, or to Nietzsche, on the other hand. The problem is that what he proposed is something, in my mind, quite new. "The other," he says, is not outside you. "The other" is in your self. The unconscious is "your other." "The otherness" is in your self. If I am emphasizing this, it is because it is interesting not only from the psychoanalytical point of view but also because when you say that "the other" is your self, you mean that the stranger is in your self, and this can reach the problem of migration. How can you educate people to meet "the other" in talking to them about the fact that they are "others," they are strangers, and there are aspects in them that correspond to the Arabs, to the Koreans, or to different people that come into their country whom they cannot tolerate? They cannot tolerate them because they project onto them what is "the otherness" in themselves, and if you can try to educate them to reconcile their own "otherness" in themselves, maybe they will be less aggressive to "the otherness" of the migrants. I do not mean that the psychological device will be a miraculous solution to the problem of migration, but it could help educate these people.

**Yamaguchi:** The theater of Noh, as Paul Claudel made clear, was the technique of confronting "the other." The mediator is like an itinerant priest who feels something, and, in his daydream, it becomes a monster figure, "the other." Those dead and "other" categories just appear and start to perform, making appeals to the mediator. So this could be one of the ways that the Japanese tried to incorporate "otherness" in their own identity—by theatrical means. I think that in Western tradition beyond literature or writings you have some artistic expression, such as the temptation of St. Anthony. St. Anthony was confronted with thousands of devils who had their own charm in the name of the "other." So if you extend your scope, you will be able to efface the difference between West and East.

**Bulliet:** I hope my remarks do not appear too parochial, but I am speaking on this topic from the perspective of someone who is very deeply involved in the study of Islamic movements in the world today and, further, from the point of view of someone who believes that we are today seeing the implantation of a structure of hostility based on religion that has the potential to blight the next century on a scale equal to the anti-Semitism that has blighted this century. That is to say, I believe that the construction of Islam as an enemy of modernism of the West and the politicization of this in the policies of numerous countries, including that of the United States, represents a profound danger to many of our most optimistic conceptions of the future.

I feel that a great deal of the hostility that is being manifested at the present time arises from ignorance and from a disinclination actually to examine what is happening among Muslims around the world, a group of people some 800 million to a billion strong. It is characteristic of the constructions of Islam that they are seen as reactions, responses, resistances, to something else, and they are conceptually denied autonomy. In as much as they are conceived of as resistances, only those aspects of them are studied which fit the preordained model of resistance. That is to say, these are viewed as traditional, conservative, fundamentalist, whereas, in fact, in most cases they are not conservative, traditional, or fundamentalist, but there is a reluctance actually to examine what is happening.

To the degree that the model of resistance fits, we are dealing with religious expressions that are resistance and reaction to certain things. They are resistance and reaction to a totalitarian police state oppression, to unrelieved poverty and a major decline in living standards, to a perceived state of cultural imperialism in which secular nationalism is viewed as an instrument of Western-oriented elites to try to make Muslim populations subordinate to the intellectual constructions and will of Westerners. They are reacting to a profound turning away by governments in Muslim states from service to the public.

When we are talking about these movements as traditional, or conservative, or fundamentalist, it is often not realized that these are movements that bring medical services, potable drinking water, and other social services to poor people, that these are movements that are profoundly based upon service to the public, rather than simply the promulgation of religious dogma, that these are movements that are suffering under profound police suppression which is supported almost without demur by Western states, whether European or American, and we are dealing with movements that are extremely modern within their own traditions.

The point is that if we continue to adumbrate intellectual constructions that solely regard a profoundly important movement as being a reaction to something and as not having an autonomous appeal, in the first place we will be unable to understand why the movement is so popular and why it is on the verge of popular electoral success in a number of countries. We will be unable to understand why it is most popular among the most selective, elite, and intelligent faculties in Islamic universities or universities in Islamic countries. That is to say, these are not obscurantist. These are the people in the scientific faculties that are particularly drawn to this movement, who will be unable to understand the dynamic that is bringing the movement to popularity and power and will be unable to understand what the positive appeal of this movement is.

We have heard statements about the peculiar accomplishment of European society in constructing a theory of "the other." I believe many people have read Edward Said's book *Orientalism,* and they will see that the theory of "the other" can become a perversion if "the other" is a totally imaginary construct that is created solely to serve the interest of the person trying to deal with his or her own identity within Western culture. I know very little about this philosophy, but if there is a theory of "the other" and an openness to seeing other perspectives in the Western tradition, it is not being developed or expounded or put into public discourse with respect to Islam. Rather we are facing a situation of public blindness, benighted policy, intellectual silence, and a general disinclination to deal seriously with one of the most profoundly important phenomena and problems at the end of the twentieth century.

**Stern:** The main thing I missed in Hutchison's paper is the degree to which the Church, the Christian churches, in the nineteenth and twentieth centuries in the West and, certainly including the United States, with a few exceptions, have assimilated nationalism, have exalted nationalism, have been subservient to the state and, therefore, that the historian who deals, as it were, with public affairs and affairs of the state, etc., was more concerned with what was going on and subsumed, unfortunately—unfortunately in the sense of the effect on political development—subsumed the Church, as one of the pillars of the establishment. There have been challenges to this, particularly in our century, in all our countries, and they have been very important, but I think in this coming to terms with—and I would even say, in some cases, subservience to—capitalism, nationalism, and so on, prevailing mores did do the Church itself a great deal of harm.

When Kristeva was talking about the new maladies of the soul, I instantly thought of Nietzsche, and it did seem to me that so much of what has been said really was first seen very clearly—and in relation to the absence of religion or to the doubts about religion—by Nietzsche. His diagnosis of our troubles and our diagnosis of the soul's maladies, which is a term that would not be alien to him at all, was very penetrating and terribly important.

**Mayall:** In discussing the relationship between religion and nationalism it would be helpful just to make the point that the great religions, do, at one level, all offer an option of transcendence and, therefore, while they can become linked with nationalism, it is ultimately a contingent, not a necessary relationship, whereas nationalism, I think, despite a very attractive vision offered by Herder, is basically solipsistic. It can only generate the tragic vision of human affairs in the sense that we can accept that we belong necessarily to human communities and have necessarily identities, and we can empathize with people in a similar situation, but it cannot itself, I think, generate any transcendent order.

The second point I would make—and I go back to Harkabi yesterday saying that we ought to start our understanding of world order—is that the present world order has its structural origins in, as it were, a religious ceasefire in Europe, which had the result of internalizing religion. Subsequently, certainly in Western liberal democracies, there was a feeling that religion should be privatized, and that is a different movement which, in a sense, raises different kinds of problems. Once you have internalized religion, then its relationship with nationalism becomes an empirical question which you must pursue by looking at different countries with different historical experiences, where religion is related to the political order in different ways.

I suppose if you accept my basic narrative, one of the frightening aspects of it in relation to the tendency to demonize Islam at the present time is that, of course, Islam was outside and had a very ambiguous relationship to this world order that was set up by a religious ceasefire. Although we have been talking about expansionary missionism, certainly there were advantages in being the outsider.

Wherever British imperial expansion came into contact with Islam, they gave it privileges which have had extremely fateful consequences in a number of places where, in fact, it was taken up as nationalism. For example, in Eastern and Western Nigeria, and particularly Eastern Nigeria, it was taken up by people who were not so privileged, who were open to Christian and, therefore, ultimately Western and secular education, where Islam was maintained as a sort of culturally isolated bulwark against modern influences. This also has had long-term consequences for the twentieth century and, no doubt, beyond.

**Kristeva:** The Western tradition conceptualized "the other," and it is quite different from the theatrical experimental presentation of "the other." This is also the case with "identity." The Western tradition conceptualizes the idea of "identity," although it exists in every other kind of society. My emphasis of "the otherness" in Western tradition is a little polemical in the sense that I believe that we have to defend some positive aspects of Western culture. For years now, we have developed an essential point of our Western tradition, which is its capacity to negate itself. We have attacked it, we have de-constructed it from the leftist point of view, from the Third World point of view, and from other different points of view. I belong to the generation that accomplished this very important work of negation, doubt, and, even in a more mild sense, just interrogation.

I think that the point now is to rehabilitate some positive aspects of this Western tradition, and one of the issues of the twenty-first century is not to protect Western culture negatively or defensively but to try to encourage a revival of our values in order to confront Eastern as well as Western problems. Malraux said that the twenty-first century will be the "century of nationalism." I would say—and maybe I will shock some people here—that the twenty-first century could also need the protection of the positive values that we have to extract from the Western tradition.

Just one remark about Bulliet's very interesting intervention in connection with the fact that we consider the Muslim religion or any other religions merely as defenses. I share an atheistic point of view, and in my mind religions are protections and defenses, but this does not mean there is something negative. The modern development of the psyche to which I referred is a very dangerous one. It is an unbearable one. It is something unsupportable, and defense is not necessarily something negative. In one respect, people are attracted to those religions because they find shelter and answers to these discrepancies.

I am not sure that in the traditional religions we can find answers for this development of the modern personality. The point is whether we agree or disagree about the fact that there is a development of the personality. If we think that the personality is the same as it was 2,000 or 200 years ago, maybe religions can answer these new questions, but if we accept that there are new phenomena—genetic experiment, sexual freedom, autism, abortion—I am not sure that ancient religions are equipped to deal with these. They will develop, some of them, as Christianity developed in this sense, but there is a long road ahead, and I am not sure that this will happen without an internal transformation of the religious disposal and religious set itself.

**Hutchison:** In the social sciences and among historians there is a substantial amount of work that is on the fringes of discourse about the connections between the collective and the individual, important work on the formations of identity, colonial, post-colonial, the malformations of identity and the ambiguities of identity in those situations. We have considerable literature on the decline of civilizations, and specifically Western civilization, that does not make any attempt to analyze the social history or individual history related to this; very few others do, except in very specific contexts.

I would be willing to make the assertion that most political extremism, whether in the Moslem world or other parts, should not be blamed on religion at all. It is not that religion is not importantly invoked and involved, but that is political extremism. I think maybe our terminology would be clarified somewhat if we erased the term "religious fundamentalism" from much of it.

We have already said that many of the happenings and the perils of the end of this century are not new but are quite old. That is healthy as far as it goes. Surely, there is a great temptation to suppose falsely that if something in the human condition is not new, it is not worth discussing, and I hope that we have escaped that fallacy in this meeting. We must be even more reflective, I think, and ask whether we are talking about the human condition or—as an assemblage of G3 representatives, an intellectual trilateral commission here—we are talking, really more often than we are aware, about the G3 condition. I do think that that is a danger when we discuss challenges to identity, whether collective or personal.

Challenges to identity are somewhat an old story, even for the hitherto dominant societies in the West, for example. There are far older stories within the modern era for Africans, for American Indians, and many others—yes, for the Japanese of Admiral Perry's time. One could say, I'm afraid, that Westerners and Christians are once again, or still, practicing the old Orientalism and the older or eternal solipsism; that is, expressing alarm about allegedly universal new problems, such as identity, but defining them unconsciously probably within parochial categories. Much of the vast literature on identity, it seems to me, does that. It is a bit like the terrible new drug problem in the United States. This was a terrible old problem in the ghettos of America and became a terrible new one only when it reached suburban streets and high schools.

# Discussion (continued)

**Iriye:** The purpose of this session is to resume our conversation about the implications of the collapse of communism as well as the future possibilities of our democratic government. We raised a number of questions about such matters as the economic implications or the economic foundations of political change, whether in terms of the viability of a post-communist society or the future of democratic systems. We talked about the moral or spiritual foundations of those political changes, the danger of fanaticism, cynicism and, in a somewhat different vein, we talked about nationalism and democracy, nationalism and communism.

In subsequent sessions further insights were added to those questions when speakers and commentators raised other kinds of questions or broadened their perspectives by talking about, for example, international relations as they hinge upon the future of democracy, or the future of a post-communist society. Much has been discussed about the question of identity, personality types, understanding "the other," and it seems that these are all relevant to our discussion of democracy as well. We spent some time discussing international migrations, population movements, and how those might impinge upon the future of democracy as well.

Now, in all these discussions, I was struck—and I think a number of you have been struck—by the fact that we have tended to focus our attention on the G3 world, the advanced countries, particularly Europe and the United States, and, therefore, the time may have come at this point to open our discussion or dialogue, bringing the Third World, the non-Western part of the world, into it. At least I would like to propose that we begin looking a little more at other countries in Asia and Latin America. Junker did talk about Latin America, but that was not sufficiently followed up by our discussion, so since we have spent so much time talking about the crisis and post-crisis and various future directions of Western civilization, as we resume our discussion about democracy might it not make sense to bring in other perspectives or other areas in the world?

**Ishii:** What I am going to say is about the situation in Southeast Asia with reference to the relationship between religion and democracy. The term "democracy" increasingly claims a universal application, and no political leaders of any Southeast Asian nation can dispense with the term. Hence, in Laos, which is a socialist country, they have now dropped the term "socialism," and call their country "Lao Democratic Republic." Even with such notoriety for killing and atrocities, Pol Pot called his country "Democratic Kampuchea." The word "democracy" has become generalized. Incidentally, in Japan "democracy" is most frequently used by the Japan Communist Party. For them "peace and democracy" is a sort of cliché. I do not know whether the concept of democracy is properly appreciated or understood by the Asian people.

When we talk about this, we should not forget that democracy is a concept rooted in Western tradition. Therefore, in its application, in our attempt to apply the concept of democracy to a non-Western political-cultural milieu, I think the religious-cultural substratum should be given due consideration. This is the case particularly with Southeast Asia, which is sometimes called a "religious mosaic." There, with its 300 million or more population, we find Indonesia, the largest Islamic country in the world, much larger than the big countries in the Middle East, and in mainland Southeast Asia we find as many as 100 million Buddhists. These religions are internalized. In Mayall's words they are already internalized. Therefore, when you speak of anything, religion comes first.

In this connection, may I refer to a Buddhist legend which you can find in Pali. Pali is the language of Theravada Buddhism, now being followed by the people of Myanmar, Thailand, Laos, and Cambodia, including Sri Lanka, of course. The legend concerns the birth of the first king of humankind. At the very beginning of this world, peace used to prevail, but, as time went on, within the mind of the human being greed and conflict gave rise to the chaotic situation that you see. Then, in order to restore peace and order to society, the people elected a king, known as "the great elect." But this king could not be despotic because he was expected to abide by the ten kingly virtues identified by his electorate, to bring these people peace and equality. When justice and righteousness prevails, the king is praised with the words, "You are Dhammarajah, the king of righteousness." But if the king deviates from that expected path and becomes tyrannical or despotic, then he can be justifiably eliminated, revolution will follow, and the people will say: "You are rejected because you are no longer Dhammarajah. You are Adhammarajah, the king of unrighteousness." A king is always watched by the people who elected him. This story is not just a religious myth; in the people's mind this legend still persists. I will give you a concrete example.

When the so-called student revolution took place in Thailand in 1973, the government of Thanom Kitikachorn and others, the "three rascals," was condemned by the people as *adhamma*, "without righteousness." So when we talk about "without righteousness," or *adhamma*, in people's mind this religious legend is always present. Therefore, whether the government is acceptable or not is judged in terms of this internalized Buddhist value. It applies in Thailand, but also in Myanmar, in Cambodia, and in Laos. Pol Pot is a typical *adhammarajah*; he is condemned simply because, according to the Buddhist standard, he is totally unrighteous. They understand the legitimacy of modern government as an extrapolation of this religious concept of kingship. I do not know whether this is democracy or not. Sometimes democracy is contrasted with totalitarian rule, which is not a parliamentary type of democracy. We cannot flatly deny this type of democracy. Should we therefore stick faithfully to the Western concept of democracy?

Suppose in Cambodia the United Nations were content that an election had been properly conducted with a poll of, say, 90 percent of the electorate. But that would be overlooking the fact that probably more than 90 percent of the voters had no idea whatsoever about democracy and probably voted on the orders of the boss or the village headman. Nevertheless, the result satisfied the United Nations. Reality was hidden by the success, the apparent success, of this sort of operation.

I do not know whether I am allowed to use this analogy—but since I am teaching at Sophia University, which is a Jesuit educational institution, may I refer to the wisdom of the Catholic Church. The Catholic Church, by definition, is claimed to be universal, but it was not until the Second Vatican Council *aggiornamento* edict that the faithful could worship in the vernacular. The Thai can now pray in Thai and the Japanese attend mass conducted in Japanese; there is a Japanese version of the Catholic faith, and a Burmese version, without jeopardizing the integrity of the Catholic Church.

What about democracy? Can we talk about the Burmese version of Western democracy? Could we allow the Japanese version of Western democracy? Are we too adamant about the veracity and applicability of the Western concept which is democracy?

I am afraid that, as is shown in the case of Cambodia, we tend to hide actuality. We are satisfied and are probably betrayed by superficial success, which complacency might jeopardize an imagined embryonic form of democracy. I am, however, rather optimistic about embryonic democracy simply because I have observed political developments in Thailand over the past four decades.

I first went to Thailand in 1957. At that time democracy scarcely prevailed there, although in 1955 Field Marshal Pibun Songkram, after his state visit to the United States, suddenly changed policy and promulgated a law on political parties, which resulted in scores of big and small political parties, as a parliamentary system was discussed. The situation only led to a coup d'état and the installation of a very despotic government. Much later it was found that this government was very development-oriented and the justification for Sarit Thanarat's despotism was to make Thailand more prosperous materially and bring about economic development. In any case, democracy collapsed, but, thanks to the developmental policy introduced by Sarit Thanarat, who was termed a sort of "benevolent despot," the so-called middle class emerged numerically and the city of Bangkok changed totally. This economic development brought a change in the minds of the people. Now, only recently, when the despotic government was crushed by a demonstration in which the now democratically minded middle-class people participated, views on how the government should be administered and managed were articulated. Therefore, what I want to ask is whether or not we can wait another decade or, even two, for this embryonic democracy eventually to flourish. In order to foster the germination of embryonic democracy, we should be patient instead of approaching everything with a fervent missionary spirit, however sincere. We should not repeat the spirit of the *mission civilizatrice* manifested in the nineteenth century.

**Ueno:** If people cannot see others as equals, how can democracy be established? So I would revert to the issue of the "otherness" of identity which we discussed earlier. While I was listening to Murakami, I anticipated he would explain the difference in the Japanese feeling of identity, but that was not the case.

I do not want to impose an Orientalist view of Japaneseness or to make Japan a particular subject, but as a sociologist by discipline, who learned the Parsonian theory of the personal system which presumably requires integrity, I was annoyed by that concept. So maybe I already live a so-called disintegrated self in post-modern Japan.

If identity is conceived as such a solid entity in the Western tradition, what we should do is to reverse the question itself rather than talking of the different concept of identity among the Japanese. We should question what really is "identity" and why it requires integrity. From this point of view, no doubt, religious and national identity takes the form of expansionism imposing its own principle on others. So it is also an origin of racism.

Kristeva said that Western civilization has developed the theory of "others," but it is no wonder that the theory of "others" is the other side of the coin of this solid concept of identity. In this context, as Kristeva argues, the new malady in terms of the loosening or the dissolution of family and social bonds, the weakening of authority, is also being experienced in modern Japan, and, in spite of the existence of non-Western Japanese thought, which might fit in with her eclectic happiness, young Japanese are now attracted by new forms of religion. As Kristeva said, religion will exist but transform itself in a new form.

What we see now in the 1990s in Japanese society is the rise of the so-called new new religions that came after the "new religions," the secularized forms of traditional Buddhism and Shintoism. Up to the 1960s the secularization theory of religion was valid insofar as these "new religions" were concerned. But now new new religions, taking the form of occultism, determinism, and mysticism, all intolerant of others, attract young people in a manner based on what I would call the "fear of others." In this sense, it might be said that there is a lack of religious fundamentalism in the Japanese context, but this rise of new forms of religion might be called a Japanese version of fundamentalism.

So, in this sense, what we see now is rather a fear of others rather than the development of an encounter with others. So just as Stern hoped to have misunderstood what Kristeva foresees, it might be too pessimistic to share her prediction that the twenty-first century might be the time of the coming of new forms of fascism. Instead, perhaps, we are talking about how we could see "others" as equals in a different sense, but it seems that it might be the fear of "others" rather than the acceptance of "others."

**Kosai:** I will make three points. Kristeva said the twenty-first century could be a century of fascism. I am shocked by this final comment in her paper. Because of the progress in information technology, identity or individuality is being jeopardized. This is part of the background to this pessimistic prognosis. Certainly, information can be a tool for manipulation of the masses, but the progress in information technology also has another more positive aspect. Information technology can cultivate more dialogue between people, in which case progress in information science does not necessarily mean the de-construction of the identity but, rather, the building of a network of people with different identities. I think this raises the possibility of democracy rather than fascism in the next century.

The second point refers to Ueno's observation on the question of identity in language. There was some doubt about the presence or absence of the very concept of identity in the Japanese people. I am not a specialist in psychoanalysis, but I am reminded of the novelist Mori Ogai. In his novel *Illusion*, the hero thinks about his death, which he does not fear, but he does fear that his family and friends will mourn it. In this sense, he has a sense of relational or relative identity.

I now propose that the concept of relational identity should be involved in the process of building a network of people. This could, of course, lead to fascism, but alternatively it could lead to a healthy emergence of community, as Morin suggested at the outset. Now, this relational ability works very well and is a very operative concept in the structure of the Japanese economy. For example, "contract." In Japan what is understood implicitly is more important than the letters of a contract. The relational contract is more important than the written contract and this, for instance, is a very familiar pattern of behavior in the Japanese economy. So this concept of relational identity may be an added element in our consideration, in addition to what Ishii so ably introduced us to.

Earlier we discussed the relation between nationalism and religion. Well, we social scientists have talked about the relation between religion and capitalism, between religion and economic development, and between nationalism and economic development since the classic work of Max Weber argued that Protestantism would lead most effectively to economic development. But, as I said in my paper, when we look at economic development in Asia, Protestant capitalism is not the only way to economic prosperity.

Junker referred pessimistically to Latin America and Eastern Europe, but think of what the economic level was in Asia. Only twenty or thirty years ago they complained that there were no market structures or economic know-how in Asia, including Japan, but in the last thirty years Asian countries have managed to achieve great economic development. Perhaps you should not overemphasize the difficulty of economic development in areas where at present the circumstances seem to be so formidable. For instance, economic development in Thailand will promote the democratization of Vietnam, and it will improve conditions in neighboring countries and promote their economic development.

**Bulliet**: With respect to the new maladies of the soul: Do we visualize the world acting in simultaneous fashion or are there some things happening in some parts of the world that might not occur elsewhere for another generation? Changes in psychology, identity, and so forth can be perceived as worldwide or as specific to certain areas at certain times.

For example, the ethos of the Islamic movement is opposed to the notion of seeking office or promoting one's qualifications for office. Muslims are often horrified by Western democratic procedures, and to see what we do in the United States in the name of "democracy," particularly the presidential system. They cannot believe that any human being would ever get up and claim to be the most highly qualified person in the entire country to lead the country. They basically feel that anyone like that obviously is a lunatic. But they seriously study the question of nomination, who determines whom, and how running for office is determined. They observe that in Western democracy—whatever its origins in terms of an Athenian model where people knew one another, or a town meeting model—today in America achieving nomination and election depends enormously upon commandeering financial resources, controlling media appearances, and other things that do not appear to be part of a basic democratic concept.

I think that one of the questions about democracy in the future is whether democracy can be multiculturalized, that is to say, whether it is possible to recognize that there are other possible sources of contribution to democratic theory than simply the Western cultural source, and whether people in the West coming from that tradition are willing to listen to critiques of their democracy and to accept the possibility that an improvement or a refinement of democratic theory and principle could be achieved through the incorporation of other cultural approaches instead of through the continued assertion that only the West truly understands what democracy is.

**Windsor:** Two brief points. One is in response to what Ishii was saying, and with which I very much agree. There is not a single model democracy, but nonetheless it seems to me that the democratic framework is the framework of freedom of choice, and without talking about that one would not be talking about democracy at all.

But, while accepting a plurality of frameworks, I think there is one other thing which is very important. Democracy is not an end in itself, not a transcendent end, but there is a sense in which democracy is an end in itself, and one that has seen people risking or losing their lives, for example, in Haiti for the right to vote. Maybe in Cambodia they did not know what voting meant, but in Haiti they are dying for it, and in that sense we are talking about an end in itself. People in the slums of Bombay, living in the most degrading circumstances and whose lives were utterly impoverished, also fought for the ballot, and for them the word "democracy" meant something beyond the immediate circumstances of their daily life. In that sense, to talk about democracy means getting away from one of the most pernicious legends of the last couple of hundred years, namely, that democracy comes after development. It does not, and Bertolt Brecht could not have been more wrong when he said "*Erst kommt das Fressen, dann kommt die Moral.*" And, in any case, democracy can also provide a framework for development.

**Hutchison:** I thought Ishii's final comments, his call for more patience, were right. Certainly, the Christianizers, the missionaries, needed at least that in the past, and that is needed still, but yet there are tremendous difficulties which I am sure we will hear a great deal more about when we talk about human rights. Patience is fine, but of course the American Congress or some other entity has to decide whether or not to pass a bill now in view of alleged torture somewhere. That is, the human rights issue comes before them and must be decided, and patience only works in certain contexts. Yet Americans must acknowledge that there was slavery and segregation and so on in America, that our democracy has not worked. My impression from constant Indonesian discussions and many others is that much of that kind of modesty is uttered by Americans and Westerners, but often it is lip service. It does not go very deep. It is not a very fundamental kind of modesty, and perhaps we are even talking here about an aspect of all religious traditions that should be thought about: we have to talk about humility, more than just modesty. That would depend on some kind of recognition of transcendence and would mean Westerners acknowledge that republics in the West have precisely misused the term democracy. When we acknowledge this we do so out of a real depth of modesty that would better be called humility. I think that probably has not been fully expressed.

**Stern:** There was, especially I suppose in America, the naive notion that capitalism would bring about democracy, that if you have capitalism, then very likely you would have democracy. This is theoretically unlikely. In practical terms, all you have to look at is Singapore, where you had tremendous economic development but hardly a democratic system, and the same for Pinochet's Chile.

The second point I want to make is, again, on the question of patience: patience and humility in the face of people trying to establish a polity that we would recognize in some ways as being democratic, yes, but that patience must not extend to seeing obstacles to democracy being introduced, and the greatest obstacle to democracy, it seems to me, is the existence of torture, the systematic violation of human rights. Here, it occurs to me, since we keep talking about the West we should not arrogate to ourselves certain roles and we should be modest. For Europeans, for the self-liberation of Eastern Europe, the Helsinki Charter was very, very important. Why could it not be that the Japanese and others have a similar charter for Asia whereby you have a yardstick by which you could judge violations of human rights? It does not have to be the West. It could be you yourselves.

**Nivat:** When we ask whether democracy can triumph, I feel, indeed, rather uncomfortable about that expression because I would say triumph where and when and on which level, because democracy must be revitalized. When Windsor reminds us that people may die for democracy, we feel there is another dimension, which is more existential, that the links with life and death are often forgotten.

The territory of democracy is very important as we have been reminded. First of all, it was the agora. In Switzerland in some cantons it is the small canton with so-called direct democracy. The territory and the stage and where democracy is—that is to say, that freedom of choice—are important, and I would like to recall that in a Christian view, everything is important on the earth until the end of history because history has a beginning and an end, and the end of history is important from the Christian point of view. In *Three Conversations*, the Russian philosopher Soloviev has discussed how we can think, and how we reflect modern thinking on the end of history. For him the end of history was a sort of fake Kingdom of God, which might be democracy and which might be a gross, primitive and, in fact, unjust democracy, and that would be the anti-Christ.

I would just like to remind you of that because I don't think that democracy as a philosophy is the real expression of the West and of Europe. It is part of its philosophy, it is integrated, but it came out of Christianity more than out of Athens where, after all, there was freedom of choice for the citizens and not for the slaves, and it is integrated in a philosophy which looks at the end of history.

**Junker:** I would like to make a comment on Ishii's tale about the founding myth of a good government. Now, we have had this myth around for several thousand years in several countries, so my main point would be that you cannot base modern democracy just on the concept of a good king or good government, but modern democracy has to be more precise, and in this I agree with other speakers here.

If you talk about modern democracy, the very basis is not the notion of a just government because this can be abused, but it is really the dignity and integrity of the individual and human rights. So if there is a tradition of good government, that is no justification to call this government a democracy. Call it something else, but I think you have to be very careful with this founding myth lest we lose any meaning to the term "democracy."

**Likhachev:** In the process of democratization, let me tell you what is actually taking place in our country. Nivat made a comment similar to mine. It is with a sense of fear that everything is being done under the name of democratization. All sorts of things are done. We need to reject the use of such an ambiguous word. Democratization and democracy—in the name of these beautiful words, minorities are trampled on. The democracies of minorities are being trampled on. For the last thousand years, three hundred different minorities have occupied Russian territory. Officially, at present the number has been halved, but in reality still less than half are still present because it has been legally prohibited to speak in the vernaculars of the minorities. That is to say, since democracy is rule by the majority, in the cultural field these cultural minorities were completely ignored, overwhelmed by the majority.

The rule by majority certainly is a principle of democracy, I agree, because democracy is a representation of the voice of the majority, but those in the majority very often make mistakes. For instance, in the field of science, can you decide scientific research by democratic processes, by majority rule? What would have happened to Einstein? Minority opinions would never have blossomed. Take the field of art. Can you assess the value of art by majority? I will not say anything about new music, but take impressionism. How do you evaluate impressionist works of art? Many people have come to appreciate impressionism, but when it first came on the scene what was the reaction?

In time of war, are military strategies and tactics going to be decided by a majority? In 1917 soldiers in the trenches tried to settle the war by democratic means. It was a very primitive form of decision making. All these examples point to the fact that majority rule is not the absolute, sole guiding principle of democracy.

At present we are living in a world controlled by language. What is cultural behavior? We have to define, verbally define, what is meant by cultural behavior. If democratization should be guided by a primitive notion of majority rule, in the Caucasus and Central Asia and in various component countries of the old Soviet Union where Bolshevist legacies are still very much alive, politicians of the old generation are despots, but they have all been elected by due process of democratic election.

**Gold:** A very brief comment about science and democracy, and I will draw on what Kristeva said, in part, to illustrate this caution. Kristeva gave a beautiful description of the necessity for valuing the treasure of the inner self and for nourishing its complexity and its capacity to appreciate complexities as a means of facilitating our ability to appreciate the wonder of "the other." At the same time she mentioned that we must be careful about science because it may significantly diminish our psychic curiosity, and in that regard there may be a tendency for philosophically oriented, social scientist-oriented individuals to see science as "the other."

I believe that it is very important to recognize that science really only will provide methodologies and data but will not create meaning, and you as philosophers and social scientists and economists must not ascribe that function to the scientists. They do not want to dictate to us necessarily what our concept of humanity will be, but we cannot afford, I think, to be technophobic in the twenty-first century. I think, at the very least, each philosopher and social scientist must have a rudimentary understanding—and that is all that is necessary—of what the genetic code is, how these methodologies may be utilized, what the limits of their applications are, and what kind of data they are going to provide for you to be able to interpret and provide meaning for that information, and I am afraid if you do not do it then those who are much less qualified will, and that would be a tragedy.

**Mayall:** If I may be ironic, perhaps because I am not an American, I am rather more impressed by the worldwide attraction of some of what have been called "Western values" rather than the overweening arrogance. Just two examples. I believe at the Vienna Conference of 1993 there were, of course, a number of Asian protests that this was a Western imposition. What is less reported is the number of opposition groups which were, of course, very strongly in favor of these universal concepts. The point that I am really getting at is that we are, in a sense, caught in a system of no escape. We cannot avoid being caught up in a world where ideas have common appeal even if they have different interpretations.

I was very struck by the fact that Ishii—and I entirely agree with him—referred to legitimacy. It is interesting that that is the first time, I think, in our discussions that the word "legitimacy" has come up. The difficulty is if we could find a standard, a way of being sensitive to other cultural standards of legitimacy, it would be excellent, but it is difficult to accomplish within a global environment.

Just one final example since Africa has not been mentioned much. Morin, quite rightly, said that the experiment with democracy in many African countries was rather short-lived and, sadly, I suspect I agree with him, although it is in many cases a failure which is not a total failure. I think many brave people who have opposed their governments are now able to sleep slightly safer in their beds at night as a result of that move. That may not be a very heroic conclusion, but it is one that I think deserves our support.

Basil Davidson, an Africanist who long romantically identified himself with a particular notion of a particular African nation-state, has recently written a book saying that the nation-state was an appalling Western imposition on Africa. What he fails to point out is that it is the only thing that any particular political class that you could find in Africa wanted, and that is a very important point. We cannot go constantly in search of authenticity from outside as a form of indulgence and therapy when people all over the world actually wish to participate in a common humanity which endorses the politics of consent and freedom.

**Perczynski:** We have adopted a very important topic for our symposium. I cannot resist making some comments on that because I fully agree that there are numerous institutional forms of democracy, and of course parliamentary democracy in Western Europe is only one, but probably in Europe it will persist for a long time.

What is more important, however, is that democracy is a certain pattern of human behavior, and it is we human beings who are choosing for ourselves the forms in which we could express and defend our interests. This is the biggest problem in creating democracy in post-communist countries, in which the democracy is an end in itself because without that no other transformations are going to be possible. It seems to me that the damages we are facing in our economies, in our societies, are damages which are not to be expressed only in a material sense, but they are damages done to the society as such. In communist times we were building the society of the new man. Instead, something has emerged which is now called by some scholars *homo sovieticus*, who is scarcely able to create a democratic way of life. I fully agree with Likhachev that sometimes, by introducing certain formally democratic institutions, we may face the situation in which that *homo sovieticus*, who belongs to the new forces of building the new society with a psychology deeply rooted in the old times, may produce a very damaging effect on the creation of a real condition for development.

Of course, I again agree with Likhachev that the only way is to increase the level of culture, and together with that we will have the new society. But this is a very long process. We must decide something now to prevent a return to the old times. There are, of course, possibilities to marginalize such tendencies. One of them, which I do not have time to develop, is a deepening of the process of integration of post-communist societies of Eastern Europe with the outside world so that they can join the mainstream of civilizational development.

# THE ENVIRONMENT: A NEW DEFINITION OF NATURE

# THE ENVIRONMENT:
# A NEW DEFINITION OF NATURE

KYOGOKU Jun-ichi

*"We govern people by words. Which word is correct, no one knows."*
—Benjamin Disraeli

In the human history of ideas the concept of nature was introduced very early. It is now more than two thousand years old and has been through a multifarious development in recent centuries. The concept of nature was born through the efforts of man trying to know and understand himself. We have developed myth, religion, metaphysics, philosophy, science, literature, and art. A basic element of human self-understanding is the distinction between what is human and what is non-human. It has been called nature and the supernatural for many centuries.

Between the seventeenth and twentieth centuries the metaphysics of "rationalism" and accompanying "rationalist" and "scientific" understandings of nature came to be generally accepted. The supernatural was relegated to the backstage of the universe, then forced to make its exit. Its remains were handed over to religion and superstition. The human being was given the scientific name of *homo sapiens*. The process of evaporation of the supernatural and emancipation of *homo sapiens* was called disenchantment (*Entzauberung*) by Max Weber. During the same period, being deprived of the aura of the supernatural and the awe inspired by it in the human mind, defenseless nature was subjected to human dominance and ruthless exploitation. The human being was given the additional name of *homo faber*. In modern industrial-technological civilization, not only the fauna and flora on the surface of the earth but also deep inside the earth, the stratosphere, and the bottom of the oceans are all the objects and arenas of human engineering activities.

In the nineteenth century, industrialism brought many changes in nature that were often viewed with distaste. Industrialism itself was accepted as an essential foundation of "civilization." In order to ensure the coexistence of industrialism supported by nature and nature unaffected by it, the new concept of nature conservation was proposed. By the turn of the century, conservation of nature had become accepted. The National Trust for Places of Historical Interest or Natural Beauty was founded in England in 1895, and the National Trust Act was promulgated in 1907. The National Trust for Scotland was founded in 1931. Even today some people see nature as composed of two parts, the first part polluted by industrial civilization but the second part untouched by it, and that nature conservation is an effective method for keeping the second part safe and intact. But, unfortunately, conserved nature is not always free from pollution and degradation.

In 1962 there was a flash of lightning. Rachel Carson published her book *Silent Spring*. It contained a thunderous message that no part of nature was left unaffected by the evil of industrial civilization. An awakening took place and many researchers began to reappraise their positions. Since the late sixties there have been many publications on ecology. "Environment" became a popular word. It also expressed a subconscious anxiety and fear that human beings were surrounded and besieged by the evil produced by themselves. On the one hand some ecology groups partly renounced the benefit of industrial civilization by employing such methods as natural food and organic farming. On the other, environmental issues became increasingly political both domestically and internationally. In 1972 the first United Nations Conference on the Human Environment (UNCHE) was held in Stockholm. In 1992 the U.N. Conference on Environment and Development (UNCED) was held in Rio de Janeiro. The Rio Declaration endorsed the concept of sustainable development, which was originally proposed in the 1987 report "Our Common Future," produced by the World Commission on Environment and Development (WCED). As we near the end of the twentieth century, the environmental issue has become globalized and thoroughly intertwined with the issue of developed versus developing countries. It is also connected with the issue of equity between and among human generations.

In early modern times there were the rather simple issues of "man and nature," both of which were clearly and distinctly different. Now we have to confront many complicated issues between man and nature: man and man-conserved nature; man in man-polluted nature; and man-processed (possibly polluted) nature in man.

Nature itself has grown into the "environment." In the following pages we will observe some aspects of the recognition of and response to the "environmental" issue, which are not only scientific and technological but also economic and political.[1]

## CITY, COUNTRY, AND "FAR OUT" LAND

In many cultures, the world inhabited by human beings has long been divided into three broad categories; city, country, and "far out" land. This trichotomy refers to the degree of civilization achieved through generations of human activity. The division was established and disseminated by articulate people living in the city. The categories are geographic ones, but they are also part of a value system which is incorporated into the traditional system of culture.[2]

The growth and development of town, city, and metropolis in many countries has a long history covering many centuries. Cathedrals, palaces, government offices, markets, stores, banks, and other institutions provide urban inhabitants with opportunities to rise in the world and accumulate wealth. Many people who come to live in the town are drawn by its charm; at the same time they are pushed there by the misery and want in the countryside. As the population increases, a town grows into a city, and a city into a metropolis.

Towns, cities, and metropolises often have two faces, a characteristic common to the urban areas of many cultures. On the bright side, they are centers of manners and civility, of pleasure and amenities, and of high culture. On the dark side they are places of hypocrisy and vice, of sweat and toil, and of a variety of crimes. Before the modern restructuring of city management, the physical environment of the city was not very enjoyable. Many people lived in dismal conditions. Streets were used as rubbish dumps, full of dirt and waste. Fumes and soot filled the air, and the sky was overcast with smog. Rivers were clogged with debris. Outbreaks of fire and contagious disease were frequent, and mortality was higher than in the country.

In the nineteenth and twentieth centuries, many cities introduced new public services, such as effective police protection, fire prevention, public transportation, traffic control, and sanitation, as well as amenities such as public parks, zoos, museums, concert halls, gymnasiums, libraries, and schools. All were essential to ensuring a decent standard of living in urban centers. In the early to mid-twentieth century, many cities suffered disasters visited on them by the Great Depression and World War II. But by the fifties and sixties, metropolises were once again centers of pleasure and entertainment.

Traditionally, the city and the country had contrasting images. In contrast to the image of the "nightless city," a place of pleasure, the country, amid nature untouched by human hand, was long viewed as rustic, dark, and untamed, inhabited in the main by wild animals, trolls, and demons. But the growth of cities and the extensive cultivation of rural areas in the eighteenth and nineteenth centuries brought about a dramatic change in the moral and aesthetic sensibilities of urban inhabitants, especially those of the middle class. The country came to be regarded as a place for relaxation, refreshment, moral healing, and spiritual regeneration.

To enjoy both the comforts of city life and the pleasures of a country sojourn, urbanites began to live in the city and the country alternately. Affluent families lived in their city houses for three seasons, and in the summer they stayed at their country houses. Slowly, this alternation came to be a weekly one and weekends in the country became common. Retirement to the country has come to be embroidered into this pattern of alternation. In the late twentieth century, affluence and the increase of vacation time has made it popular for people to travel abroad, on safari, to fashionable resorts, or on ocean cruises.

As nature became increasingly viewed as having aesthetic, moral, and spiritual value, its conservation was deemed by many to be a self-evident necessity. Hence, the founding of organizations such as the National Trust in England. The "religion" of nature in an age of secularization led to the naturalist worship of youth, health, and longevity, as well as to a high sensitivity to the various hazards of human life. This sensitivity paved the way for a receptivity to environmental issues in the late twentieth century.

Traditionally, the materials necessary to keep the economy running were not produced in the cities but had to be brought in from other places. Staple food could be satisfied from the nearby countryside, and some rudimentary raw materials were also available. But the more industrialization proceeded in cities the more it became necessary for materials to be brought to the cities from the "far out" land, sometimes even from foreign countries. "Far out" land is an area which is so far away that ordinary city people know it only by name and pay it very scant attention. Historically, the adventurous traders and, later, colonists visited and stayed there.

Between the sixteenth and early twentieth centuries, certain Western countries acquired colonies and built empires. In the "far out" land new colonies were developed and plantations of cotton, rubber, coffee, pepper, and sugar, etc., as well as ranches with cattle, sheep, and other livestock were established. In forests, timber was felled and lumber was exported to make furniture and wooden buildings. Diamonds, gold, silver, copper, iron, tin, coal, and uranium were mined. Colonies produced materials which helped to keep the industries in the home countries running. Affluence in the cities back home was supported by the "far out" land. After World War II, however, the colonies became independent and entered the global scene as developing countries, many of which have their own trichotomy of city, country, and "far out" land.

## DEGRADATION: CITY

In the twentieth century, many people in many countries become comfortable with the trichotonomous notion of city, country, and "far out" land. They happily visited the country and the "far out" land to spend money, but they were not particularly concerned about the conservation of nature. After about mid-century, however, circumstances in many places throughout the world began to deteriorate rapidly, and living conditions were perceived by experts to have entered a serious phase. Some city people became aware of the problems and, in seeking an answer, the ecology movement was born.

As urbanization and industrialization proceeded in the twentieth century, industrial plants were increasingly mechanized and automated, requiring fewer workers. More and more people came to work in the so-called tertiary sector. High-rise office buildings took up more space in the inner cities of metropolitan areas. High land prices in the business districts made it impossible for middle-class people to live in the inner cities, and they made an exodus to the newly developed suburbs. In many cases, people came to rely upon commuter trains to travel to work. In some places, the system became overloaded during commuter hours, with the volume of passengers far exceeding the capacity of the system. In Tokyo, the term "commuter hell" was coined.

In some metropolitan areas, however, commuting by car was a very natural solution, especially where there was a lack of efficient public transport. This in turn brought about the now common problem of metropolitan air pollution caused by automobile exhaust, nitrogen dioxide ($N_2O$). The most serious case can be observed in Los Angeles. An overabundance of carbon dioxide ($CO_2$) has also become a problem. Its sources are many: the passenger automobile; long-haul trucking; power plants burning coal and petroleum to generate electricity for factories and offices equipped with air conditioning and central heating (highly concentrated in metropolitan areas); and incinerators burning plant, office, and home waste. $N_2O$, $CO_2$, and several other elements, in large quantities, are said to lead to global warming, the elevation of the temperature of the earth's atmosphere. It is called the greenhouse phenomenon. That phenomenon, in turn, can lead to a rise in sea level, resulting in the submersion of land in many coastal areas around the world. It can also have serious effects on the earth's ecosystem. To counter this hazard, the Framework Convention on Climate Change, an international treaty, was signed by 155 countries in 1992 at the UNCED in Rio de Janeiro. It has not yet taken effect, however.

Human activity brings about many changes in the ecosystem. As an example, the heat island phenomenon (elevated temperature due to the topography and functions of a city) has long been observed in cities. Another example are the side- and aftereffects of petrochemical products. Industrial civilization has created synthetic materials, such as nylon, plastics, and vinyl chloride, that cannot easily be disposed of either by the natural process of decomposition, or incineration. Streets, sewers, and rivers in metropolises are, consequently, filled with such debris, vinyl chloride presenting a serious hazard to wild life.

In the suburbanization process aforementioned, low-income groups living in the inner city could not follow suit and relocate. Despite well-intentioned assistance from city administrations, slums could not easily be demolished, and poorly funded public services tended to be meager in many places. The whole situation was exacerbated by the loosening of family ties and the disintegration of social cohesion. Eventually, the former "nightless city" became a place for unlawful activities. Drugs, violence, bombings, and other brutal crimes in many metropolises now draw attention to some of the symptoms of serious malfunction in the urban ecosystem.

## DEGRADATION: COUNTRY

The country has also been the scene of dramatic change since

World War II. As Rachel Carson expressed so eloquently in *Silent Spring*, when spring returned in rural America, the birds did not. They had died out. Not only singing birds but also other forms of life such as plankton, worms, insects, amphibians, and fish in the rivers, lakes, and marshes had disappeared.

Before and during World War II, synthetic chemical industries grew rapidly. The battles fought in the South Sea islands hastened the demand for mass production of effective new insecticides, pesticides, and herbicides. After the war, organic chloric chemicals, such as DDT, and organic phosphoric chemicals, such as Parathion, were utilized in large-scale mechanized farming. This was principally accomplished by spraying large quantities of chemicals from aircraft. Elements poisonous to organic life rained down on farmland, woodlands, rivers, lakes, and marshes. These poisons, entering the natural process of the food chain link by link, were killing wild life in large numbers. *Silent Spring* was a real warning.

The poisonous elements entering the food chain not only damage wild life, they also kill human beings. In Japan, there have been very serious cases of poisoning, some of which have led to lawsuits. The most famous cases are the Minamata and Aganogawa cases. Two chemical companies were manufacturing acetaldehyde, utilizing mercury chloride as a catalyst. Waste water containing very small amounts of methyl mercury had been draining away for many years. Progressing along the food chain to fish and shellfish, the methyl mercury was condensed and finally made its way into the human population. Paralysis of the nervous system and loss of coordination with high mortality followed. As a result the use of mercury as a catalyst has been halted. Another well-known case is the so-called ouch-ouch sickness, which occurred in Jintsugawa. For many years waste water containing a small quantity of cadmium drained away from a local zinc and lead mine and it, too, eventually reached the human population. Presence of cadmium in the human body induces very small amounts of calcium to be discharged from the bones, resulting in patients suffering repeated bone fractures. Another symptom was arthralgia, or acute pain of the joints. This pain was unbearable, and the condition came to be known as the "ouch-ouch sickness."[3]

Large-scale mechanized farming depends upon chemical fertilizers. Traditional farming had relied on organic fertilization from compost and other natural elements, but this method became uneconomical after the mass exodus to the city. Soils in mechanized farming tend to be easily eroded and land degradation follows. The alternative sometimes seems either to give up farming or move to new, uncultivated land. As land degradation has proceeded on a large scale, and soil sprayed with poisonous elements has been eroded by rain and floods into the rivers and oceans, the ecosystems of river, lake, marsh, and ocean have undoubtedly been much disturbed, although there is a paucity of data on this.

The country is also influenced by industrial activities in the city. Power plants and factories burn coal and petroleum to operate machines and to generate electricity. The smoke forms ionic sulfuric acid and ionic nitric acid, and is precipitated as acid rain, damaging buildings and monuments in the city. Downwind, acid rain renders lakes and marshes so acidic that they become uninhabitable for fish. Acid rain also falls on "far out" land some three to six hundred miles distance from the source, killing countless trees, sometimes destroying entire forests. The Black Forest is one of the most serious examples of this damage. In order to tackle the problem of acid rain, the Convention on Long-Range Transboundary Air Pollution was signed in 1979 and became effective in 1983. The reduction of sulfuric acid exhaust ($SO_x$) was addressed by the Helsinki Protocol in 1985, and the reduction of nitric acid exhaust ($NO_x$) was addressed by the Sofia Protocol in 1988.

There have been several methods adopted to dispose of industrial and city waste. One is incineration; another is as landfill in coastal areas, and sometimes country dumps are utilized. Poisonous waste must be de-toxified before disposal but sometimes de-toxification is so expensive that poisonous waste is exported to other countries. There have been stories of cargo boats loaded with toxic waste wandering the Atlantic. Recognizing the potential hazards in transporting poisonous waste led many countries to become signatories of the Basel Convention in 1989, which became effective in 1992. The convention controls the international transboundary movement of poisonous waste, its basic tenet being the obligation to dispose of waste in the country of origin.

The accumulative effect of the phenomena described above is that many areas of the country have ceased to be places of relaxation for city people in the late twentieth century.

## DEGRADATION: DEVELOPING COUNTRIES

After World War II, the former colonies became independent and joined the U.N. as member states. Environmental problems began to beset these developing countries.

There were several conditions which initially characterized these new countries. The first was the political situation. Colonies were the result of territorial struggles between the big powers. Colonial boundaries were drawn on maps as a matter of convenience by these powerful countries, irrespective of the group identity of the native people living there. When the colonies gained independence, colonial boundaries became national boundaries. Many of these new national entities adopted Western-type constitutions of democratic government. For a democratic government to work in an orderly fashion, however, a feeling of national identity, national unity, and responsibility for a nation must be shared by politicians. Unfortunately, where the identity of the populace is based on tribal and/or religious unity, these conditions are very difficult, if not impossible, to realize. As a consequence, the period after independence saw the emergence of many autocracies— extravagant corruptions which derived not from national but more often from tribal and/or local definitions of the role of politicians. To redress the perceived injustice of this situation many civil wars— in effect tribal wars—followed. Political discontents often became intertwined in the machinations of the Cold War. Civil wars became surrogate wars. In some cases socialist governments were set up. The collectivization of land led to lower agricultural productivity, less food, and even to famine. Warfare with advanced armaments supplied from outside left behind a debris of weapons, of which land mines are the most dangerous hazard to farming and traffic.[4] It is in this way that the political situation has, on occasion, led to serious environmental degradation.

The second initial condition which characterized these new countries was the economic situation. Before independence and the arrival of industrialization, many colonies had two-sector economies, one sector being the plantation and/or mining economy of a monoculture and the other being the traditional economy of subsistence, including artistic handicraft. After independence, many gifts from industrial civilization were offered. Advanced medical systems were introduced. Antibiotics and other medicines dramatically decreased the mortality rate for babies, infants, and young people of both sexes, resulting in a population explosion. More jobs, more houses, more clothes, and more food became necessary. The economies of the new countries had to grow to feed the populace. The economic growth, which in the developed countries had taken several hundred years, had to take place almost overnight in the newly independent countries.

Unfortunately, the expatriation of former colonials who had managed farms, plantations, and mines led, in some cases, to lower productivity and even shortages of food. Those who could not be supported in their birthplaces flowed into the towns and cities to earn a livelihood. Very rapid urbanization took place, and for urban residents to survive there had to be secondary and tertiary industries in towns and cities. Industrialization became an urgent task, and consequently many environmental troubles were created in connection with urbanization and industrialization in the new countries.

For example, air pollution became a serious problem in the cities of developing countries. Without sufficient public transportation, automobile travel causes chronic traffic problems and air pollution. The case of Bangkok is well known. The pollution of rivers in cities by poisonous effluence is not infrequent. Pumping out subterranean water for industrial use leads to ground subsidence. Insufficient provision of sewerage and sanitation creates public health hazards that can lead to outbreaks of epidemics.

Some developing countries are located in the tropics, where in tropical forest areas a method of shifting cultivation known as slash-and-burn is practiced. As a result of population pressures, untrained groups join in slash-and-burn agriculture. Forests are felled to provide firewood, lumber, farmland, and pasture. Forest land rich in leaf-mold soil can hold water for a long time and prevent landslides, avalanches, and flash floods. As de-forestation proceeds, large-scale floods become more frequent. Moreover, as de-forestation decreases photosynthesis, there is concern about the disappearance of tropical rain forests. There are also arid areas in the tropical zone. These areas face a different problem: desertification caused by overgrazing of livestock. In the mid-1980s, droughts in the arid grasslands of Africa caused more than 30 million people to endure great suffering, and 10 million among them had to migrate. These latter people were known as "environment refugees."

A different type of environmental problem must also be noted here. Tropical "far out" land was for centuries a place for trophy hunts. Exotic fauna and flora were brought home to decorate the castles and mansions of the developed world. The tradition has continued, despite efforts to curtail it. People at both ends of the trade still unlawfully traffic in rare plants and animals. To prevent indiscriminate hunting and eventual extermination, the Convention on International Trade in Endangered Species of Wild Fauna and Flora (CITES), known as the Washington Convention, became effective in 1975.

## THE POLITICS OF INTERNATIONAL REGULATION

In the early twentieth century, conservation of nature was regarded not as a global but a local activity, limited to city and country areas within one national territory. However, advancement and global dissemination of industrial civilization caused not only the globalization of environmental problems already present in developed countries but also fostered new kinds of environmental problem such as global warming, which could affect the sea level. Another is acid rain, also described above.

Excessive amounts of chlorofluorocarbon (CFC) are damaging the ozone ($O_3$) layer. Recent reports on the destruction of the ozone layer in the stratosphere and the creation of a hole in it high above Antarctica have received a great deal of attention. The ozone layer absorbs the ultraviolet rays in sunlight and prevents health hazards such as skin cancer and cataracts, which can be caused by excessive exposure to ultraviolet rays. Ultraviolet rays also kill plankton in shallow water, and disturb the food chain and the ocean's ecosystem. In order to protect the ozone layer, the Vienna Convention and the Montreal Protocol were adopted in 1985 and 1987, respectively, to regulate the production and consumption of CFC.

Ocean pollution is another new problem. Poisonous waste is dumped into the sea, and pesticides, insecticides, and herbicides settle on the ocean's bottom. Floating plastics, vinyl products, and oil slicks are hazards to marine birds and animals. More serious than these are the cases of mammoth tankers shipwrecked or run aground. In response to this threat, the London Convention (effective since 1975) controls dumping in the ocean. The Marpol 73/78 Convention (adopted in 1978) regulates pollution caused by seagoing ships. In addition, the aforementioned Basel Convention regulates the hauling of toxic industrial waste by cargo boat across vast stretches of sea.

Global problems have to be dealt with through international cooperation. There have been many U.N. conferences organized, U.N. declarations issued, and conventions and protocols signed and ratified in addition to numerous other small programs and working U.N. organizations. There are also regional and bilateral agreements, such as the Bilateral Agreements on Migratory Birds. Of course, the biggest example of international cooperation is the Rio de Janeiro U.N. Conference and the Rio Declaration on Environment and Development of 1992, which reveals, in its twenty-seven principles, the complex situation which makes up the contemporary global environmental situation.

When the National Trust for Places of Historical Interest or Natural Beauty was founded in 1895, the procedure was relatively simple. Some comparisons across a century are useful. The purposes of the ecological movements then and now are not much different in a sense. Both want to conserve something. The National Trust wanted to conserve "places," while the present movement seeks to conserve not "places" but industrial civilization itself. To be conserved, "places" must be maintained in their original condition. In the case of a civilization, conservation means that some activities must be either stopped, changed, or eliminated and must be paid for.

Conservation of "places" involves either buying, receiving through donation, or acquiring ownership as a matter of property right in civil law; other parties are not usually involved. In contemporary cases, potential environmental problems often come to light when scientists or other experts issue warnings. Conventions are often signed and ratified after specialist international conferences have been held for several years. Declarations are made, and international regulations begin to be applied through the legal cooperation of the governments involved. Effective national regulation in countries which ratify the convention is vital. Although the participation of all national governments is often desirable, some governments, for domestic reasons, may be unwilling to join, while other governments may be unable to enforce compliance by their citizens.

In the case of the National Trust, the initiative to conserve places comes either from the National Trust itself or from individuals who want to assign their property during their lifetime or on death. The change of ownership is easily supported and welcomed by the public, since historical interest and natural beauty are criteria based on traditional moral and aesthetic sensibilities. But in contemporary civilization, if some activities need to be stopped, changed, or eliminated, an accommodation of conflicting interests becomes necessary in many cases, since individuals, families, communities, labor unions, companies, industrial organizations, pressure groups, bureaus and departments of government, the military, politicians, political parties, and even a unified national interest can be aroused. Very often compromises such as postponement, a reduction in quantity, or the payment of compensation have to be made.

International regulation of environmental degradation not infrequently is unable to avoid the issue of developed versus developing countries. Sometimes cost, damage, and loss caused by degradation are not equitably shared, while the national interests of developing and developed countries can be basically different and not easily reconciled. The Rio Declaration contains principles of diplomatic compromise. First, Principle 2 confirms national sovereignty and states as follows: States have, in accordance with the Charter of United Nations and the principles of international law, "the sovereign right to exploit their own resources," pursuant to their own environmental and developmental policies, and the responsibility to ensure that activities within their jurisdiction or control do not cause damage to the environment of other states or of areas beyond the limits of national jurisdiction. Principle 7 refers to differentiated responsibilities: States shall cooperate in a spirit of global partnership to conserve, protect, and restore the health and integrity of the Earth's ecosystem. In view of the different contributions to global environmental degradation, "states have common but differentiated responsibilities." The developed countries acknowledge the responsibility that they bear in the international pursuit of sustainable development in view of the pressures their societies place on the global environment and of the technologies and financial resources they command.

There is another point on which developmental national interests differ. Developed countries, well equipped with the fruits of modern industrial civilization, consume far more resources than developing countries. Several generations from now, when the developing countries have caught up and consume in equal proportion to the developed countries, there is the possibility that resources will be exhausted, leaving very little for future generations. This possibility should make it clear that equity between and among generations, in terms of development and consumption of resources, is vitally important. This anxiety is shared by many. Principle 1 reads: Human beings are at the center of concerns for sus-

tainable development. They are entitled to a healthy and productive life in harmony with nature. Principle 3 states: The right to
development must be fulfilled so as to equitably meet the developmental and environmental needs of present and future generations. No one can predict the needs of future, unborn generations,
let alone the changing needs of the present generation. Predicting
the future of a civilization is beyond the ability of humans. The
concept of sustainable development appears often in discourses on
the environment. It is the morally exhortative expression "Do not
waste. Think of Posterity." in disguise and recalls the traditional
value system that was effective before the advent of mass consumption.

## THE POLITICAL PROCESS
## OF ENVIRONMENTAL REGULATION

If present society hopes to eradicate environmental degradation,
the necessary steps must be supported by the populace. But the reasons why certain steps are necessary are not always easily understood. In contemporary society, in every activity there is a basic
dichotomy—specialists on the one hand and laymen on the other.
In the mouths of professionals, explanations can become very esoteric, foggy, and beyond the comprehension of laymen. What laymen can digest is, very often, a simple message that human health
and life are in danger and that the necessary steps, proposed by
ecologists, to alleviate the problem should be followed obediently
by them. Warnings verging on menace and desperation work well
in times of imminent danger and emergency. But in ordinary daily
life they do not work effectively. Common people are not scared so
easily. Finding no followers, the voice of the anxious, concerned
expert is, sometimes, like a voice in the wilderness.

An additional problem for the ecologists is the scarcity of data
on the environment. Data collected covers a rather short period of
time, a century or two at the most. Very often we do not have con-
clusive, scientifically verified evidence and have to depend usually
upon extrapolations based on very meager data. Environmental
problems are ambiguous and, in ambiguous situations, as is well
known, some people maintain their equanimity very naturally
while others lose their emotional stability, become anxious, and, to
relieve their anxiety, hyperactive. So you have in many movements,
past and present, quite a few vanguards, zealots, and true believers
(Eric Hoffer)—the people of authoritarian personality. Provided

with charismatic leadership they come to believe that they have acquired the "sacred, final truth." In addition always you have the indifferent, unconcerned people. As the history of Nazism shows, a group of true believers can subjugate the indifferent and enforce an ideocratic autocracy on them. Thus, while an ecology movement can serve as an outlet for the anxiety generated in an ambiguous situation inherent in "environmental" problems, it can be an outlet for the energy of politically hyperactive people.

The sacred, final truth can also be provided by a system of culture to which one has a feeling of belonging. The system of culture imprints and transmits common habits of sense, emotion, and intellect, that is, common habits of perception, evaluation, and selection through language. Since these habits are shared by other members of the same culture, they do not need constantly to be explained. Here, in ordinary daily life, we have the sacred, final truth, if somewhat inarticulate, which can be the basis of any type of group-centrism. One example: "All animals are equal. But some animals are more equal than others." In *Animal Farm* by George Orwell, the pigs got more equal. But which animals are to be more equal? It depends on the culture. In many cultures different animals are more equal. In some cultures the selection is literally the sacred, final truth.

Both a system of culture and the plurality of systems of culture are parts of the human environment, being man-processed nature. The experiences of World War II, Nazism, and communist despotism exposed a new environmental issue on a different level. Systems of culture produced true-believers in the sacred, final truths, who manufactured tremendous hazards to human health and life. After World War II there emerged the issue of the multiplicity of cultures. This issue came to be related to the problem of racism and feminism. But it is also related to the separation of Western Christian culture, which is local and not global, from industrial-technological civilization, which certainly originated in Western Europe and America but is now globalized and appears to be even universal. The process of global dissemination of industrial-technological civilization was accompanied by the export of a system of formal institutions. Such political institutions as a written constitution, popular election, presidency, parliament, and cabinet, and also such economic institutions as banks, currency, stock companies, and stock exchanges were exported. But it did not mean the global dissemination of Western Christian culture and its value system. In fact, the separation of Western Christian culture from industrial-technological civilization—a basic tendency from the beginning of the twentieth century—has become more and more apparent. An illustrative example is the warfare in and between Islamic countries. The weapon systems developed by industrial civilization are operated very effectively by Muslim soldiers.

Everywhere a traditional system of culture is the central component of personal identity. Many people tend to believe that every aspect of their perception, evaluation, and selection is universally valid and a manifestation of the sacred, final truth. In order to be able to accept the plurality of systems of culture and approve the relativity of cultures, you have to be gifted with very strong intellect and willpower. It seems to be very difficult, especially for citizens of Western developed countries, to admit the relativity of their own Western Christian culture, since the global dissemination of industrial-technological civilization seems to confirm the universal sharing of Western Christian culture. In such a situation, difficulty arises when one particular preference, derived from a traditional, particular culture and charged with the emotional intensity of true believers, is produced as a manifestation of the sacred, final truth. Quite naturally, other people of different cultures do not give their consent. There are two possible ways out of the situation. One is to accept the negative response of other people as a matter of fact, withdraw the pretense of universal validity, and adopt the path of coexistence between multiple cultures with courteous tolerance. The other is to adopt the path of cultural imperialism and subjugate other people of different cultures by force.

In the late twentieth century, industrial civilization has so developed that everywhere, from stratosphere to Himalayas to ocean bed, there is almost no nature left intact. We have also found many hazards to human health and life caused by industrial civilization itself. Since human beings seek a high quality of life and to avoid these hazards, what is needed is enlightened and organized self-control. Since human nature, as it is, is subject to original sin or radical evil, enlightened and organized self-control is only possible by effective regulation, control, and coercion through the offices of political and legal institutions.

The politics of environmental issues, as a drama, have three groups of actors on the stage. The first, the proposal group, is composed of three types of people. The first type consists of researchers and experts who propose new regulations and control on the basis of scientific findings; the second is the concerned true-believers who, as the cadre of activist groups, loyally and enthusiastically support the new regulation, while the third is the mass media which, as an auxiliary corps, helps promulgate the great cause of new regulation. The second group, the procedure group, is also composed of three types of people: the politicians who are the specialists of negotiation and compromise; the bureaucrats, who man the government agencies and execute the new regulations; and the business executives, whose companies might be regulated and controlled anew. The third group comprises the indifferent, unconcerned general public, who can be aroused by propaganda activities.

The scenarios of the environmental issue drama do not vary much. The first is the common, ordinary type. A new regulation, proposed by an ecology group and supported by the mass media, is taken up by politicians and goes through the regular political process of "negotiation and compromise," involving government agencies and business groups. Finally a new regulatory law is enacted, sooner or later.

In the case of international regulation, there is an international community of researchers and experts who share a common culture of science and technology. There is also an international community of bureaucrats, who man the environmental agencies in each country and share to some degree a common understanding. So with due respect to differing national interests, it is not very difficult to arrive at an international convention. The difficulty, more often than not, lies in the ratification process in each country.

The second type is the "direct action" scenario. Proposals by activist groups are rejected by government and politicians on the grounds of national security and/or national survival. Examples of such proposals are not few: abandonment of thermonuclear weapons; cessation of activities such as the testing of thermonuclear bombs, the processing of low-level plutonium to refuel nuclear power plants, the opening of nuclear power plants, etc. If the activist group, being a small minority, cannot organize adequate popular political support, it has to choose between abandoning its activity or taking some kind of "direct action," such as picketing.

The third type is a scenario of internationalization. A group of ecologists in a country conceives a new international regulation, which is to be applied mainly to peoples of other countries. The legitimacy of the regulation is well supported by the culture traditionally obtaining in their country. The group arouses their general public and, through the pressure of the popular vote, induces the politicians to support the new regulation. The political leaders of the country organize an international conference and, with the help of international political pressure behind the scenes, conclude a new convention embodying the new regulation. An example is the prohibition against whaling enacted through an international organization (IWC). Incidentally, for many American people the legitimacy of prohibition was self-evident, since it was rationalized in terms of Western Christian culture, but to many treaty-abiding Japanese people, who do not share Western Christian culture, the selection of the whale as an animal "more equal than others" did not appear persuasive—a case of the multiplicity of systems of culture.

## POSTSCRIPT

In the late nineteenth century the idea of the "conservation of nature" became accepted, while in the twentieth century the institution of national parks was internationally endorsed. Areas of natural scenic beauty were categorized as national parks throughout the world. Many tourists visit these parks in various countries to see and spend time in the midst of nature. This is an example of the concept of man and man-conserved nature. In the mid-twentieth century experts and citizens in developed countries were alerted to the danger of the side- and aftereffects of industrial civilization. The environmental issue was politicized nationally and internationally, sometimes to the point of fanaticism. Human beings had been exposed to the evils which they themselves had manufactured, an example of man in man-polluted nature. There is also a third concept: nature in man. There are many ways to improve the functioning of human organs. The first is to rely upon artefacts, such as false teeth, spectacles, contact lenses, hearing aids, walking sticks, and wheelchairs, etc. The second is medication. The third is surgery, such as the implant of metal joints or organ transplants. Currently, there are reports of genetic engineering, which could have effects on future generations. Quite apart from the functioning of the human organs, in the realm of the human senses, the emotions, and the intellect, we have the grave problem of the plurality of systems of culture, which have produced serious hazards to human health and life. Thus we have examples of the concept of man-processed nature in man. The twentieth century has added several new aspects to the age-old concept of nature.

# Notes

[1] I am very much indebted to Keith Thomas's book *Man and the Natural World: Changing Attitudes in England, 1500–1800*, published in 1983 (now in Penguin Books). I particularly appreciate the basic framework of his town and county contrast, as well as his detailed exposition of changing ideas and attitudes. In addition, the *Dictionary For Global Environment* (Japanese version), produced by the Global Environment Department of the Environment Agency, is a very useful handbook.

[2] The human being has developed, as an expression of an innate, biologically endowed, gene-controlled capacity, various "local" systems of language and culture. A traditional local system of language and culture controls the habits of sense, emotion, and intellect, that is, habits of perception, evaluation, and selection of its members. And the multiplicity of systems of language and culture, which is a part of man-processed nature in man, is one of the confounding elements of the environment's problems. But it also seems to be one of the guarantees of the survival of human beings as a species.

[3] A digression: In laboratories, scientists try to establish causal relationships identifying one element as a cause and another element as the effect. This one to one correspondence can only be identified by keeping other conditions equal. From the scientific findings of laboratories, entrepreneurs turn out marketable industrial products. The negative side- and aftereffects of mass use are not usually well studied; by definition, they are outside the scope of the original laboratory research. New experiments and surveys in the field are very often regarded as unnecessary expenditure by the entrepreneurs who often view negative effects as rare and negligible.

[4] According to a U.N. report, 100 million live land mines are left buried and unmarked throughout the world. (*International Herald Tribune*, November 4, 1993.)

# COMMENT ON
# THE KYOGOKU PAPER

UMESAO Tadao

Although I am by profession an ethnologist, I initially started my studies in biology, particularly in the field of ecology. It is from my background as a student of ecology that I should like to make my comments on Kyogoku's presentation.

Man's recognition of nature on the surface of the globe developed and advanced greatly in the twentieth century. Geographical characteristics of the earth, such as continents and oceans, mountain regions and plains, had been discovered and mapped out by the nineteenth century. By the end of the same century, understanding of the state of vegetation covering the face of the earth was also quite comprehensive. *Cosmos,* a great work by Alexander von Humboldt, illustrates the extent of understanding of the time. But the dynamic relations among plants that exist in a range of vegetation were still ambiguous. It was in the 1920s that the development of the field of ecology gave leverage to finding the answer.

The study of ecology, in the context of morphology and auto-ecology, had already begun in Europe in the nineteenth century, but the relationship between plant communities in the botanical realm and its dynamism came to light in the continent of North America in the twentieth century. The forests and the pampas of the American continent provided ample data to form the basis of those discoveries.

The most important idea of this new discipline is the one called "succession." This is a concept designed to explain the rules of the life cycle of vegetation. This idea led to the discovery of the fact that a mature state of vegetation peculiar to the land existed. The term for the last stage of succession is "climax." Since climate is the decisive factor in the course of succession, it is also called "climatic climax." Topographical classifications of the surface of the earth soon appeared in accordance with climatic climaxes. This naturally coincides with the distribution of climate types. (The discovery of all the climate types that exist on the earth was also one of the major events in the twentieth-century quest for knowledge.) The most famous map of global climate types was created by Professor Wladimir Köppen. This became the basis on which we now define the global ecological map. In other words, global ecological distribution became clear only in the twentieth century.

Nevertheless, the concept of climatic climax proposes that a peculiar state of vegetation will flourish only if one leaves a plot of land alone for a long period of time. Yet in reality the demographic explosion that occurred at the beginning of this century destroyed inherent characteristics of land in vast proportions. This caused the natural environment to undergo an exceptional change, a process that is still going on.

We cannot underestimate, however, the resilience of nature. This power is so strong that man has yet to achieve the ability to change the climate. There are people of the opinion that various human attempts to change nature might in effect result in the total destruction of the environment, a catastrophe that might happen at any moment. I am against this idea. The natural environment is basically stable. And presently there is no reliable evidence of any qualitative change.

Desertification is often cited as an example of the destruction of nature. I am aware of many reports about desertification progressing in Africa, Central Asia, and in many regions of the world. But in reality, this is not true. There are, indeed, certain areas of the globe—for example, steppe lands—that have suffered from some degradation due to excessive overgrazing. But this does not mean that desert lands are expanding. There are examples of dunes moving among the peripheries of arid zones. People often confuse dunes with deserts. Dunes do shift places, but they are not extensions of deserts. Television programs sometimes depict domestic animals dying in the midst of a desert storm in order to illustrate the expansion of desert lands. It is very easy to produce such film artificially. Deserts are based on an equilibrium of the earth's waters and solar energy, and so do not easily change their geographical positions. Desertification does not occur simply because of some sheep grazing on the land. I rather think that the concerns expressed about the crisis of desertification are due to some political or diplomatic consideration. The climate of the earth has not basically changed since the Ice Age.

There is much talk about the changes taking place in the global environment, the rising levels of carbon dioxide and its effect in global warming, the freon gases destroying the ozone layer, etc. There might be a few issues here that are really serious and true, but I think the majority are merely suppositions and speculative concerns. I say this because there is a crucial lack of reliable data. The data may be exact; they may be false. Likhachev mentioned in his comments that half of what the Communists say might be true, the other half might be untrue. The same thing can be said for most of the concerns about the degradation of the global environment: half may be true, half may be false. At any rate, we are not at a stage where we can make a decisive comment about this matter.

Nevertheless, there is a possibility of such a crisis becoming a reality, and this uncertainty has provided fertile ground for anxiety. Thus, the so-called ecological movement urging people to "repent" has emerged. Being a student of ecology, I have been surprised to find the term "ecology" manipulated so that it ultimately has become a slogan for such a movement. Conservation movements of this sort may have a glimmer of truth in them, and yet they may simply be means of political agitation. At this stage, however, it is next to impossible to silence the global chorus in favor of the movement.

The ecology movement and other conservation movements are in theory very easy to understand and are even persuasive. In that sense, these movements and communism that emerged at the beginning of this century have much in common. Indeed, in Japan, just as in many other countries of the world, the ecological movement has developed as a successor to communism. I have a friend, a plant ecologist whose name is Dr. Sasuke Nakao. One of Dr. Nakao's works, entitled *Principles of Classification*, deals with various modes of taxonomy. He attempts to classify the religions of the world according to diverse characteristics, pseudo-scientific religions being one of them. Communism is the first item classified under this heading. This illustrates the fact that he has no qualms about identifying communism as a religion. He regards it as a type of pseudo-social science. The second item under the heading of pseudo-scientific religions is the ecology movement. Dr. Nakao defines this movement as pseudo-natural science and perceives it as a successor to communism, a fanatical movement that frequently incorporates violence. I cannot make judgment on whether this perception is right or not, but would like to present it to you as one among many other possible perceptions.

# Discussion

**Murakami:** If my understanding is correct, "civilization" as an English word appeared in the early eighteenth century, reflecting a solid ideology, I think, to separate human beings clearly from nature; to civilize people at least partly implied, and still implies, negation of the dependence of man on nature. That means the separation of man from nature. Man's dependence on nature became a sign of anti-civilization. The phrase "uncivilized people" implies people who depend fully on nature. Consequently, the modern world view of nature stemmed directly from the ideology of civilization, where human beings were to be separated from and become independent of nature. And that ideology allowed human beings to exploit, dominate, and conquer nature.

**Kosai:** Kyogoku and Umesao tend to regard the ecology movement as a political movement, based on insufficient data or half-lies. It may be true. But I think the acid rain in the United States and Canada, and in the northern part of Europe, is an established fact. The smog in Tokyo, Osaka, and London is a clear fact. The Edogawa, the Sumidagawa, and the Thames are cleaner today than half a century ago. So I think the environmental movement or the ecology movement has some sound basis which should be incorporated in our democratic society. We cannot wait another million years to have sufficient data; we must decide today. This is a problem of rational choice.

**Gasteyger:** I, too, was rather surprised to hear Umesao compare the ecology movement with that of communism. I think those of us around this table would agree that we are really talking about two very different movements, however politicized some of the ecologists may be. Kyogoku's presentation shows us quantitative changes that to some extent are measurable, and here I agree with Kosai that quantitative changes are likely also to have qualitative effects. One does not need to be an alarmist to consider oneself an ecologist. I consider myself an ecologist, but I have never considered myself a follower of communism. I think it is dangerous if we have this kind of comparison between the two. The problem obviously is the one which Kosai has raised, namely, that of rational choice: On what kind of basis can we make this rational choice? There are a number of data where, in fact, one does not know for certain how established they are. That is, for instance, the case with climatic change. There are various views that have good points and not so convincing points. The death of the forest, which was eight years ago one of the major subjects in Europe, today does not seem to be a major concern. On the other hand, there are some facts and figures that are relatively well established, and to some extent even predictable, such as demographic growth and water resources.

We have—and this is certainly true for the United States, Canada, and for practically all West European countries, though I do not know whether it is true also for Japan—a clear polarization between ecologists and what I call developers. Today no West European politician would dare not to be concerned about environmental issues, and the electorate, certainly in Western Europe, is at least partly concerned about ecology.

**Nivat:** There was no preoccupation with ecology in the cult of industrialization in communist countries. In a way there was a sort of ecological disaster in those countries because of overindustrialization, but nowhere have the living conditions of workers been given less attention than in some Siberian factories, for example. Ecological preoccupation has played a role, not in the crumbling of communism, but in the weakening of communism. In the 1970s, when the industrial establishments formulated the famous plan to reverse the course of all the Siberian rivers, there began a movement, headed by writers and people like Valentine Rasputin from Irkutsk, warning against the destruction caused by climatic change. There was some sort of Christian philosophy saying that, maybe in a more orthodox way than Western Christianity, some sort of respect and veneration for creatures in God's House is being totally lost.

**Gold:** It was noted that the nature is resilient and that the world is resilient, and that may be true. But specific biological systems are less resilient, and certainly a concern among many biological scientists has to do with the impact of toxicological pollution on the viability of the survival of many species, including humans. For instance, a piece of data that is disturbing to me is the fact that the sperm count in humans has fallen 50 percent in twenty years. That is quite clearly documented, although whether it is toxicological or from other sources is unclear, and whether that trend will continue is unclear. The rates of malignancy are rising: the more we learn about DNA, the more fragile we find it is in the face especially of certain novel chemicals that the organism has not evolved to confront in the past. I think these points have to be raised, because biological species are really quite fragile.

**Junker:** At this conference one of the main themes, of course, is the limits of the nation-state. I cannot emphasize too much that the nation-state is too limited to handle the question of the environment. Just to give you one very ironic example, Brazil as a nation-state has found out that it has a very new weapon in its foreign policy. The interest of mankind in the survival of the Amazon's forests has resulted in Brazil deliberately trying to attract funds from the outside using the survival of the Amazon as a lever. This credit will be used for further industrialization.

**Nakamura:** Technology, in particular so-called high technology, has the power to change the world for good or ill more profoundly and more quickly than ever before, I think. If we wish to change our world for the better in the next century, it is essential to utilize high technology effectively, instead of rejecting it. I would like to point out that we should reconsider the nature of technology and our attitude to it. First, we should treat science and technology as the flowering of human creativeness, not like a fact beyond our control. If we fail to retain control, technologies could trigger a chain of biological destruction.

Second, we should reconsider our value system underlying science and technology. Science was derived from the value system of Europe designed to reveal universality in nature. However, since science itself has made clear recently that diversity is an important aspect of nature as well as universality, we need to develop a science and technology based on not only universality but also diversity.

If we try to control science and technology under the new value system, we can use it to solve our present problems and prevent disasters in the future. For instance, the technology of genetics can contribute to conserving plants and animals in the rain forests. They could help us transform the economics of developing countries and create a new world order. For those purposes, it is necessary that particularly the leaders in politics, economics, philosophy, religion, and so on in the world, should be much more familiar with science and technology.

**Likhachev:** The word "ecology" is used like an ambulance these days. It is like a medicine, a good dose of medicine for the world. Ecology, however, should be established on a certain philosophy of nature, a view of nature. One significant book is by Lossky called the *World as an Organic Whole,* published in 1916. According to this book, the world was created by somebody, probably by God, in a variety of interlinkages, and nobody can destroy that interlinkage.

By paying attention to this linkage, we can consider the goal of the linkage or the grand design of God. The way the world is made is so that humans can exist on the face of the earth. All biological and material entities and the entire cosmos itself exist in the context of this linkage; all plants in the world and man are destined to be born and be able to live in this network of linkages.

However, not all things on this earth are perfect and good. Even among humans, there are factors of incompleteness or of evil nature. I will not refer to the details of this negative aspect. What I would like to emphasize here is that the ecology of science, or ecology as an ambulance, should be rooted in a certain philosophical view. Revisions should be limited to rare and minor occasions. Only when nature fails to realize itself completely do we need to make the slightest possible revisions. The world as an organic whole needs to be preserved, conserved, and human assistance to nature as an act of conscious interference, intervention in nature, has to be carefully examined.

Let me add one thing. One very special feature of *homo sapiens* is that we can speak. Therefore, it is the obligation of humans not only to protect individual obligations, rights, and interests, but also to respect and preserve the rights and interests of nature. Animals have rights, plants have rights, fish have rights, and insects have rights. Mountains, forests, and natural scenery have rights that need to be conserved and protected. In my view, all existences have not only a moral but legal right for being what they are.

**Stern:** I found the comparison between the ecological movement and communism deeply deeply disturbing. I do not know whether it is more shocking to see in it the trivialization of communism or the demonization of the ecological movement. I would also say that we do not need a philosophy of nature to fear a repeat of Chernobyl or to understand the relation of pollution to disease. It is perfectly true that ecologists may exaggerate, but it seems to me that the exaggeration can be corrected, and that what at bottom most of them—or many of them who are not ideologists but pragmatists—are trying to do is to protect us from ourselves or from our past.

**Murakami:** The paucity of data does not enable us to say anything decisive, but only to suggest possibilities. This means that by the time enough data is available it might be too late to prevent disastrous results, which might possibly be anticipated on the basis of the little data available right now.

**Junker:** Men of all colors, races, classes are using up resources. This, of course, is our basic problem, and within it comes one of the fundamental ironies. We all know that only after development demographic increases slow down. But in order to achieve that, you have to use up resources. So one of the most urgent practical things is to stop this demographic explosion. If we do not do that, all other efforts are of no use.

**Ueno:** Pollution takes place usually at the local level. And there is a party responsible for causing that disaster. Take Minamata: When pollution occurred there, environmental degradation reached a level where the environment cannot be restored for succeeding generations. If we have to wait until sufficient data is available, it will always be too late. As Kosai said, we have to make a rational decision for the responsibility for such actions. For example, the Japanese government's regulations on pollution removed responsibility for a disaster from the victims to those who had caused it. Instead of the victims having to prove the cause of the pollution, the onus was on the accused party to disprove their guilt by providing sufficient data.

**Gold:** I am a bit surprised, in a conference on the twentieth century, that one of the elements on the human landscape and human ecology has not surfaced at all once in three days. And that is that we are in the midst of a global epidemic of AIDS, a disease which is unprecedented in modern history, that threatens to wipe out entire continents for the first time even in the developed nations and threatens people of all walks of life. It is the leading cause of death in individuals under thirty, and for those of us lucky enough to be prosperous, still for the first time in several generations we must face the contingency of the vulnerability and potential death even of our children.

I do not think there is any data to suggest that this illness has emerged as a result of the scourges of modern civilization—technology and toxic pollution—although people have made such suggestions. But it is a debate, I suppose, that raises questions about freedom of migration. If a cure to this illness is not discovered, and if it keeps proliferating, it will change the human landscape in the twenty-first century.

**Kyogoku:** We cannot wait until the end of human existence to collect all data in order to make a proper judgment in the field of political science as well as human life. We have to make decisions with insufficient data. I think it is human destiny.

When we make decisions without waiting for the data, various problems arise. But through negotiation and compromise, mankind has been muddling through with varying degrees of success. In my paper, I quote Principle 2 of the Rio Declaration where various sovereign states maintain that they have right to exploit their own resources. That was a result of negotiation and compromise, from the standpoint of issue groups. On whaling, Japan and the United States can negotiate through diplomatic channels, and if limitations or bans are introduced, it is a case of the success of diplomatic negotiation and compromise. Principle 1 of the Rio Declaration states, "human beings are at the center of the concerns for sustainable development." Now "sustainable development" is at the core of the ambiguity. Can we develop in a sustainable way? We can talk about it in terms of language, that it is just words, but language can change the world.

**Umesao:** I am an ecologist in the true original sense of word "ecology." To me, there are too many things in this sphere beyond our comprehension regarding the environment. That is why we need to make decisions on various fronts. In many areas we have learned a great deal and already many findings and discoveries have been made. But yet there is so much that we do not understand. I hope that science in these fields will advance much faster. All the environmental destruction and degradation has basically come from the very explosive increases of population on the earth. The growth has been so fast that anything could happen and is the source of so many troubles and difficulties for us.

# TOWARD
# A NEW
# ANTHROPOLOGY

# MEN AND WOMEN: BOREDOM, VIOLENCE, AND POLITICAL POWER—PROSPECTS FOR THE TWENTY-FIRST CENTURY

Linda K. KERBER

My title comes from a lecture prepared by the distinguished American lawyer and civil rights activist Dorothy Kenyon, written in 1971, the last year of her long life. So far as I can tell, the speech has never been published or even quoted in print.[1] She knew she was passing a baton to a younger generation, and she wanted to say something meaningful about relations between the sexes—as they were, and as she hoped they would become. The themes she chose epitomize the central contested sites of gender relations in her own time, themes which—like much of her career, seemed idiosyncratic at the time—resonate in the present moment as central subjects of feminist discourse. Kenyon's words and her work link the problems of sex relations across the long twentieth century, offering a ground on which we can stand as we squint into the future.

Dorothy Kenyon was born in 1888 and graduated from college twenty years later. Late in her twenties she entered New York University Law School, one of the few major law schools that welcomed women, and was admitted to the New York Bar in 1917. Entering the profession as the United States entered World War I, one of her first jobs involved research for the 1919 peace conference. For the rest of her life social justice at home and internationally would absorb her energies. When the League of Nations established a Committee for the Study of the Legal Status of Women in 1937, Dorothy Kenyon was the American member of the group of seven jurists who comprised it. The committee struggled to do its work even after the outbreak of war. It was reconstituted after the war as the United Nations Commission on the Status of Women; Kenyon served as the U.S. delegate from 1946 to 1950.[2] As she conducted her own private legal practice, she also maintained her concern for women's condition internationally. She kept up a vigorous career as an advocate for civil liberties and for a broad interpretation of the implications of the Fourteenth Amendment's "equal treatment" provisions as they concerned women. At the end of her life she initiated ACLU discussion of abortion rights for women. Ruth Bader Ginsberg, who was recently appointed to the United States Supreme Court, built upon Kenyon's work and is in some ways her direct intellectual successor. The clues Kenyon left in her unpublished papers encourage us to study continuities in relations between men and women across the twentieth century. They remind us that our generation is not the first to understand that relations between men and women are socially constructed.

In her 1971 speech, Kenyon referred to "boredom." She meant the emotional state men often displayed when the subject of *women* was raised, the assumption that "the woman question" is tediously devoid of interest or trivial and frivolous. Kenyon interpreted that boredom and frivolity as "a shield, a protection of some sort," a strategy which gave men permission to ignore intractable problems. By "violence" she meant to convey that unequal relations between the sexes are invisibly sustained by the fear of the violence men are capable of exhibiting if they did not have their way, just as hierarchical race relations are also sustained by a violent subtext.[3] And, finally, Kenyon was convinced that change for the better in relations between men and women was a political matter. She wrote just before the Supreme Court, for the first time in its history, declared discrimination on the basis of sex an example of unequal protection of the laws, but lower-court decisions were already pointing in that direction. Kenyon had worked throughout her life in expansive political movements which sought to develop equal, rather than unequal, relations between men and women, not only in the United States but throughout the world. The implications of these themes—boredom, violence, political power—still resonate for us.

***

The League of Nations was founded at a moment not unlike our own. It was founded at a time of enormous optimism about the prospects for a revitalized and peaceable international order in which the quality of life for all people, all over the globe, would improve and flourish. It was founded at a time of a strong feminist presence on the international scene; indeed the word "feminist" had only recently been coined in English. In the United States and in the United Kingdom, women had at last won the right to vote; in the Soviet Union, women were members of the Executive Committee of the Bolshevik Party and their role in the state and party was asserted to be central. An energetic international movement to make birth control information and technology available flourished. It was increasingly recognized that in all cultures women were less likely to be literate than men, have less access to health care than men, be more vulnerable than men to sexual exploitation and to oppressive working conditions. It was increasingly recognized that relations between men and women, even men and women of the same families, were usually hierarchical, were rarely authentically reciprocal. These generalizations remain accurate descriptions of contemporary life.

Women's issues were implicit in the agendas for the League's work and for the committees that sustained that work in Geneva. It was generally assumed that women's problems would be included in more general headings: "Welfare," "Diseases," "Refugees," "Slavery," "Nutrition." As improvements were made in these areas it was thought that women, like men, would necessarily benefit. But even so, the League added other categories. Early in its existence, the League sponsored an International Conference on Traffic in Women and Children (Geneva, June 30–July 5, 1921) and, taking the advice of the conference, established in 1922 an Advisory Committee on the Traffic in Women and Children. In 1936 this committee was, along with the Child Welfare Committee, merged into the Advisory Committee on Social Questions. The League's Legal Section early marked the problems of the legal status of women under international law as difficult ones. For example, in places where women derived citizenship from their husbands' status they were particularly vulnerable to statelessness. Toward the end of its life, the League established a Committee for the Study of the Legal Status of Women (September 30, 1937). This committee—on which Kenyon served—struggled to do its work even after the outbreak of war. The committee provided, in turn, the basic foundation for the United Nations Commission on the Status of Women, which has continued into the present, emphasizing the codification of international law relating to women and expressing a concern for improving women's status in an international context. The "Scheme of Work" devised by the League Committee for the Study of the Legal Status of Women does not seem outdated.[4]

The United Nations continued this commitment by developing its World Conferences on Women, which have met every fifth year, and by establishing the United Nations Convention on the Elimination of All Forms of Discrimination Against Women (CEDAW). CEDAW was opened for signature and ratification in 1979.[5]

When I examine the agenda of the men and women who, like Kenyon, sought in the 1920s and thereafter to assess the relations between men and women and to change those relations in the direction of increased equity, equality, and reciprocity, I find myself somewhat less impressed by progress and more impressed by the extent to which the agenda which we face is similar to the agenda that was outlined nearly a century ago. To inspect the work of the League of Nations on relations between men and women is to be humbled by the recognition that many of the most intractable problems we face are not new problems. The League reports, the early U.N. reports, and the reports of the U.N. International Conference on Human Rights in Vienna last spring are congruent documents.

When the League and the U.N. gather information on the status of women they are in fact measuring *relations* between men and women. The allocation of social resources that establishes status is an expression of power relations. For example, early in the twentieth century, the League undertook the first substantial systematic investigation of the international dimensions of the "traffic in women."[6] In our own time, the collapse of the Soviet Union and the Warsaw Pact has resulted in aggressive "trade" in vulnerable women for prostitution rings in arrangements all too reminiscent of enterprises which flourished in the first two decades of the twentieth century.[7] State power, as embodied in border patrols and in civilian and military police, is complicit in this construction of females as potential objects of pleasure for men.[8]

The war in the former Yugoslavia has demonstrated the systematic use of sexual violence as a strategy of war, calling our attention not only to its use in the present but in the past. Rape is a protected form of torture; protected in the sense that the perpetrator "explains" that he is only expressing "natural" urges, and protected in that structures of shame in civilian society often inhibit victims from reporting their experiences, lest they be subsequently regarded as tainted.[9]

The League worried about infanticide. In our own time, we know about the widespread use of ultrasound technology in China to guide the abortions of female fetuses; it is estimated that more than 12 percent of all female births have been aborted. Misuse of amniocentesis for similar purposes is widespread in India.[10] These accounts of female infanticide or selective abortion tell us also of relationships in societies that choose boys over girls. We will not be surprised when demographers find, as the distinguished economist Amartya Sen has so effectively reported, systemic deprivation of food and basic health care to girls as compared to boys. Gendered disparities can be observed "in the division of labour within the household, in the extent of care or education received, in liberties that different members are permitted to enjoy."[11] The United Nations estimates that in Asia and Africa, women work as much as thirteen hours more per week than men do.[12] These are measures not only of the status of women but of the relationship between men and women; the subtext, as Kenyon suspected, is the violent denial of social resources to females and the allocation of these resources to males.

The terms of the Convention on the Elimination of All Forms of Discrimination Against Women are encouraging. Among them is the principle that women should have citizenship in their own right and not as a derivation of their husbands' status, an issue which was contested in the United States in Kenyon's time and took more than twenty years of vigorous political work to change. When Kenyon served on the League's Committee on the Legal Status of Women, vulnerability to statelessness was a major problem for women; although it has been resolved in the United States, it remains a problem elsewhere and is highlighted in CEDAW. But the principles of CEDAW remain matters of dispute and there are no enforcement mechanisms. Many parties signed with reservations; some, like the United States, signed but did not ratify. Yugoslavia signed and ratified CEDAW more than a decade ago, but the effect on gender relations inside the region is not today discernible.[13]

United Nations' reports describe three systems of relations between men and women in the world today. In the "developed world," female literacy, education, and access to health care is increasingly comparable to that of men. That is to say, in the societies of the developed world, girls and boys, women and men can make roughly similar claims to the resources of their families and of society. They remain constrained by their class positions, it is true, and maintaining equal access in practice often requires political action and attention. But women and men have roughly equal access to education and health care at virtually all levels; we can observe women increasingly claiming competence in fields which had been previously monopolized by men, and we can note that men and women are increasingly likely to relate to each other as colleagues as well as kin and lovers.

But there are two other worlds—a "developing world" of Latin America and North Africa; and an "underdeveloped world" of sub-Saharan Africa and southern Asia, and, it should be said, sectors in the societies of the "developed" world—in which limited resources are clearly allocated differentially on the basis of gender as well as class. These are societies in which women work harder than men, die younger than men, are less literate than men, and have virtually no role in social decision making. In these worlds, Amartya Sen's terrible statistics tell us—as the best social science almost always does—that the surface of what counts as "normal" hides unpleasant social secrets. In this context, what are we to say of relations between women and men? What words can we use that do not signal tension, resentment, and exploitation—however implicit or unconscious—of one sex by the other? There remain many in whose interest it is to insist that women's issues are boring and tiresome; many who live in societies in which resources are violently torn from some and given to others. In all worlds, as Dorothy Kenyon discerned, relations between women and men are a matter of politics as well as a matter of emotion.

*\*\**

Future public policy is rarely the historian's métier. We dream of shaping the future by telling ever more precise stories of the past. For historians like myself, two major theoretical shifts have taken place since Kenyon wrote that have changed the questions we ask of the past and the strategies we use for developing our answers. They make possible more precise analysis and perhaps offer grounds for optimism about progressive change. The first shift was articulated powerfully by Mary Beard shortly after World War II and again in the early 1960s by David Potter. By 1971 historians were taking up their challenge, which required that we question generalizations by asking whether they hold for women as well as they do for men. Virtually no generalization in the major historical narratives held up against that question. American historians, for example, who had long considered the frontier the major locus of social and economic opportunity, found that generalization is gender specific; the city, not the frontier, was more likely to be a site of opportunity for women. The effects of social and intellectual change also turned out to be gender-specific; eras that seemed to improve the status of men—like the Renaissance—could be periods of decline and demoralization for women. The insight was a simple one, but it required a reexamination of many conclusions about the past that had been regarded as well established. It meant that the grand narratives we have inherited, built as they were on the assumption that men's experience is normative and women's experience is trivial, are partial narratives. It required that historians recognize women as historical actors, vulnerable as men are to forces beyond their control, striving as men do to shape the contours of their lives as best they can. The new approaches sustained a generation of exciting and productive scholarship across a wide spectrum of historical topics.

By the mid-1980s, the new lines of investigation were leading almost inexorably to the second major theoretical shift: to introduce into historical work the analysis of gender relations. The work of women's history expanded to include not only those experiences particular to women but the complex relations between men and women. Asking questions about how men and women construct meaning for their historical experience, historians now understand that gender itself is socially constructed. Gender is a culturally specific system of meaning that, as Alice Kessler-Harris has observed, "orders the behavior and expectations of work and family, influences the policies adopted by government and industry, and shapes perceptions of equity and justice."[14]

Dorothy Kenyon understood that women had interests to which male legislators generally did not respond. What she could not understand was why when she raised those issues, male eyes glazed over; in the speech from which I have been quoting, she said frankly "I sense [a] little hostility in the air....Nothing seems taken very seriously....One feels somehow or other put in "one's place," whatever that is."[15] We can now say that Kenyon felt that discomfort because she lived in a culture which constructed men as the ungendered norm. Only women were thought to have gender; in such a culture, it was almost impossible to situate a gendered self as a professional colleague. In America whites were not understood to have race; only blacks had race. Other cultures racialized other marginal groups, not necessarily on the basis of skin color—Jews, Gypsies, untouchables in India, the people who used to be known as *burakumin* in Japan.[16] Every society is capable of creating an unracialized norm and a racialized Other. The physical body of the asker is itself part of the discourse. Like all academic and professional women of her time, Kenyon found that almost anything that she said or wrote was treated, at least in part, as what Foucault has called "subjugated knowledge"—knowledge marked by the knower's gendered social identity—as though no other knower also had gendered social identity. Since the community of historians had already concluded that the history of women was not serious, it became necessarily radical to claim women as the object of knowledge if one were oneself a woman. Understanding gender as a social construction helps us understand why women like Kenyon, who, in the post–World War I world, thought that the accomplishment of suffrage was a sign that they could enter politics, the academy, and workplaces as equals, were bound to be disappointed.

Understanding gender to be a social construction also helps us comprehend how it happened that the serious and extensive work on relations between men and women undertaken by League committees and United Nations commissions bore so little fruit; we may get some clues about how to interrupt this unfortunate pattern. For all their detail and force, the reports about women, especially when women were linked with children, were received as "subjugated knowledge"—marginal, separate from the "real work" of the League, which involved negotiations over reparations, or over boundaries; separated from the "real work" of the U.N. To resituate these reports as something more substantive, another theoretical move was required.

That shift involved the recognition that generalizations need to be tested simultaneously by their resilience in the face of differences of race and class as well as gender. What had been separated as political history, diplomatic history, working-class history, women's history, and the histories of races marked by skin color or of racialized ethnicities we can now try to place in dynamic relationship to each other on battlefields of contested historical knowledges. Class resides in class formation; gender lies in the process of naming, displaying and giving meaning; race in the social construction of the other. The triad of race, class, and gender is *not* a mantra; and it should not be the monopoly of left-leaning historians or of social historians. It is not only a set of abstract concerns but modes through which relations of power are claimed and constructed. In most recent investigations, it has become increasingly clear that race, class, and gender are not separate modes of analysis but are inextricably linked in complex relationships, each participating in the construction of the other in ways of which we have been only dimly aware, and all participating in the construction of political and economic power relations.

The "Scheme of Work" that guided the League Committee for the Study of the Legal Status of Women sensed this challenge. The committee was warned that the category "woman" was not monolithic; they were not only to "describe the position of women as such but also to deal with differentiations made between women themselves on the ground of marriage, age, education, number of children, etc." For the most part, however, the committee was instructed to gather descriptive information, for example: "I.f. Position of women as regards personal freedom and safety, liberty of speech and of assembly; I.g. Fiscal laws affecting women as such. II.b.e. Right of a married woman to carry on business or industry. II.B.a. Law of adoption as it affects women. III.e. Prostitution and traffic in women. III.f. The law of vagrancy as it affects women."

Framing the assignment in this way meant the League Committee would discuss the structure of law relating to women as though it stood alone, unrelated to the structure of law covering men with which it was always necessarily in dialogue. This structure was maintained even though, as they worked in the late 1930s, fascist politics were not only effectively marking Jews as targets but constructing Jewish men as effeminate and Jewish women as masculine; that is, reconstructing gender and race simultaneously. Kenyon would later be impressed by the work of Gunnar Myrdal, whose devastating study of American race relations blamed a "paternalistic order of society" and linked the problems of women and African Americans. In recent years, scholars whose work has been informed by post-structuralist analysis have urged us to understand language not only as systems of words and grammatical rules but as systems of thought through which meaning is constructed. As Jane Sherron De Hart has put it, through language "meanings are reproduced differentially, through contrasts and oppositions, and hierarchically, through the assignment of primacy to one term and subordination to the other. Pairings such as objective/subjective, public/private, equality/difference, and male/female are key examples."[17]

These pairs convey, superficially, that they name symmetrical relationships, but invariably they describe asymmetrical relationships, relationships in which the first part of the pair is privileged and the second is understood to be supplementary. The superficial equality between the two has the effect of masking the power relationship between them. For example, the public/private dichotomy has often been accompanied by a description of women as living in a "separate "sphere" or "private sector" of their own. In this language, "public" and "private" seemed to be reciprocal social constructions.[18] But this discourse masks the way the power of the state intrudes upon and shapes intimate, "private" relationships—by laws governing marriage, by systems of taxation, by rules of divorce and child custody, by cultural climates in which literacy is differentially available—reifying difference and sustaining the dependence of women on men. When the League's "Scheme of Work" listed topics in law "as it affects women," it also inadvertently conveyed that it is possible to speak of one part of the pair without necessarily constructing meaning for the other part.

Scholars from a variety of disciplines have also come to understand "the contingent, constructed character of presumably neutral, universal concepts and principles."[19] Carole Pateman has argued that even the abstraction "the social contract," in which individuals are understood to legitimate civil government by voluntary and free "exchange [of] the insecurities of natural freedom for equal, civil freedom which is protected by the state," describes in fact not "all adult individuals" but only relationships among men. The liberal order in which every man claimed, in Locke's words, "a property in his own person" did not sustain women in claiming a property in *their* own persons. Pateman argues that lurking behind the social contract that sustains liberal society is a *sexual contract* which defines women as politically irrelevant and personally subordinate.[20] The rational individual on whom liberal political theory is based, one who can display autonomy and independence, is necessarily an adult male unmarked by class or race.[21]

Pateman's work helps explain why even in liberal, egalitarian political systems, even when they are of the same families and the same economic classes, men and women are differently situated in relation to the social order. Indeed, for those who are differently situated, it is possible for the application of equal rights to be punitive. Kenyon's contemporaries could not explain this fully, but they could sense it; the beginning of the "Scheme of Work" carries the warning that "In some cases...a law which *prima facie* affects both sexes equally is in reality of a nature to operate adversely to women." The "Scheme" went no further; but it was pointing to the phenomenon which the lawyer Martha Minow has recently characterized as "the difference dilemma."

By the difference dilemma Minow means that the very act of naming difference is to risk reifying it. "[S]ocial and legal constructions of difference have the effect of hiding from view the relationships among people, relationships marked by power and hierarchy," Minow writes. "...Difference, after all, is a comparative term. It implies a reference....A short person is different only in relation to a tall one. But the point of comparison is often unstated. Women are compared with the unstated norm of men, "minority" races with whites...." It is more important, Minow suggests, to be skeptical about what counts as difference, and to examine not the "traits inherent in the 'different person'" but rather "the relationships between people who have and people who lack the power to assign the label of difference."[22]

As we develop new and more expansive historical enterprises—global history, environmental history—we will need to resist the temptation to write a history driven by abstract "forces." We need to strive, instead, to link social transformation to political and economic change. We will not be able to adopt national histories as traditionally written, for they convey primarily what has traditionally counted as centers of authority—emperors and popes, patriarchs and legislatures—activities by which men claim, articulate and enact relations of power, without much attention to how the participants in these relations are named or chosen.[23] Traditional historical practice has generally failed to interrogate the ways in which the invisibility of women sustains the power of the men of their class and kin. Driven by a need to understand how difference is enacted even while it is denied, we can insist on asking—of any society— questions that haunt us now. Many are like the questions which the members of the League committees struggled to articulate nearly a century ago. Now, one hopes, we can frame the problems with more precision and address them more successfully.

We can, for example, resist treating as "natural" relationships which we know are socially constructed, named "natural" by state power which seeks to make itself invisible. We can recognize that gender is implicit in many questions which have been assumed not to involve gender at all. When we study routes to public authority, whether legitimate or illegitimate, we can ask not only who has traveled them successfully but also examine who found resistance when they embarked on the journey. We can investigate how gender, race, and class have affected access to authority and to power. We can ask what happened to gender relations during the Nazi and fascist achievement of power? Or during the U.S. Occupation of Japan? Or in the course of revolutionary transformations anywhere, including the last four years in Europe after the fall of the Berlin Wall? We can ask how changes in gender relations in moments of violent social upheaval have participated in changing power relations, understanding that it is likely that these changes were not necessarily peripheral but may have been central to the new configurations of social power. We can ask under what conditions ethnic differences have been marked as racial. And under what conditions has it become imperative to effeminize racially marked men.

Asking questions like these may have significant policy implications. For example, studies of intellectual history undertaken in this spirit will take as their subject the knowers as well as what is known. Before we complain about the absence of female intellectuals, we need to ask who learns to read, and we will come up against the harsh statistics of female literacy. In the United States, the first census which showed women as likely to be literate as men was not taken until 1840, and there is evidence that this relationship did not persist after the great waves of immigration at the end of the century. In the world today, 40 percent of young women, and 75 percent of women over age twenty-five are illiterate in much of Africa and in southern and western Asia.[24] Our account of the social history of intellectuals, or of the absorption of colonial intellectuals into metropolitan culture must recognize that the sites of argument—universities, journals, even coffee houses and taverns—have for much of the past been gendered as spaces accessible to men.[25]

The most heartbreaking problems are gendered: Who is fed in time of famine?[26] Who gets to be a refugee? Who gets left behind? Because single men travel alone more easily and invisibly they have had somewhat more success fleeing oppressive regimes.[27]

*\*\**

Dorothy Kenyon concluded her 1971 speech by observing that relations between men and women involved political power. The reason that women had no influence in government for so long, she pointed out, was that in order to get the vote they had to persuade men to give it to them; only in France had the decision on votes for women been opened to a national plebiscite in which women voted. But suffrage alone, Kenyon warned, could not revolutionize political relationships; so long as "men controlled every policy making agency in government," women would have little voice in choosing candidates, setting agendas, managing legislative bodies, choosing what is to be debated and the order of debate.[28] Recent political experience in the United States, when the Anita Hill/Clarence Thomas hearings set off a firestorm of political activity which resulted in the election of more women to Congress than ever before in its history, sustains Kenyon's point, and suggests how heightened gender consciousness can be related to heightened political activism and efficacy.[29]

The work of women's historians in the three decades since Kenyon spoke has made it possible for us to address the issues she raised with more precision, but the categories she identified remain salient. As we face the twenty-first century, we would well to do to heed Kenyon's warnings, guarding against the temptation to marginalize women as different and understanding that the language of marginalization is itself a clue that power relations are at work.

### Notes

[1] The manuscript can be found in Folder 241, Box 23, Dorothy Kenyon Papers, Sophia Smith Collection, Smith College, Northampton, MA.

[2] Dorothy Kenyon Papers, Smith College, esp. Boxes 51–52, 56–64.

[3] She had in mind Gunnar Myrdal's work on race relations, as well as the "sadistic displays of brutality and cruelty" in television and movies which, she believed, instruct "all our male children, as the younger generations came along, the niceties of killing and gun play generally."

[4] See, for example, the "Report on the Progress of the Enquiry, Adopted on January 10, 1939" and *Legal Status of Women: A Survey of Comparative Law* (Rome, 1942). See also "Confidential: Not for Publication. Committee for the Study of the Legal Status of Women. Scheme of Work. April 12th, 1938," Folder 504, Box 51, Dorothy Kenyon Papers. A very helpful map of League concerns is Hans Aufricht, *Guide to League of Nations Publications: A Bibliographical Survey of the Work of the League, 1920–1947* (New York: Columbia University Press, 1951).

[5] The convention was drafted in 1976. A revised draft was passed by consensus in the General Assembly at the end of 1979; by the Copenhagen Conference on Women in 1980, 52 states had signed. CEDAW is in force as of Sept. 1981; in 1993, 119 states had signed. The Committee on the Elimination of Discrimination Against Women is chosen pursuant to CEDAW; it called the Second World Conference on Human Rights, held in Vienna in June 1993. See Lars Adam

Rehof, *Guide to the Travaux Préparatoires of the United Nations Convention on the Elimination of All Forms of Discrimination Against Women* (Dordrecht: Martinus Nijhoff Publishers, 1993).

[6] *Report on the Traffic in Women and Children* (1927), discussed in H. Wilson Harris, *Human Merchandise: A Study of the International Traffic in Women* (London: Ernest Benn Ltd. 1928?) pp. ix–x; see also pp. 259–70.

[7] *Time*, June 21, 1993, pp. 45–51.

[8] Historian Bruce Cumings has written movingly of "the social construction of every Korean female as a potential object of pleasure for Americans" over the entire course of the American relationship with Korea from neo-colonial authority to ally between 1945 and the present, analogizing the "free" enterprise of prostitution under American occupation to the "comfort girl" system under the Japanese occupation. See Cumings, "Silent But Deadly: Sexual Subordination in the U.S.–Korean Relationship" in Saundra Pollock Sturdevant and Brenda Stoltzfus, eds., *Let the Good Times Roll: Prostitution and the U.S. Military in Asia* (New York: The New Press, 1992), pp. 168–69. On the policing of prostitution in the environs of the U.S. Naval Station in Subic Bay, see Aida F. Santos, "Gathering the Dust: The Bases Issue in the Philippines," in *Let the Good Times Roll*, pp. 32–44; also Cynthia Enloe, *Bananas, Beaches & Bases: Making Feminist Sense of International Politics* (Pandora Press, 1989; American Edition, University of California Press, 1990).

[9] Amnesty International has recently undertaken a major project to identify gendered practices of violence in more than forty countries.

[10] Nicholas Kristof reports that the number of male births in China has skyrocketed from the normal ratio of 105 for every 100 female births to 118 males for every 100 females; there is real reason to suspect that girls whose births come as a surprise because the ultrasound tests were misleading are abandoned, killed, or sent for international adoption. *New York Times*, July 21, 1993.

[11] Amartya Sen, *Inequality Reexamined* (Cambridge, MA: Harvard University Press and the Russell Sage Foundation, 1992), pp. 122–24. See also Amartya Sen, "More Than 100 Million Women Are Missing," *New York Review of Books*, Dec. 20, 1990, pp. 61–66; and Marge Koblinsky *et al.*, *The Health of Women: A Global Perspective* (Boulder: Westview Press, 1993). UNICEF has described what are sometimes called "cultural discriminations"; in Malaysia, for example, the weekly duration of work for little girls aged five to seven is 75 percent longer than that for boys of the same age, without counting the "invisible" work they do at home. In Jordan, baby boys between four and eight months are four times more likely to be well nourished than baby girls. Sixty percent of children in the world who have no school education are girls. *Women of Europe*, No. 68, February/May 1991, p. 35.

[12] *The World's Women, 1970–1990: Trends and Statistics*, Series K, No. 8, Social Statistics and Indicators (New York: United Nations, 1991), p. 1.

[13] This discrepancy between statements of principle and lived experience are not unusual. For example, the United Nations' most recent summary statement on the status of women observed that "the Bangladesh Constitution guarantees the equal rights of men and women and sanctions affirmative action programmes in favour of women but...the status of women in Bangladesh is among the lowest in the world." *The World's Women, 1970–1990*, p. 7.

[14] Alice Kessler-Harris, "A New Agenda for American Labor History: A Gendered Analysis and the Question of Class," in J. Carroll Moody and Alice

Kessler-Harris, eds., *Perspectives on American Labor History: The Problems of Synthesis* (DeKalb: Northern Illinois University Press, 1989), p. 226.

[15] "Men and Women...," Dorothy Kenyon Papers, p. 6.

[16] For a thoughtful examination of the racializing of Gypsies, see Katie Trumpener, "The Time of the Gypsies: A 'People without History' in the Narratives of the West," *Critical Inquiry* XVIII (1992), pp. 843–84.

[17] In much of what follows, I am indebted to Jane Sherron De Hart, "Equality Challenged: Equal Rights and Sexual Difference," *Journal of Public History* VII (forthcoming, Jan. 1994). See also Joan W. Scott, "Deconstructing Equality-Versus-Difference: Or, the Uses of Poststructuralist Theory for Feminism," *Feminist Studies* XIV (1988), pp. 32–38.

[18] I have discussed this point at length in "Separate Spheres, Female Worlds, Woman's Place: The Rhetoric of Women's History," *Journal of American History* (1988), pp. 9–39.

[19] De Hart, manuscript, p. 29.

[20] Carole Pateman, *The Sexual Contract* (Stanford: Stanford University Press, 1988), pp. 4–9. I have discussed the impact of these disparities during the revolutionary era in the United States in "The Paradox of Female Citizenship in the Early Republic: The Case of *Martin v. Massachusetts* (1805), *American Historical Review*, April 1992.

[21] Martha Minow, *Making All the Difference: Inclusion, Exclusion, and American Law* (Ithaca: Cornell University Press, 1990), p. 147: "Rights analysis offers release from hierarchy and subordination to those who can match the picture of the abstract, autonomous individual presupposed by the theory of rights. For those who do not match that picture, application of rights analysis can be not only unresponsive but also punitive....In short, rights analysis preserves rather than alters the dilemma of difference: difference continues to represent deviance in the context of existing social arrangements...."

[22] Minow, pp. 22–23. We reify difference, for example, when health insurance systems cover all non-pregnant persons, a strategy which apparently treats men and women equally, but which leaves women without medical coverage for an expensive disability which is marked female. For the litigation of this issues, see *California Federal Savings v. Guerra* 107 S. Ct 683 (1987).

[23] Two recent issues of the *American Historical Review* filled with fine review essays on the state of the field for histories of Eastern Europe and of the Middle East are instructive for the virtual absence of attention to the relationship of social relations and structures of political power. But now that new archives are opening up—at least in Eastern Europe—we will find that we need not be dependent on inherited histories as written.

[24] *The World's Women, 1970–1990*, pp. 46–47.

[25] David Hollinger has thoughtfully observed that intellectual history "focuses on arguments made by people whose chief business it was to argue." See David Hollinger, "Historians and the Discourse of Intellectuals," in John Higham and Paul K. Conkin, eds., *New Directions in American Intellectual History* (Baltimore: Johns Hopkins University Press, 1979), pp. 47–49.

[26] Paul R. Greenough considers gender-selective survival strategies in *Prosperity and Misery in Modern Bengal: The Famine of 1943–1944* (New York: Oxford University Press, 1982).

[27] See the essay by Sybil Milton in Atina Grossmann *et al.*, *When Biology Became Destiny* (New York: 1980s).

[28] Kenyon, "Men and Women—Boredom, Violence and Political Power," conclusion. Folder 241, Box 23, Dorothy Kenyon Papers.

[29] See Sue Tolleson-Rinehart, *Gender Consciousness and Politics* (New York: Routledge, 1992).

# COMMENT ON
# THE KERBER PAPER

UENO Chizuko

Kerber's paper discusses continuity and change in gender issues in the twentieth century, spanning the half-century between Dorothy Kenyon and herself. I must confess that I am somewhat depressed by the fact that Kenyon's argument is still valid fifty years on. Kerber's paper has two virtues that impress me: first, she does not limit her argument to issues concerning American women only but discusses them internationally. Second, she puts the gender issues in context with class and race. The United States is, after all, the country where the politics of gender, class, and race are intermingled. In general, I agree with much of her argument, and there is little with which I would disagree. My comments, therefore, provoked by her paper, are intended to take our discussion a step further.

First, she is right to raise the problem of gender issues not in terms of the status of women but in terms of the relationship between the sexes. As she states, it is a power relationship, based on the exploitation of labor and sexuality of women by men, where you see the biased allocation of resources on a worldwide scale. It might be possible to achieve gender equality in developed countries, but if the prosperity and equality women in the developed world enjoy is based on exploitation of the underdeveloped societies, it is illogical to argue that gender equality can be exported to the latter. In her discussion of "invisible" labor, or more precisely the unpaid labor of women, Maria Mies, a leading German feminist, argues that the accumulation of world capital is based on the "housewifezation" of women, that is to say, the exclusion of women from the labor market. There seems to be a structural zero-sum game in gender, class, and racial relationships in regard to scarce social and natural resources. Realistically speaking, it is impossible for those living in developing and underdeveloped societies to catch up with the consumption level of energy and resources in developed societies, unless the natural environment of the entire earth is destroyed. I sometimes hear American optimism echoed by American feminists as if they imagine they could "export" gender justice and gender equality to less developed societies without changing their own society. If the modern age, as was the case with the Renaissance, is the time when the status of the human, or more exactly the male man, was liberated at the cost of women's sacrifice, this has resulted in the establishment of a gender dichotomy, or gender gap in reality, that will inevitably lead us to questioning those concepts of "modernity," "development," and "human rights."

I had the opportunity to stay in Germany for a year between 1991 and 1992, where I conducted research into the experiences of women in the former GDR during the process of reunification. The result was depressing. My co-researchers and I decided to call our forthcoming book *Are Women the Losers in German Reunification?* With the country thrown into the market economy, there is a marked increase in the gender-influenced allocation of resources. It reminds me of the experiences of Japanese women since the introduction of the Equal Employment Opportunity Law, which resulted in exposing them to intense competition, competition defined according to male standards in the name of "equal opportunity." Most Eastern German leaders in the autonomous women's movement, in the process of democratization, told us frankly that they lacked alternative visions. Apart from the state-controlled economy, they needed to seek alternatives in the process of adjustment to the brutality of a free-market economy.

Second, in a political context, Japan has the particular double-sided locus of both victimizing and being victimized. Let me avoid any misunderstanding of Japanese "particularism" by using the term "particular," which might be targeted for attack by American revisionists. Japan has had an historical specificity from the beginning of modernization; it has been victimized by the West by being threatened with violence, while it has victimized other Asian countries. Both threads are so strongly entwined that the right wing uses this victimization as justification of the advance into Asia and the inevitability of the attack on Pearl Harbor. They describe Japan as a woman, a poor woman raped by the West. Western discourse on early modern Japan is full of Orientalism, effeminizing Japaneseness. Theories on Japaneseness, or *Nihonjinron*, formulated by

Japanese male intellectuals, take the form of a reversed Orientalism in order to restore national pride. They debate Western discourse and reverse its value. As the West says Japan is mysterious, yes, it is mysterious. The West says the Japanese are group-
oriented, yes, we are more "contextual" than "individual," that is to
say, a more mature society. The shift from negative to positive in
discussing *Nihonjinron* has become clear since the mid-70s, when
the U.S.–Japan balance of power started to change, correlated with
the rise in the value of Japanese yen. When it comes to gender
terms, it is annoying, because those male intellectuals, progressive
or conservative, take over the feminist discourse and say, "Look, we
are already feminine enough. How can we be more feminine?"
There is the popular argument of matrilineality, or the authority of
mothers in Japan. Japanese women already have the real power,
and there is no need of more liberation, they say. In reality, modern Japan is a patriarchal society that exploits women's labor as well
as sexuality. But the reversed Orientalist discourse, full of gendered words, obviously man-made, obscures the gender issues, or at
least intends to do so.

Take the example of the traffic in women which Kerber addresses.
Japan was "exporting" women, known as "*Karayukisan*," that is,
women sent abroad for prostitution, up to World War II. The
belief prevalent among GIs regarding the "social construction of
Asian women as a potential object of pleasure for Americans," was
familiar to Japanese women both in occupied Japan and around
the U.S. bases. But at the same time, Japanese men were guilty of
the sexual exploitation of Korean, Chinese, and other Asian
women, known as "comfort women" during the war, and today as
prostitutes known as "*Japayukisan.*" As a result of Japan's affluence,
the traffic in women has been reversed. This places Japanese
women in a somewhat ambivalent position in relation to Asian feminism. The recent rise in interest in feminism among Asian women
may be attributed to so-called internationalization, while Japanese
feminists, who have long been under the influence of American
feminism, in turn consider Asian women's issues but, this time, on
the part of the oppressor. When Japanese women say "we Asian
women" in an effort to establish sisterhood among Asian societies
to promote non-Western values, they always face the question
raised by other Asian women, "What can you do with your government's exploitative policies?" This is increasingly a major issue for
Asian women concerning the disbursement of ODA and compensa-

tion for the former "comfort women." One of the outcomes is the rise in "self-reflective women's history," which investigates the active participation of women in the war and sees Japanese women not just as victims but also as oppressors.

Third, while Kerber poses the question of gender bias in the acquisition of knowledge itself as "Who learns to read?" I would like to put the further question "How is knowledge structured?" Women's participation in decision making is important, but if the system of production of knowledge is gender-biased, women's participation might result in women becoming male clones. Unlike American feminists, who have fought for a woman's presidency, British feminists have no fantasy about a "woman on top." They had Mrs. Thatcher on top and she was notorious for promoting policies unfavorable to social minorities, including women. There is now a greater presence of women in unconventional fields, but those elite women tend to take up more universal issues such as international politics, regarding women's issues as local and peripheral. They are caught in the trap of mistakenly believing that by neutralizing their gender and internalizing male values they are on the path to success and equality. Boredom is dominant even among women (especially among young, elite women) in some so-called advanced societies where feminism is said to have achieved its goal and died. It might be possible to achieve gender equality within a limited group of elite women in developed societies at the sacrifice of ordinary women in underdeveloped societies. President Clinton's failure to appoint two women candidates as attorney general illustrates the complicated politics of gender, class, and race. We need to restructure the entire system of the production of knowledge, and it goes without saying that Kerber's work is a positive contribution toward making this change.

# Discussion

**Kristeva:** First of all, I would like to say how essential it is in my view to discuss women's issues in this prestigious, predominantly male audience today. I agree with the arguments of Kerber and Ueno, and I will limit my remarks to the distinction between women's rights and the feminist movement. My intention is to ask both speakers to clarify their positions on this distinction, on which I think we profoundly agree. It seems to me that in a period of social recession such as this, it is not surprising that feminism is no longer a major public concern, even among women themselves. It does not mean that its goals have been attained. Of course, they have not been achieved in the developing world, the Third World, or Muslim society, etc. But they have not been attained even in Western countries. For instance, on this panel, there are only four women, as everybody has noticed.

But something else bothers me more. Feminism—and I notice that Kerber does not use this word, maybe because her focus is on women's rights—the feminism that pushed women's rights further seems to have accomplished its program in what I will call—and the mass media has already labeled—the "super-woman," a strange combination of professional woman, housekeeper, spouse, and mother, a very heavy burden that in fact has destroyed many women and pushed them into psychosomatic illness or depression. Of course, on the contrary, there are those who demonstrate an extraordinary female character, a combination of wisdom, strength, and delicacy that is rare in men—I beg your pardon, gentlemen. This is maybe one of the main characteristics of this century, and probably of the next. It seems to me there is a lot to be done in society to further women's emancipation, precisely taking into account the religious and social particularities of every society.

After these general remarks, I have two more precise comments. First, the term "gender equality" bothers me considerably. I prefer to differentiate between gender difference and social equality, that is, political, professional, and legal rights. We have mentioned the enormous work of Miss Kenyon. For my generation, there is a philosopher I must mention here, Simone de Beauvoir, who has emphasized the necessity of gender equality. But for the generation that comes after Simone de Beauvoir, the problem is not equality. It is gender difference. I will try to explain very briefly.

The claim for "gender equality" can lead to a real war between the sexes, which is a deep reality, maybe, of the human psyche. Men and women do not have the same sexual interests, pleasures, and rewards. Feminism has, in my mind as a psychoanalyst, a tremendous obligation to review this rivalry between the sexes. But this truth of the rivalry, and even the war between the sexes, can lead to considerable difficulties in couple relations and can destroy the very possibility of eroticism. So the problem seems now to be to restore harmony between men and women, and even revive the very possibility of family. How diversified and free could be the models of this family. In my mind, it would be better not to speak about "gender equality" but "social equality," in order to prevent excesses of that kind. In this sense, "different" is not inferior; it is not necessarily marginalized but means the necessity to consider the singularity and particularity of the feminine approach and contribution to civilization and to society.

Second, it seems to me that the model on which the feminist movement was built is the model of liberation movements following Marxism, leftist movements, etc., with essential differences but with some commonalities. Consequently, those movements and the feminist movement also share the logic of the master and slave relationship, and can repeat or even exaggerate the features of the enemy. There is, as everybody knows, a feminist fundamentalism. My question, therefore, is what could be the way to prevent such deviations and excesses in order to allow women to take their real and singular place in the development of society?

**Kerber:** I guess that Kristeva and I are going to have to agree to differ, because I do not concede most of her givens, beginning with her last assumption that there is a feminist fundamentalism of the sort that she has described, that feminism shares the model of a master–slave relationship, and that the feminist movement was built only on the single model of what we are offered by liberationist movements. I will not enter into an attack on an ill-defined feminist fundamentalism. I think that I will find it more profitable to address her previous set of remarks, actually both of them. One is the assumption that the feminism that has pushed for women's rights in the last half-century has accomplished its program. I do not believe it has. And I think that the image that what was accomplished, the development of a model of super-woman, is what resulted when feminists were able to make some changes, but the least difficult changes, that were part of their agenda.

The goal of the super-woman, the goal of the woman who has a professional career, runs an elaborate household, runs an elaborate child-nurturing program at home, and does all that in a world in which men's behavior does not change was, I want to argue, never the feminist goal. It was certainly not the goal of American feminists, nor was it the goal of the feminist community that I entered in the early 1970s. Rather, there was an image of a different kind of social life, in which certain behaviors which had been marked as "male only" would be made more accessible to women, and behaviors which were marked as women's behaviors would be made more accessible to men.

What we have found, I think, what we have all seen, is that some entry into certain aspects of life—access to the professions, schooling, jobs, and careers—has increased markedly in the Western world. But what counts as a professional life has not changed. We have not embedded into our definition of how one makes a professional life the understanding that men and women need to be good mothers and fathers, need to have time to be good mothers and fathers, and to reconfigure the terms of what is professional life. In the United States we still run our universities on men's biological clocks, not on women's biological clocks. We have not reconsidered what it would mean to structure a university so that men and women had equal opportunity to develop their careers. If feminists in America, whom I know best, ended up playing the role of superwoman, it was because the resistance to what they wanted to accomplish was so very great. I share with Kristeva the understanding that this was a burden too great to be borne, that it did plunge many women into a sense that they were inadequate. But I do not think it was the fault of the vision; it was the reality and the resistance that they met.

Second, you have attacked the term "gender equality," and I am not quite sure that I used it in my paper, but I take your point that you want to differentiate between "gender difference" and "social equality," and to avoid a war between the sexes. Unless we acknowledge that in our society power has been claimed differentially by class, by race, and by gender, we will not solve the problems of disparate power relations.

Underneath the relations between man and woman there have been differential power relations—I think we see that now, with the revelation of the great, and in some ways surprising, amount of domestic violence existing throughout the world. I think we must name it and in naming it we can address it. If we do not name it, we cannot address it. I am afraid that there are elements of our lives in which there is a war between the sexes, and that war is taking place in the form of domestic violence; it has taken the form of the right of men to beat their wives in the context in which police come and say: This is a private battle; we will not intrude. I do not know how else to describe this except as publicly supported power relations. I think that kind of violence also removes the possibility of erotic relations between men and women. By the way, most feminists I know have very good love lives.

**Ueno:** Kristeva has exactly met my request to discuss the concept of equality. I agree with your use of the terms "social equality" and "gender difference," rather than "gender equality." In my view, gender difference lies mainly in the reproductive aspect of human life. My point was that if social equality is defined by male standards, which we can now see in the Japanese market economy, it is very deceptive and destructive to women and children.

I would like to make comments on two of Kristeva's points. First, as for the perception of feminism achieving the goal of superwoman, we must not ignore that there are diversified feminisms. I would like to use the plural rather than singular. And it varies with cultures. So far I have been trying to establish the indigenous feminism within the Japanese cultural context. I have seen a huge cultural gap between American and European feminisms. The second point is that if you criticize all the various forms of feminisms because of feminist fundamentalism—and I am disturbed myself by them—it is like attacking all forms of ecology because of ecological fundamentalism, as some people did in the former sessions.

**Kristeva:** Just one word. I think the maturity of the feminist movement and the women's rights movement is measurable in its capacity to be self-critical.

**Yamaguchi:** We also need to extend our point of view in terms of the problem of nature itself. When we talk about individual rights we usually tend to be human-centered, human-centric, and forget about the rights of nature. Likhachev pointed out that trees could have rights, and I should think that when we talk about the inferior position of some beings in society, it could be extended to the right of the constituent elements of nature. Our imagination may discuss the position not only of disadvantaged people but also of disadvantaged natural elements. This will strengthen our position toward the problem of inequality. When we imagine each particular problem in which people are suffering, we always try to ameliorate the situation. We should take a similar stance with respect to nature.

**Iriye:** As a historian I deeply appreciated Kerber's contribution. She was right in reminding us that the kinds of issues that all too often appear to be very contemporary had been there, or have been with us, for some time before. It is very important to remind ourselves that so many of the issues that appear as rather recent occurrences have had a long history. It does not mean that we should congratulate ourselves that things have been with us for such a long time. Maybe we should ask why those issues that were raised seventy years ago have taken so long to elicit any kind of adequate response. In this connection, Ueno's paper, too, had some historical observations, and I would agree with her concluding statement that we need to reconstruct the system of knowledge production.

As a historian, I would take that to mean that we ought to be willing to redefine the past, reconstruct the past, taking into consideration many feminist theories, many of the agenda kinds of questions that have been raised. But in doing that, we should avoid the danger of reconstructing the past as we wish it to have been, or as the ideology would force us to define it. The past should be closely examined on the basis of the data we have, on the basis of the evidence. I do not think there has been any major change with regard to that, to the task before us. In knowledge production we must, more than ever before, avoid the temptation of letting our polemical viewpoints, ideology, determine how we should do it.

In this context, I have been struck by the fact that despite the tremendous amount of historical information stemming from women's studies by American historians and others in the past fifteen years, we still know so little about women and international affairs. I mean, my field is international affairs, and I am looking for good empirical studies of the relationship between gender and international affairs. We are waiting for more important contributions, but until we have more empirical studies of gender relations as they affect international relations, it would be rather dangerous to generalize about the past and historiographical trends.

One footnote to Ueno's comment. I find it particularly interesting that she talks about male-dominated views of Japan's history. It may be that Ueno accepts the male-dominated view of Japan's past aggression when she says that Japan was an aggressor in Asia, but that Japan was victimized by Western aggressiveness or Western violence. My view of Japan's past is that there really was no time in Japan's recent history when Japan was victimized by the West. I think it has been the other way around. Japan victimized the West. I mean it was Japan that threatened Russia in 1904. Russia did not threaten Japan. It was Japan that threatened the United States in 1940. It was not the United States that threatened Japan. To say that there is a parallel between Japan being victimized by the West and Japan victimizing Asia is in my view a rather male way of saying things. I do not think it is true. It is just one example where we need more empirical study. And I think you are right in pointing out that Japanese women have been just as aggressive vis-à-vis other countries. I would not say that Japanese women have been victims. I think we should say that Japanese women have been quite aggressive, not just vis-à-vis other Asian countries but vis-à-vis Western countries as well.

**Kosai:** Ueno argued that brutal market forces are threatening the female position in Eastern Germany, but as far as I can see the Eastern Germany problem is not a problem of the market economy *per se*. It is a problem caused by the transition from a command economy to a market economy. It is rather a transitional problem. And history shows, as far as I can see, that a well-functioning market economy helps to raise the status of women. If you have full employment, then the legitimate demand for women's participation is more widely admitted by conservative males. So I think Ueno's attack on the market force is a little misplaced. On the other hand, I fully agree that we need some new pattern of economic development for the next century, different from the nineteenth or the twentieth century.

As we discussed in the last session, we are witnessing a population explosion in the developing economies, and as is the case with the environment, the evidence is insufficient. There remains much, much ambiguity. But I think there is some reason to assume that if female human rights are assured in these developing economies, a population explosion might be avoided, or mitigated at least.

I support Ueno's position from an economic point of view by admitting the legitimate demand for female human rights in the whole world. We can thus have a new pattern of economic development. In both the Western case and the Japanese case, only after industrialization have we had a decline in population and a rise in human rights for women. Perhaps in the next century this order might be reversed.

**Nivat:** I have a question to the authors of both papers about changes in the production of knowledge. The part of women in that production of knowledge is developing, but do you mean that the results of the production of knowledge will change, that—apart from enlarging some areas, adding some areas—something essential will change in the production of knowledge? I would like you to clarify this idea.

There is one area in which complete equality between men and women has been obtained, and that is in twentieth-century Russian poetry. We have four poets, genius poets—two men, two women: Mandelshtan and Pasternak, Akhamatova and Tsvetaeva. I think nobody, knowing Russian poetry, would disagree with that. How that was achieved and why, I do not know. The result is not completely different poetry on either side, although there is no question that the poetry from the two women comes from women, and it achieves the same archi-human penetration as the poetry of the two men. That is the reason why I ask what you mean by changing the production of knowledge.

**Mayall:** I was deeply struck by the title taken from Dorothy Kenyon, and particularly the reference to boredom. I confess I have always regarded myself as a closet feminist, but I would also confess frequently to having glazed over. Why have I glazed over? I would not want to think that I have glazed over, because I had accepted that the woman question was of marginal significance. I believe I have glazed over because of two things: on the one hand, a sort of deep embarrassment about what I have felt to be the truth of some of the points that were being claimed and, on the other, what I believe is knowledge—if we can say anything about knowledge— and that is that while men and women construct their social relations, they are not free to construct them in any manner they please. And so there is a sort of feeling of impotence in the face of this dilemma.

Now, I am afraid I must be a little autobiographical to make my point, and I would like some help, because I do not have a real way of thinking about it. I was brought up by a mother who was, I think, a very straightforward and not particularly articulate feminist, who as a young woman living in Khartoum was, because she was attached to an imperial setup, in a position to intervene. And she intervened, against the advice of my father and of the whole establishment, in trying to proselytize amongst women against the practice of clitoridectomy. Many years later I had a graduate student with whom I had lost touch, and then met in Canada. She had been teaching in a high school in Kenya and had been apparently trying, in the 1970s, to do in a quite different context much what my mother had been doing in the 1920s. She had got nowhere because, of course, her students could not separate the practice from their identity.

I am left with this dilemma that, in a sense, people can only free themselves, that we all go to hell in our own particular way, and that therefore—something which I do not really want to accept might be the case—that feminism, as it were, must stay at home. This is a discrete problem: the end is a universal one—that it is extremely difficult, especially in a revolutionary interventionary way, to change human relations. We can articulate what we believe to be the case, but if we try to become revolutionary, there are great dangers that the revolution will be subverted in the way we have been discussing.

**Stern:** I hope Kerber will understand the unease that I feel when I hear the term "feminist historian." I think I am going to talk to you as a fellow historian. And how might I define myself? I am not a feminist historian. I think we are all historians primarily, and the very term raises difficulties, about which I was wondering whether you would say a word or two.

Let me make three points very quickly. My one great disappointment in your very good paper—and in the discussion, too—was that the enormous strides made by the women's movement in the nineteenth century were neglected. I am talking here particularly of European, but also of American movements. The position of women in the nineteenth century changed significantly. In some ways, if only out of historic justice, it seems to me that that work—which probably was at least as hard today, and even harder because it was a pioneering effort—ought to be remembered.

The second point I want to make is the question of power. Obviously, we cannot possibly go into this in any depth. Let me simply say again, with great diffidence, that women are subjected to male power, or to social power. This can be demonstrated in certain fields and certain realms, and that has been done very effectively and very importantly. Power relations, let us say, within the family, it seems to me, are so intricate that to talk about them simply as if they were the same kind of power raises some questions in my mind. If I think of the great novels of the nineteenth century, which very often deal with this subject, they deal with a nuance and a subtlety that certainly transcends the word "power," and yet does justice to women and to difficulties that women encounter.

The third point I want to make is, in a certain sense, purely political, and looking forward. It seems to me that one of the great problems the women's movement—and I have a great deal of sympathy with what Mayall said earlier about being sympathetic to the women's movement—is going to face is in the transformation of work in industrial society that is likely to happen. I am talking about the enormous unemployment, and the question of unemployment that will take place at certain unexpected new levels.

**Gold:** I would like to refer to Ueno's comment that we are less individualistic, more contextual, and therefore more mature. Here, I start with a brief personal vignette. When I was completing my psychoanalysis I remember regretting the fact that I had not completely overcome my reticence to approach confrontational issues. My analyst indicated that this was not surprising, that I would always be biased in the direction of reticence. But, at least, now I had gained the flexibility to approach some confrontational situations if I felt strongly enough about them. In that regard, I do not believe that it is desirable or necessary for people, either men or women, to differentiate into other postures that permit infinite flexibility in accommodating to a context, or into a position of rigid individuality that does not permit a willing accommodation to a context. Rather, it may be optimal for individuals to have the flexibility either to accommodate to context and/or promote communal goals, or to assert individuality, based on the confluence of a variety of factors, including intuitive and concrete apprehension of what constitutes oneself. We are all biased toward one or other of these polarities, either biologically or culturally.

My simple-minded sense is that there is a bias in Japan toward the capacity to sense the nuances and needs of the context and to contribute to them, in contrast to a bias toward individualism in the West, although I assume that under the best of all possible circumstances, each has flexibility to go in either direction.

**Junker:** I would like to follow up the questions of Nivat from a different point of view. Listening to the precise reasoning of Kerber, Ueno, and Kristeva, I realized that they used the same kind of analysis, logics of conclusions, modalities of reasoning, as the male participants. Now, this reinforced what I had learned from Hegel and Kant: if you think about the structure of knowledge, how knowledge is possibly structured, the question of age, gender, class and so on, plays no role whatsoever. So, my question is how knowledge is structured? Is it an epistemological question, or would you regard it as a gender question? You may answer from Kant's point of view, or from Hegel's as well. Is this a social question, a question of age, or whatever?

**Kerber:** I would regard this as a social question.

**Ueno:** To answer Junker's question related to that of Nivat, about the meaning of the restructuring of the production of knowledge, and if it is limited to the result of the production of knowledge, well, I do not see any change. There are supplementary findings made by feminist historians. But I mean by the word "restructuring" a rather essential change, how to create new concepts to view our world in a new light. If learning just means to adjust ourselves to the existing conceptual apparatus, it is just applying seemingly the gendered and, in fact, male-biased view of the world. In order to create a new concept one has to change the battlefield of the concepts and the discourses on how to see the world.

And so far what we women did was to listen to our own experiences, and to find new concepts and words. Actually, as Kyogoku said this morning, it is the word which controls and dominates people and the world. And so for Junker's question about the model, whether it is epistemological or gendered, it should be both, as I said, if knowledge is a battlefield of the concepts and discusses how we see the world in different ways. So that should be taken into account from the other side of society, like social minorities and underdeveloped societies.

One more point: To answer Kosai's comment if the change experienced by East German women is just transitional, it sounds like a hope that the problem will be solved in the near future. But what I see is that they all have this prediction that women's participation in the labor force will be closer to the level of Western German women, which is actually lower than the participation level of the former East German women. As a result, the divorce rate has dropped, and at the same time the birth rate has suddenly dropped. So, in this sense, if the outcomes of the market economy are working for women and filling the gender gap, compared with the former regime, we do not see any improvement for women in this change. I just do not see these changes as transitional but rather an inevitable outcome of the free-market economy.

**Kerber:** Let me start with Junker, because that is an easy question for me. As you can see from my essay, I really can only deal with a matter of changes in knowledge in the sense of who gets to read in the first place; who gets access to books and ideas; who gets to write books which describe the ideas of the uneducated; who gets to say the generalizations by which we live. It seems to me that what we face is a problem in the sociology of knowledge as much as anything else. I am quite conservative on this point, but I add a footnote to what I say. I am not looking for different terms of what should ultimately count as knowledge. All I wish to do is hold this up to the standards that I think all of us, as people who want to be members of something called an intelligentsia, hold.

On Stern's very important point that we should think about nineteenth-century feminism, I can only underline and claim some impotence in the face of trying to say things in terms of a short paper. But this gives me a chance to say that Dorothy Kenyon herself is in effect an artifact of nineteenth-century feminism. She was born in the late 1880s into a wealthy family. Had she been born into the same family half a century before, there would have been no Smith College for her to attend. And her college experience was very important for her. The college itself was founded as part of a nineteenth-century movement to open access to women to a variety of fields. There are no clean breaks between the nineteenth century and the twentieth century. Her view of the world was shaped by the suffragettes and the feminists of the early twentieth century. One reason why she is so important for our purposes is that she bridges the world of the nineteenth century and the late twentieth century and reminds us that if there seems to be a space in the 1930s, 1940s, and 1950s in our history of activist women playing a vigorous role in the world, it is not because they were not there, they did not try, but because the resistances they met, particularly in the late 1940s and the 1950s, were so severe. Her career is a good way to think about the role that feminist movements have played in the world. At the end of her life, she marched in one of the early feminist parades.

As for power in the family, again I want to be very modest in the topic that I am inquiring into. This is where perhaps I have difficulty with Kristeva as well. I really cannot deal with psychotherapeutics or emotional relations. But as a historian I am aware that the law of the family, the American law of domestic relations, that every country has a law of domestic relations, and that law of domestic relations shapes the boundaries of the family, whether the family knows it or not. In nineteenth-century America, deep into the twentieth century up to the early 1970s, however loving the family was, husbands controlled large amounts of women's property. Ruth Bader Ginsberg made her first Supreme Court brief (she didn't appear, but she wrote it) in resistance to an Idaho statute that said that if a child died without a will the father automatically got to deploy the estate. Now, this may seem a minor point, but it meant that while whatever living relations they developed inside that family space was their affair, the shaping of that space was the public affair. And it is that space that we can criticize and we can work to change.

That brings me to Mayall's very moving testimony. I do not know how to think about intervention, but I do know that no one can make a revolution for anyone else. That is why, in effect, the women's movement has to be done by women claiming their voices, making their analysis of the situation they face. I do not think it means that your mother had to be silent in the face of what she perceived as violence. But I suppose it meant: How did the resistance to clitoridectomy fit in the larger agenda of her analysis of the world?

Finally, on Iriye's point about our needing more work on women and international relations, and absolutely we do, I have two things to say. One is why was it left to women historians to do this work? There are lots of people who have been working in international relations. The other thing is that I think that in some ways no historian, male or female, feminist or not, could as easily understand the relationship between gender and foreign policy as we may be able to start to see now. Take the efforts of people like Jane Addams and the international movement of women for peace, which have been treated as marginal movements by international historians. I think now we are in a better situation to ask how those movements are in dialogue with the efforts of people who are undertaking negotiations. How much of those movements were they aware of? How much did they take them seriously? And we are perhaps better situated than we once were to ask more capacious questions. That certainly is the way I would like to think about it.

# "THE G-3 WORLD"
# AND
# THE THIRD WORLD

# "THE G-3 WORLD,"
# THE THIRD WORLD,
# AND THE WORLD COMMUNITY

Akira IRIYE

One of the first instances of Third World assertiveness may have been Wellington Koo's speech at a League of Nations meeting held on December 10, 1920. The delegates were discussing the composition of the council, to consist of four permanent and four rotating members. The nations comprising the former group had already been designated: Britain, France, Italy, and Japan. (The United States would have been the fifth permanent member if it had joined the League.) Of the four non-permanent members, Koo, the Chinese representative, proposed that three should be from Europe and North America, and one from "Asia and the remaining parts of the world."[1]

"Asia and the remaining parts of the world"—that was how the areas outside of Europe, North America, and Japan were characterized. Today we would variably call the latter category of nations "the West," "the North," "the advanced countries," "the tripolar world," "the metropolitan powers," or, as an abbreviation, "the G-3 World," while the rest would be referred to as "the Rest," "the non-West," "the South," "the developing areas," "the periphery," or "the Third World." What each "world" contains and whether there are other "worlds" may be debated. Should the nations of Eastern Europe and those belonging to the former Soviet Union be considered a separate entity, part of the G-3 World, or of the Third World? Should the Latin American countries be included in the Third World even when some of them, at least, have not so regarded themselves? For the purposes of this essay, all European nations, the United States, Japan, and such other countries of European origin as Canada, Australia, and New Zealand will be considered to constitute the G-3 World, and the rest assigned to the Third World. Such a division makes sense in a discussion of twentieth-century history, for one key theme of that history has been the replacement of an international system defined and dominated by the European powers (including, of course, Russia) by a tridimensional one in which the United States and Japan have joined them and together exerted tremendous influence over the fate of mankind, militarily, geographically, economically, and culturally. Asia (minus Japan), the Middle East, Africa, and Latin America have constituted "the other," their peripheralness aptly described by the term, "the remaining parts of the world." But they have by no means been passive receptacles of G-3 influences but have steadily developed their collective self-consciousness, whether they have called themselves the Third World or by other terms. Thus, another theme of twentieth-century history has been the increasing self-awareness and assertiveness of these areas and countries against the G-3. This essay will focus on changing conceptions of the relationship between the two as one way of understanding how we may see "the future in the past."

To go back to Koo's address, it is remarkable that he should have insisted on only one seat out of eight in the council for the Third World. It is no less interesting that his modest proposal met with strong opposition on the part of some European delegates. Whereas the Chinese diplomat was in effect advocating international affirmative action, arguing that only a representative of a country from outside Europe and North America could speak for the interests of the rest of the world, the Dutch delegate said that such a formula was too rigid. In effect he was stating a case for the principle of Western superiority, saying that the interests of all areas of the globe would be fully discussed by the council regardless of whether or not it included any member from the Third World. Supporters for Koo's proposal insisted that Third World representation would ensure "universal cooperation" which was "essential for the effective maintenance of world peace and the advancement of the common interests of humanity." But the opponents countered that "neither the Asia–Africa–Oceania group nor even Asia or Africa separately can be considered...entities sufficiently homogeneous to supply a legal basis for representation on the Council."[2] It made little sense, in their view, to institute a quota system under the circumstances. A subcommittee charged with the task of reconciling the two positions came out against the Chinese proposal, but the League Assembly endorsed it by a vote of thirteen to twelve, the former consisting of all Asian and other non-Western countries. A small step in itself, the episode marked an important point in the annals of modern international relations when the Third World asserted itself with one voice.

The significance of the episode also lay in the fact that Koo's proposal suggested an internationalist framework in which the Third World question could be dealt with. It may be said that this was a vast improvement over the prewar pattern of the G-3 powers acting as imperialists, whether unilaterally or collectively. Japan establishing its colonial control over Taiwan and Korea, the United States intervening in Central American affairs in the name of the Monroe Doctrine, or France suppressing Indochinese nationalists would be examples of unilateralism, while the international expedition to China to subjugate the Boxer rebels and the various "ententes" among colonial powers to respect each other's spheres of influence would be instances of cooperative imperialism. Either way, the G-3 powers before the war had not developed a systematic approach to the incipient challenge of the Third World. That is why the early discussions at the League of Nations were so important. For, by stressing international cooperation as a framework in which to discuss G-3/Third World relations, the Chinese official was introducing a new vocabulary into the discourse.

To be sure, neither the concept nor the practice of internationalism was new. But it is important to recall that internationalism as it had developed in the West had not envisaged anything global, conceptually linking all parts of the world. F. L. S. Lyons's pioneering work, *Internationalism in Europe* (1963), lists some 466 "international" organizations that had come into existence since the mid-nineteenth century, but, except for a handful such as the Universal Postal Union, these were predominantly European bodies, although some had the participation of the United States. In 1910 a Union of International Associations was organized in Brussels, but here again the organizations affiliated with the Union were all European and American. Japan, which was missing from these lists, had, nevertheless, begun to be included in some "international" activities. At a World Congress of Arts and Letters, held in St. Louis in 1904 in conjunction with the world's fair, a small number of Japanese scholars were the only non-Western participants among the hundreds of prominent scientists, jurists, novelists, artists, and others who gathered together to celebrate the achievements of modern civilization. Characteristically, a University of Tokyo professor read a paper on the development of modern law in Japan, implying that, having successfully undertaken legal modernization, the nation had now joined the ranks of the great powers. This was important in international affairs, as internationalism at that time was often equated with the development of international law. It is no accident that in the United States, too, its emergence as a world power coincided with the organization of societies for the advancement of international law. But international law did not imply a view of a global community. Rather, it postulated rules of conduct among "civilized" nations as they carried on their affairs throughout the globe. (This is not the place to examine in detail the concept of "civilization" as it applied to the G-3 powers, but it may be noted that all of them were supposed to possess, in varying degrees, such features of modern nationhood as industrialization, political democracy, and a concern for social welfare. Nations sharing such characteristics were presumably in a position to abide by some common rules. In other words, they could begin to experiment with a kind of internationalism. But that was not the same thing as envisaging a structure of international relations where all countries were to be invited to cooperate.)

Before the war, it would have been unthinkable for a Third World spokesman (or for a G-3 World spokesman for that matter) to call for "the cooperation of all parts of the world" in the maintenance of peace, as Wellington Koo did in 1920. It would be difficult to say whether the newer conception of worldwide cooperation would have emerged sooner or later even without the Great War. But it could be argued that it was not so much the war as the peace conference out of which the League was created that provided the first significant opportunity for the airing of collective self-consciousness ("national aspirations," as it was called) on the part of Asian, Middle Eastern, or Latin American countries. (In a recent monograph a Chinese historian writes that China's participation in the Paris peace conference showed its "desire to become part of the world." This was the first time "that China concerned itself as a member of the global international society with international affairs, [indicating its] perception of common interest with other members of the international society."[3] Similar observations could be made of other Third World countries that joined the League in 1920.)

In other words, postwar internationalism was the setting in which the new nationalism was expressed. The picture is not fundamentally altered by the fact that the more radical nationalists in these countries turned to Bolshevik Russia for support. For the Bolsheviks were, at least initially, developing their own internationalist agenda. Bolshevik internationalism and League internationalism represented two attempts at redefining international relations, and from the beginning both attempts assigned a significant role to Third World nationalism. If such an analysis is plausible, then it suggests that a new conception of the G-3/Third World relationship was emerging out of the ashes of the Great War, a conception in which G-3 internationalism would seek to accommodate Third World nationalism. Contemporary observers were struck by the revolutionary implications of such a conception, for it implied significant changes in the nature both of nationalism and of internationalism. The challenge now was to take cognizance of the new kind of nationalism and to incorporate it into a new internationalism. Not the older internationalism of advanced, "civilized," and imperialistic nations, but a novel formulation that encompassed the whole world and could become the basis for the postwar peace—that was the agenda the world was being presented with.

There would be other ways of defining the G-3/Third World relationship, but the stress on internationalism as a framework for dealing with the equation would seem to have been one of the contributions the twentieth century has made to the vocabulary of international relations. At the 1983 symposium on the twentieth century, I argued that the century had failed to produce novel ideas about war and peace. "It may be," I wrote, "that about the only significant contribution the twentieth century has made to theories of war and peace is the Orwellian dictum that 'war is peace.'"[4] Benjamin Schwartz added his observation at the same symposium that "a good deal of twentieth century thought is basically continuous with nineteenth and even eighteenth century [Western] thought."[5] Without contradicting these assertions, it may nevertheless be pointed out that this century has significantly altered traditional Western conceptions both of nationalism and internationalism, and that this alteration has had much to do with the challenges posed by the Third World. War and peace, which had earlier been comprehended as a clash of, or an accommodation among, different national interests, would now be seen as a breakdown or a preservation of an international system encompassing the whole world. If, in twentieth-century terms, war and peace have tended to be conceptually blurred, it may have been because the connections between nationalism and internationalism are always extremely complex. Nevertheless, it would seem that the idea that a broad, global framework of internationalism, not just the juxtaposition of disparate national interests, is a prerequisite for a stable world order has gained increasing acceptance during the course of the century.

International affairs during the 1920s provide a good example. Geopolitically, Europe, the United States, and Japan still dominated the world; their combined armed force overwhelmed the rest, they controlled the production and marketing of manufactured goods globally, and they were the principal creators, consumers, and distributors of technological innovations such as automobiles, telephones, movies, and radio sets. But the G-3 nations were increasingly aware of the need to take seriously national aspirations and anti-imperialistic sentiments in various parts of the world and often did so by adapting the framework of international cooperation to the new challenge. The powers would cooperate where possible in order to accommodate Third World nationalism, and they would also expand the scope of cooperation to include cross-cultural activities.

The various treaties signed at the Washington Conference (1921–22) were an example of the G-3's readiness to respond cooperatively to Chinese nationalism. Although the United States did not join the League, this did not prevent it from assuming a leading role in bringing the European powers and Japan together to agree, at least in principle, to help promote China's economic development and political reform. To a lesser extent, the European powers and the United States began to coordinate their policies in Turkey, Iran, and elsewhere in the Middle East to encourage their modernization. Even in Central America, where the United States retained its hegemonic position, it was willing to modify its unilateral interventionism and to respond to the area's nationalism by developing a regional system of cooperation. (Some countries, like Costa Rica, sought to counter American influence by turning to the League of Nations, an interesting example showing that the new internationalism was being viewed as an alternative to imperialism.[6])

At the League of Nations, in the meantime, already in 1922 a decision was made to increase the number of non-permanent members in the council from four to six, to be selected "with due consideration for the main geographical divisions of the world, the great ethnical groups, the different religious traditions, the various types of civilization and the chief sources of wealth."[7] This formula went

a step beyond the 1920 quota system and revealed how fast the consciousness of global diversity was penetrating the minds of world
governments. Such awareness was also behind the creation, by the
League, of a committee on intellectual cooperation. The idea, as
Henri Bergson, one of the major inspirers of the organization, said,
was that "when the mentality of other nations was understood, the
world would be much more ready to agree" on matters of war and
peace.[8] It is not surprising that from the beginning the committee
on intellectual cooperation had the active support of men and
women (the committee especially stressed the importance of including women) from various countries. For instance, the list of fifty-
eight prominent intellectuals who constituted the core group
charged with the task of preparing for the establishment of the
committee, included those from the United States, Britain, France,
Germany and other European countries, Japan, India, Brazil,
Uruguay, Argentina, Paraguay, and Colombia.[9] When the committee on intellectual cooperation was launched in 1922, intellectuals
and artists from the United States, Europe, Japan, China, India,
Egypt, Mexico, Brazil, and Venezuela proved to be among the most
active. (It is to be noted that individual Americans and Germans
were deeply involved in this work, although neither the United
States nor Germany was a member of the League.) Although it cannot be denied that European, particularly French, intellectuals
played leading roles in the committee's activities, there was shared
awareness that all were engaged in promoting cross-cultural communication and that only through such work could nationalistic
and parochial excesses be surmounted.

Interwar international relations have tended to be dismissed as
having been but an unfortunate interlude between two world wars,
but one would miss its real significance unless one noted these contributions to internationalism. True, the 1920s were also notable
for the persistence of nationalistic ambitions and rivalries among
the powers, on one hand, and for the radicalization of nationalism
on the part of some Third World countries, on the other. But
because of the very intensification of these two kinds of nationalism, serious efforts were made to supersede or at least curb them by
erecting internationalist mechanisms. And these efforts, frustrating
as they often were, would never disappear but would constitute an
important force in subsequent international relations.

In such a perspective, the 1930s can best be seen as a period
when some of the G-3 powers abandoned internationalism for a

blatantly aggressive variety of nationalism, while the Third World once again tended to become the great powers' spheres of influence. Japan tried to combine with part of Asia to turn the region into a new region independent both of G-3 and Third World influences, with disastrous results. The picture, however, becomes complicated as the Axis powers (including, for a time, the Soviet Union), undertook their own cross-cultural programs, while in the Western democracies nationalism (isolationism in the United States) reasserted itself. Moreover, there were frequent exchanges among all these (and many other) countries, the Berlin Olympics of 1936 being a conspicuous example. A conference organized in Hamburg that year on "leisure time and recreation" was attended by delegates from sixty-one nations, who resolved to dedicate themselves to the "development and cultivation of direct relations among the different countries" for promoting recreational activities, "a language which all nations understand."[10] The fact remains, nevertheless, that the kind of G-3/Third World cooperation that the idea of internationalism had begun to connote disappeared during the 1930s, a decade in which the G-3 powers once again prepared themselves for war against one another, and when neither the League nor any other organization survived to provide the Third World with a milieu for asserting their interests.

It is all the more remarkable, therefore, that visions of internationalism were kept alive during World War II—not an internationalism in the form of wartime alliances but one that harked back to the post–World War I days. The winning side of the second G-3 war did not want to keep the world divided after its expected victory. Although the Axis members of the G-3 would be severely punished for their aggression, they would not be permanently ostracized or expelled from this group. Even more important, the G-3 allies would resume the task of integrating Third World countries into the international community. Not surprisingly, they once again resorted to international schemes to bring this about: the United Nations as well as the Bretton Woods system for trade and economic development. They were established in the same spirit of internationalism that had produced the League, but there were also significant differences. For one thing, the United Nations, even at its inception, had many more Third World members than the League. The new Security Council included five permanent members, of which one was China. It was not that China now replaced Japan as a G-3 power. (Japan would retain that status, albeit as an economic, not a military, power.) Rather, the significance of having China on the Security Council lay in the fact that this was the first time that a Third World country had been given such a pivotal status in world affairs. And American officials who, during the war, had pushed for China's postwar status had justified the policy precisely on those grounds; as State Department officials had noted in 1943, if there were to be "an increasing measure of political stability and economic, social and cultural welfare" in the world after the war, then cooperation among the United States, Britain, the Soviet Union, and China was of crucial importance. To give China a prominent role in international affairs would "go far to advance the United Nations' cause in the eyes of all Oriental and colored peoples." Otherwise, China's and other peoples' nationalism might become too narrowly focused and endanger international stability.[11] Thus, giving China a permanent seat in the Security Council was a way of ensuring that Chinese nationalism, and by extension the nationalism of other Third World countries, would be accommodated through an international framework.

The United Nations was more "inclusive" than the League of Nations in other ways as well. Whereas at the Paris peace conference the Western powers had rejected out of hand Japan's and China's pleas for having a racial equality principle included in the preamble of the League, the United Nations charter from the beginning contained a ringing endorsement of the same principle. The 1946 Declaration on Human Rights by the United Nations Educational, Scientific and Cultural Organization left no doubt that the postwar world organization considered the ideas of freedom, justice, and human rights applicable to all people everywhere. The UNESCO itself was a continuation of the League's committee on intellectual cooperation, and the 1946 declaration that peace "must be founded upon the intellectual and moral solidarity of mankind" echoed a prominent interwar theme. It was as if the war which had produced so much race hatred, genocide, and mass destruction made it inevitable that the earlier visions of internationalism be reaffirmed, strengthened by an unambiguous assertion of national, ethnic, and racial equality. As the Cuban delegate at the preparatory commission for establishing the UNESCO observed, the organization's primary aim was to be "action which benefits the greatest number, and touches the lives and welfare of the masses of men and women in all lands."[12] He went on to suggest that one of the first tasks of the UNESCO should be the reduction of inequalities in educational and cultural opportunities within each nation and among the member states comprising the United Nations. These and many similar expressions by Third World representatives (besides Cuba, the preparatory commission included delegates from China, Mexico, and South Africa, in addition to the United States and several European countries) indicated the shared belief that nationalism and internationalism were more closely intertwined than ever, that Third World nationalism and international organization reinforced each other.

Although the Bretton Woods system's principal goal was the restoration of world trade which had been disrupted by the economic nationalism of the G-3 powers during the 1930s, its underlying principles were unmistakably internationalist. Not only were the International Monetary Fund, the International Trade Organization, and other mechanisms designed to expedite the restoration and expansion of trade among the G-3 nations, the economic development of Third World countries would be assisted through the Bank for International Reconstruction and Development, popularly known as the World Bank. The United States and other advanced countries would contribute funds to the bank so that it would distribute them among developing nations to help their industrialization projects. In the meantime, the United Nations Relief and Reconstruction Agency would alleviate the suffering experienced all over the globe because of the devastation brought by the war. With the Soviet Union tentatively participating in such projects, it might have seemed, in the early postwar years, that the G-3/Third World relationship could finally be stabilized to the benefit of both.

That this did not happen—that it has not happened—is a major theme of postwar (and contemporary) history. Of course, it is easy to argue that such a visionary arrangement could never have been realized. But to do so is to ignore an important legacy of interwar history and to underestimate the renewed determination of internationalists all over the world to work for their ideals. It would be too simplistic to say that the "realities" of the Cold War and other well-known postwar developments eclipsed and overwhelmed these ideals. The significance of the Cold War in the context of our discussion lies in the fact that it served to prolong the G-3 powers' domination of world affairs; having survived their divisive war, they now concentrated their efforts on reestablishing and maintaining a balance among them, efforts in which the reentry of the former Axis enemies into the G-3 World played a crucial role.

This was a different sort of "internationalism" from the one envisioned in terms of G-3/Third World cooperation. The G-3 powers "cooperated" in monopolizing nuclear weapons and maintaining their hegemonic position in the world, not only militarily but economically and culturally as well. Their dominant position in the global economy was unmistakable; the United States and its European and Japanese allies, of course, benefited from the Bretton Woods arrangements and expanded their production and trade tremendously, but even the Soviet Union and its European allies, which did not choose to subscribe to the arrangements, registered higher rates of growth than most Third World countries. As late as the 1960s, the G-3 powers accounted for over 80 percent of the world's total gross domestic product and export trade. What is perhaps most important may have been the G-3's ideological hegemony over the Third World. Not simply the Cold War ideologies of capitalism and communism but the concept of "nation-building" itself was largely of G-3 origin. Whether a new state undertook nation-building along "liberal developmental" or socialist paths, these ideas were, as Samir Amin would write, products of "Eurocentrism."[13] Both the capitalist and the communist halves of the G-3 World brought unprecedented numbers of young men and women from the Third World to train future leaders of their countries.

In Britain, which, perhaps because it had a socialist government after the war, took the education of Third World youths very seriously, a National Association of Labour Student Organizations was established in 1947 in the belief that "the peaceful future of mankind is dependent on...the relationship between the advanced nations and the underprivileged."[14] But this relationship was conceptually more often than not defined by the West, or by the East as the case might be, not by the South. Some in the Third World did try to develop their own perspectives to free themselves from dependence on the G-3 powers. The Bandung Conference of 1955 may be taken as a good example. The fact that this gathering of Asian and African countries took place outside the United Nations may have indicated their unhappiness with the big-power domination of the latter organization. (Of course, China might have taken such an initiative within the United Nations if the new Beijing regime had been admitted into the world organization.) Japan, which, too, was not yet a member of the U.N., sent a delegation to

Bandung but did not noticeably contribute to its deliberations. Instead, leaders from China, India, Indonesia, and Egypt seized the opportunity to assert the Third World's interests as distinct from those of the G-3. They enunciated "five principles of peace," a general statement on peaceful coexistence and reciprocity derived from a Chinese–Indian declaration of 1954.

Although none of the "five principles" was uniquely Third World, they might have served as a statement of collective identity on the part of its constituent members. They were not, however, long able to maintain their unity. Within a few years after Bandung, China and India, two leading embodiments of its spirit, were at war against each other, and the former came to espouse much more radical ideas of national liberation than implied in the principle of "peaceful coexistence." Indeed, Beijing came to denounce this principle as a mask for perpetuating G-3 domination, but others did not share such radicalism. Intra–Third World tensions mounted, partly a product of Chinese initiatives to spread its influence throughout the world, and partly due to local antagonisms of the more traditional sort (such as the India–Pakistan war of 1965). Ironically, just as intra–Third World conflicts increased, the G-3 powers in the United Nations agreed to call the 1960s "the decade of development," and in 1964 a U.N. Conference on Trade and Development (UNCTAD) was convened. But without the participation of China in the United Nations, and with the energies of Europe and Japan still devoted to their own economic agendas, there was no perceptible improvement in the relative economic position of Third World countries throughout the decade. Many of them experienced internal difficulties as well as conflicts with their neighbors. Indeed, it could be argued that if Asian, Middle Eastern, and African countries had not taken on each other, their economies might have grown faster. But could they have done otherwise, now that they had emerged as sovereign entities? Could they be expected to behave any differently from the G-3 powers in this regard? Was something wrong with the idea of nation-building itself? (It should be recalled that the United States justified its support of South Vietnam in the name of nation-building, just as North Vietnam viewed U.S. policy as an intervention in its own nation-building efforts.) Neither the G-3 World nor the Third World had satisfactory answers to such questions.

They still do not, but at least since the 1970s, it would seem, there has been a relaxation in the pattern of G-3 domination and with it a certain change in G-3/Third World relations. The American failure in Vietnam; the "oil shocks"; the U.S.–PRC rapprochement; the crisis of the Bretton Woods system—all these developments in the late 1960s through the early 1970s indicated the passing of an era of G-3 domination. The recognition by the United States that it could not prevent Vietnam from being unified by the Communists, and the decision to reverse its twenty-year old policy toward China by dealing directly with the government in Beijing, were both expressions of that change. Henceforth, the United States, and its European and Japanese allies as well, would be more willing than hithertofore to bring China and other Third World countries into the international system. That system itself would be redefined; in Henry Kissinger's formulation, it would consist of the superpowers, the industrial democracies, and the Third World. The formula itself was little different from the juxtaposition of the G-3 powers (Kissinger's first two groups) and the Third World that had long existed, but now the latter would be recognized as an important component of what Kissinger called "the new structure of peace." If additional evidence was needed, the "oil shocks" provided it; the petroleum-producing countries of the Middle East and elsewhere were now calling the tune insofar as international economic matters were concerned.

Drastic social and cultural changes in the industrial democracies confirmed the growing influence of the Third World. Among the exponents of the counterculture movement were those fascinated by China, Cuba, and other representatives of non-capitalist countries that seemed to offer alternative ways of life to what was perceived to be the malaise of capitalist democracy. Civil rights and women's movements could be readily translated into a global concern for the rights of colored races and for the health of women and children. Protests against the war in Vietnam often escalated into a revisionist critique of the Cold War and to a condemnation of big-power domination over the rest of the globe. The wisdom of unlimited economic growth through industrialization and trade came to be questioned when it was realized that these had taken place at the cost of polluting the air, water, and soil not just in industrial countries but also in less developed areas of the world where forests, rivers, and seaboards had been mercilessly subjected to exploitation and where rare animals, birds, and plants were becoming even more so.

What these changes implied was that the G-3 domination of

world military, economic, and cultural affairs was eroding. The G-3 powers still predominated in nuclear armament, and their military incursions into Third World countries did not stop. But the importance of military affairs in international relations was diminishing, while that of economic and cultural issues grew. This may have been the most crucial development of the recent decades, for the changing patterns of G-3/Third World relations reflect the latter's economic and cultural challenge of the former. The increasing economic power of Asian countries and the intensity of religious fundamentalism in Islamic nations are good examples. Already in 1991 the combined trade of the NIES and ASEAN countries approximated 12 percent of the world's total, not too far behind the United States' share. The per capita incomes of Hong Kong, Singapore, and several others had surpassed those of Portugal or Greece. What the "rise of the Asia–Pacific region" indicated was that at least in economic terms one part of the Third World was coming to approximate the G-3 nations. The fact that China, hitherto the leading anti-G-3 nation, began eagerly to adopt a competitive economic system so as to increase its production and wealth appeared to indicate that sooner or later it, as well as other Asian countries, might join the G-3 powers, even as some of the latter, especially the former Soviet Union, might lose their status, at least as far as economic performance was concerned. On the other hand, Islamic fundamentalism and other religious movements in the Middle East and elsewhere posed a different kind of challenge to the G-3 world by questioning its cultural hegemony, in particular the notion of nation-building as essentially a secular undertaking to effect economic and political development. As Cornelius Castoriadis has noted, development implied "a total transformation" of a society, indeed of man, something fundamentalist Third World leaders (even with a Western education) refused to accept for their countries.[15] Ethnic revivalism in many parts of the globe, including some G-3 countries, reinforced such anti-developmentalism.

These challenges to G-3 domination provide an opportunity for a redefinition of G-3/Third World relations. In a sense, this is what the current search for "a new world order" means. But it should be put in an historical context. As this essay has tried to suggest, the challenge to G-3 domination is not a recent phenomenon but goes back to the first decades of the twentieth century. The G-3 World has sought to respond to it by expanding the traditional framework of internationalism to incorporate Third World components. The new internationalism has remained an ideal, but for a long period of time, during the 1930s through the 1960s, it was frustrated by G-3 rivalries as well as by intra–Third World conflicts, with the result that the gulf between the two worlds remained, if it did not actually widen. Now, the increasing prominence of economic and cultural questions may awaken a new realization of the need to bring the G-3 World and the Third World closer together as members of the world community.

Will the G-3 nations be equal to the challenge? Pessimists will point to such instances as the recent moves in Europe for restricting immigrants from Africa and the Middle East, acrimonious trade disputes between the United States and Japan (and with China and other Asian countries), and the reluctance on the part of many advanced countries to increase economic aid to the poorer countries as examples indicating that internationalism has no more chance of success today than earlier. Not only might the G-3 nations fail to integrate the Third World into a stable international order; they themselves might abandon internationalism and pursue their respective national interests without regard to the consequences of such behavior for the world's future. Or else these nations might revert to the turn-of-the-century practice of banding together to preserve their collective superiority. Samuel Huntington suggests as much in a recent article on "the clash of civilizations" when he says the West "must maintain the economic and military power necessary to protect its interests" from the non-Western civilizations "whose power approaches that of the West but whose values and interests differ significantly from those of the West."[16] But such a strategy—which seems identical to one advocated by earlier realists like Alfred Thayer Mahan—is no more likely to work than pre–World War I imperialism, and the Third World's power and self-confidence today are, of course, infinitely greater than a century ago. Besides, if the key global question today is cultural conflict—here I would agree with Huntington—no use of military or economic power will ensure success, for by their very nature cultural clashes are a cultural phenomenon calling for a cultural solution.

If perpetual G-3/Third World tensions or intra–G-3 and intra–Third World conflicts were all that the twentieth century could bequeath to the twenty-first, the world could only look to a dismal future. It is to be hoped that another legacy of the present century, that of internationalism, will yet be confirmed and strengthened as a guide to the next. The tenets of interwar internationalism are still valuable today: international organization, cross-cultural communication, and cooperative efforts at solving global issues. But the principles would need to be brought up to date. The G-3 nations would have to be willing to yield even more than they have to Third World countries in economic and cultural matters, while the latter would have to be prepared to give up part of their sovereign rights, especially the right to armaments. In the meantime, both the G-3 World and the Third World should welcome the transformation of some of the latter into the former, for that could bring the two closer, especially if the newcomers accepted the principle of internationalism. It may very well be that only when, through such steps, the distinction between the two worlds became blurred, would there finally emerge a vision of common humanity.

**Notes**

[1] FO371/5486/W3259, Dec. 10, 1920, Public Record Office.

[2] FO371/5486/W3321, Dec. 16, 1920, PRO.

[3] Zhang Yongjin, *China in the International System, 1918–1920* (New York, 1991), p. 97.

[4] Nobutoshi Hagihara *et al.*, eds., *Experiencing the Twentieth Century* (Tokyo, 1985), p. 31.

[5] *Ibid.*, p. 143.

[6] Richard V. Salisbury, *Anti-Imperialism and International Competition in Central America, 1920–1929* (Wilmington, 1989).

[7] FO371/8335/W9237, Sept. 29, 1922, PRO.

[8] FO371/8308/W10463, Aug. 5, 1922, PRO.

[9] FO371/8308/W2564, Mar. 16, 1922, PRO.

[10] International Central Bureau of Joy and Work, ed., *World Congress for Leisure Time and Recreation* (Hamburg, 1937), p. xiii.

[11] Akira Iriye, *Power and Culture: The Japanese–American War, 1941–1945* (Cambridge, 1981), pp. 135, 143, 144.

[12] FO924/294, Feb. 11, 1946, PRO.

[13] Samir Amin, *Eurocentrism* (New York, 1989).

[14] Radomir Lazo, *History of the International Socialist Youth Movement* (Leyden, 1970), p. 135.

[15] Cornelius Castoriadis, "Reflections on 'Rationality' and 'Development,'" *Thesis Eleven*, nos. 10/11 (1984/1985), pp. 18–36.

[16] Samuel P. Huntington, "The Clash of Civilizations?" *Foreign Affairs*, summer 1993, p. 49.

# COMMENT ON
# THE IRIYE PAPER

Richard W. BULLIET

Iriye concludes his analysis of internationalism and nationalism in the twentieth century by concurring with Samuel Huntington's observation that "the key global question today is cultural conflict" and adding that by their "very nature cultural clashes are a cultural phenomenon calling for a cultural solution." The solution he outlines, drawing on the history of internationalism in the twentieth century, calls for a renewal of the main tenets of internationalism in a form that "yields" more to Third World countries in economic and cultural matters while those same countries relinquish some measure of sovereignty by agreeing to arms-limitation regimes and perhaps other international strictures.

The representative example he gives of cultural challenge to G-3 hegemony—and the one Huntington cites as well in more apocalyptic and xenophobic terms—is "Islamic fundamentalism." Leaving aside the ambiguity of this much-debated term, the issue is, indeed, as Iriye has said, one of cultural hegemony. At a popular level, advocates of Islam as a basis for social, moral, and political life often couch their struggle in terms of trying to prevent G-3 consumer culture, entertainment styles, moral values, and intellectual discourse from overwhelming peoples with rich and different cultural and religious traditions. At a political level, they argue that the secularly educated leaders of their own countries, with notable exceptions in Iran and Sudan, are in thrall to foreign ideologies, whether nationalist or internationalist, and have betrayed their fellow believers by leading them into a new post–World War II world of nominal national independence but actual subordination to the economic and cultural power of the G-3 world. The power and persuasiveness of the Islamic critique of G-3 hegemony is apparent in the rapidly growing numbers of its adherents, disproportionately drawn from the brightest and best-educated Muslim youth. A movement that began in the 1950s with small bodies of followers has developed into a powerful political force in virtually every Muslim country.

Some observers have abandoned efforts to explain the phenomenon away as an aberration of lopsided economic development, a narrow and isolatable sectarian fanaticism, a generational revolt, or an unforeseen channeling of dissent in a religious direction caused by autocratic limitation of political participation. They have rejected the idea that resort to police control can stifle the movement and have recognized it as a powerful cultural force that will eventually find political and social expression at national and international levels. In short, they see it as a model of the type of cultural phenomenon Iriye foresees for the next century.

Fearful of a successful political outcome for "Islamic fundamentalism," other observers have supported police suppression of religious political opinion and have portrayed the Islamic movement, or movements, as intrinsically anti-Western or anti-modern using distinctly cultural formulations. Some have gone so far as to visualize competition between "the West" and "fundamentalist Islam" as a world-structuring struggle potentially equivalent to the Cold War, though without its underlying motivation in economic theory. The instruments they see as appropriate to this new global conflict include support for "anti-Muslim" or "pro-Western" regimes in their resort to police suppression; arming of such regimes against potential "fundamentalist" aggressors; vigilance against Islamic subversion, terrorism, and foreign infiltration; and cordoning off politically and economically "outlaw" nations that are seen as the international sponsors of "Islamic fundamentalism." In other words, the same economic and military instruments used in the Cold War are to be redirected toward this perceived new threat.

At the same time, the social composition, ideological content, and attitudes of "Islamic fundamentalism" toward other cultures remain largely uninvestigated, and such writings as there are tend toward sensationalism and alarmism. In short, the G-3 world increasingly regards "fundamentalist Islam" as a problem with a cultural basis but responds economically, militarily, and politically rather than culturally. Far from yielding to new cultural expressions from the Third World, the G-3 nations increasingly voice positions of rigid rejection reminiscent of a premodern crusading mentality.

As the new century begins, Islam will probably be the first test of the capacity of the G-3 world to adapt to a truly multicultural world. The international institutions of the twentieth century, as well as its nationalist ideologies, were crafted for the most part by Europeans and Americans, or by Third World scholars and diplomats with similar educational backgrounds and acculturation. While these Third World participants were culturally Hindu, Muslim, African, and so forth by origin, most of them shared a universe of intellectual discourse with their G-3 interlocutors.

The challenge for the future will be to communicate and negotiate with Third World leaders, who may well understand the G-3 world intellectually but who will insist on reciprocal understanding and acceptance of alternative domains of discourse. This conflict is already joined in the clash between activist Muslim thinkers and G-3 politicians and diplomats over mutually agreeable understandings of concepts like "democracy," "human rights," "equality of gender," and "political participation."

As Iriye astutely points out, it would unreasonable to expect movements and national governments that define themselves in terms of cultural distinctiveness vis-à-vis G-3 hegemony to relinquish elements of sovereignty for the sake of world peace and stability without a compensating acceptance of their self-proclaimed cultural identities. In a world teeming with weapons suppliers, it is unlikely that efforts to stem the proliferation of missiles and other modern weaponry by coercion or embargo will be very effective. More likely they will simply harden emerging patterns of cultural hostility.

The new internationalism that Iriye advocates cannot achieve its goals of peace and stability without an acceptance of the validity of articulations of modernity (or post-modernity) deriving from cultural bases currently neglected, derided, or feared by many G-3 governments. The old institutional bottles of twentieth-century internationalism must be filled with a new wine that tolerates and values not just "Islamic fundamentalism," but other constructions of human meaning and worth emanating from cultural sources that do not accept G-3 cultural hegemony.

Iriye's synopsis of twentieth-century internationalism highlighted the participation of Third World states in various international deliberations. In the future, having representatives of Third World governments at the negotiating table will be less important than whether those representatives are seen as clones of G-3 diplomats sent by leaders whose power is based on exogenous political and philosophical theories or whether they are seen to represent the autonomous cultural identity of their peoples.

Japan and, to a lesser degree, China seem already to have achieved this combination of cultural autonomy and international legitimacy. Islam will prove a more difficult case. The hostility toward the Islamic religion so deeply embedded in European cultural history will have to be overcome at the very moment when responsible leaders and thinkers of European cultural heritage are preparing themselves and their followers for apocalyptic religious, or cultural-religious, conflict. The historical trajectory so eloquently delineated by Iriye points to Islam as the crucial test of the world's capacity to transcend G-3 hegemony and rethink internationalism in a truly pluralistic cultural form during the coming century. The road to achieving this goal is difficult. It will require tolerance, humility, and profound reeducation. Failure in following this road, however, will produce a century of hatred and conflict comparable to the one we are on the verge of surviving.

# Discussion

**Harkabi:** I contend that in discussing the Third World, we have first to try to identify what part of the world is the "world order" and consider the expression "world order" as dynamic. Some countries in Asia that previously considered themselves Third World have developed, and perhaps redeemed themselves from that status. The center of gravity of the Third World is now Africa, and perhaps Latin America, but it does not seem to me that the Third World gets much attention. On the contrary, I would maintain that the Third World gets too little attention, and the reason is that the developed countries do not need the raw materials and do not need these countries.

From time to time there is starvation in Africa. Some help is sent, and that's all. I am afraid that after the Somali experience there will be less willingness to intervene on humanitarian grounds. In some Third World countries we see certain changes, and the changes come about not because of influence from the outside. It is not a question of dialogue but simply change because of the need to change. For instance, one of the most prominent trends in recent years has been the democratization of many military regimes in Latin America. That was not done because anybody had a blueprint of internationalization of nice souls at the time of the League of Nations. Simply they came to the conclusion (and that, too, in the Soviet Union) that, despite all the descriptions of democracy as unstable, as a bad system, it was better than anything else.

Thus, we see a trend toward democratization, but it does not come through any decision about world order, and here I do see a difference in the way that I use the term "world order" and the way Iriye uses it. It seems to me that he uses world order as one that people want to establish, and I use world order as the kind of world which we find now, which has already been established by the efforts of different countries. Therefore, my use of world order is pragmatic, it is not prescriptive, and I think that that is a very important difference. At the time of the League of Nations, world order denoted the kind of a world we wanted to establish, and I use it simply to characterize the relationship between nations (as we, of course, conceptualize them because that is all we can do).

Another difference is internationalism. I believe that there is a trend now toward internationalism as a prudential policy, that is to

say, countries understanding that they have to take into consideration wider factors than those which concern them directly. Take
Israel, if I may. The Israeli problem is not the Palestinians. The
Palestinians could be easily smashed. Israel's need to reach a settlement with the Palestinians is because of other factors in the world
which Israel has to take into consideration—an indication, it seems
to me, of the increase of the influence of the international factor in
the world.

I believe that many people have read that brilliant article by
Huntington. But it is incorrect that the difference between civilizations as he described them will be the next source of wars and, more
specifically, Islam and Christianity. We have seen war between civilizations. We have to go back to the war between the Greeks and the
Persians and to the Crusades. In all other cases, the wars were not
between civilizations but between states. I do not see that Islam is
united. One of the big mistakes of Orientalists at the beginning of
the American–Iraqi war was that they said that there would be a terrible reaction all over the Islamic world against the interventions by
the United States and its allies. I do not see Islam as united to wage
a war of civilizations.

I do believe that there are problems, but I do not think that you
can export a solution to the Muslim world. The problem is within
Islam, and there are difficulties in Islam which are, I would say,
similar to difficulties which I find in Judaism of adjustment to the
modern world. In Judaism it is easier. In Islam itself there are great
problems besides the political clashes as such. But I do think that a
certain progress has been achieved in the world since the time of
the League of Nations. Sometimes we are greatly tempted to an
ostentatious realism, and that means cynical realism, as described in
"nothing has changed, you have to prepare yourself for the worst,"
etc. I would say that nothing is more blinding than when people
pretend to be realists.

**Kosai:** Iriye emphasized the importance of the cultural problem. He was too modest to offer the cultural solution directly, but I
sense that his solution lies in the direction of equality of races, gen-
ders and states and nations, tolerance or toleration, peaceful coexistence, non-interference, and dialogue. So far I have nothing to
disagree with but, at the same time, there is no denying that there
are several actual more urgent questions which must be solved, as
he will agree, according to his paper.

First, in economics. The Third World in general emphasized a new international economic order, while Korea or Taiwan or such successful industrializing nations accepted the current regime as far as it goes. There are wide differences within the Third World as far as economic policies are concerned, and how to reorganize the world trade regime is not a cultural problem but, rather, a pragmatic problem.

The second is, of course, the security problem, and how to deal with the Third World, for the G-3 countries remain contingent on developments in the Third World. Perhaps our attitude toward the Third World will affect its own development, but we cannot control what will be the China or what will be the India in the next century. So I think we need some contingency plans to deal with the security problem for the next century.

As an example, I would like to add one other question: that is, the reorganization of the United Nations. I am not propagandizing or demanding that Japan should be admitted as a permanent member of the Security Council, but at least currently the United Nations is organized on quite a dual principle. One is equality of nations, equality of states in the General Assembly, and the other the oligarchic structure of the Security Council, although the Security Council includes China as a former Third World country. So if equality of nations or states should be the principle of our policy toward the Third World, the reorganization of the United Nations must be resolved in some way compatible with that principle.

I think the cultural problem is quite important, but if the emphasis on the cultural side diverts our attention from the pragmatic urgent problem, it might be counterproductive.

**Stern:** I would like nothing better than to talk as historian to historian on Iriye's really splendid paper, but that would get us into a purely historical discussion, and I am afraid that is not what we are here for. Let me just make a couple of points about the paper. In dealing with the question of Europe's relation to what we now call the "Third World," one has to understand that its position was shaken from the very beginning of the century, by the Boer War, the Russo–Japanese War, etc. Europe was in retreat, as it were, from its arrogant supremacy, expressed also in racial terms, before 1914.

Needless to say, I agree completely about the admirable attempts of internationalism in the cultural realm, in particular, but not only in the cultural realm. It was, it seems to me, in the context of the cultural realm that the Briand-Stresemann Agreement, the Locarno Agreements, could have been made. In other words, however, there is a spill-over effect, and this is meant to strengthen the argument that cultural reconciliation can have its political repercussions. We have seen that. After all, what the first half of the twentieth century showed was not only the struggle between Europe and the outside but the struggle within Europe. Today symbolizes more a degree of progress, and here I want to echo what Harkabi says— that a pessimism which never acknowledges any successes is really deeply erroneous and injurious. The Franco-German reconciliation after 1945 is, in part, based on a cultural reconciliation, as is the entire European reconciliation after 1945, so all of this is meant to suggest simply further evidence for your basic thesis.

I am puzzled by some of the things that Bulliet has said because actually they suggest, if I may put it this way, a degree of certainty and almost one-sidedness that is in itself troublesome. I remember distinctly the days after the Algerian election and my own deepest puzzlement. I thought it was a heart-breaking problem for a democrat—and perhaps it is not only a problem of Islam but in general— that of whether, within a democracy, you allow a shifting plurality to inflict what were assumed to be intolerant measures that would subvert democracy. Whether you allow it or not is a major problem for practical politicians, for thinkers about democracy. When you speak with assurance about popular will in Algeria and Egypt, I would simply say: Yes, of course, it was an expression of a part of popular will. The tragedy, it seems to me, in Algeria, and as far as I understand in Egypt, is that within democracies you have shades of difference. Equally, the West, and not only the West, would be appalled by a situation in a country where one of the authentic heroes, I think, of the decades, Sadat, would be assassinated, but also that fact it would be celebrated by so many people as a very good thing and that others are threatened by the same fate. You would understand them but it seems to me that it is not only that we have to understand but that we want to hear that you understand. Again, I use the example of Sadat's assassination as one of the principal shocks that we have had.

**Nivat:** I have a question for Stern. I did not quite understand the point on democracy and popular will in Algeria. First, you seemed to say that an undemocratic will should not be allowed even through some sort of democratic process and, then, it seemed to me that you said that you are not sure that it was a real popular will.

**Stern:** What I meant to say was that in any case it is not a particular problem of Algeria, though I experienced it as a particular problem. It was a choice between two evils, I thought. I see as a general problem in any polarized political democracy what you do under that kind of circumstance.

Then I, secondly, picked up separately—but linking it not only to Algeria, but to Egypt as well—Bulliet's remark about popular will because it seemed to me that we are talking about a deeply divided society. So those in my mind are two separate issues.

**Mayall:** Could I first just make a comment on Iriye's fascinating paper, and then link it to something that is troubling me with Bulliet's argument about the diplomatic system. From Iriye's paper I have a sense that internationalism, as it has developed in the twentieth century, has had two components. One was the gradual expansion of international society so that, for the first time, it becomes a truly global society. I suppose if one wants a shorthand or symbolic date it is Resolution 1514, because it means that from then on, 1960, formal empire is no longer accepted as a legitimate political form. The other strand of internationalism is an attempt to make international society into a kind of purposive organization, so by analogy ultimately into a kind of global welfare state and that, I suppose, is an inheritance from nineteenth-century progressive thought. It was not only an international duty to incorporate the world and to make it more tolerant but it was also meant to be going somewhere. There was a common destiny, and I think that strand is much more problematic when we come to think about where we are going now because one way you can characterize this strand of international relations since 1945 is the dream of a quick fix.

The quick fix was to be brought about by economic development, and I think if you look at the way, not in which knowledgeable technicians studied problems of development, but the way in which the diplomacy of development was conducted, what you see is a series of searches for a catalytic agent. First, in the manner of Walt Rostow, financial transfers were to move the vast majority of mankind to a position of self-sustaining growth. Ten years later, it was—if only the industrial Western countries would get rid of their escalating tariffs on semimanufactured goods—a catalytic agent. Since the vast majority of Third World countries were condemned, anyway, to be for the foreseeable future the producers of raw materials, it was the structure of commodity pricing which would somehow bring about this change. All of those suggested that the quick fix had to come from outside.

Now we are in just as pernicious a sort of dream, it seems to me, because we are told, against all pragmatic expectations, that the fault is purely internal, that there is nothing outside. It purely has to do with getting the prices right (or whatever) internally. So, in a sense, the fact that we know that there is no quick fix is a net advantage as we approach the twenty-first century, but it also makes the problem of the diplomatic system and its heterogeneity more, not less, problematic. It makes the importance of a diplomatic system even greater than it was before.

The Western origin of the current global system is almost a contingent factor, and a diplomatic system arises to cope with problems of cultural diversity amongst other kinds of diversity. I was reminded of reading a marvellous book—not much read now perhaps—by the anthropologist Professor Isaac Shapiro, about tribal government and politics amongst Botswana people living on the edges of the Kalahari Desert who constituted in the pre- and partly during the colonial period, a world of their own. During the transition they produced a different diplomatic system which has all of the same components as the one characterized as deriving from Westphalia and then being spread around the world.

As the world we are involved in is a single system, which is more culturally diverse, it becomes more important, not less, that even if there is a price to pay, diplomats should play the same game.

**Yamaguchi:** The contrast between pragmatic and cultural approaches was mentioned by Kosai, but I think Iriye's reminder that we should reflect on the 1920s and 1930s shows that pragmatism and culturalism should not be opposed to each other. I think the two are complementary. Pragmatic solutions have to do with the technology of politics, economy, etc., but you need cultural imagination to keep technologies and practical solutions really viable and sustainable.

**Perczynski:** What bothers me is that still the G-3 world is divided. Whether the division will deepen or will move toward a more global and unified solution depends on the direction of the development of integration on a regional scale. But there are tremendous polarization processes going on in the Third World, and this is a really dangerous question. That polarization is also due to the fact, a very positive one, that we are living in the period of scientific technological revolution, according to Rostow. Because of the possibility of absorbing the achievements of that revolution, we have newly industrialized countries which not long ago were very backward but have found their place in the world economy.

On the other hand, we have countries unable to utilize the achievement of that stage of evolution, and we are facing a growing absorptive capacity threshold for the new technology in a very large number of countries. One cannot expect that the diffusion of technological progress, so much connected with the achievement of that "Fourth World Industrial Revolution," will influence the situation in Zaire, Bangladesh, Somalia, or elsewhere in Africa, in Latin America and Asia.

The profound problem then arises of how to deal with this group of countries which we cannot count, and whether the achievements of the current stage of industrial revolution may change their position. I would like to ask Iriye which option could be taken into consideration. The first is not to intervene and to rely on the rationality of the invisible hand of the market. There is such an option, and probably a very realistic one, although I do not think that this is a solution of the problem. The second is to encourage the search for a certain "third wave" solution, still popular in this Third World, but, frankly speaking, I have not seen any successful attempt to build a strategy based on "third wave" assumptions.

The third option is based on regional solutions. These are very pragmatic in certain areas. I am optimistic about the role of regional integration in the Third World countries of Eastern Europe. In many respects, they are Third World countries, but they have a chance to join European civilization. I see opportunities in North America with, among others, the North American Free Trade Association. There are some chances in Asia, with a regional center of gravity like Japan, and an integrational grouping, ASEAN. Still, the regional solutions are very far from the group of countries which find themselves in an extremely desperate position, one which has not only a human dimension but also a tremendously dangerous political dimension.

There is the last solution, the hope of establishing a new international economic order. The last serious attempt failed and probably there are few chances of establishing a new international order by passing another United Nations resolution and embarking on some strategy never to be fulfilled. Of course, there is a small avenue opening to create global partnership arrangements, but these call for elaborating something on which the global partnership may be based, namely the principles of global rationality. Is it possible to build this principle of global rationality, to engage in global efforts to solve the question of those countries so terribly hit by the history?

This is a question which I think calls for discussion, and on which I would like also to have your opinion.

**Iriye:** I think Harkabi is absolutely right in saying that Third World is a term that conceals many different kinds of Third World countries, different regional varieties, different types of economic development, and so on. I think I said somewhere toward the end of my paper that some of the Asian countries, at least economically speaking, may be beginning to leave the Third World and may be joining the G-3, but it would seem to me that still leaves the cultural question. When we talk about cultural differences, democracy, human rights, China comes to mind as well. It does seem to me that there are these cultural questions that have to be faced, too, no matter into how many pieces we subdivide the Third World, but in any event I am in agreement with Harkabi on this. I also agree with him about our different uses of the two terms "world order" and "internationalism," or "internationalization." I think we are using these terms more or less in a complementary fashion.

Kosai said that if we are too preoccupied with cultural questions that might divert our attention from other issues like security or economic questions. I agree, but at the same time we can turn it around and say that if we focus our attention too much on security and economic issues we may somehow forget the cultural question which, to me, is perhaps as important as the others. I mentioned the human rights issue, and I think we are going to come back to that. In terms of rational choice, while I could believe and trust Kosai to come up with rational solutions to economic development and other issues, I am not sure if rational choice can solve cultural questions, and that is why I think we have to be aware of the need to come to grips with those kinds of questions.

I am grateful to Stern for reminding us that even when we talk about cultural communication, understanding, reconciliation, there are political repercussions, and he cited some very good examples of what has happened in this regard, for example German–French reconciliation. Another potentially good example might be Japan and China. No matter how many treaties they sign with each other, no matter how much money is being invested by Japan in China, no matter how economically developing China might be, there does still remain today, I think, the question of cultural reconciliation, and without that I do not think China and Japan are going to be equal partners in building a new world order.

Mayall's point about the need for a diplomatic style is more than ever relevant even in this world of transition where cultural issues might become very important. We are going to need some kind of traditional international framework and diplomatic effort. It does seem to me that interwar cultural internationalism, that is, advances manifested in the diplomatic arena of the League of Nations, became vulnerable and crumbled as soon as Japan withdrew from the League of Nations. That was abandoning a traditional diplomatic attempt, so that today, more than ever, I would agree that diplomatic initiatives and efforts are going to be as important.

As to Perczynski's very perceptive enumeration of different alternatives, not being an economist I cannot answer his question as to which of these alternatives is the best. I hope I can agree with him that a sense of global rationality is possible in a world of cultural diversity. If that were to come about, that would be my utopian vision.

# CAN JAPAN
# BE A
# MODEL?

# CAN JAPAN BE A MODEL? REFLECTIONS ON ARTICLE 9 OF THE CONSTITUTION

HAGIHARA Nobutoshi

I feel reluctant to discuss whether Japan can be a model for other countries. Such a question should properly be addressed by a non-Japanese observer. The Japanese, of course, have had a long tradition of looking for a model in the outside world and imitating it zealously, whether the model be Chinese or Western civilization. Although such imitation has been less wholesale and blind than selective and even creative, the fact remains that Japan is looking for an external model even today. Recently, however, as it has become harder to find a suitable outside model, foreign observers have been increasingly interested in drawing lessons from Japan's postwar economic successes. Thus "Can Japan be a Model?" may no longer be as preposterous a question as it was several years ago.

In considering this question, I should like to focus on the postwar constitution, especially its Article 9. Today I am more than ever convinced of the relationship between Article 9 and Japan's potential role in the world. I remain very proud of that article and the principle of pacifism that is behind it, but I also feel, in this post–Cold War age, at a time when Japanese politics appears to be reshaping itself rather rapidly, that some modification of the article may be called for.

As is well known, Article 9, entitled "renunciation of war," states, in the first paragraph, that the Japanese "forever renounce" the "threat or use of force as a means of settling international disputes," and, in the second, that they undertake not to maintain "land, sea, and air forces, as well as other war potential" and not to recognize "the right of belligerency of the state." This article remains a declaration of the ideals of pacifism, derived from our reflections on Japan's past aggressive wars, and it has been accepted by the majority of the Japanese people.

At the same time, however, we cannot deny that some uneasy feeling has been entertained even by those, including myself, who strongly support the pacifist constitution. For example, although the constitution states that Japan is not to maintain "land, sea, and air forces," it actually possesses armed forces of 270,000 in strength, the so-called Self Defense Force, and annually spends one percent of its GNP on defense, an amount which exceeds the defense expenditure of all but two other countries in the world.

Moreover, the constitution has been interpreted in such a way as to legitimate the participation of the Self Defense Force in "peace-keeping operations," as happened in September 1992 when a small force was dispatched to Cambodia to assist the United Nations' mission in that country.

Clearly, such ambiguities and expanded interpretations need to be checked if the constitution is to be maintained as the basic law of the country and if Japan is to define anew its role in the world. This would call for some serious national debate on the constitution before it gave rise to cynicism at home and doubt overseas regarding the meaning of Article 9.

In the general election of 1955, the question of constitutional amendment was faced by the electorate, but at that time the leftists, who opposed any amendment, succeeded in securing over one-third of the seats in the House of Representatives, a minimum necessary for forestalling any amendment. Since then, however, there has been no opportunity to test popular sentiments on this issue. Today, I think we must reopen the debate on the constitution, ending its thirty-eight-year "freeze," and reconsider whether we shall further continue to maintain the constitution as it stands or whether certain modifications may be introduced. This is a matter that should be put up to a national referendum. It might be argued that since the Socialist Party, the major force opposed to constitutional revision, has joined the new coalition government, it will be more difficult for the Diet to take the initiative in this direction, but because of this very development I believe the party should be ready to play a role in moving the constitutional question into the public arena. Whatever the result of a national referendum, it should at least help the Japanese make the issue their own, to, as it were, internalize the principles embodied in the document.

Specifically, I believe the following steps should be taken in order to make Article 9 more compatible with the realities. The first paragraph of the article should be kept as it is, but the second paragraph should be amended so as to make the Self Defense Force constitutional. At the same time, its role should be limited strictly to three objectives: self-defense, disaster relief, and participation in peace-keeping operations of the United Nations. If we think what Japan should do in the post–Cold War world and how it can cooperate with the United Nations whose role is constantly expanding, I do not think we can avoid coming to such a conclusion.

In this connection, we should strongly support the indefinite extension of the Nuclear Non-Proliferation Treaty, which expires in two years, in order to make absolutely clear to other people that Japan has no intention of becoming a nuclear power. This will also ensure that our debate on the constitution will not mean Japan intends to become a great military power again. As for the possibility of Japan's becoming a permanent member in the Security Council of the United Nations, we should be very careful, however much we may feel such a position is justified because we pay so much for the U.N.'s operations. We should not forget to state clearly that our contribution in the United Nations will be limited to a basically non-military role. That may make it difficult for Japan to gain a seat on the Security Council.

I fully recognize that such changes as I have advocated are unlikely to be effected in the near future. Not only would there persist a reluctance in government circles to undertake constitutional revision as too destabilizing for domestic politics, Japanese public opinion will remain too deeply committed to the value of peace to consider tinkering with Article 9, however modified it may in practice have been. Moreover, the neighboring Asian countries will probably not accept a significant revision to the article as it may imply some sinister moves away from pacifism.

Nevertheless, I believe we cannot escape coming to terms with Article 9 in a changing world. As I stated at the outset, I remain proud of the constitution, but I also believe its significance has been too focused on Japan's own postwar experience. The time has come to try to universalize the experience to be able to say, this is how Japan seeks to contribute to the world through taking the initiative on behalf of world peace. But that will be possible only after the Japanese people have squarely faced the ambiguities that have developed in interpreting Article 9 and, through a national referendum, indicate what roles they feel the nation can play in the post–Cold War world. If, after such a referendum, we can, with a renewed sense of commitment to the spirit of the constitution, participate in peaceful roles in such areas as disarmament, environmental protection, and refugee relief, then it will be possible to hope that others will regard our efforts as proper and decent, and begin to see our constitution as a model for their future as well.

# COMMENT ON
# THE HAGIHARA PAPER

Michael R. WINSTON

Although Hagihara decided to defer analysis of the question "Can Japan be a Model?" he has provided a provocative basis for exploring the broad but quite pertinent issue of the foundation for Japanese leadership in the emerging post–Cold War world. He has placed at the center of his concern the relationship between Japanese public opinion as expressed in a democratic political process and Japan's role as a major force in international relations. As he has pointed out on other occasions, the pacifist values of Article 9 of the Japanese constitution may very well have propelled Japan to a new plane in international affairs, focusing its energies on economic development at a time when other major powers were driven by the national security imperatives of the Cold War. The diversion of economic and scientific-technical resources to the essentially non-productive military sector can scarcely be thought of as a net benefit to those societies.

Hagihara, however, has maintained that whatever the benefits of Japan's non-military course, imposed initially by the American Occupation and pursued later by Japan's business and political elites, there remains the issue of legitimizing Article 9 by the test of a referendum. While this can be debated from a number of angles, I would suggest that the most fruitful way to discuss the issue is in terms of its relationship to the larger question of Japan's role in the post–Cold War world.

A generally accepted postulate of international relations is that there is a reciprocal, though not symmetrical or predictable, relationship between a nation's domestic politics and its capacity to project power and influence in international affairs. The Hagihara position on Article 9 is the kernel of the major question about the interaction of Japan's public opinion, and Japanese political and economic institutions, and any role that Japan will play in world affairs beyond the boundaries of its formidable economic activities.

From the perspective of an outsider, it is not difficult to recognize that there are no objective factors that would disqualify Japan from playing whatever military role its economy and political system could sustain, within the parameters of the "great power" system. To argue the converse of this position is to maintain in effect that Japan should be, militarily speaking, in some kind of presumptive pariah status (or at least function as a "protected" or "special" state in the "great power" system). By 1995, World War II will have been over for fifty years. Given all that has happened since, the issue raised by Hagihara is not different in potential impact from the reunification of Germany. Indeed, in light of Japan's current economic capacity and the rapid alteration of the Cold War "great power" system, Japan's departure from its current course could have a far greater impact than the reunification of Germany. But I would go further than Hagihara's explicit discussion of legitimizing Article 9. In addressing this issue, there opens the new opportunity to reconsider Japan's role in the world as a "great power," not in traditional military terms.

For the twenty-first century, international leadership is not likely to be linked so tightly to military strength *per se*, especially in light of the ambiguous "benefits" derived from it, in social and economic terms, by the Cold War superpowers. (The case of the latest Bosnian crisis may be instructive, since tactical deployment of military force has been decisive for the belligerents, but no great power or surrogate alliance organization has exerted strategic military force in the situation.) Could Japan provide the international leadership that would mobilize greater resources for economic and social development in the "Non−G-7 World"? Here may be one of the more fateful questions of our time. Having been excluded from the disastrous social consequences of the militarization of the economies of the Cold War superpowers, can Japan now exercise international leadership in the enormously complicated and conflict-ridden challenges of development in the non-European world? Willingness to exercise global leadership in a non-military posture would also place in a new context the question of a seat for Japan on the Security Council of the United Nations. Such a role is far broader than simply being a source of venture capital for poor countries. It entails considerable political leadership and social vision, of a sort once contemplated by liberal opinion in the United

States in the late 1940s but eclipsed eventually by the global tragedy of the Cold War. Such a role also has the obvious requirement of a political and social system that could sustain it over time. The current upheaval in Japanese politics makes the question of the form of Japan's future international leadership a practical question for the first time since World War II. The character of the Japanese public's response to the question "Can Japan be a new type of international leader?" will be one of profound importance for the next century.

# Discussion

**Hutchison:** We could greatly enrich the discussion, and in very specific ways, if we make sure that we maintain a connection with a broader context of cultural considerations. I mean, for example, Japan has been a model for a very long time to Americans on Asian culture broadly. And Asian cultures, religions, aesthetics, philosophy have been models in entire areas of Western thought. So can Japan be a model? If we take the term "Japan" to represent something more, or even if we just take it to mean Japan, Japan has been a model for a very long time in the cultural area, and I mean "model," not just an "influence" at certain levels.

**Kerber:** It seems to me that one result of taking the challenge of this conference seriously is, as we look to the twenty-first century, to try to see the twentieth century as a whole, to understand that the generations flowed inextricably one into the next, to see the League and the United Nations as part of one long story, and to insist that the next chapter be written in terms of the United Nations so as not to let it end here and to feel we have to start all over again, but to continue working out in some way the dreams of the late 1940s.

I think that Hagihara's very sensible, very exciting, and potentially of great significance rethinking of what a constitution born in defeat might mean for victory of a cosmopolitan sort in the future is something that gives us great cause for optimism. One would like to see other nations absorb or reclaim their own versions of Article 9.

**Murakami:** In the Cold War regime, there was an ideology-based system of values within which decision making was between the choice of the two well-organized systems. Almost always politically and economically, and even culturally and religiously, the choice was between A or B, at the international level. However, at present, whether we like it or not, economically and culturally and socially, pluralism is the key word. Pluralism is here, we must accept it, and that has, in fact, come to the fore as a very positive value appreciated by many. In Japanese society there is an approach whereby in every single situation we always try not to create an absolute loser. This has been the pattern in our society reflected in the decision making process. This has been the dynamics in Japan. It may be suggested as one possible alternative.

**Junker:** I am struck by the similarity between the Japanese problem and the German problem. Except for minor deviations, you could almost take the whole discussion and say this has been the debate in Germany. Of course, I would strongly agree with Hagihara that it is always good to reconcile doctrine with reality: so make the Self Defense Force constitutional. That is true of Germany's constitution. The other suggestions combined lead to the inclusion of what you have here as a model of self-constraint, but the problem is a model for what? If this is to be regarded as a model for the world, that would mean that the United Nations, as a body of collective security, would no longer be functional, and Japan as the model of self-restraint means that the dirty work has to be done by the United States and other nations. So as sensible and as pragmatic as your solutions may be, I still have to find the rationale behind the idea that this is a model.

**Hagihara:** For many years I thought that Article 9 was a very good one, but, as we discussed at the last symposium ten years ago, there are contradictions inherent in the constitution. Unless we eliminate this inconsistency, then Article 9 cannot really become effective. I came back to the same issue again, for I feel guilty personally. A model for what, you ask me. The idealism embodied in this constitution, how can this ideal be mobilized to serve "others," not only the Japanese ourselves? I do not know whether you accept this as an answer, but I thought I should acknowledge that I am still groping for an answer.

**Iriye:** If Japan were to join the Security Council as a permanent member without revising the constitution, that will make Japan a rather different kind of member. I mean Japan is going to be not just the only member of the Security Council without nuclear weapons, but it may be the only country in the Security Council that cannot use its military force. What kind of Security Council is that going to be? It may very well be that by Japan joining the Security Council, it might even lead to some transformation of the Security Council itself, but that is really beside the point here.

**Yamaguchi:** We were made to believe that the constitution should not be changed, but we should be freed from such an inflexible attitude. Winston has encouraged us to be much more cosmopolitan for Japan to become a model, and this simply means that Japan should be opened up inside before it is opened to the outside and reaches cosmopolitanism. For instance, at the level of the university, there is very little interchange among the staff, and only during the past ten years have Japanese universities reluctantly started to open their posts to non-Japanese, but still you cannot be appointed a teacher at the primary and secondary level unless you have citizenship. It is reported in the newspapers that there is some discrimination even against Japanese citizens of Korean origin and then, in general, in Japanese companies there is very secret discrimination against the outcast people called *burakumin*. The structure of Japanese society has been producing structural failures; we have developed no mechanism for a dialogue with those who have failed. This is what Kristeva stressed when she talked about dialogue or confrontation with the stranger or "the other." So we need to revise the Japanese system of making selection by origin and by class.

**Kyogoku:** Let me talk about the circumstances surrounding the birth and growth of Article 9 of the constitution of Japan. In August 1945 Japan surrendered to the allies and was occupied. The Occupation forces came to Japan on August 28, and General Headquarters produced a draft constitution on February 13, 1946. This was imposed on the Japanese, and a new constitution, which has Article 9 in it, came into effect on May 3, 1947. On June 25, 1950, North Korea suddenly invaded South Korea, and on July 7 or 8 General Headquarters ordered the Japanese government to organize a National Police Reserve, which is the forerunner of the Japanese Self Defense Force. This was an order from General Headquarters.

Among scholars it is a minority view that the constitution was revised by order from above. The San Francisco Treaty was signed in September 1951, and Japan became independent. Together with the Peace Treaty, Japan concluded a Mutual Security Treaty with the United States; that was Japan's choice to shelter under the umbrella of the American military forces. In due course, the role of the Self Defense Force was changed; the Police Reserve was transformed into the SDF. This is revision of interpretation by the Japanese authorities. Constitutional scholars are not agreed whether the revision has already been completed or interpreted or whether the constitution has not been revised at all because the phrasing of the first clause of Article 9 is still preserved intact. Pro-Soviet forces in Japan insisted the constitution remained intact, and they used it as a political tool, while the Liberal Democratic Government, the conservative regime, asserted that the Self Defense Force is constitutional according to interpretation of the original wording of Article 9, and that state of affairs remains. The Occupation forces, after the constitution took effect in 1947, concealed the fact that the constitution had been an American initiation and the *de facto* acceptance by the Japanese authorities was hidden from the general public.

The result of the last general election can be interpreted in different ways. The eight coalition parties did not compete with the LDP on policy platform matters. The LDP split into two parties, and sizeable numbers of the LDP split from the party. That is why they lost their majority in the House of Representatives and had to hold a general election. Since they at least maintained the number of seats they had before the dissolution of the Diet, the LDP does not think of the last election as a complete loss. Now, as for the coalition of eight parties, this octopuslike presence is committed to continuing the policies of the LDP government. They had to commit themselves to the LDP policies for two reasons. For one thing, the LDP has been in power for so many years and was embroiled in corrupt practices, which is one of the reasons they lost the election, but the voters, the constituents, while they were happy that a corrupt party had been thrown out of office, nevertheless do not want any change in the long tradition of conservative policies followed by the LDP.

So the strange thing is that only the party in power was switched from the LDP to the eight-party coalition without any tangible difference in policy. A revision of the constitution is, therefore, out of the question. It is not the policy of the coalition to abolish the SDF in strict conformity with Article 9. The Socialist Party's seats were reduced from 130 to 70, so the Socialists are no longer in a position to call for the abolition of the SDF in accordance with a literal interpretation of Article 9. There is a stalemate. Whether it is good for us or convenient for us, whether or not it is effective or convenient for Japan is another matter. But the gist of the fact is the party's name has changed and there is a different cabinet, but policy-wise there will be no change.

**Hagihara:** I'm quite confused about this whole topic of the revision or non-revision of Article 9. As Yamaguchi was trying to suggest, I think we should be very careful about tampering with the constitution. You notice I belong to the same generation as Yamaguchi. We fear that the participation of the Socialist Party in this eight-party coalition could mean that the issue of the constitution might again flare up sometime. But undoubtedly the people, the constituency, do in general want stability.

**Watanabe:** Reliable historians in Japan do not explain how Japan "succeeded." We do not like to brag about our "success." In this sense, we could be a model. We are not aggressive enough in selling ourselves. We find a virtue rather in being reticent. And this has to do with the point Murakami raised about how decisions are made in Japan. This is not a principle. It is not a theory. It is a nebulous practice.

On the question of "Can Japan be a leader?" if you look at Japanese politicians, do they look like "leaders"? We doubt whether the Japanese public perceives their politicians as leaders. One, though not the only, reason for this is that no general theory or principle has explained man's position in Japan. Since at least the seventeenth century this has been a distinctive feature in comparison with China, Korea, and even Western Europe. The Japanese regime which was established in the seventeenth century was a perfectly secular structure, rejecting all transcendental values or theories. Accepting no superior power or authority, the shogunate persecuted the Christian religion and placed Buddhist sects under government control. Different from the Chinese emperor, the shogunate even did not worship heaven. The entity they worshiped is the first-generation patriarch of that particular clan which formed the government. They never sought to legitimize their authority by worship of something transcendental. Thus, Japanese society has been secular since the seventeenth century; the government itself did not try to explain or legitimize its position by general theory, and secularization quickly proceeded.

Now, after the Meiji Revolution, it was decided to follow the Western model, so Japanese government officials went to see how things worked in the Western world. They noticed that religion was a prevalent influence in Western societies. They perceived Christianity to be the integrating device used by Western leaders, so they decided they would have an equivalent of Christianity in Japan as a unifying force. But since it was impossible to diffuse Christianity immediately throughout Japan, they thought: We have no Christ, so we will use the emperor instead. This really was said at a conference by a member of the committee drafting for the imperial constitution.

Now, the emperor is a human being and not a theory. So this power, which cannot be explained in terms of general theory, was still allowed to continue. In 1945 a descendant of this regime was toppled and we have now a new constitution formulated basically at the initiative of the United States, based on general principles. This Article 9 has a particularly distinctive feature, compared to Western constitutions. It was the case after a long interval of several hundred years, that a general theory—paradoxically particular to Japan—was combined with political power. In various aspects the Japanese have relied on Article 9 when they think of their distinctive characteristics, and it causes a problem still now. But, as I said, the Japanese people are generally not accustomed to generalizing about their position in Japanese society.

**Winston:** Perhaps the most important thing I could say is that, with all due respect, I remain unconvinced that Japanese society is, in some way, uniquely constrained and trapped by its past in ways that other societies would not be; that is, I think one of the characteristics of modern societies is a greater capacity to transform themselves. As an American looking at the history of Japan, particularly since the Meiji Restoration, I am very struck by the number of times there has been an intentional break with the past and the development of the capacity to change. It is certainly one of the most striking features of that, so that in my comment on Hagihara's paper there wasn't the expectation that a change of direction is possible at jet speed, but it is certainly possible once, as Yamaguchi suggests, there is the opening of the discussion as to what is this marvelous thing for, what is the purpose, this achievement of the last twenty years, particularly, after the high growth rate of the 1970s.

The question now becomes probably the most difficult one any society can face—that now that that task has been achieved, what is it for? Is it just to be more and more a consumer society? Is there some higher purpose that this is all for? I do not think any answer is immediately forthcoming. I would not expect it to come out of a conference but to come out of a process. So the issue would be: What is the most reasonable way to create a process within Japanese society so that public opinion is, in fact, interacting with policy in a way that it did not before? I remain an optimist about what is possible. I simply do not think that Japanese society could not change or that American society could not change. I think that is one of the things becoming a modern society makes possible.

**Hagihara:** As a matter of fact, starting with Winston and Hutchison, you offered very kind advice and helpful suggestions. My own paper was very crude, just material for discussion. I wanted to elicit your reactions. As Winston said, in the final analysis we must endeavor to change Japan into a more open country, cease merely to be a beneficiary of the international community, and strive to make Japan a more positive contributor in a non-military way to international society.

# CULTURAL
# DIALOGUE IN
# HUMAN RIGHTS

# CULTURAL DIALOGUE IN HUMAN RIGHTS

Philip WINDSOR

The whole notion of human rights represents an extraordinary confluence of different and partly conflicting Western traditions which has now come to the centre of international debate. Before considering some of the difficulties and implications of that debate, I shall try to elucidate the different Western traditions, since I believe that only by doing so can one help to resolve the difficulties. But a preliminary word of caution is necessary. To say that the idea of human rights derives from Western tradition is obviously not to say that other cultures did not have any notion of people's rights. The Koran, for example, is very specific about the rights of women, even though it is even more so about their obligations. And it is probably true to say that any anthropologist could demonstrate how a particular society views the rights and obligations of its members, usually defined in terms of their roles. But human rights, independent of obligation and undefined by role—that is a very Western idea; and it is sometimes hard to know what it means. That is why it is worth examining the traditions first.

In part, the concept is inherited from neo-Platonic interpretations of Natural Law. In that tradition, humans, as humans, are endowed by God with Reason, and human dignity is therefore universal. No human being has the right to deprive another of that which inheres in being human. That is the foundation of the universalist approach to the question of human rights: I have human rights because I am a human being. Within the context of the Christian faith, one can indeed so argue; but it depends on the priority of faith. Unless one believes that God created us, the statement that one has rights because one is human is very vulnerable to any other human who simply disagrees. But that is where the second tradition comes in.

In this case, the notion of human rights is derived from the Enlightenment attempt to reason the order of society without antecedent faith. In some respects this was an heroic undertaking, one which argued that people of different religious beliefs, or none at all, could live in peace in the same civil order. Faith was now optional, but liberty was not. Instead, liberty became the new antecedent to the exercise of reason. But equally, society became the condition of liberty. Hence, the most famous declaration of human rights in history defined them as *les droits de l'homme et du citoyen*. But did that mean that society now defined what human rights were? If so, that is the opposite of the universalist approach. Even within the framework of liberty, the definition of human rights can vary from one society to another. Many societies, for example, have been, and still are, notoriously chary about extending "their" human rights to foreigners living in their midst.

There are two ways of attempting to reconcile the clash between these first two traditions. The first is simply to cheat, whether consciously or not. The American Declaration of Independence, which preceded the French Declaration of the Rights of Man by a few years, admirably represents such a manoeuvre. Its language is that of Enlightenment Reason, holding certain "truths" to be self-evident; but the basis of its argument is that of religious faith, in that it asserts that all men were endowed by their Creator with certain inalienable rights. But putting the Declaration into practice was an exercise which soon made it clear that the extent of these rights was determined not by the Creator but by society. When Thomas Jefferson argued in the Commonwealth of Virginia that if the Declaration meant what it said, slavery would have to be abolished, he was treated with near-derision. To the contemporary mind, it is virtually inconceivable that a country which based its existence on the proclamation of human rights should continue to tolerate slavery. But the fact that it did so for a further three generations indicates the social limitations on the Creator's endowment.

The second way out of the dilemma was not so much to cheat as to replace one act of faith with another. It was the Romantic notion that the essence of humanity lay in man's affinity with Nature, usually but not always with some sort of pantheistic implication. In such a view, liberty and human rights were part of nature itself; and it was the duty of society, so frequently the enemy of Nature in the Romantic version of things, to liberate the full potential of humanity. Rousseau's "man born free but everywhere in chains" would have his fetters struck off once society returned to Nature. Echoes of this view can still be heard in the Green movements in various countries; but many Greens, like their Romantic predecessors, tend conveniently to overlook the fact that Nature is also "red in tooth and claw," and that if we were simply to return to our natural condition there would be precious few human rights left, and Hobbes would score an easy victory over Rousseau. Yet the Romantic legacy is important in the subsequent development of thinking about human rights, not least because it has an implicit evolutionary appeal.

A more comprehensive attempt to reconcile the principles of faith and social reasoning than those represented either by the American muddle or the Romantic turmoil lay in Kant's *Critiques*. Indeed, his whole work can be read in one sense as an impassioned struggle to establish the universality of human rights. Having reasoned out Reason, he turns to the applicability of Reason to human affairs, to the creation of just and constitutional government, and to perpetual peace among nations. In a sense, one might say that his vision has come half-way true: it is by now a truism to say that, whatever their conflicts of interest, liberal democracies do not wage war on each other. Yet he has come only half-way true. Those same liberal democracies have frequently shown their willingness to fight against different nations and cultures, partly in the name of interests but also partly in the name of values. Apart from particular and proximate causes, the reason is not far to seek. Kant's work was undertaken on the basis that what he himself called "the leap of faith" preceded both the elaboration of pure reason and the assessment of its applicability. And his leap of faith had a distinctly Christian content, depending as it did on the existence of God, the immortality of the soul, and the freedom of the individual will. (It is this last which makes it distinctively, though not quite exclusively, Western. Space does not permit any discussion here of what I understand by the individual will when defined in different cultural terms.) But Kant's universal applicability of reason to human rights becomes in that sense a triumph of European ethnocentrism, however noble and non-imperial his aspirations might have been. Yet it is also part of that confluence of Western traditions on which the generalized concept of human rights is based today.

In contrast to Kant who based Reason on the leap of faith, Hegel identified the two. For him, Living Reason was the unfolding and self-realization of the Spirit in and through the agency of human consciousness. And it was human consciousness which created human rights, and reconciled the state, society and the individual in the continuing expansion of freedom, even though he drew sharp distinctions between the three. "The substance of the Spirit is freedom. From this, we can infer that its end in the historical process is the freedom of the subject to follow its own conscience and morality, and to pursue and implement its own universal ends....The end of the World Spirit is realized in substance through the freedom of each individual." (*Lectures on the Philosophy of World History*) Here, Hegel, voicing the legacy of both the Enlightenment and the Romantic movement, is arguing in essence that Living Reason enables human rights both to evolve and to be created through the activity of human consciousness. By now, we have come full circle from the Natural Law tradition, which suggests that human rights are inherent, to an entirely different position, which suggests that we make them ourselves. Yet that, too, has become part of the contemporary discourse, as all manner of discussion about "raising consciousness" amply testifies.

The Hegelian legacy, however, was also to take another turn in the work of its rebellious adherent, Karl Marx. In eliminating the Spirit from history and focusing consciousness on the understanding of material conditions and social forces, Marx came very near to denying the notion of human rights altogether. His attack on liberalism in the *German Ideology*, for example, or his views on politics in the *Grundrisse*, made it clear that he regarded human rights as the codification of a particular set of values in the superstructure at a given historical moment. In that sense, they are not fundamental to the wider emancipation of humanity which was his declared aim. One can see his point: discussion of human rights is impossible outside any historical context—unless, that is, one still believes in Natural Law. But, unfortunately for him, his contribution to contemporary debates on human rights is that the Marxist tradition has made it possible for many, whether benevolent dependency theorists or downright despots, to argue that what really matters is the overhaul of the infrastructure; and that until that is achieved questions of human rights are at best of marginal relevance.

To sum up this sketch of the different forms of thought which are involved in discussing human rights, one can illustrate what is involved with a simple example. To the question: Do women have the right to vote?—the neo-Platonist or Natural Lawyer would answer yes, and they always have had whether men recognized it or not. The child of the Enlightenment would probably say: never heard of it, but might concede that it is a social possibility. Kant would show that Reason gives women that right. Hegel would argue that they have created it. Marx would answer the question with another: Could women have the right to vote before there were elections? Yet all these traditions are present when questions of human rights are raised; and the rights involved are, if one accepts that they exist at all, much more fundamental than even the right to participate in politics. Given both the importance and the difficulty of the questions, is it possible even to address them in a dialogue between different cultures?

***

Any form of dialogue between cultures demands a certain tolerance—some will even argue mutual respect. But that immediately raises the central difficulty: Is it possible to believe both in tolerance and in human rights? In theory, the question has already been answered by the United Nations. The Universal Declaration of Human Rights of 1948 has the countries of many different cultures appending their signatures to a document which outlaws discrimination against anyone because of religion, race, or sex. Yet, as the Vienna Conference on Human Rights of 1993 amply demonstrated, there is very little agreement when it comes either to the interpretation of what discrimination means or to the prioritization of attempts to deal with it. And in any case the very act of interpretation can sometimes be seen as an affront to a particular culture. In the summer of 1993, the Minister of the Interior of Saudi Arabia, for example, explained to a Dutch journalist who had questioned him about the arrest and disappearance of a group of human rights activists there that there was no need to agitate for human rights since the country already comprised a perfect society, based as it was on strict adherence to the teachings of Islam. In fact, the question of how to reconcile tolerance with a concern for human rights has hardly yet been addressed, let alone answered.

Most discussions of the issue tend to polarize the participants into sharply conflicting groups, accusing each other of cultural imperialism on the one hand and mindless relativism on the other. One way of inching out of this impasse might be to draw a verbal distinction between tolerance and toleration. The need for this distinction is apparent when one considers the Enlightenment tradition of human rights. As I argued at the beginning, toleration between people of different religious beliefs was essential to the development of a civil society—and indeed John Locke virtually defined civil society in those terms in his famous Theory of Toleration. But this did not imply unlimited tolerance: the framework for toleration is precisely that everybody obeys the same rules, whatever the nature of their beliefs. Similarly, toleration is indispensable between cultures, but that does not imply tolerance of practices which are clear violations of human rights. At this stage, however, the distinction only serves to beg the question. After all, agreement on what human rights are, and on what constitutes a violation, is necessary before toleration can be distinguished from unthinking tolerance.

What *are* human rights? One is tempted at this point to remember Bacon's words about Pontius Pilate: "'What is truth?' said jesting Pilate, and did not stay for an answer." But an attempt to persevere leads to the conclusion that the different traditions outlined above have produced genuine and perplexing antinomies. In the United States for example, the battle over abortion has been cast in terms of the "right to life" (Natural Law) versus the "right to choose" (post-Enlightenment). Even then, neither of these positions is absolute. Proponents of the right to choose virtually all agree that some limit should be set to the length of the pregnancy which can be terminated. And even in Ireland, where the Natural Law tradition has survived to a greater extent than in any other Western country, the Bench of Bishops recently went through extraordinary intellectual and moral contortions in order to justify allowing a teenage rape victim to travel abroad for an abortion.

If even the right to life cannot be said to be either absolute or unambiguous, what hope is there for clear-cut guidance on other rights? Theorists of justice, such as Rawles, have tried valiantly—but it seems to me in vain—to create a schematic framework within which human rights can be charted; but they still do not get past the problems of the antinomies. To some extent, it must be allowed that human rights are circumstantial: what is a right in one context might not be a right in another. (This question comes up again and again in discussion of such questions as what constitutes legitimate self-defence.) But if human rights are only circumstantial, does not this open the door by which toleration gives way to unthinking tolerance? Does it not make it impossible to conduct any cross-cultural dialogue about the question at all?

There are two possible answers to that question, one provisional and one more discursive. The provisional answer is that while it might be difficult, if not impossible, to define human rights in positive terms, a negative definition becomes increasingly feasible. (The word "increasingly" there conceals the more extensive answer.) And indeed, the negative definition has a long ancestry. A famous sentence from the *Magna Carta*, while begging at least three questions on the way, makes the point: "To no free man will we deny or delay the right to justice." And it is still true today that Amnesty International, when publishing its graphic and increasingly voluminous reports of human rights abuses in the world, relies on the negative definition. In terms of any of the traditions outlined above, it is accepted that people have the right not to be arbitrarily imprisoned, tortured, raped, or murdered. The negative definition of human rights might at least provide a minimalist basis for consensus between cultures. But it has two drawbacks.

The first is that much of its content depends on the assumption of the due process of law. People do not have an automatic or inherent right to freedom from arrest whatever they do (that is also implicit in the Theory of Toleration); their right lies in freedom from arbitrary arrest. But due process can be very circumscribing in terms of rights. Nor can it answer questions pertaining to fundamental rights. The difference between lawful execution and judicial murder cannot be resolved by appeal to the due process of law, either in the terms of Dostoevsky's impassioned rejection or of Joseph de Maistre's view that the executioner was indispensable to a civilized society. In that respect, the appeal to the legal system can help to establish rights in the terms of safeguards against arbitrariness, but it does nothing to move the question beyond the existing social norms. In such terms, Karl Marx was quite right; and his views are indeed borne out in the sentence quoted from the *Magna Carta*. Even among countries which still accept the death penalty, there is no scope within the terms of the negative definition of human rights as to what crimes might merit it and what crimes do not.

The second drawback to the negative definition has already been suggested in the discussion of the first: it allows for no extension of human rights. While it might be agreed that there are certain horrors or indignities to which no human being should be subjected, it is much harder to reach agreement on the access to new and even perhaps newly created rights, or even the access of certain categories of people to older, well-established rights. Rights in suffrage, property, personal representation in law all provide instances where some categories of people inherently enjoyed them and others were absolutely denied them. The negative definition can take no account of such matters. And there is no cross-cultural consensus on such matters. That raises the second answer to the question asked above: the discursive rather than the provisional.

In terms of that answer, the suggestion here is that one cannot say that human rights *are*, but that they *become*. Obviously, this draws on the Hegelian tradition. But after the experience of the twentieth century, it is to say the least problematic to view world history in terms of the Objectification of the Absolute Spirit. So what are we left with? It seems to me that we find ourselves in a most peculiar moral and philosophical position, in which, even while drawing on Hegel we are obliged to take a kind of existential bet of the kind to which Hegel would have objected most strenuously. Yet, had he lived now, he might have accepted the terms: its nature is that the discourse of human rights is redefining the meaning of ontology in categories which are concerned not with being but with becoming.

That is of course a contradiction in terms. But it seems to me that the hitherto unacknowledged task with which any discussion of human rights is implicitly preoccupied is precisely that of reconciling the contradiction. Despite Rousseau, Man is not born free, but can become free. Is Man even born Man? Certainly not in terms of the questions of human rights. In terms of the existential bet, however, human beings can become human.

But playing Hegel in aid of an existential bet exacts its price. It is that the discourse of human rights now reenters history with a vengeance. For Hegel, that would not have been a problem—more like the definition of the answer. But that was because for him there was only one history, the history of consciousness, which precluded the subjects of Oriental despots from entering into history, let alone such societies as those of Africa, which, he roundly declared, had no history at all. But if the very basis of cultural dialogue is the acknowledgement of different histories, and if on the other hand human rights demand a common ontology of becoming, where does one go from there? To see human rights in terms of becoming gets us out of the trap of unthinking tolerance, but does it provide for the development of human rights within the framework of toleration?

\*\*\*

Before even attempting to answer that question, it is convenient (and necessary) to get a couple of obvious points out of the way first. These have in the past bedevilled the question of the relationship between human rights and cultural dialogue. The very phrase "cultural imperialism," at best an inapposite analogy, at worst an attempt deliberately to translate questions of humanity into questions of power, indicates the confusion that has arisen between politics and the relations between states on the one hand, and rights and the relations between cultures, on the other. A number of considerations need unpacking here, however. The first is that part of the difficulty in addressing questions of human rights at the international level is that it was originally couched in terms of a clash between one self-consciously "becoming" culture (the West) and other "being" cultures, less self-conscious perhaps but more attuned to identity in the world and less concerned with the painful clash between identity and authenticity which has been so characteristic a feature of the Western experience. The supreme attempt to translate authenticity (which might be characterized as "true" becoming as opposed to false becoming) back into identity can be seen in the history of fascism and Nazism. But, short of that, the West attempted to impose its own history of the awareness of "becoming" on to the "being" of other peoples through the process of imperialism. The *droits de l'homme et du citoyen* became *la mission civilisatrice.* (Or, in the case of Britain, "The White Man's Burden"— but few remember that this particular bit of elevated doggerel was addressed by Kipling to the United States as a form of accusation, reproaching Americans for their reluctance to take up the imperial role of sweat, sorrow, and duty.) Given that background, the category-errors which are involved in the term "cultural imperialism" are perhaps understandable, though errors they remain. But there is a further complication.

When the United States did indeed decide to assume the burden in the years after 1945, it was not concerned with the civilizing mission as between cultures but with the containment of a threat to Western civilization from within an extraordinary province of Western culture. What made this province so extraordinary was not only that it had been in its own terms an imperial power but that it had extended its own rule of "being" (having missed out on most of the Western forms of "becoming" ) over other cultures of "being"—

from the uplands of the trans-Caucasus to the plains and deserts of Central Asia. It had then indulged, however, in a frenzied process of becoming, in which its own history and that of all the peoples it ruled were now subjected to a redefinition of themselves in the future. And it was that redefinition of the future which the United States sought to contain when it did take up the burden.

America—in many ways the expositor, though not the originator, of the notion of the human quest for "becoming"—was now, however, defending a codification of human rights which could be defined almost entirely in terms of being. The antinomies had not yet burst forth, the questions of the extension of rights had scarcely surfaced, the problems of who would be able to participate in acknowledged rights had scarcely been addressed, let alone become a matter of consciousness. The voices of Martin Luther King and Kate Millett had not yet been raised. In a very peculiar sense, the island, as it saw itself—the planet even—of becoming had now become the redoubt of being. The two offshoots of the European form of Western experience had now switched roles. The old Russia had now become the sinister form of Soviet becoming; the American enterprise had now been redefined in terms of defending the *status quo*.

But that defence of the *status quo* also took the form of power. In two forms. The first was, as far as possible, the imposed extension of human rights, as hitherto conceived by the United States, upon other peoples. Japan is a notable case in point. The second was the battle about the nature of human rights with the Soviet Union—and this battle took the form of a struggle for power.

In other words, America had now assumed the demi-imperial role of imposing human rights on others but while also subsuming such questions into questions of power. The culmination of this process was evident under the Carter presidency, and in the aftermath of the meetings of the Conference on Security and Cooperation in Europe, when, in the review conferences the U.S. adopted what might be called a forward strategy on human rights. That, by its very nature, was really an attempt to translate the rules of power politics into a form of procedure for the adoption—or at least acknowledgement—of human rights themselves. President Reagan continued in the same tradition—at least until he saw, at last, that Mr. Gorbachev was trying to change the rules of the game.

But by then changes in American society had begun to ensure that human rights were now to be defined in terms of becoming rather than in those of being; and Gorbachev's abjuration of the old principles of Soviet becoming led to the possibility of a new dialogue. Yet the principle of power was still seen—at least by many Americans and their adherents in other Western countries—as essential to the intercultural definition of human rights.

Here, we have two historical forms. The first, that of Western imperialism, imposes becoming on being. The second, that of the Cold War, translates the original conflict into a new one: that which was the old becoming into a new form of confrontation with the old being which had now turned into the most condign form of becoming. The result is that, caught between these different forms of historical criteria, the whole question of human rights has become both fissiparous and static. Fissiparous in the sense that within the interacting conflicts of social relationships inside a country, on the one hand, and the requirements of international society, on the other, rights become arbitrary, determined by governments jumping between domestic constituencies and international interests, and therefore ultimately more of a tool of management than a principle of either being or becoming. Moreover, the fissiparous nature of the rights at issue, when seen in this context, tend to heighten the antinomies suggested above. Human rights, as in the case of abortion, are no longer the binding forces of society but the questions which set its members apart from each other.

In general, then, human rights cannot be imposed by power, nor can they be tools of management of society by government. The dialogue between cultures can seldom if ever be conducted as a dialogue between governments—if only because some governments just don't like human rights and other governments can't make them. But, as the case of Russia shows, such governments can also fall victim to the dialogue between cultures. Occasionally, too, non-governmental organizations can help: Oxfam's agronomic work in Africa, for instance, has entailed a very active cultural dialogue, which has done much to extend the ideas of rights independent of roles through the transformation of traditional agricultural practices, and has done so without any hint of "cultural imperialism"; but at the same it has done so only by indirection. The real question which this section addressed is whether these matters can be directly addressed without the instrumentalities of power or management. Once these have been cleared out of the way, is there a basis for dialogue?

I would suggest that there is, but that it depends on one initial distinction. All cultures depend on translating certain underlying values into the norms of social behaviour. For the most part they promptly proceed to confuse the two; so that any criticism of a given social norm is regarded as an attack on the values which it is supposed to represent. Yet toleration implies respect for other people's beliefs and values, without necessarily implying that the social norms should be condoned. To give an example: York Minster in the North of England is one of the outstanding European cathedrals. Its architecture and its stained glass are the evidence of a monumental faith. (It is also a miracle of modern technology in that it is hydraulically afloat on a bed of oil in order to protect its structure from the vibrations of traffic.) Yet between the monumental faith and the modern technology, what has the Minster witnessed? It has seen one of the early mediaeval pogroms of Jews carried out by the Christians who built it. It has seen a frenzy of witch-hunting and witch-burning some centuries later. Not long afterwards, during the Puritan ascendancy, it was witness to the solemn trial and execution of a cat for catching a mouse on a Sunday. All these social acts were carried out in the name of Christian belief. Today, for those who worship there, the faith remains, but such norms have vanished. And that is exactly the concern of toleration: never to lose respect for the values but to be vigilant about the norms which are deemed to be their expression.

If it is the business of toleration to distinguish between the two, between the expression of faith embodied in York Minster and the identity of which it is a monument, on the one hand, and the massacre of Jews and the burning of witches on the other, then a central element of cultural dialogue is criticism. Unthinking tolerance or a commitment to relativism preclude all criticism, and with it, as suggested earlier, any commitment to human rights. Toleration, in the sense in which I have used it here, demands criticism precisely because of a commitment to such rights—and does not allow a Saudi interior minister to get away with the conflation of norms and values. Once the distinction is made, cultural dialogue is, at one level at least, rather easier than it looks, if only because of the empirical argument that there is a surprising consensus on ultimate values among different cultures. Love is better than hate. Forgiveness is better than revenge. Peace is better than war. One could be tempted to leave it at that—to make, as it were, an eclectic confection of the ultimate values on which everyone seems to agree and proclaim the outbreak of universal peace as everybody listened to everybody else's criticism and adjusted their social norms accordingly. (That is perhaps what the founders of the Ba'hai faith expected.) But it is unfortunately not quite so simple.

Precisely because human rights are in part circumstantial—that is, contingent on the reinterpretation of the norms—and at the same time dynamic—that is, concerned with the interpretation of becoming rather than the static definition of being—the cultures will continue to clash, and the readaptation of norms and values will continue to be painful.

In terms of the existential bet, however, that is exactly what is required. It *is* the clash, it *is* the pain of adaptation, which lead to the extension of human rights to greater numbers of people and to the creation of new rights. There are two implications here, one concerning clashes between cultures, the other concerning the adaptation of norms to values.

In terms of the first, human rights "become" in different cultures in different ways. Sometimes they are rooted in older ideas of "being," but only explicitly "become" when they are recognized as rights. A Japanese institution makes the point. In Japan, at about this time of year, a public holiday has been inaugurated under the name of National Day of Reverence for the Aged. There are many social implications here, reflecting in part an anxiety in Japanese society that younger people were losing their traditional respect for their elders ("being") and a determination to rearticulate it (perhaps "becoming"). Yet in spite of the ambiguities, the very re-minder inherent in such a public holiday would enable any Japanese to criticize virtually any Western society for its callous disregard of older people, which deprives them of dignity and independence—let alone their social value in a world which is subject, and vulnerable, to the consequences of unforeseen change. Such an example might help to illustrate, albeit in an ambiguous and some might say caricature form, an essential criterion for the judgement of clashes between cultures. That is, that one culture might have realized far more effectively than another the human potential of certain categories of people. And in doing so it acquires, within the terms of toleration and of the ontology of becoming, the "right" to criticize others on the grounds of their human rights records. Once that potential is realized, the "right" becomes a duty. Otherwise there would be no basis for toleration.

At the same time, however, the critical basis for toleration, while perhaps providing a solution to certain problems in the discourse of human rights, fails entirely to answer the question of antinomies. As said before, human rights cannot become an instrument of social management; and in most societies one right can be established at the expense of another. Officially, Japan recognizes the rights of women. Socially, these are very often subordinate to the rights of the aged.

That raises the second implication—concerning the adaptation of norms to values. The actualization of human potential might indeed provide a criterion whereby the experience of one culture can enable legitimate criticism of another (in terms of what it has failed to realize), but it provides no guide at all to the question of how the relationships of norm and value can be readdressed. "We" cannot argue from our attempts to deal with these questions to "your" historical experience. To be dogmatic: all logic is the transformation of the perceptible into the *a priori*; in each tradition the process of apprehension by which that logic then redefines itself by questioning the *a priori*, both in terms of new definitions of the perceptible and in terms of the consequent *a priori* (paradox deliberate), is unique. It is not impervious to external influence, but that external influence becomes part of its own self-referring contingency. Only within the terms of its own contingent (which includes the external influence) can it infer the next translation of the perceptible into the *a priori*. In other words, a culture can create human rights only from the inside. They cannot be imposed, and it is probably true to say that each culture, even if, and as, the discourse of human rights becomes global, will have to wrestle with the problems of antinomies in its own way.

What all this suggests is that while there can indeed be a basis for a dialogue on human rights between different cultures, it cannot be based on the universalist approach, nor can it be based on a single history; rather, on the gradual and painful elaboration of a set of criteria which might help to establish the ontology of becoming. The "species being" of Karl Marx might never become a teleological achievement, but in spite of his disciples it could yet become the criterion for a common enterprise in which the different variations of "blood, sweat, toil and tears" are nonetheless recognized.

\*\*\*

That leaves a last, and most important, consideration, almost a codicil to the Will of the Enlightenment. I suggested at the beginning that the notion of human rights represented a confluence of Western traditions, and suggested later that these had been foisted on to the world in various ways. But the adoption, or creation, of human rights in other parts of the world does not mean a global process of Westernization. Citizens of each culture must achieve their rights in their own way. Hitherto the whole debate on human rights has been bedevilled by Western ideas and imperialist connotations. And perhaps it is true to say that even the search for a consensus on what constitutes these rights is itself an outcome of an earlier Western framework of thought; but the argument put forward here implies that the search for a consensus is itself part of the problem, prolonging the connotations of imperialism rather than leading to any solution. The clashes between culture are more productive—and can help each society to produce its own agenda for human rights in indigenous terms—once the enterprise of the Enlightenment has been divorced from the legacy of imperialism. To give one example, much of the literature of Arab feminism comes from Algeria, and all of it was written after French colonial rule had come to an end.

That example raises the full implications of this final consideration. The establishment and advance of human rights in any society proceeds by a continuous challenge to traditional identities—to roles and norms. The challenge will always provoke a backlash, whether from fundamentalist zealots or plain vested interests. But, even so, the very nature of the struggle between the challenge and the backlash broadens the scope of the dialogue on human rights, and (as long as governments don't interfere too much) helps to make it more genuinely international. As each culture begins to learn the difference between the Minster and the witch-hunt, it becomes possible for all cultures to understand and respect each other's achievements better. That won't lead to a single history but it might help to establish something like a common humanity rooted in cultural diversity. But there the criteria of common humanity would be almost the opposite of those of the Natural Law with which this paper began: one defined by its engagement in becoming, not by its origin in being.

I have dropped enough names in this paper but am tempted at the end to quote one last philosopher whose work is certainly not generally associated with the concept of human rights, but which is nonetheless indispensable to the ontology of becoming. "What," asked Friedrich Nietzsche, "might yet be made of Man?"

# COMMENT ON
# THE WINDSOR PAPER

WATANABE Hiroshi

F ranklin L. Baumer once characterized the basic trend of European thought during the period from the seventeenth to the twentieth century as a gradual shift from the supremacy of the idea of "being" to that of "becoming."[1] Now Windsor, being a good twentieth-century European thinker, has even placed the concept of human rights in the realm of "becoming." His motive is laudable. On the one hand, he wants to abstain from imposing "universal" criteria based on ethnocentric arrogance upon other peoples with different cultures. On the other hand, he wants to secure the possibility of the extension of human rights, not only to greater numbers of people but also to the creation of new rights (including animal rights?). He believes that by adopting the "ontology of becoming," cross-cultural dialogue in human rights will become more fruitful.

This is a stimulating quest for a noble cause. Naturally my thoughts were stimulated to come up with various ideas and questions concerning the paper, three of which I outline below.

First, according to Windsor, it is difficult, if not impossible, to give a definition of human rights in positive terms that might be universally persuasive. The negative definition that might provide a minimalist basis for consensus between cultures is deeply flawed, too. Thus, he proposes to see human rights in terms of "becoming" rather than "being." In other words, rather than absolutizing a certain set of human rights, he places them in progressing time and extending space. I wonder, however, is that not a kind of relativization of human rights after all? If it is all right for "each society" "to produce its own agenda for human rights in indigenous terms," probably there will be Hong Kong residents' human rights of 1997 and North Korean human rights of 1984 as well as British human rights of 1993. But I am afraid that if the validity of a human right is limited to the members of a certain society of a certain period, it is not a *human* right any more. Rather, it becomes some people's privilege.

Yet, as a matter of fact, Windsor is not a pure relativist. He supports "toleration" of different beliefs, but he denounces "unthinking tolerance." One must have "respect for other people's beliefs and values," although this approach does not require that one should condone all the social norms related to those beliefs and values. Simultaneously, he finds "a surprising consensus on ultimate values among different cultures." (I suspect that Windsor is a relativist of culture, but not a relativist of values, after all.) I wonder whether this argument is tenable. Take one of his examples, namely the value judgment that "forgiveness is better than revenge." Unfortunately, this is the exact opposite of the teaching of some cultures of machismo, including the Japanese samurai culture (think of the most popular Kabuki play, *Chushingura*). Moreover, I think some "values and beliefs" are not worthy of respect at all, even though I might tolerate the existence of the people who have such beliefs. Remember Nazism.

Thus, I think there are several problems concerning both Windsor's concept of human rights as "becoming" and the way he distinguishes between "toleration" and "tolerance."

Second, since Windsor is against the imposition of Western culture on non-Western peoples, he emphasizes the fact that there are many different cultures and different histories other than those of the West. He even contrasts the "self-consciously 'becoming' culture" of the West with "other 'being' cultures" of the non-West. (This reminds me of a nineteenth-century cliché, "the dynamic [or progressive] Occident and the static [or stagnant] Orient." It seems to me, however, that a simple opposition of Western culture to all the non-Western cultures has already become obsolete because almost all non-Western peoples have been "becoming" bicultural, whether they like it or not. Western culture has already become an integral part of many non-Western cultures and societies. (In this sense the Westerners are a peculiar exception in today's world in terms of their monoculturedness. Probably that is one reason why they tend to overreact to the prospects of "the clash of civilizations." As a matter of fact, Western civilization has been continuously clashing with other civilizations outside the West for several centuries.) Therefore, the advancement of science and technology in their societies is not regarded as "Westernization." It is their own "modernization." To many, Mozart and the Beatles are their own musicians. Soccer is their own sport. Although nationalism is an invention of the West, most nationalists do not consider themselves to have been "Westernized" because of their nationalism. They just "woke up" or "stood up." To many non-Westerners, democratization is their own "political development."

If this is the case, "the adoption…of human rights in other parts of the world does not mean a global process of Westernization," to borrow a phrase from Windsor. He seems to suggest that a Western set of human rights is not necessarily suitable for non-Westerners because they have different cultures, but I assume that today's many bicultural non-Westerners prefer genuine Western human rights to locally tailored ones, just as they love real soccer games with the same universal rules. As far as these non-Westerners are concerned, to play a game of Western origin does not mean that they have been forced to join the "global process of Westernization." Rather, to become a good player of this world sport is their genuine hope in the process of their own "development," or, if I may use an old-fashioned term, "progress." I wonder what Windsor thinks of these non-Westerners.

Third, I would like to introduce an historical example which suggests that acceptance of the concept of human rights is not necessarily an imposition by the West. It is late nineteenth-century Japan.

Within ten years of the Meiji Revolution (1868), the word "freedom" became very popular in Japan. The anti-government "Popular Rights Movement" was powerful and influential in the 1880s, and in 1889 the Constitution of the Empire of Japan, which guaranteed various rights within the limits of the law, was promulgated and a legislative parliamentary system was established. Though this was a notoriously insufficient guarantee of human rights, one cannot deny that it was a remarkable achievement for a country which had been governed until two decades previously by the hereditary samurai (warrior) class, who bore two sharp swords all the time. Why were the concepts of freedom and rights accepted (to some extent) so quickly?

One reason is that such acceptance was believed to be the key to "civilization" because "civilized" Westerners themselves believed so at that time.[2] In order to ensure a secure national independence vis-à-vis Western powers, Japan had to be "civilized." For that purpose the freedom and rights of the Japanese people had to be realized. This was not, however, the whole story. Freedom and human rights were not mere instruments of "civilization." Leading intellectuals often regarded them as inherently valuable because such concepts were in accordance with their own Confucian ideals.

According to Neo-Confucian doctrines, Nature (or Heaven) endows every person at his (or her) birth with one and the same universal moral principle, which must be realized through each person's effort. If one abandons this principle under the influence of one's selfish desire or under the pressure of those in power, the result is that one loses his (or her) human nature. Thus, loyalty to one's inner self and moral integrity are the same thing. To be ethical and to be public-spirited are regarded as actually one and the same (公 , *ko* in Japanese, *gong* in Chinese). Also, humanity and benevolence to others are expressed by the same word (仁 , *jin* in Japanese, *ren* in Chinese).[3] Therefore, rulers, who are supposed to be the living models of morality, must reign over their subjects benevolently in order to make people's lives secure and ethical, while humbly listening to public opinion. If everybody realizes his (or her) inner principle under the aegis of good rulers, there will be no conflicts and wars in the world.

Imagine: What did an intellectual who had been nurtured by these teachings think when they heard about the Western ideal of individual moral freedom based on natural right? How did he feel when he heard of the Western societies which have no hereditary privileged classes? And what about republicanism and democracy? In fact, leading Japanese intellectuals sometimes considered that Western society embodied important Confucian values much more than China and Japan and that it was only natural that the Western countries were so prosperous and powerful. This understanding of the West may sound preposterous to the people who believe in the profound chasm between "the East" and "the West." However, books on world geography written in nineteenth-century China praised the Western parliamentary system and the republic in North America from the same standpoint,[4] and New Confucianists in mainland China, Taiwan, and Hong Kong, who are becoming more and more influential in recent years, on occasion write virtually the same thing.[5] It may not be a sheer misunderstanding.

Therefore, it is perhaps not true that the West always imposed its concept of human rights on other reluctant peoples. Even though it is "an extraordinary confluence of different and partly conflicting Western traditions," I believe it was and still is possible that the concepts of human rights have somewhat happy encounters with other traditions.

**Notes**

[1] Franklin L. Baumer, *Modern European Thought: Continuity and Change in Ideas, 1600–1950*. New York & London: Macmillan, 1977.

[2] Windsor wrote in his earlier paper, "The idea that freedom might itself be a requirement for effective development is generally accepted when applied to the history of the West." Nobutoshi Hagihara, Akira Iriye, Georges Nivat, and Philip Windsor, eds., *Experiencing the Twentieth Century* (Tokyo: University of Tokyo Press, 1985), p. 347. This idea was applied sometimes to non-Western histories. Who could easily deny the authority of the representative scholars of "civilized" countries, such as François Guizot and John Stuart Mill, who preached that there would be no progress without freedom? (A Japanese translation of *On Liberty* by J. S. Mill was published in 1872 and was very influential.)

[3] As a matter of fact, researchers of Chinese thought in the English-speaking world use both humanity and benevolence as a translation of "*ren*" ("*jin*").

[4] 魏源 『海国図志』 (1847, 1849), 徐継畬 『瀛環志略』 (1850).

[5] One of the representative New Confucianists published a book titled "Confucian Political Thought and Democracy, Freedom, Human Rights."徐復観 『儒家思想與民主自由人権』 台北：学生書局, 1979.

# Discussion

**Ishii:** Windsor's paper allows us to consider the problem of human rights in a broad context. I especially appreciate his definition of human rights as a process of becoming to redefine humanity.

I have a Burmese student who worked with me at Kyoto University and obtained his doctorate four years ago. And he went back to Burma just to be arrested. He is now in jail, suspected of an espionage operation, helping the Karen and Shan insurgents. I wish to help him by writing a letter or doing something. But the more I do that, the more it jeopardizes his position. I do respect the concept of human rights, and in fact, at this particular moment, my former student is deprived of his human rights and suffering in jail, about which I can do nothing.

Nevertheless, I am more optimistic than pessimistic. I believe that the time and aspiration of the people who are in search of human rights may improve the situation, as is taught by the case of Thailand. Thailand forty years ago was far from being a democratic country. But the despotic government introduced a policy of industrialization, which resulted in the emergence of the so-called middle class, which became strong enough to topple the despotic government. Through their continuous efforts, the Thai people obtained their rights within four decades. Let us help them in whatever way we can, but let us not push them to adopt one single solution.

**Stern:** I want also to compliment Windsor on a superb paper that combines philosophical and practical questions and accounts historically for the evolution of human rights.

I think Rousseau's aim was not to throw off fetters but to see whether there was a possibility of legitimating authority in a social contract. And it seems to me that one omission from the paper is the notion of civil rights of the social contract.

Second, the idea of toleration came to Europe after the fanaticism of the religious wars. I see a certain parallel in that our efforts at human rights, as enshrined in the United Nations, came after the West experienced its own brutality in the first half of the twentieth century. Until then, very often, it exported its brutality.

The third point: If we could enshrine and protect minimal rights, we would already be doing a great deal. It would be a very great leap forward. I entirely agree with you, if I read you correctly, that minimal rights, the freedom from torture, from rape, and so on, can be asserted to be universal rights.

My final point is your discussion of the link between human rights and power. You mention Amnesty International as an example. It does seem to me there is a certain amount of hope—and I have great faith in Amnesty International—that a good deal can be achieved. It's a slow process; it's a becoming. But for the first time, we have international organizations that are non-governmental committed to the protection of minimal rights.

**Nivat:** I was very impressed by both papers; by Windsor's paper with the dialectics of "becoming" and "being," and Watanabe's pointing out to us that we Western people are the only monocultural people. It seems to me that in the Western, Judeo-Christian civilization, human rights are given by God in the Bible. Even the Enlightenment, in my eyes, derives its roots from that Judeo-Christian message. But, of course, the Enlightenment is also a philosophical revolt against religious faith. We in the field of human rights derive many things from revolts and from schisms. Schisms are necessary. A unique religion leads probably to a denial of human rights, although it comes from God and from the affirmation of human rights, because man is the image of God. So the link between the absolute, coming from a religious root, and the becoming is probably very important. Amnesty International, in our generation, has educated thousands and thousands of people to know what are human rights concretely. Let us put politics and political philosophy aside and confine ourselves to considering, only on the small scale, an experimental defense of human rights.

**Kristeva:** I was very impressed by Windsor's brilliant paper, which is implicitly connected with the discussions on democracy, identity, religion, women's rights, information, etc.

First, two general observations related to the notion of universality, which underlies human rights, and also the relativity of different national conceptions of rights. I think that the universal reason underlying the French Enlightenment and the Declaration of the Rights Man of 1789 implies sacrifice. I would like to emphasize this notion of sacrifice underlying universality. In other words, to be free and equal, each individual or each identity, be it ethnical, national, etc., has to concede something, has to sacrifice something, not in order to sacrifice something outside but in himself or herself. But we often forget that universality implies sacrifice, that tolerance is based on internalized sacrifice. Modern individuals want to be total. "We want everything" was the slogan of 1968. The right to have and to be all is an extraordinary pretension of modern mankind. The West, the East, men, women, etc., everybody wants to be total. I think that no global partnership would be possible on these grounds, and we have to make an extraordinary effort in order to reintroduce in modern society and in its greed for total satisfaction this notion of incompleteness of internalized sacrifice.

The second general question is connected with the fact that Hegelian history, to which you refer, is a history of consciousness, but it does not take into account different cultures. And here Watanabe's paper tries to introduce differences in cultures. Do you not think that, besides other cultures, what we have to introduce in this history of consciousness and the notion of universality in order to make human rights more complex is also unconscious logic? I mean different modalities of logic—prelinguistic, non-Cartesian, non-Kantian, or non-phenomenological—taking into account the preferable aspects of human behavior, gestures, feelings, images, etc.

Now I will come to some very brief, more concrete remarks, again in connection with universality. It seems to me that there is a great challenge to human rights to be found now in some religions, partially resolving their fanaticism and developing social doctrines. The Catholic Church now, in its attitudes toward migration, unemployment, the Mafia, genetic experiences, etc., appears as an ally of human rights. So, it seems to me that, in order to encourage their better development, the history of religions should be urgently introduced in schools and universities.

There is another aspect of universality today, and this is the universality of the mass media, which is of course a tool of information and fills up the abysses between cultures. Winston talked about this yesterday evening. I do not devilize information, but I am really alarmed by the abuses and stereotypes and some schematic patterns of behavior that are imposed by some universal aspects of the mass media. The standard American film in all countries, children absorbing new games, or the reduction of the human mind to genetic codes by the media, such uniformization of culture through universal information is really a soft fascism. I think we need here a new human right, which will be a sort of ontology of the mass media that doesn't exist.

I think that we have to consider two kinds of frames, two regimes in which we have to shape each problem. Shape A, which will be the universality of reason, as Watanabe said, is for everybody. In this connection, I think there is no feminist mathematics, and I doubt even that there is feminist writing. The question is more complicated here. On the other hand, and this is Shape B, as far as the specific subjectivity is involved, differentiation occurs. I call this level a semantic one. And there is a French, a Japanese, a feminist contribution to anthropology, to history, to literature, to the conception of rights, eventually. This position selects angles of analysis and results in the themes developed, the themes of Virginia Woolf, another theme of James Joyce, or even in the types of logic used, for instance, foreigners presented by argumentation in Western tradition, and foreigners presented by theatrical rhetoric, as Yamaguchi related. So we find here that there are mentalities that ask us to widen the notion of human rights. I say in conclusion that these two regimes of the notion of universality can be compared to a piano with its black and white clavier.

**Junker:** I think these two important papers raised deeply philosophical and practical questions at the same time. The basic philosophical question is how to justify the universality of human rights, how to justify universality irrespective of any situation, circumstance, location, area of the world. Unless you are able to do that, you do not have a general theory and a general argument. Now, I am deeply convinced that the only philosopher who has successfully done so was Kant.

**Harkabi:** There are two systems, the moral system and the legal system. And they are not identical. The problem is whether human rights are part of the legal system, or part of the moral system, or are they part of both? Let me give an example. Colonialism was part of the legal system. It was perfect in the legal system. When the colonies were divided into Africa, it was done according to the legal system. There were contracts between states. And as far as legality, it was perfect. However, it was not perfect according to the moral system. What we see, it seems to me as a universal trend, is that the legal system runs after the moral system and slowly adopts precepts—moral precepts become legal precepts. But of course, until now, it has not been identical. There is always a gap.

The legal system provides for the enforcement of measures by codes of law. The moral system, however, has no power of enforcement, except some moral judgment and consciousness. It seems to me that the trend should be that the gap between the moral system and the legal system should be as small as possible, although of course there will be always this gap. Now, I will join this gap between the two categories of "becoming" and "being." This closing of the gap is the "being" aspect between legality and morality. And I think that that is the trend. When Kristeva spoke about universality, it seems to me that she spoke on the moral level. As to the legal system, we do not yet have a universality in the legal systems. Each country has a different legal system. But we have to exert ourselves to narrow the gap between these two systems, the legal and the moral.

There is, of course, another problem for which I do not have a solution, and that is how to define what is in the moral system. For religious people there is no problem here, because they would say that that is what is in the Bible. Kant defined what is moral by saying, do whatever you do in such a way that you will wish it to be a universal law. That is to say, it is up to us as human beings to decide what is morality. But let us acknowledge there is a difficulty here.

**Kerber:** I was pleased to find myself in agreement with Kristeva, particularly her point that tolerance is based on hesitation to claim everything, that it is based on some element of internal modesty about what is claimed. It has struck me, listening to this conversation, that one of the grounds for conversation among various cultures may be that it is very hard to articulate what rights we claim, but it is easier to articulate what we believe ought not be done, so that perhaps it might be easier to find a narrow ground for shared human rights. It is that negative notion of the things majorities may not do.

**Yokoyama:** Inspired by the reports from Windsor and Watanabe, I have been led to think that there may be a possibility of redefining the notion of civilization for the twenty-first century. Looking at the situation we are now facing, we find that many, including animals and forests, are obliged to assume a certain kind of civility, attaching to each other a sort of small quality of deity. This reminds me that the old notion of civilization in China, which is called "*wenmei*," and "*bunmei*" in Japan, has a similar epistemological tradition to the West. "*Wenmei*" basically meant a society which was interwoven, every being was densely interdependent. Yet there was another important aspect of "*wenmei*," which was not dark. How to attend to this sort of quality is the task which I think can be taken seriously in the next century.

**Bulliet:** I was very impressed, as everyone else has been, by Windsor's paper, and, indeed, had it not been for Watanabe's paper, I might have been convinced by it. But Watanabe brought up a problem, and the more I have heard the debate and pondered on it, the more serious I think it is. It has to do with what constitutes a culture, who is in the culture, who is a cultural interlocutory, and whether there is a kind of idealistic reification of the notion of culture in Windsor's paper that does not match very well with reality. Watanabe talked about bicultural individuals and observed that Western culture is perhaps the only monoculture left in the world.

I was struck by a comment in the very first paragraph of Windsor's paper where he says: "The Koran, for example, is very specific about the rights of women, even though it is more so about their obligations." I was struck by the fact that if anyone talked about women's rights in the West, they would not quote the Bible. They would, in fact, avoid quoting the Bible, because there are a lot of things in the Bible that are not very favorable to women's rights. I was interested that in talking about another culture, the citation was not of Turkish laws about women's rights or status, or Tunisian law, or Egyptian law, or any of the actual legal situations in Islamic countries but rather of a document that is fourteen centuries old and has gone through fourteen centuries of interpretation, none of which interpretation ends up being cited. It raises in my mind the question whether Muslims belong to a culture that is developing or hopefully "becoming" in the direction of human rights? Does the secular national government of Iraq form the same category culturally as the revolutionary Islamic government of Iran? Do we classify Muslims as a culture, or do we see their several cultures? Do we see here a bicultural situation of the sort Watanabe pointed to? When we talk about "becoming," in order to become, you must predicate an entity that becomes. What is the entity? And does that entity have a coherent profile?

I would suggest that we have a tendency to have a rather out-dated notion of culture that goes back to the nineteenth century. Unless we get more in step with what is actually being thought and actually being written about, we are going to have a very difficult time recognizing "becoming," because we will not know what it is, what the entity is, that is in the process of becoming.

**Gold:** The inevitability of loss and sadness, the impossibility, and, indeed, the destructiveness of the pursuit to perfection, the necessity for sacrifice, the requirements for compromise in all systems, including biological ones, as a condition of a tenuous adaptation and a sense of well-being—that, in a tragic view, seems to frame a vision for the twenty-first century that can incorporate religious, philosophical, and political concepts of what is required for a new universalism. Human beings are one part of the world; we are not necessarily here to dominate the world. Indeed, the world may be devising ways of ridding itself of the threat of human beings to survive the threat that human beings pose to its ultimate survival.

In this regard, there is a further irony. Our ultimate triumph over the earth will result in our ultimate destruction. And it is only in a certain submissiveness to its laws and our own lack of capacity to ever get it just right that we can perhaps truly survive the next century.

**Kosai:** I was much impressed by the exciting discussion this morning. But it seems to me the discussion is going in this framework: human rights must be universal. In some cultures, human rights are admitted, but there is another culture which denies human rights as universal. But this dichotomy is a little exaggerated. Even in Western culture, human rights are not so clearly defined. Freedom from torture is a human right. But how about the death penalty? Within the same Western culture, we need a cultural dialogue on human rights.

**Kyogoku:** Looking at human rights should start from a moral ideal. But moral sensibility is not necessarily shared by different cultures. Thanks to the mass media, moral sensibilities are becoming more widely shared than before in other cultures. Therefore, when moral sensibilities change, political movements could be triggered which lead to a legal system which guarantees human rights. There is a linkage, a step by step process, of piecemeal engineering. I suggest this as a way of approaching the problem. What is important in piecemeal engineering is the notion of self-help. It is unnatural to intervene from outside to create a system of human rights. It does not work. Self-help is the important element.

At the same time the help and encouragement of others, particularly providing illustrative models, are also important. When you proselytize, there are two ways of proselytizing. One is through language, theory, or doctrine. The other is by example. These two forms of proselytization are applicable to all cultures. Thus, Western Judeo-Christian cultures have given us one model after another over the years, and that is a commendable achievement.

**Watanabe:** About "being" and "becoming": To consider human rights in terms of "becoming" does not sound very persuasive to me. If you think of it in terms of becoming, what kind of human rights are we going to achieve? There seems to be no guarantee, for we are opening up infinite possibilities. We are obliged to accept human rights as "being," assuming that there are many ways to interpret or realize them.

**Windsor:** I would like to say first that, although Watanabe does not agree with my approach, I have found his paper extraordinarily interesting, and it has certainly helped me to modify the way I think about these things. I do not agree that Confucian harmony is the same kind of thing as human rights in the way that we were discussing. That depends on too many rules. But never mind. I basically find that very interesting.

I found the whole discussion this morning very challenging, and it raises a number of themes which are of great relevance in trying to codify what is at stake here. I find it very interesting to see that different approaches were adopted toward religion and human rights, and the way in which the role of religion could be either hostile or fundamental. And it could be both, according to a particular situation and a particular religion.

The other interesting point, and that goes back very much to what Kristeva was saying: the need for the acknowledgment of sacrifice in the maintenance of any kind of human rights society. And I think it is also fundamental that, to use the terms I used, toleration demands a form of self-awareness, which totality or the totality demand does not.

# GLOBALIZATION
# AND THE FUTURE
# OF NATIONALISM

# GLOBALIZATION AND THE FUTURE OF NATIONALISM

James MAYALL

T he trouble is the data do not speak for themselves. The nation-state, we are told, is an anachronism. "Today goods, capital, people, knowledge, images, communications, as well as crime, culture, pollutants, drugs, fashions and beliefs, readily flow across territorial boundaries."[1] In particular the internationalization of production and the globalization of financial markets are said to have undermined the claims to sovereignty of modern states. For example, in April 1989 "foreign exchange trading in the world's financial centres averaged about $650 billion a day, equivalent to nearly $500 million a minute, and forty times the amount of world trade a day."[2] Controlling financial flows of this size and velocity is beyond the power of even the strongest states, and indeed most of them, making virtue out of necessity, have sensibly given up the effort. For many people, brought up in the belief that form should follow function, there is something aesthetically displeasing about such wanton abrogation of responsibility. What is needed, it will be said, is some new, and more appropriate, framework of political regulation.

If these arguments arouse a sense of *déjà vu*, it is because the challenges which globalization poses have been around for most of the twentieth century. Towards the end of his neo-Malthusian tract about the twenty-first century, Paul Kennedy quotes *The Economist* for October 11, 1930:

> The supreme difficulty of our generation...is that our achievements on the economic plane of life have outstripped our progress on the political plane to such an extent that our economics and our politics are perpetually falling out of gear with one another. On the economic plane, the world has been

441

organized into a single, all embracing unit of activity. On the political plane, it has not only remained partitioned into 60 or 70 sovereign, national states, but the national units have been growing smaller and more numerous and the national consciousness more acute. The tension between these two antithetical tendencies has been producing a series of jolts and jars and smashes in the social life of humanity....[3]

So what is new? The inhabitants of Sarajevo or Mogadishu could be forgiven for asking the question. Of course their scepticism would not be wholly justified. Much has changed since 1930 apart from the increase in the number of states to nearly 200, and the mobilization of national consciousness amongst ethnic groups who apparently favour fragmentation being extended indefinitely, or at least until it embraces themselves. There is now a whole range of problems that can only be comprehended globally. We can hardly fail to be aware that our collective efforts to harness nature have produced, not merely unprecedented material affluence but also international public bads (that is, evils which are produced by the market but whose consumption cannot be privatized within national frontiers). It may also plausibly be claimed that the revolution in communications and information technology has so increased the mutual sensitivities of national economies that the volume of transactions is bringing about a qualitative change in the nature of international environment. Traditional interdependence, in other words, is being transformed into genuine globalization.

Something is clearly going on: a sense of turbulence, of a world out of control, of collapsing moral and cognitive foundations—such premonitions are widespread. Yet the nation-state has survived "the end of geography" and the creation of a global marketplace, just as a generation ago it survived its alleged military and strategic obsolescence.[4] In the face of such resilience, how are we to understand globalization? No doubt, as Anthony Giddens assures us, there is now a "global human condition" arising from the growing interpenetration of global forces with the particularities of place and individuality.[5] But what does this really mean?

On an intuitive reading of the data, we might have expected the processes just described to have reduced the appeal of nationalism as a political doctrine. Indeed, Eric Hobsbawm concluded from the recent expansion of scholarly interest in the subject that the age of nationalism was drawing to a close.[6] As the owl of Minerva finally spreads its wings, he argued, the academic vultures were closing in on the corpse.

So long as the communist system had not actually collapsed, it was still possible, if you were so minded, to believe that God might be dead, but the surrogate gods of nineteenth-century historicism were alive and well. To hold such a position now represents the triumph of hope over experience on an heroic scale. Perhaps, therefore, before trying to come to terms with the political and moral dilemmas of the contemporary world, we should reexamine the conventional assumption that globalization and nationalism are contradictory trends.

## THE DEATH OF THE SURROGATE GODS

Nationalism, in Elie Kedourie's celebrated definition, "is a doctrine invented in Europe at the beginning of the nineteenth century." It asserts that humanity is naturally divided into nations, and, on this basis, "pretends to supply a criterion for the determination of the unit of population proper to enjoying a government exclusively its own, for the legitimate exercise of power in the state, and for the right organization of a society of states."[7] Arguably, this account conceals the extent to which nationalism was the child of both the eighteenth-century Enlightenment, and of the Romantic movement, the counter-Enlightenment which elevated the values of cultural distinctiveness and particularity over those of cosmopolitan universalism. This dual ancestry is important since it locates the origin of the contemporary debate between the proponents of civic nationalism and those of ethnic self-determination. Nationalism, as Tony Judt reminds us, "far from being incompatible with universalist human sympathies, is—for a Frenchman, though not for a German, for instance—the very condition of their realisation."[8] Nonetheless, if nationalism was originally conceived as a vehicle for purveying the humane and civilizing values of the Enlightenment, it is true that its worldwide appeal owes more to the strategic alliances which nationalists made with historicism.

For the nineteenth-century systems builders, whether Marxist or liberal, human freedom was the end state of an evolutionary process. In both systems, the nation had no independent status: it was either ignored as irrelevant to the cognitive mapping of the world, or regarded as a regrettable but temporary stage in the history of social and political development.

Historical evolution was not only explicit but central to Marxist philosophy, although nothing as idealized and abstract as the nation could be allowed more than a walk-on part in the story. But just because nationalist sentiment would eventually be exposed as false consciousness, Marx was able to support, or oppose, particular nationalist movements depending on his judgement of how they would contribute to the overthrow of capitalism, the one development he considered of genuine historical significance.

The historicism of nineteenth-century liberalism was implicit. The idea of inalienable human rights, which lies at the heart of all liberal thought, constitutes a claim to universal values which is essentially context-free, that is liberated from the constraints of time and place. In principle, therefore, nationalism with its emphasis on the historical development of "communities of fate," represents a challenge to the autonomous self-determining individual. In practice, most nineteenth-century liberals were deeply impressed by evolutionary theory, and operated sometimes openly—more often tacitly—on the assumption that the then current distinctions between civilized, barbarian, and savage peoples represented stages in human and social development.

This still left open, of course, the basis of the constitution under which liberal society should be governed. But by mid-century, John Stuart Mill, perhaps the thinker who saw the dilemma most clearly, was prepared to throw in his lot with nationalism in the interests of democratic government.

> If it be said that so broadly marked a distinction between what is due to a fellow countryman and what is due merely to a human creature is more worthy of savages than of civilized beings, and ought, with the utmost energy, to be contended against, no one holds that opinion more strongly than myself. But this object, one of the worthiest to which human endeavour can be directed, can never, in the present state of civilization, be promoted by keeping different nationalities of anything like equivalent strength under the same government. In a barbarous state of society the case is sometimes different. The government may then be interested in softening the antipathies of the races that peace may be preserved and the country more easily governed. But when there are either free institutions or a desire for them, in any of the peoples artificially tied together, the interest of the government lies in exactly the opposite direction. It is then interested in keeping

up and envenoming their antipathies that they may be prevented from coalescing, and it may be enabled to use some of
them as tools for the enslavement of others.[9]

Where Marx saw class warfare as the mechanism driving historical progress, Mill placed his faith in education. Having confidently
asserted that "one hardly knows what any division of the human
race should be free to do if not to determine with which of the various collective bodies of human beings they choose to associate
themselves," he faced the problem of secession. He could not conceive that the cause of liberty would be served by the breakup of
France or Britain, and he wriggled out of the impasse in which he
found himself (as he had wriggled out of his more famous argument with Bentham over pushpin) by assuming that any properly
educated Breton or Highland Scot would opt for rule from Paris or
London, just as education would liberate the bowling addict for the
superior delights of poetry.

This is a more sympathetic solution than that offered by Marx to
the moral problem of how to reconcile our need for an identity
with the operation of hidden (albeit progressive) historical laws.
However, it is hardly more satisfactory since it apparently insists on
regarding the values of liberal education as both privileged and
self-evident.

Alone amongst the nineteenth-century thinkers, Hegel succeeded in reconciling liberal values with an evolutionary theory,
although his solution depended on refuting the claim that they
could be context-free. In his view, not just anybody had a right to
declare themselves a nation and set up a state on this basis:

> A nation does not begin by being a state. The transition from a
> family, a hoard, a clan, a multitude, etc., to political conditions
> *is the realisation of the Idea in the form of that nation.* Without this
> form a nation as an ethical substance—which is what it is
> implicitly, lacks the objectivity of possessing in its own eyes
> and in the eyes of others, a universal and universally valid
> embodiment in laws, i.e., in determinant thoughts, and as
> such it fails to secure recognition from others. So long as it
> lacks objective law and an explicitly established rational consti-
> tution, its autonomy is formal only and is not sovereignty.[10]

The advantage of this formulation is that it differentiates

between liberty as a formal value and its true realization as fully developed, and therefore presumably internalized, human consciousness. There is no room for squeamishness here. Hegel continues:

> The same consideration justifies civilized nations in regarding and treating as barbarians those who lag behind them in institutions which are the essential moments of the state. Thus a pastoral people may treat hunters as barbarians and both of these are barbarians from the point of view of agriculturalists, etc. The civilized nation is conscious that the rights of barbarians are unequal to its own and treats their autonomy as only a formality.[11]

On Fukuyama's reading of Hegel, the victory of liberal democracy in the Cold War has brought about the end of history.[12] If so, the passages just quoted would seem to provide a somewhat permissive set of criteria by which to judge the actions of the "advanced" countries toward the less fortunate—those, mostly in Asia and Africa, which find themselves caught in a time warp. There is indeed some evidence that the great powers are willing to sanction action in the Third World of a kind they would be reluctant to support nearer home; and are even less tolerant than their predecessors of "stateless" territories, those peripheral semicriminalized international slums where guns can be run, drugs landed for onward shipment, and money laundered.

However Fukuyama's reading is open to three serious objections. First, while some kinds of society and state are due for extinction, this apparently does not apply to its highest form—the constitutional nation-state properly understood. But if there is an evolutionary principle of social and moral development at work, why should history have an end? Secondly, to free liberal values from their universal application in time and space may allow us to reconstruct how they came to be established, but robs them of much of their practical appeal and power. There is only a small distance between the view that holds that the civilized can dispose of the barbarians at will, and the relativist position that anything goes, that criticism of practices in other countries, however arbitrary and cruel, is misplaced providing the practices in question are sanctioned by culture and custom. Thirdly, Hegel's method notoriously gives us insight, including moral insight, only after the event: its power is critical and analytical rather than prescriptive or normative.

In recent decades, modern technology has enabled naturalists to make films of great beauty and authority which are regularly beamed into our living rooms at peak viewing hours. The image of the natural world they portray is one which originated with Darwin's *Origin of Species*. As we watch in slow motion and hideous closeup well-camouflaged insects luring and then devouring their prey, or packs of ferocious wild dogs isolating and terrorizing the weakest or slowest antelope in the herd, we are consoled to learn that this is nature's way of preserving the ecological balance. It has always been so: wherever there is something to eat, there will be something to eat it. It is a powerful argument, but it seems an appalling metaphor on which to base a political and moral order. No one would question our need for both criticism and analysis, but there are strong grounds for questioning the evolutionary model—in any of its nineteenth-century variants—as the best way to interpret social, let alone political or moral, development.

## NATIONALISM AND GLOBALIZATION

If we discard the evolutionary assumptions of nineteenth-century thought, the relationship between globalization and nationalism may appear in a different light. On this view, the two trends are not contradictory but symbiotic, appearing in the world together and constantly reinforcing one another ever since. The rise of nationalism was a response to a globalizing process, just as globalization itself, or rather what kept the process going, was largely a consequence of nationalist competition. There is no reason in principle why the nation-state should last forever, since it is only the most recent in a succession of political forms which have passed into oblivion, but neither is there a technological imperative requiring its surrender, nor a plausible hypothesis of what might take its place. There may be something to be said, therefore, for attempting to unravel the relationship itself, rather than to predict the outcome of a largely imaginary contest.

**Nationalism as Globalization:** A Kikuyu proverb has it that when two elephants fight, it is the grass that suffers. Much the same could be said about the truth in scholarly disputes. Much ink has been spilled over the question of whether nations existed before nationalism. The answer seems fairly clear—some did, most did not. Simi-

larly, the argument about the causes of nationalism—Was it a consequence of the propagation of subversive ideas or of the progressive
breakdown of traditional agricultural society?—is either insoluble
or beside the point.

Whatever the truth about the historical origins of nations, the
doctrine of nationalism—roughly speaking one culture, one state—
is modern. It was formulated, on the one hand, at the time of the
political revolutions in America and France and, on the other, in
the context of the social and economic transformation of Europe as
a result of industrialization. For present purposes the dispute
between chicken and egg may be put aside; what matters is that,
both at the level of ideas and of material life, the rise of nationalism
was a response to forces which were, and were perceived at the time
to be, universal in scope.

The French Revolution was not a parochial affair. In this it was
unlike the Iranian or Ethiopian revolutions of recent times, let
alone the numerous Third World coups d'état whose perpetrators
have sought to dignify their seizure of power by proclaiming their
revolutionary credentials. At the same time it was undoubtedly
French. To quote Judt again: "Because France, especially the France
of 1789, incarnates universal values, to be a patriot in France is to
be a patriot for peoples and nations everywhere."

If Napoleon's export of French universalism was partly responsible for the later flowering of an anti-Enlightenment romantic
nationalism, the idea that the state belonged to the people, and not
the people to the state, was a genuinely liberating idea which
retained its global appeal. Over the next two hundred years it was
frequently perverted, but it was, and is, impossible to gainsay. If
prescription is no longer a basis of legitimate authority, the only
alternatives are popular sovereignty or dictatorship. Few modern
tyrants are honest: they all pay the price of vice to virtue and claim
to rule in the name of the people. But if the people are sovereign,
they have to be a named and bounded community in contact with
but separate from other similar communities. A national state
depends for its existence on a society of states.

Before contact with the Hudson Bay Company, the Eskimo
called themselves Inuit—the people—although they had fifteen
words for snow; but in time the generic term was attached to a self-
conscious ethnic and cultural identity. It seems reasonable to pre-
sume that this was roughly how naming occurred worldwide. The
growth of national consciousness and the political claims of nation-

alism were from the beginning part of a globalizing process. It is
true that the success rate amongst potential nation states is very
low—less than 200 out of a possible 8,000[13]—but while this refutes
the primordialist claim that national identities were dished out at
the Creation, it does not support the counterclaim that new identities can be engineered from on high to coincide with each and
every level of market integration. What keeps the nation-state alive
is not that its frontiers coincide with those of its economy but the
lack of an alternative basis of legitimacy to popular sovereignty.
And this idea continues to have a more secure (in the sense of more
deeply felt) global reach than the fact that we can now bounce pic-
tures of one another off a satellite, or deal in shares across time
zones on a round-the-clock basis.

**Globalization as Nationalism:** No one has yet provided a satisfactory general explanation of why Britain, France, Japan, and a
handful of other countries were centralized, and at least partially
nationalized, prior to industrialization. Nor can one do more than
speculate about the connections between national consolidation in
preindustrial civilizations, subsequent technological and industrial
innovation, and the development of democratic political cultures.
There are strong reasons for maintaining, however, that those who
came late to industrial civilization could not have made the transition without the support of a national state. Ernest Gellner has
argued elegantly for the functional necessity of nationalism during
the transition from mechanical to organic forms of social organization. Essentially, the argument turns on the need in modern societies for an educated work force. The stability of agrarian polities
may actually be enhanced by the coexistence of distinct ethnic folk
cultures which are unlikely to unite in rebellion against the state.
By contrast, industrial societies depend on the basic education of
the whole population. Industrial societies which are deeply divided
along ethnic, linguistic or religious lines, and where consequently
people have to confront one another on a daily basis in the work-
place, tend to be inherently unstable.

Herder, one of the more sympathetic of the romantic nationalists, had envisaged a world in which each national group, secured
in its own unsullied cultural autonomy, would blend with his
neighbours in the same way as flowers in a herbaceous border. The
international order to which this vision gives rise is much like a progressive primary school, in which the different creative talents of

all the children are carefully nurtured except for those which release their competitive instincts. Unfortunately, the vision was obscured as quickly on the playground as by the harsher realities of domestic and international politics.

Domestically, while nationalists often idealized the folk ways of rural society, their appeal was to an increasingly urban and industrialized population. Traditional society did not break down everywhere at the same time or at the same speed—there were still peasant communities in the Haute-Savoie in the early 1970s as there still are in Kossovo today—but the erosion was nonetheless a global process, in the sense that no society was able to resist altogether the social and political dislocation brought about by modernization. Indeed, nationalist politicians were usually modernizers, if only for the unromantic reason that their followers needed jobs.

Industrial society depends on capital accumulation and investment to a much greater extent than agrarian society. In other words it depends on economic growth. Until the collapse of communism revealed that the centralized command economy could no longer deliver the most basic political and economic goods, it was *not* obvious that industrial society required a de-regulated market economy. Nor was the commitment to full employment (or what passed for it) a communist monopoly: the social democratic governments which established the welfare state throughout Western Europe after 1945 also made that commitment, and were, therefore, inevitably involved in income redistribution and economic management. The welfare state was a much more nationalist project than its founders would have hoped—since the extension of entitlements implied a criterion of exclusion, and so raised the price of citizenship everywhere.

International society under the *ancien régime* was already highly competitive. Indeed, as Raymond Aron once noted, for the mercantilists trade was essentially war carried out by other means. The two activities were driven by the same bleak perception of all exchange as zero-sum. At the same time the level of technology available to sovereign states limited the damage they could inflict on one another. The takeover of the system by nationalism did nothing to soften the competitive aspects of international relations; rather it both reinforced and dynamized them. The national empires completed the enclosure of the world during the nineteenth century, establishing the infrastructure for the world's first global economy in the process. The wars of the nations were also more deadly than those of the dynasts. Moreover, where the competition of the dynastic states had been largely confined to territory, the dependence of the nations on trade gave the strongest of them—first Britain, followed by Germany and the United States—an interest in penetrating foreign markets.

Fichte's vision of a *Closed Commercial State* (1801) was as inappropriate to the world of modernizing nations as Rousseau's dream of an international society composed of small self-sufficient rural communities. The best latecomers could do in response to the powerful new economic machine was to develop strategies for national and infant industry protection. The ideas of List and Alexander Hamilton were the precursors of the modern theory of targeting markets which in recent decades has been used with such success by the governments of Japan, Korea, and other newly industrialized countries. Protectionism should thus be viewed not as a preparation for autarky, but as a prelude to more effective national competition in the global market place.

If there was any doubt that there was no alternative to participation in the global economy, it was dispelled during the 1930s. The Great Depression spread like an epidemic from one part of the industrial world to another; while the self-defeating adoption of "beggar-your-neighbour" policies established that interdependence was already irreversible. The contemporary relevance of this episode is not that it proved the nation-state to be an anachronism, but that its competence, at least in peacetime, is much more limited than governments would like. Group identity seems to be relatively unaffected by market changes, except possibly over the very long term. Adam Smith was concerned with enriching a population whose national identity he took for granted. In the same spirit Robert Reich has recently argued that the ownership of the American corporate sector is relatively unimportant in defining American identity:

So who is us? The answer is, the American workforce, the American people, but not particularly the American corporation. The implications of this new answer are clear: if we hope to revitalise the competitive performance of the United States economy, we must invest in people, not in nationally defined corporations.[14]

Smith foresaw the possibility of a global market; Reich is reacting to its existence and the confusion which this has engendered amongst national governments. In this context, a final speculation on the relationship between nationalism and globalization seems appropriate. If the impact of globalization is to reduce still further the competence of the state, at least so far as the economic sphere is concerned, the result may be to strengthen rather than weaken the appeal of nationalism in two kinds of circumstance. The grounds for this view are not just that the turbulent social and economic conditions have traditionally been the seedbed of militant nationalism, but also that as confidence in the regulatory capacity of the state fades, national groups which have a strong internal sense of cohesion and order, and are therefore relatively less dependent on an external framework of law, may be better placed than others to respond flexibly to increasingly rapid changes in the international environment. If the rise of Sikh nationalism in the wake of the Green Revolution is a typical response to the first kind of circumstance, the success of East Asia in world markets may be an example of the second.

## NATIONALISM IN THE NEW WORLD DISORDER

To recapitulate: The assumptions inherited from nineteenth-century evolutionary theory, in all its variants, are at best questionable, at worst simply false. The nation-state is not a way-station en route to a wider and higher form of political organization. Nor can one deduce from the emergence of regional and global markets a transfer of political loyalties from the nation to a putative community of mankind. From the beginning, communitarians and universalists have struggled to claim the nation for themselves. If there is a truth to be uncovered here, it is that, like a bickering old married couple, nationalism and globalization remain mutually dependent. Economic activity cannot be wholly privatized and globalized; and the democratic state cannot easily, therefore, be de-nationalized.

If the argument is broadly accepted, what are its implications for international society? The first is to acknowledge that the repeated attempts to devise an international constitution in the twentieth century have all been based on the need to reconcile the claims of nation and humanity. More particularly, after 1945, an attempt was made to reconcile the protection of human rights—including the right of all peoples to self-determination—with the principles of state sovereignty and territorial integrity. This could only be achieved by defining self-determination in a highly restrictive manner. When the world was reborn in San Francisco, those who were present at the creation were simply deemed to have exercised their right at some point in the past; those who had been colonized by the West Europeans were to be allowed to exercise it in the future; and those who might subsequently wish to recommend a further territorial revision were to be denied the opportunity. Not only was secession ruled out as an acceptable method of state-creation, but national minorities lost even the theoretical right to protection (i.e., as members of a minority rather than as individuals) that they had enjoyed under the League Covenant.

We cannot know whether this remarkable formulation would have survived had the structures of the Cold War not been superimposed on the U.N. constitution. But we do know that a strong preference for the territorial *status quo* was one of the very few issues on which there was a consensus across both the East/West and North/South divides. Between 1947 and 1991 only Bangladesh was created as the result of a secessionist rebellion against the central state authorities; and this success was in circumstances in which the influence of the world powers cancelled one another out.

The end of the Cold War, the collapse of communism and the disintegration of the Soviet Union exposed the fragility of the U.N. compromise once it was required to stand alone as the framework of international order. To some extent it is probably more fragile now than it would have been had the Cold War never happened, since the capability and competence of the major powers has been weakened by the development of global economic and technological structures that took place, so to say, under cover of darkness. Current speculation about the possibility of, and prospects for, a democratic world order, the emergence all over the political landscape of irredentist and secessionist demands, and the associated clamour for humanitarian intervention and minority protection are all global challenges to the moral order of the nation-state and the society of states. How are we to address these new challenges?

**Sovereignty and Non-Intervention:** The principle of non-interference in the domestic affairs of other states is the secular descendant of the principle of *cuius regio eius religio*, without which a political settlement to the seventeenth-century European wars of religion would not have been possible. In its modern version, it remains an essential legal prerequisite of intergovernmental cooperation and is enshrined prominently in the U.N. Charter (Article 2.7). Indeed, so long as distinct political communities must coexist within a competitive environment, it is difficult to see how any order could be maintained except on the basis of some such self-denying ordinance. Amongst the present permanent members of the Security Council China has already signalled its opposition to any international attempt to impose cosmopolitan values through the United Nations.

It is important to be clear about what is *not* covered by Article 2.7. It does not prohibit mutual involvement, merely coercive interference. There is no theoretical contradiction, therefore, between the continuing importance attached to sovereignty and the emergence over time of an interdependent world economy, although from a practical point of view governments will find themselves constrained by having to operate within it. In principle, they can, and indeed have, created numerous international regimes to reduce the costs of these constraints, although, as is becoming clear in the European Community, there are limits to what can be achieved in this way, at least amongst democratic states.

The contemporary challenge to the principle of non-intervention arises primarily from the breakup of the Soviet Union and Yugoslavia, broadly along national lines, although it is not confined to the ex-communist world. The turbulence that accompanied these historic events posed two questions for the international community. When and on what basis to recognize the new states? And whether to assert a right of humanitarian intervention in cases where ethnic conflict over the political map is accompanied by massive and systematic abuse of human rights? I will return to this second question shortly; here the point to stress is the inadequacy of the international response to the first question.

In this case, historical precedent was unhelpful. In the nineteenth century the great powers did not accept that the principle of non-intervention applied to their relations with Asian and African countries, most of which they conquered or brought under indirect control. In the twentieth century, once the state system had been globalized, self-determination was defined as de-colonization, and no further questions were asked about the basis on which the new states had been constructed or the way in which their governments honoured (or in many cases ignored) their commitment to protect the human rights of their citizens.

The collapse of communism created an entirely new situation, since it led to a relatively large number of demands for recognition by ethnically defined national movements. The response of the powers was to ignore these demands for as long as possible and to urge instead democratic reform within the existing state frontiers of the U.S.S.R. and Yugoslavia—as late as the spring of 1992, for example, the British Foreign Secretary was still urging the Yugoslavs to follow the African practice of insisting on the sanctity of colonial frontiers.

The mistake did not lie in the reluctance to address the question of territorial change. Indeed, in most parts of the world it remains as difficult as ever to create ethnic states without at the same time creating entrapped or threatened minorities. The mistake lay precisely in the failure to address the internal criteria necessary for recognition.

Admittedly, it is easy to be wise after the event in this regard. Governments everywhere are facing an unprecedented situation. It is not merely that the Cold War resulted in a decisive defeat for the Communists on a battlefield of their own choosing, namely that of economic performance, but that this defeat was largely self-inflicted. Moreover, it was inflicted not by a superior and well-organized army, but by a rival system that was finding it difficult to deal with the consequences of its own success. There were two implications of this apparent paradox. The first was that the new nationalism had to be cast in a liberal rather than a collectivist mould—what was wanted was both national autonomy and the right to participate in an increasingly de-regulated global market economy. The second implication was that the Western democracies, particularly in Europe, were so preoccupied with trying to renegotiate their own political arrangements in the global context that they were totally unprepared for the new geo-politics. In particular, they failed to acknowledge that, at the point of recognition, neither non-discrimination nor non-intervention—the two concepts on which liberal international society rests—were appropriate as criteria for recognition.

The new states and would-be states of the former communist world want access to the liberal world order from which they were excluded during the Cold War. This order was one which separated, not completely but to a substantial extent, the respective spheres of civil society and the state. Non-intervention applied to the detailed constitutional and political arrangements of the state; non-discrimination was an insurance principle, the minimum commitment that governments would accept on behalf of their citizens if they were to open their markets to their competitors.

At the technical level, access, for example to the GATT, could not be granted without preconditions for the simple reason that, to operate non-discriminatory trading rules, a market system requires a certain kind of constitutional arrangement amongst its members. At the political level, what is required is representative government, not the implementation of a standard constitution. The West European mistake in the former Yugoslavia was first to have encouraged elections without paying attention to the inevitable minority fears that would be aroused in a deeply divided society; then to have recognized Slovenia and Croatia indiscriminately and again without imposing conditions at the one point when third parties indisputably had a legitimate right to do so; and finally to have recognized Bosnia, which manifestly lacked either the civic culture or the ethnic solidarity to defend itself against the imperial ambitions of Belgrade and Zagreb, without simultaneously providing credible international guarantees of its independence.

**Democracy and Minority Protection:** It is unfortunate that the resolve of the international community in its attempts to fashion a new world order is being tested in parts of the world—Bosnia and Somalia—where the prospects for success are minimal. In the first case, outside the cities, whose civic identity has now been virtually destroyed, there is no overarching political culture which can stand alongside, let alone above, Serb, Croat, and Muslim communal identities; yet unless the "national" state can invoke loyalty, it is difficult to see how a democratic system can be constructed, let alone survive. In the second case, while national identity is not a problem—it is about the only thing that unites Somalis—the whole organization of society is conflictual, based on the structured opposition of clans, sub-clans and extended families, a feature which enormously complicates the task of establishing a legitimate central government.

If, in the new global context, there is very little chance of societies conforming quickly to a single political or moral set of standards, the principles of sovereignty and non-interference may still serve a useful function in demarcating spheres of responsibility and reducing the costs of coexistence. At the same time the end of the Cold War has stripped away many of the conventional constraints that shielded governments everywhere—and not just in the communist world—from being held to account with respect to their performance on human rights and other political commitments they had freely entered into. Amnesty International's report for 1993 reveals over 160 countries against which charges of major human rights abuses have been made.[15] Many of the gruesome stories which the report uncovers are connected to the proliferation of ethnic and nationalist conflicts in a period of unusually severe political, social, and economic dislocation.

In these circumstances we urgently need a better understanding of the relationship between nationalism and democracy. In the West, the Wilsonian assumption that the two concepts were mutually reinforcing fell into such disrepair during the interwar period that afterwards most West Europeans were happy to overlook the extent to which their own democracies rested on secure national foundations. Nationalism was frequently equated with irrationalism. This claim is not incorrect in itself, but, as Ghia Nodia has pointed out, it ignores the fact that:

> Popular sovereignty consists in the claim that "We the People" are only going to play by rules that we ourselves freely choose....This "game-like" aspect of democracy supposedly shows it to be completely rational. If we push the analogy further, however, we uncover non-rational aspects of the democratic enterprise. In addition to rules, a game requires a community of players and a playing field. Democratic laws...may be consensual products of rational decision-making, but the composition and territory of the polity in which the laws will have force cannot be defined that way.[16]

Nodia's analysis goes to the heart of the problem posed by the new nationalism. Throughout the century nationalists have pressed their claims in the name of popular sovereignty, that is, they have claimed the right of self-government for their own distinct community. In a few cases this claim was accompanied by a genuine commitment to democratic procedures, so that minorities were able gradually to merge with the rest of the population, or, if they chose not to, did not feel threatened by the new political dispensation. But in most the introduction of a democratic constitution led to the capture of the state by an ethnic or religious majority and the establishment of a system of either legal or structural discrimination against minorities.

The reasons for such discrimination are not difficult to understand historically. The peoples of the Baltic Republics felt that they had been robbed of their own countries as a result of massive Russian immigration, and the official policy of Russification during the period of Soviet rule. Similarly, indigenous people of Fiji resented their minority status in their own country, as a result of the immigration of Indians during the period of British rule. But while collective humiliation imposed by one people on another in the past may feed a nationalist movement, it cannot justify what amounts to the legalization of revenge. At least, regimes which insist in behaving in this way—denying their minorities citizenship or otherwise disenfranchizing them—should not expect to escape international criticism. Nor should they be allowed, even before they had been recognized as sovereign states, to receive economic and other support, while simultaneously claiming, as it were in anticipation, protection under Article 2.7 of the Charter.

The uniqueness of the present situation deserves emphasis. The collapse of communism has left people free to remake their own future: in this sense it signals a kick-start to history, not its demise. While it may appear that liberal democracy has triumphed—and it is true that most people given the chance would opt for OECD living standards—the force of global economic integration has weakened the liberal state in the area where its achievements have been most admired—the ability to balance the requirements of social justice with those of efficiency and the demands of equality with those of liberty. It is already clear that, for reasons well described by Gellner and others, the nationalists are the most likely to move into the ideological vacuum. They generally profess a belief in democratic values but in practice find it difficult to construct political systems of a non-discriminatory nature.

The situation is unique, but not, unhappily, its most likely outcome. The history of modernity could be written in terms of genocide, the forced movement of peoples, or their equally forced assimilation. Parodying Renan, the nation can be ironically defined as a group of people united by a common error about their ancestry. How else, indeed, could the amazing diversity of human cultures have been reduced to politically and economically manageable proportions? What shocks us about the current wave of "ethnic cleansing" is that it is occurring, not on the opposite side of a war in which we ourselves are engaged, or a revolution, or some historical dark age, but in full daylight within a world order ostensibly devoted to the protection of individual human rights.

In the final analysis there may be little that the international community can do to protect the innocent from the guilty. But at the margin—and certainly at the time of diplomatic recognition— there are things that can be done and conditions that should be insisted upon. The instruments already exist in the Council of Europe's criteria for admission of new members and in the authority vested in the CSCE's Commissioner for Minorities. The creation of these mechanisms no doubt represents an advance over what existed before—it at least suggests that a problem that was systematically ignored throughout the Cold War has now been recognized— but the record of the past three years hardly provides ground for optimism.

What then should be done? It is tempting to follow Ibsen in his famous verdict in *An Enemy of the People*—it is not merely that the majority is sometimes wrong, the majority is always wrong. On this view, the end of the Cold War has created a window of opportunity: we should be prepared to strike in the name of universalist values wherever minorities are being persecuted. So far as nationalism is concerned, however, the majority is not invariably wrong. As students of civil war know, there is always a minority within the minority, for whom the *ante-bellum* is to be preferred over a secessionist state. It is in this context and in the hope of establishing transparent criteria that international lawyers are debating the desirability of codifying the grounds that would justify a humanitarian right of intervention. If that path were to be followed, it would logically require specifying the conditions that would justify a secessionist right of self-determination, a position that few of them had been prepared to adopt and which governments would certainly not endorse.

No doubt their reasons are self-serving—they are scared of demonstration effects. But in a world increasingly characterized by global forces beyond the control of governments, their prudence may also, unwittingly, be morally wise: the only way of proving that politics requires freedom. Some national minorities no doubt deserve support, and indeed have derived from their historical experience a fierce attachment to democratic principles and practice; others do not. The same could be said of national majorities.

A desire for legal consistency and transparency, admirable in themselves, cannot replace the need for responsible and humane political judgement. In this sense, politics will always be as much about discrimination as about the creation of non-discriminatory rules. In *The Human Condition,* Hannah Arendt wrote that law should never attempt to cover the whole of human life. It was at best an island of predictability in an ocean of chaos. She believed that if law aimed to cover all possibilities, it would inevitably serve a totalitarian purpose. Many world problems are now genuinely global, beyond the capacity of any single state or group of states; for others the existing nation-states—more often multicultural than monoethnic in character—are often too large and impersonal to allow genuine participatory politics to flourish. In attempting to navigate in these turbulent waters, Hannah Arendt's advice seems more relevant than ever.

### Notes

[1] David Held and Anthony McGrew, "Globalization and the Liberal Democratic State," *Government and Opposition,* Vol. 26, No. 2, Spring 1993, p. 262,

[2] *Ibid.,* p. 269.

[3] Paul Kennedy, *Preparing for the Twenty-First Century,* London: Harper-Collins, 1993, p. 329.

[4] See John Herz, *International Politics in the Atomic Age,* New York: Columbia University Press, 1959.

[5] A. Giddens, *Modernity and Self-Identity,* Cambridge: Polity Press, 1991, p. 187, quoted in Held and McGrew, *op. cit.*

[6] Eric Hobsbawm, *Nations and Nationalism since 1780,* Cambridge University Press, 1990, p. 4 and p. 183.

[7] Elie Kedourie, *Nationalism,* London: Longmans, 1960, p. 9.

[8] Tony Judt, "Chauvin and His Heirs: The Problems of Adjusting to a Multiracial France," *Times Literary Supplement,* July 9, 1993, pp. 11–12.

[9] J. S. Mill, *Representative Government,* chapter XVI.

[10] G. W. F. Hegel, *Philosophy of Right,* translated by T. M. Knox, Oxford University Press, 1979, part 3: Ethical Life, (iii) The State, (c) World History.

[11] *Ibid.*

[12] F. Fukuyama, "The End of History?" *The National Interest,* Summer 1989.

[13] E. Gellner, *Nations and Nationalism,* Oxford: Blackwells, p. 83.

[14] Robert Reich, "Who is Us?" *Harvard Business Review,* January–February 1990, pp. 53–64.

[15] *Amnesty International Report 1993,* London: Amnesty International Publications, 1993.

[16] Ghia Nodia, "Nationalism and Democracy," *Journal of Democracy,* Vol. 3, No. 4, October 1992, pp. 3–31.

# COMMENT ON THE MAYALL PAPER

Maciej PERCZYNSKI

Mayall's paper is an extremely original and profound attempt to define the relationship between the two major tendencies shaping contemporary world affairs, namely the tendency toward globalization on the one hand and nationalism on the other. These are well-known facts of life which, however, "do not speak for themselves" (as the author underlines). Most frequently they are described as processes contradicting, if not excluding, each other. Growing interdependencies in the sphere of economics and politics on the global scale are accompanied by the infusion of new life into nationalistic drives and aspirations. New national states emerge, and the search for a more adequate definition of *raison d'état* preoccupies the minds of politicians everywhere. At the same time arguments are heard more frequently that in view of the vigorously progressing internationalization of social and political life nationalism has outlived its days and the nation-state has become an anachronism.

In my view the most creative and valuable element in Mayall's approach to the discussion of the relationship between globalism and nationalism is his idea that "the two trends are not contradictory but symbiotic, appearing in the world together and constantly reinforcing one another ever since. The rise of nationalism was a response to a globalizing process, just as globalization itself, or rather what kept the process going, was largely a consequence of nationalist competition."

I fully share this view. It has been remarkably well documented and convincingly proved. The only reservation I have relates to certain nuances in the author's approach to nationalism, which he treats, in my perception, almost as a homogeneous notion instead of showing its highly diversified nature. The merits and demerits of nationalism were and are extremely differentiated, according to the time, place, and conditions in which it appears.

It is particularly important to take this into account when assessing its relation to globalization in the second half of our century. Probably nobody will deny that the current structure of world relations was shaped under the influence of two major events in recent history: the first is the political de-colonization of areas subordinated to the imperial powers which emerged at the turn of the nineteenth century; the second, the collapse of "real socialism" in Central and Eastern Europe and the subsequent dismantling of the Soviet bloc.

It is important to stress that in both cases the tendency toward nationalism played a distinctly positive role and contributed effectively to the demolition of the entire structure of imperial and Soviet domination. Under the new circumstances, the character and content of the tendency toward nationalism changed substantially. Mayall splendidly describes and appraises its new qualities, particularly with regard to the new contradictions that have sprung from ethnic questions, the aspirations of national minorities, and issues of human rights. However, in covering a very broad spectrum of problems, he touches only briefly on some aspects of the new wave of nationalism which, in my view, are very crucial to appraisal of its impact on globalization. Following the logic of the author's analysis, I would like to develop some additional arguments showing the interdependent relationship between the two processes. I have in mind, above all, the specific relationship between nationalism, hegemonism, and regionalism.

## NATIONALISM AND HEGEMONISM

A natural tendency of nationalism and particularly "victorious nationalism" (in contradistinction to "oppressed nationalism") is a strong proclivity and drive toward hegemonism. In the case of large nations and states this drive usually transcends local or even regional boundaries and gives rise to ambitions to rearrange the entire world order. There is no need (and also no possibility in my short intervention) to elaborate at greater length on the historical experience connected with the hegemonistic drive of nationalism. It is enough to mention the examples of Hitlerite Germany or Stalinist Russia to perceive the consequences of this type of evolution, which culminates in an attempt to establish world hegemony. In this context it is worth noting that contemporary developments in world affairs have *decisively* undermined nationalism's chances of evolving in the direction of hegemonism. The erosion of hegemonism is due to at least two sets of reasons. The first obviously stems from the collapse of the Soviet version of socialism. Its direct consequence—disintegration of the Soviet bloc—has eliminated the sources of hegemonistic tendencies based on the assumption of world revolution and international class struggle and an historical confrontation between East and West.

The second reason is of a different nature. It is connected with the current stage of industrial revolution (the so-called information technology or microprocessor revolution), which has created entirely new conditions for economic and social progress. The traditional factors of economic power, such as territory, natural resources, population, geographical location, have ceased to determine a country's position in the structure of world relations and the dynamic of its development. These factors are gradually giving way to new ones among which the *accumulated knowledge* capable of generating technological progress and absorbing it for productive purposes plays the most important role. The information technology revolution was highly conducive to speeding up the diffusion of technological progress, particularly among those countries which were equipped to utilize the achievements of modern civilization. This is why in the last couple of decades there has been a clearly perceptible tendency toward reduction of economic and technological differences within developed industrial countries and areas. At the same time, the gap between the less developed economies, which have not passed the absorptive capacity threshold of the new technology, and the developed world has increased tremendously. As a result the bipolar structure of world relations, which existed until recently, is being replaced by a multipolar structure. One part consists of three distinctly formed centers of regional gravitation, namely the U.S.A., the European Community, and Japan. To the other part belong the underdeveloped countries and areas of Africa, Latin America, and Asia. In this world architecture, competition between different groups of countries will tend to increase and even sharpen (particularly in the economic sphere), but there are good reasons to believe that in its competitive content creative elements may prevail over destructive ones. The threat of global confrontation is disappearing, and there is little chance of one of the emerging centers of regional gravitation being able to aspire to global hegemony. Given the radical change in the function of traditional and modern factors of growth and power (as noted earlier), territorial expansion and political domination outside nation-state boundaries are becoming more and more costly and therefore economically unprofitable. The social byproducts of political expansion are usually so burdensome that the danger of de-stablization of the world system of relations discourages attempts to expand by force and to dominate. Under these circumstances nationalism's natural tendency to seek domination is losing its hegemonistic perspective. There is little chance of a global leader reappearing and successfully performing the function of watchman, guardian, or policeman of the existing world order. This does not mean that in certain political circles nationalistic tendencies toward domination will die forever, but there are no grounds for believing that they might determine the main direction of nationalism and its evolution. This is made even less likely by another factor determining the relationship between globalism and nationalism—namely the tendency toward regionalism.

## NATIONALISM, GLOBALISM, AND REGIONALISM

Regional integration is not only a fact of life which should be taken into consideration in assessing regional arrangements; it has become a category of international relations actively influencing the direction of globalization processes. Regionalism is an *intermediate link in the chain* leading to the emergence of a new global structure. It may complicate or smooth the dichotomous interdependence between nationalism and globalism. European regional integration has a special part to play in speeding up and deepening the systemic transformations in the countries of Central and Eastern Europe and enabling them to rejoin the mainstream of change in modern civilization. It is in this perspective that one should also assess the role of nationalism versus regionalism, particularly at a time when the post-communist countries are searching for a new place in the emergent system of intra-European relations and the new framework of international security. As we have said, nationalism does not have only one face. During the period of Soviet hegemonism it contributed immensely to the erosion of the pillars which supported the whole imperial structure, particularly in Central Europe. It is nevertheless a fact that after the collapse of the system the direction of the nationalist tendency radically changed. Its main current is, we fear, creating the most difficult barrier to pan-European integration and the parallel drive to build a market economy and complete transformation of the socio-political system in Central and Eastern Europe. This is a very complicated problem which cannot be addressed without first identifying the reasons for such a negative, not to say dangerous, evolution of nationalist tendencies. Some of them are simply of a banal character and, if it were not for the scale of the phenomenon, would probably not merit serious consideration. We are thinking in the first place of a legacy of the past (not only recent but also more distant), which manifests itself in xenophobic prejudices, parochial feelings of superiority, pseudo-patriotic demagoguery, etc. All such sentiments (none of them very new) are deeply rooted in the mentality of certain social groups, ones that are usually passive and closed to the outside world. As a rule this part of society is characterized by a comparatively low level of education and culture although, it now appears, not without surprising exceptions. These social groups ceased, however, to be closed and passive when faced with a drastic deterioration in living standards and lack of any immediate prospects of improvement. On the whole, these people are not supporters of the old regime; however, they expected something different from the change in the system. It goes without saying that the socio-political transformations currently under way were bound to be costly even if mistakes in economic and social policy could have been avoided (which is also an unrealistic assumption). But the reform process has also turned out to be much more costly than predicted and involved greater social sacrifices than expected. Thus, there has inevitably arisen a syndrome not only of false expectations but also of unfulfilled promises.

In such a situation the easiest solution is to look for somebody *alien* to the given society to blame for all these disappointments. This opens the way to demagogic claims that it surely must be outsiders who wish to take advantage of the new conditions at the expense of the truly native population. One can hear frequently that foreigners are coming and buying out the national wealth for almost nothing while the nation-state is helpless and passive because it has to subordinate itself to "Europe." Although the real problem is not an excessive inflow of foreign capital but the lack of it (which limits the possibility of economic reconstruction), it is all too easy in these circumstances to appeal to "national," "patriotic," and even "Christian" values, which are being destroyed at the price of rapid entry into the European Community.

From this soil there emerge populistic movements with a decidedly nationalistic and xenophobic orientation. Anti-Semitic tendencies have reappeared vigorously even in a country like Poland where there are almost no Jews and a considerable part of the population was witness to the most horrible of crimes against humanity—the Holocaust—which brought the extermination from Polish society of several million Jews.

Though all such phenomena deserve to be treated with the utmost disgust and condemnation, one must also be aware of how dangerous they are. However, it is also necessary to learn carefully the lessons of the first years of transformation because it is not taking place in a vacuum. There is undoubtedly a chance of marginalizing populistic tendencies and nationalistic extremism, but one should be aware that jumping natural stages of socio-economic and political evolution, even if necessary and justified, is always likely to produce the aftereffects of shock. These may set in motion social forces capable of de-stabilizing the rational development of historical processes. There is also a need for very careful judgment of the pace of the transformation process, the permissible limits (at the given historical stage) of its profoundness, and, last but not least, the degree of social acceptance of the ongoing reforms. Besides, this last requirement reflects the most fundamental principle of democracy which is being built in the post-communist societies.

Nationalistic extremism is not capable of reversing either the tendency toward globalism or regionalism. A rational nationalism, accommodating to the objective development of global interdependencies, could even add some positive values to the emergent system of world relations. This process cannot be helped, however, by the premature elimination of institutions which, though belonging to the vanishing epoch, are still needed and essential in the process of global and national transformations. One of the most important is the nation-state, which cannot be treated as an historical anachronism. Thus, the proposition, popular here and there, to minimize the role of the nation-state and maximize the space for the free play of forces (plus supra-national regulations) does not seem to me the best answer to the assumed aims. Mayall is in my mind absolutely right in saying that "the nation-state is not a way-station en route to a wider and higher form of political organization. Nor can one deduce from the emergence of regional and global markets a transfer of political loyalties from the nation to a putative community of mankind."

I might add that it is only by ensuring the practical use of that approach that one can hope that the objectively justified tendency toward globalism will develop without excessively high social costs and be much more immune to irrationally perceived and historically realized nationalistic concepts and politics.

# Discussion

**Junker:** I am really thankful for these two papers, and I would like to start with a small commentary on the paper of Perczynski and then go on to Mayall's. I just notice that in your evaluation of the situation in Eastern Europe, you have been as pessimistic as I have been when I talked about the future of democracy in Eastern Europe, and I realize that you basically gave the same reasons for that—an excessive ethnic nationalism, lack of tradition of liberty, property, and entrepreneurship. You added anti-Semitism, which I was not aware of, and you mentioned the cost of the breakdown. So, though you ended on a hopeful note, I would say it was just like the old Latin saying: Hoping against hope.

I completely agree with both commentators that nationalism and liberalism appeared at the same time, and liberalism partly broke down. I will just remind you that when Bismarck was appointed prime minister of Prussia, the first thing he had to do was to fight the liberals and the constitutional movement, which is one of the tragedies and ironies of German history. The other thing about a legal solution to the dichotomy of, on one hand, the sovereignty of the nation-state and, on the other, the upholding of human rights. I offered a solution in the name of Kant earlier, and this is the only solution. If a nation-state denies human rights, it has no legal foundation and even no legal foundation within the community of nation-states. Such is the basic idea of Kant. So, from a philosophical point of view, I still believe that there is a solution. Of course, this creates problems, but we should be very clear about distinguishing these philosophical, theoretical problems from the practical ones; I feel we have to go back to Kant in this respect as well.

**Stern:** I thought Mayall's paper admirable in every respect. Let me just make a couple of small points. One is, if I read it carefully enough, the word "patriotism" either does not occur or is not dwelt on, and it does seem to me there is a connection here with the earlier remark about sacrifice, that the antecedent to nationalism was a patriotic sentiment which could be both benign and non-benign, just as nationalism was. Certainly, patriotism as such does not have the aggressive element that nationalism after the second half of the nineteenth century had. Here it was not only Herder, whom you mentioned, but a more activist political figure, Mazzini, who represented a kind of liberal nationalism, from which we can see that the past also offers hope rather than just warnings.

You talked a great deal about Mill, but talking about Mill for some reason made me think immediately of Tocqueville, and it seems to me that we ought to pay our respects to him in two regards. One is that he certainly was very much a defender of liberal rights, liberal rights being perhaps different from democratic rights, and that whole question of the relationship of liberalism antecedent to democracy is something that perhaps we could dwell on further. And having mentioned Tocqueville, I would just remind all of us that perhaps no one has better analyzed the cultural context of democracy than Tocqueville in his famous book. And that is, in some ways, something that very often is lacking in the kind of discussion that we have.

**Kerber:** What we have seen in the last few decades, in the increasing articulation of women's rights, has been the fusion of what we call in the United States "identity politics" with transnational—across time and space—claims of abstract rights. One of the interesting phenomena of the twentieth century if we start with the League in the 1920s, but also one that clearly is increasing in energy as we come to the end of the century (and we can predict it to increase in force), is something not so different from the nationalist identity politics that Mayall referred to in the nineteenth century. That is a transnational movement which seeks to articulate women's rights which had not been previously articulated, so that at the Vienna Conference on Human Rights very recently among the groups that came most well organized, with the clearest set of transcripts, principles, manifestos to distribute, were women's groups organized around the argument that there is a right to some kind of sexual identity that needed to be formulated and articulated in ways that Mayall's mother could not articulate two generations ago.

I think that if we are making some predictions about issues that will grow on a global scale in the next century, it will be the increased effort to bring this kind of identity politics into an international sector and to articulate a kind of identity politics which started out seeming very personal, very limited, very local, into a large international scale.

**Kristeva:** I was very impressed by the two papers and I have one historical comment and one connected with actuality. The historical one is in connection with Mayall's very interesting comment about nationalism as a romantic reaction against the universality of the French Revolution and French Enlightenment. But there is also a French idea of nationalism, and if you look at human rights you should notice that from the fourth Article of the Declaration, the reference is not "man" but "citizen," which means, of course, the "republic" against "monarchy" but also creation of a national state as an exigency of human rights.

The second observation I have is that, of course, we are now aware of the fact that we have to be against nationalism. We are full nations because of the historical situation, but what is the optimal definition of a "nation"? Here I would like to refer to two concepts we are trying to develop now in French discussions. Against the notion determined in terms of *jus soli* or *jus sanguinis,* we tried to come back to the Montesquieu notion of nation as a social contract, which means that whatever your origin, from the point of view of the soil, the point of view of blood, if you accept some rules, you belong to this nation. Maybe it is up to institutions like ours, or educational groups, to develop what seems to us to be an optimal notion of nation.

The other one is the notion of the nation as a transitional object, which is the Winnicot notion in psychology. It is used to describe the necessity for the child to have some object which is not his mother but which reminds him of his mother and makes him able to separate from her in order to go on to more complicated activities. So how to escape from the origin without losing it and to insert the individual in bigger entities. Here is a Montesquieu sentence I like to cite often, and it has been repeated in French schools. "If it is something that you cannot bear in yourself, you can go to your family; if it is something that you cannot bear in your family, go to your nation; if it is something that you cannot bear in your nation, you go to the world." You belong to each one of these entities, but there are transitional entities; you do not have to absolutize, a nation being one of the important entities but not the absolute one.

**Iriye:** It is very interesting that, as we are coming to the end almost of our conference, the participants are raising themes that focus not just on issues of globalization and nationalism but on earlier themes that we have been discussing. For example, Kristeva's comment now reminded me of a discussion we had about human migration and the crisis of demography, as hundreds of thousands of people cross national boundaries to enter richer nations. What she just said of a "scale of adherences" from the individual family to the nation and the world takes us back to the discussion we had about identities, Hutchison's presentation, and so on. So I think we are, quite rightly, bringing some of the themes back together.

**Nivat:** What is good nationalism? What is bad nationalism? The Russian philosopher Vladimir Soloviev tried to answer that in his famous *Conferences* on the national question in the mid-eighties of the last century. His answer was rather simple: that oppressed nations have a right to nationalism and that oppressor nations have no right to nationalism. I strongly disagree with many aspects of Perczynski's paper. I do not think that the return of nations in the former Soviet Union has been so ugly. I think there have been beautiful sides, and, as an observer of Russia, I have been struck by the beauty of parts of the events that have been going there, even in Russia, which was a former oppressor state, speaking in Soloviev's term, but very much oppressed in its quintessence by the communist regime and, for that reason, could be estimated as a sort of "oppressed" nation, too.

A very simple pedestrian wish I would like to formulate is that in a century's time when globalization probably has made enormous developments, people who will live after us will have the great pleasure to have all the flavors and scenes of the different nations on this earth.

**Junker:** About the dangers of nationalism, my starting point is an old Roman thinker, Cicero. He once made a very important distinction between *patria naturae* and *patria civitatis*. What did he mean by *patria naturae*? That is the surroundings, the landscape, the culture, the habits you are born into, things which you can nearly smell, which you can taste, which you can relate to with all your senses. On the other hand, *patria civitatis* is a political allegiance to a political entity. Now, I think all the dangers of nationalism come from this quarter of abstraction, because the more abstract this allegiance becomes, the more it is devoid of all the things which compose *natura*, the more dangerous it becomes, until you finally drink the absolute like water. That is the famous slogan of Schlegel, so I would say the inherent problem is with this *patria civitatis*, when it is removed from your cultural surroundings.

**Windsor:** A quick question primarily to Mayall but also with relevance to what Perczynski was saying. I was not quite sure when you said "let us get back to the history," do you mean "let us get back to the history to liberate it from historicism" or "the nature of nationalism is rooted in a certain kind of historicism, anyway"? And to understand its purpose, so to speak, in a reasonably healthy symbiotic relationship with globalization, one has to put it into contemporary history rather than in any historicist tradition. If that is the case, of course, it seems to me that Perczynski was raising a powerful question: how we actually get into contemporary history as opposed to the historicist throwback.

**Mayall:** I am not absolutely certain of my answer. The Enlightenment was subsequently historicized, so if one is saying, and I do, that one of the roots of nationalism and globalization being linked together lies in the pre-historicist history, one should try to get back into a contemporary history. We should acknowledge that the dilemmas of a nation within a global order have to be addressed on the assumption that they have a symbiotic relationship, a structural relationship, which is necessary, and not work on the assumption that there is some teleology or evolutionary goal in which we will see the nation withering away or disappearing from the political landscape. All I am claiming is that we have to face moral and political problems within the framework of the nation and within the framework of a political order, and it is a sort of fantasy to think that we can dispense with the nation.

**Stern:** If I could make a slightly inappropriate remark at this moment that just came to me, our conference started with the theme "The Crumbling of Communism" and we worked under the general motto of "The Future in the Past." I was suddenly reminded of a Soviet saying, that is to say, a saying within the Soviet Union, obviously by critics, and the saying went: "Only the future is certain; the past is very uncertain." What we have proved, it seems to me very happily, is that the future is as uncertain as the past.

**Mayall:** One of the things I skirted over and which goes right back to our first session, and on which I would like to hear some views, is how people see the relationship between nation and democracy. In my paper I have quoted a Georgian scholar who has recently written a piece with which I have considerable sympathy, which is clearly aimed at Western critics of the research on nationalism in the former Soviet Union on the grounds that they want to say that this is a form of "irrationalism." He points out in a graphic passage which I have quoted and which I suspect is drawn from that brilliant book by Huizinga, *Homo Ludens,* although he does not actually specifically say so, that you cannot achieve a democracy by rational choice, that behind every statement of "we, the people" are some very mysterious game-like evolutions by which a people define the playing field within which they are going to operate.

Now, that linked up in my mind when I listened to Morin on the first day, and it does, of course, produce a much more sympathetic relationship between nation and democracy than the one which many liberals, particularly many Western liberals, are prepared to concede, because they will not examine the sort of preexisting irrational mythical roots of their own national identities.

It does suggest that we cannot engineer democracies. It is not a question of saying right, let everybody have a nation dependent on a notion of citizenship and not on a notion of blood. I wish it were possible to engineer that, but we do not know how to do it, and we do not know how to do it partly because of those democracies which have over time evolved a patriotism to a civic democratic ideal. If you push them they may be more or less tolerant to migration, but the core of their identity tends to come from something which is pre-rational and historical.

In the face of the turbulence in Eastern Europe and the former Soviet Union at the moment, the case which I think of taken from Western Europe and hawked around in this area as a model is the case of Tirol. Here you have an agreement reached between the Tirolians and the Italians, which took forty years to negotiate—which suggests that it may be not a terribly useful model—but it is voluntarily agreed; it is politically a solution to the problem of a minority which sees itself as entrapped but sees the logic of not going for secession and, in any case, would not be allowed secession. The solution which has come up is for voluntary apartheid, a series of limitations on the freedom of movement and all the values which are elsewhere inscribed in the liberal constitution. However, I would want to contradict my own argument and at least entertain the hope that this can be a way-station rather than some kind of final solution to the problem of national groups in the global order.

**Bulliet:** Let me make a last observation on the question of what our agenda is and how we have conceived it. We have had, I think, in virtually every session a reference to Yugoslavia, a reference to the Soviet Union. While we have been meeting, one of the world's most bitter, long-lasting, and truly tragic conflicts has been coming to what appears to be a likely end. I am speaking of the conflict between the Israelis and the Palestinians. It is something that embodies issues of nationalism, issues of intervention, issues of regionalism, issues of culture. It is, indeed, a microcosm of the conflicts and tensions that in many other ways we have been talking about, and I find it extraordinary that at a moment which is—I suppose like every moment but not quite like every moment—histori-cal, when an event of this magnitude appears to be taking place, that it has had no reference whatsoever in this conference.

**Kristeva:** I referred to it briefly.

**Bulliet:** You referred to it briefly and, actually, Harkabi referred to it briefly, but it strikes me that we have gone through a week in which there has been no mention of India, even though the Bharata Janata Party has been a very controversial issue there, where we have had great bloodletting along racial lines or religious lines. We have had little reference to many parts of the world, and I think that the sorts of skills and knowledge that have been devoted to world issues in this sort of meeting are somewhat out of step with the actual character of the globe when most of the globe is not really referred to. China would be another area of which we have heard very little, and I would hope that if there is a third session of this discussion of the twentieth century that the rest of the world be let in on it.

**Junker:** I would like to come back to the theme of democracy and nationalism because this is the basic problem now facing Ger-many. In the old Federal Republic, we had modernization without a nation-state, contrary to one of your statements. We had democ-racy without a nation-state, and the population at large was happy, and the Liberals and the Social Democrats, including myself, could not see the necessity for a nation-state. We could see the need to expand democracy, at least, so that is why many thinkers in the for-mer Federal Republic tried to develop some patriotism within the constitution.

Many German students were raised in this mode. When they went, for example, to the United States, they were appalled by this orgy of nationalism, this combination of democracy, sense of mis-sion, God. They thought this was utterly outmoded, and then what happened? The revolution in East Germany started, and it started with a slogan: "We are the people!" and fourteen days later it was: "We are one people!" All of a sudden, Germany was confronted with this problem of nation-state again, and here we are, the old lib-eral wing without any orientation, and we are facing this problem quite clearly.

**Mayall:** When I was writing this paper I had a clear sense of try-ing to find my way through a puzzle, and so it was the first shot, and many things that have been said have given me, as other pre-senters have said, room for rethinking.

If I can just pick up few of the points, I think there really is very little substantive disagreement between Perczynski and myself. One of the things that always bedevils you when you look at nationalism is whether to be impressed by the fact that you are looking at one thing or looking at many things. In my paper I certainly concentrated on the common roots, but I think other interventions I have made elsewhere in the symposium showed that I fully address many of the problems which nationalism throws up. One looks at the specific histories, the specific formulations which this common kind of response takes.

About regionalism, again I have no objection, although I may be a bit more skeptical. As I say in my paper, one of the great problems of the symbiotic relationship between nationalism and globalism is that there are increasing numbers of problems, with ecological questions—perhaps one of the major fields. It is not just the question of international capital movements; it is also all of the sorts of questions which were attempted to be discussed at Rio last year. There is a whole range of questions for which the nation-state is an obstacle, and you can create many international entities to try to cope with the fact that you have got to reach solutions to what are increasingly global problems which do not respect boundaries.

If I am right in saying that the nation-state won't go away, I think there are limits to regionalism, great limits to democratizing regionalism. This is why I was very impressed yesterday with one of Nivat's interventions, suggesting that in addressing the ecological problems we cannot rely on the emergence of a global regulatory framework, and, therefore, we must think about cultivating within all our societies a sense of limitations, or what used to be called "human scales," something which the whole pressure of modernity militates against.

Just another point raised by a number of speakers and by Nivat in response to Perczynski: What is good and what is bad nationalism? I am really not coming off the fence on that. All I am saying is that the reality is that we live in a world of nation-states, and they have a potential for goodness and evil, for perversion and for developing in a civic and progressive way, and I agree with the comments that have been made about patriotism being at least historically a less-loaded frame. My worry about that, and it relates also to something that Kerber said, is that I suppose patriotism derives originally from a non-political concept, something deeply rooted in agricultural societies—love of the particular countryside where you grow up and all its resonances. If you translate "let's get back to patriotism," there is a slight tendency to indulge in a kind of romantic nostalgia. We cannot, as I have suggested, get back to Fichte.

Watanabe told me yesterday that when Fichte produced his model of a closed commercial state, which in a sense was part of the prehistory of nationalism, rather than history (you need to go to List to see the modern political economist as a nationalist), in fact he was drawing on Japan as his model, and this was, in a sense, an idealized conception of a premodern nationalized community. Many of us are tempted, and I would include myself in that number—to yearn for the possibility of a simpler world, less driven by the logic of accumulation and industrialization. But I do not believe it is possible, and I do not believe we actually want it. We simply would not be sitting around this table if we were living in that sort of world.

**Perczynski:** Of course, the most important issues which really are necessary to approach when discussing the problem of nationalism is the question of what is bad and what is good nationalism. We all feel that it is not a homogeneous notion, that there is not simply one tendency of nationalism. Probably the definition reported by Nivat that good nationalism is nationalism of oppressed nations is a too narrow one because it deprives non-oppressed nations of using nationalism in the positive and constructive sense, and there is a positive and constructive sense in nationalist tendencies.

I was saying myself that the development of nationalistic tendencies made it possible to end Soviet domination much earlier, and that was good nationalism. Sometimes good nationalism is called "patriotism." Nationalism has many faces: it is for me absolutely obvious, and I was concentrating on the ugly faces of nationalism because every second party which is now opposing the transformation, and fighting against the tendency of European integration in the post-communist party, call themselves nationalists, National Parties of something. They are appealing to the national interest and xenophobic feelings, and that is bad nationalism. They undermine the possibility of transformation, and this transformation without the trend toward a United Europe is impossible. This is why I see in nationalistic tendencies of that type the biggest danger for the process of transformation.

In fact I am rather an optimist, but if the definition of "pessimist" is that it is a well-informed optimist, then maybe there are some pessimistic tones in my understanding and in my expression. I said I am deeply convinced that we have reached the point of no return in Central and Eastern Europe as far as the development from the communist to the new society is concerned, but one cannot hope that it will be achieved soon and that Poland, let us say, or Hungary will soon be in the European Community. A lot has to be done to create compatible societies. If societies are not compatible, that will be harmful for the development of national economies and societies in the post-communist world. We are in a very crucial period now. Stern was referring to Tocqueville. I can refer to another famous saying and thesis of Tocqueville: People riot not when the situation is deteriorating, but when the situation is improving; and with an improved situation new hopes arise, and this encourages rioting.

I think that the situation is improving, and in this improving situation there is a danger of riots, protests, which may reverse, not completely, but reverse and hamper the process of socio-economic transformation and, first of all, in Central Europe, the process of really joining Europe. I do not think that the national state is something which will last forever, but I will protest vigorously if that instrument is removed as an instrument of development too early, as so many other instruments of transformation removed too early are backfiring. At this stage, national state and good nationalism adjusted to global transformations and new regional arrangements may play a very positive role in the development and help reaching the globalization goals which we were discussing in our paper.

**Iriye:** Thank you for an admirable summing up, in a sense, of not just of your own paper but many other things that we have been discussing. Now for a more formal, perhaps more personal, summing up of our session, may I now turn to May.

**May:** The Conference Politburo assigned me this task of saying a few closing words. The billing of "summary" would be wholly misleading as no one can possibly summarize this conference. Few of us, I think, should pretend fully to understand all that we have read and heard. The subject matter ranges too widely, the languages we use are too varied. I do not mean by that English, Japanese, or Russian. The translators are superb and they missed, so far as I can tell, no nuance. But I mean that an international historian, a German historian, a feminist historian, and a historian of Islam have great difficulty finding a common vocabulary; and words of common meaning become even less frequent when any of us as historians converse with an anthropologist, or an economist, or a scientist, or a psychoanalyst. On top of that, exchanges during any few minutes' discussion have been capable of covering the earth. My notes on one session ranged from Plotinus to Elizabeth Taylor. As often in these circumstances, I am reminded of an old story concerning Leonid Brezhnev. At one point, the story goes, Brezhnev complained to his aides about the size of the Soviet Union. "We have fourteen time zones," he said. "I never know the date or the time. So I make mistakes. I write to Mrs. Gandhi congratulating her on her election. I'm a day late. I write to the Pope saying I am sorry about the assassination attempt. I'm a day early."

Given all of these complications, I cannot try to summarize our conference, but what can I usefully say in this allotted time? To help figure this out, I have imagined how we would think about a conference of comparable character held in 1893 or 1894. We would look back at it and ask several questions. What did it identify as major continuing trends? What important trends did it not foresee? What can one say in retrospect about what was said and not said, about how to deal with the future that actually developed? What might the conferees have recommended that could have made the twentieth century a less awful time for those who experienced it?

The conferees would certainly have noted trends much commented on by contemporaneous journalists. In what we call the developed world, these would have included cascading industrialization, growing concentration in wealth, and the continuing pauperization of workers, both industrial and agricultural. The conferees would certainly have commented on the apparent Europeanization of the world. Colonial imperialism was then at its height. A Japanese military victory over China was about to earn for Japan status as a non-European European power. The conferees might have linked their observations on economic trends and global political trends with a phrase similar to that which British journalist W. T. Stead would soon use as the title of a book, *The Americanization of the World.*

Probably, the conferees would also have remarked on a trend toward adoption of democratic or republican forms of government. This was a common theme in contemporaneous political and historical writing as, for example, in the works of Lord Bryce and Elie Halévy. The evidence included the French Republic, the role of the Reichstag in the German Empire, and of parliamentary bodies in the Austro-Hungarian monarchy, Italy, and even Spain, the apparent direction of change in Britain, and the increasing citation of the United States as a model, or warning, of how other polities might evolve.

Finally, it is quite possible that the conferees would have commented on the fact that seven decades had passed since the last Great European War. They would not have been saying anything out of the ordinary if they concluded that the progress of civilization had made such warfare obsolete.

What the conferees would almost certainly have failed to foresee was the violence and tyranny that would characterize much of the century ahead. What they probably also would have failed to foresee was the countercurrent against European domination that would create by the end of the next century a political map of the world beside which the map of the old Holy Roman Empire seems simplicity itself.

How could these hypothetical conferees of a century ago have foreseen these hidden trends? They certainly could not have done so on the basis of what then passed for social science. They would probably have done best to let their imaginations extrapolate from popular literature, not from high literature but from middle-brow works—novels serialized in magazines—yesterday's equivalents of "Dallas" and "Dynasty," Jack London's *Iron Heel*, for example, or H. G. Wells's novels about wars involving what he called "atomic bombs." Our mythical conferees would also have done well to think of Nietzsche as a possible prophet.

What might we wish that such conferees had recommended? For one thing, we could wish that there had been prompting for more analysis early in this century of how the timbers of democracy could be shored up to withstand economic adversity and war. We could wish, for example, that there had been more understanding of how public opinion could become not only free but judicious. How could people in Europe have resisted surges of passion such as those in Germany and France in 1914 or in Germany after the war, or comparable surges in Japan in the 1930s, or the United States in the 1950s?

We could wish, too, that there had been more useful study of nation-building, more asking long in advance about what it might take for a non-industrialized colony to become an industrialized nation, with perhaps a Muslim or Buddhist or other non-European culture.

So how to epitomize this conference of ours? Anyone's response will be idiosyncratic. As I read the papers and commentaries and interpret our four and a half days of discussion, the dominant theme of the conference has been the continuing surge of democracy. Our analysis of this continuing surge of democracy has dealt primarily with two clusters of questions. One cluster concerns requirements for the implantation and survival of democratic institutions. The second concerns challenges with which democratic governments must cope if they are to fulfill their promise. The two clusters obviously link up, for if democratic governments fail to meet these challenges, they may not survive.

As our conference has had as a subtheme the collapse of communism, so a conference like ours, held in 2093 or 2193, could have as its major theme the collapse of democracy. In the first cluster of questions, the subtheme of the collapse of communism has been particularly prominent. States in Europe, formerly communist, have created parliaments and held elections. In some, the level of citizen participation in government approaches that in longer-standing democracies. Poland and the Czech Republic are foremost. Elsewhere, changes seem more superficial. In some instances, the new democracies are hard to distinguish from the people's democracies they have allegedly displaced.

Ranging beyond Europe, North America, and Japan, our discussion touched on the character of governments actually or nominally democratic in other parts of the world. Junker described the variety of actual and would-be democracies in Latin America. Others discussed the Middle East, Africa, and Southeast Asia. The question of what distinguished a hopeful case like the Czech Republic from less hopeful cases was left hanging. There did seem to be general agreement, however, on certain criteria not to be regarded as necessary prerequisites for success.

First, religion. Religious faith of almost any variety or level of intensity was taken to be at least potentially compatible with democracy. Bulliet, in particular, argued eloquently that there was no incompatibility between strong faith in Islam and democratic or republican institutions, and an Islamic republic, he contended, could be as much of a success as a Roman Catholic or a Zionist republic. Ishii cited examples in Southeast Asia where Buddhist traditions and democratic procedure seemed to be mutually reinforcing.

Second, economic development. The view was strongly stated

that economic development was not a prerequisite for democracy. It might be a prerequisite for a democracy's survival, but it was not a prerequisite for a beginning. If the second cluster of questions yielded promising answers, democratic institutions could, indeed, further economic development.

Most of the conference concentrated on this second cluster of questions. Discussion identified three sets of challenges. Not surprisingly, the more extensive the discussion, the more complications and difficulties came into highlight, and the more remote came to seem any prospects for early solutions. Some of us felt at times on the verge of descending into the clinical despair instanced by Gold to illustrate the current state of biological science.

The first set of challenges fit the rubric, "Whose democracy?" Whether new or old, democracies and, indeed, whether democracies or not, nations around the globe faced questions of self-definition exacerbated by migration. Gasteyger summarized the evidence and detailed the dilemmas. Shall nations accommodate refugees? Others fleeing famine, poverty, or disease? How? As temporary guest-workers? As citizens? As something else? Internally, how shall nations accommodate ethnic and religious divisions? Just now Mayall and Perczynski detailed evidence on the largely unforeseen force of reviving nationalism. Hutchison and Yamaguchi earlier highlighted additional evidence of the force of religious beliefs.

With evidence of national and ethnic self-identification gaining strength, and religion becoming not only a stronger force than long supposed but also, as earlier, a reinforcer of exclusionary nationalism, how are democracies to deal with age-old problems of majority–minority relationships?

An overlay of these problems is the question, stressed by Kerber and Ueno, of how societies might adjust to the reality that gender relationships have been systematically skewed by political and social institutions, and even by language and syntax commonly in use. No democracy or republic, whatever its cultural setting, could be deemed successful—even deserving its name—if, in any domain, it long embodied and enforced tyranny by any cultural or religious group, or one sex, over others.

The second set of challenges fit the rubric, "Whose good?" The period of the crumbling of communism coincided with militant promotion of free markets in major Western democracies, particularly Britain and the United States. The downfall of the communist regimes and the disintegration of the Soviet Union discredited the extreme alternative of the command economy constructed without regard to individual preferences and initiatives.

As a result, democracy and the unregulated free-market economy frequently became confused. Some of the newer democracies, or supposed democracies, have mortgaged their futures very heavily to the expectation that their populations will accept the brutally uneven distribution of goods and services characteristic in free markets. It is arguable that the widening gap between rich and poor could make democracy vulnerable even in Britain and the United States. Surely, it can do so much sooner in nations with smaller reserves of economic fat. Equally surely, the success and survival of democracy is closely tied to finding means to ensure that no substantial part of the population is, or believes itself to be, durably disadvantaged in access to goods and services.

This set of challenges becomes all the more daunting the farther one goes down the ladder of economic development. How does a democratic government sustain itself if its decisions necessarily resemble triage, if the best it can do is spread the pain of famine? The point thus underlined is that the problem of alleviating the adverse consequences of free markets cannot be conceived as a set of unconnected international problems. The surge of democracy can sharply recede if there is not significant international and transnational cooperation in an undertaking currently in bad odor in the nations most critical for any such undertaking, namely, the redistribution of wealth.

Fortunately, or half-fortunately, some of this redistribution can be produced by means other than the international equivalent of a massive "Beveridge Plan." Experience, especially in Asia, can be studied for clues as to how to make transfers of wealth to less developed countries attractive as investments. Also, as was emphasized in discussion prompted by presentations from Kyogoku and Umesao, elites in developed nations have come to recognize that uncontrolled environmental pollution endangers their societies. Less developed nations need and pursue industrial and other forms of economic development with comparatively little regard to environmental pollution. Their elites are not particularly responsive to intellectual appeals based on ecological principles. In developed countries themselves, as the political scientist James Q. Wilson comments, an environmentalist is likely to be someone who already has a summer home.

This makes an argument for redistribution from rich nations to poor nations subsidizing pollution-reducing development. This means, it is true, that environmental concerns in developed countries offer less developed countries opportunities for blackmail, even extortion. The example or precedent is alarming, for one can imagine less developed countries also seeking subsidies for refraining from torture or massacre or development of weapons of mass destruction as, indeed, some governments have already extorted concessions in return for releasing hostages or refraining from terrorism. Nevertheless, to the end of protecting the common environment, developed nations have a positive incentive for helping to meet the economic needs of developing countries.

The third set of challenges consists of opportunities and perils stemming from science and technology. The conferees focused on the example detailed by Gold and amplified by Nakamura of advances in molecular biology that offer prospects of comprehending and manipulating the genetic makeup of humankind. The practical and ethical implications of these advances could pose for democratic processes issues of difficulty beyond any ever before confronted.

Kristeva warned that a congeries of technological and social developments creates a possibility of massive psychic damage among the populations even of the most firmly rooted democracies.

Environmental pollution and startling changes in the potentialities of science and technology illustrate the point that many challenges to democratic institutions and processes are international in character.

As Iriye repeatedly emphasized, there has been recognition throughout the past century that many of the aspirations of democracy will be unobtainable unless pursued cooperatively.

Windsor analyzed on this final morning of our conference one of the most difficult and painful of these issue areas, that of human rights. He, Watanabe, and Yokoyama delineated elegantly the problems of distinguishing between universalizable norms and culture-bound social values.

If this calendar of concerns covers only those that are obvious as of the early mid-1990s, what are the problems passed over? What have we missed? What are the equivalents of violence and tyranny for our hypothesized conference of the mid-1890s? If there are contingencies not completely hidden from us, they may be among those mentioned in the course of the conference as possible but unlikely. One is a large-scale revival of totalitarianism, probably under labels other than communism or National Socialism. A second is revived risk of large-scale war among advanced, nuclear-armed states. For the immediately foreseeable future, our conferees agreed, war was unlikely to be an instrument of policy except for less developed nations coping with challenges already enumerated. The farther ahead the future, however, the less confident that forecast. In any case, with both contingencies, a new totalitarianism or large-scale war, goes a large regret factor, to borrow a term from engineering. If our assumption is wrong, the costs could be catastrophic. We should, therefore, scrutinize the possibilities even if we discount their likelihood.

How, then, to cope with all these challenges, the likely and the less likely? The general prescription is not hard to compose. We are all scholars. As a practical matter, we can speak only of what can be done by ourselves and other scholars. We cannot, in the first instance, preach to those who manage affairs in other spheres. We can, however, recommend in the most urgent terms undertakings by scholars aimed at illuminating and perhaps even guiding choices to be made in cabinet offices, legislative chambers, corporate board rooms, and other such sites (extending perhaps to voting booths, living rooms, perhaps even bedrooms).

We scholars need to understand better and explain better the topic sketched at our conference by Morin, the structural underpinnings of democracy. In practice, what have been the strengths and weaknesses of alternative means of safeguarding the interests and integrity and dignity of individuals? What has successfully ameliorated the harsh effects of free-market mechanisms? What in the past has brought resources from outside to nations struggling with economic problems beyond their own resources? What lessons can be extracted from the experience of democracies that did not go the way of the new Russian Republic of 1917 or the Weimar Republic? What lessons can be learned from past efforts to prevent large-scale war, extending at least from the Hague and London conferences of the turn of the twentieth century through the SALT and START negotiations?

For specific suggestions, we could simply recommend more conferences at the Yatsugatake Kogen Lodge or some other such idyllic spots, if there are any. I have no desire to discourage such an outcome. At the same time, I think the agenda for action has to be more extensive and to reach outside our own circle, indeed, outside our scholarly disciplines. One recourse has been suggested by Harkabi: those of us who teach could ask ourselves and our colleagues whether we are forcing these issues on the minds of our students. When we think we are doing so, or think someone else is doing so, we should see that the syllabuses reach other teachers, as the syllabus of Harkabi's course on world order has reached us. We should do what we can to ensure that suitable readings and collections of readings are available to encourage and underpin courses addressing or touching issues such as the accommodation of minority rights within, among, or by democratic states, the promotion of equality, the avoidance of war, and so forth.

To the same end but on a necessarily more extended timetable, we should undertake and encourage scholarly writing designed to give shape to such teaching and to correlative international public debate. The core of this historical writing, I would argue, should be historical in character. That is, it should analyze past experience and derive from that experience propositions potentially useful to those who have to act. This is partly counsel that historians attempt to repair some of the weaknesses in social science tactfully mentioned by Kosai, and more sharply specified by Dore. Its point of departure is, however, an observation that the most powerful and most used of the social sciences—economics—relies very heavily on generalizations from historical data.

In some respects, we had an example of what I recommended yesterday in the fascinating discussion inaugurated by Hagihara, Murakami, Kyogoku, and Winston of what Japan's past suggests about Japan's future and of Japan as a possible model for other nations.

To give some more specificity to my thoughts, let me, however, mention three possibilities. One, briefly referred to in my commentary on Wednesday, is that of systematic historical analysis of the mechanisms for the preservation of peace. I would argue that generalizations from experience in industrial and post-industrial ages should begin with the following trio of propositions:

1. Choices concerning peace or war are made by political leaders.
2. Except in extraordinary circumstances, the first concern of political leaders is preservation of their authority at home.
3. In making choices affecting relations with other governments, political leaders are guided by:
   a) Judgments concerning the extent and duration of domestic support for, or opposition to, particular options;

b) Judgments concerning the extent and duration of support, or opposition, in other policy areas.

While those propositions may strike most of you as truisms, they happen to be at odds with the fundamental premises of most current writing about international relations, where the actors are states seeking advantage from or protecting themselves from other states.

Second, I would suggest analysis of trends in opinion-formation in democracies. The premise of democracy is, after all, the capacity for choice by informed populations. As of today, one sees, on the one hand, quantum increases in the amount of information available to the citizens of democracies that pours in, much of it in the form of immediate visual imagery. Most of us saw the failure of the coup in Moscow in August 1991. On the other hand, there is an arguable progressive diminution in citizens' capacity to understand the issues before them. As just one quantitative sign, let me mention that the total number of foreign correspondents for the best American, British, French, and German newspapers and magazines has shrunk by more than one-third just in the past dozen years. Interpretation of events in areas of crisis comes thus from teams of reporters arriving with little or no sense of context, and, as is underlined by the recent McBride Report for the U.N., the problem is all the greater in developing countries where sources of information for citizens—even often about affairs in their own countries—are the parochially American or British videocasts of CNN or the BBC. This is a field desperately in need of remedial analysis.

Third and last, I would suggest systematic study of past experience in bridging, or at least controlling, the potentially malignant national, ethnic, and religious tensions highlighted throughout our conference. In the Indian subcontinent, which, it is true, we paid very little attention here, there have been many horror stories, but there have also been many communities where Hindus, Muslims, and others have lived in peace, if not necessarily in tranquillity, and certainly not in prosperity. Why and how?

Another example, possibly instructive, if not uplifting, is Northern Ireland. In few places is murderous religious antagonism more evident. Yet, statistically, Northern Ireland has less murder and other violent crime than any comparable part of the United Kingdom, indeed of almost any part of the world. The condition is scarcely the toleration that Windsor recommends, but the laws do operate equally. May there not be useful propositions to be pulled from this history? I add hastily that I do not expect anyone's propositions to be unchallengable. I am urging debate about history, not the formulations of dogma.

Before closing these closing words, I wish also to acknowledge the force of points made more than one time at our conference by, in particular, Nivat and Likhachev, and in arresting ways by Kristeva. The method of the literary scholar, depending on perception by gestalt and often on communication by metaphor, may, in some instances, be more enlightening and even more efficient than those of the social scientist or even those of the positivistic historian. This would surely have been the case for identifying and analyzing the dangers not foreseen in the 1890s. So I am not suggesting exclusively historical analyses that resemble Keynes's extrapolations from British economic history or Milton Friedman's from the American record. Rather, I think of democracy-focused analyses as varied in approach as, say, Ranke's essay on the great powers—an early sort of social science—or Henry Adams' essay on the virgin and the dynamo, a pristine rendering of gestalt.

The cumulative product of the efforts proposed would be the uncovering of some of the rubric of our conference, "The future in the Past." We could well go wrong, but it would not be for want of asking when, how, and why humans before us, experimenting with democracy, went right. I would invoke again the line from Benedetto Croce, the neo-Hegelian historian-philosopher, that I quoted in my written response to Harkabi's paper. Croce said it was the task of the historian to address urgent theoretical problems. This conference has, I think, brilliantly illuminated the most urgent theoretical problems that lie before us.

**Iriye:** Now, it is time for me to turn to Nivat for a second concluding statement.

**Nivat:** A brief word on behalf of the Steering Committee.

We have been living for five days in this island of beauty which has been, I think, also an island of very free discussion, and the typhoon has been benevolent to us. We have had an idea that Nature still has its word to say even when culture is at work, but we have been spared by the typhoon, and it has been so pleasant and agreeable to have these five days in this oval concert hall where Sviatoslav Richter has played. It was not music, it was an exchange of ideas, but at some times there was in it some harmony, at some times there was the, let us say, necessary incisiveness, irony, and emotion. Anyway, at all times the necessary tolerance.

I hope we will never have a symposium beginning with "The Crumbling of Democracy." Anyway, I suppose that it would be a contradiction in terms so there would be no such conference after the crumbling of democracy.

The excellence of the atmosphere has been also the excellence of exchange in the corridors. Each of us has probably a different experience of those exchanges.

I want to make one small correction which I received from a participant in this conference. When I congratulated Likhachev on his idea of rights for trees, and especially for insects, he suddenly said to me, "Not all insects."

I would like to say a few special words because we all know some foreign languages, and this knowledge of foreign languages is absolutely indispensable for any sort of international exchange, but none of us knows all the languages, or any language to perfection, so I must thank very specially the interpreters, knowing how difficult the task for such themes must have been, and the interpreters and the translators who have translated and who will translate, too—thank you to them.

Last, I must make a special vote of thanks to Mr. Minoru Kusuda, director of the Center for Global Partnership and the vice president of the Japan Foundation, because it was not only a pleasure but a great honor to participate in the conference and to be given a chance to express ourselves on this very important problem.

# INDEX